Domhnall ua Buachalla

For my mother, Bríghid,
her brothers and sisters

Domhnall ua Buachalla

Rebellious Nationalist,
Reluctant Governor

Adhamhnán Ó Súilleabháin

MERRION

First published in 2015 by Merrion Press
an imprint of Irish Academic Press
8 Chapel Lane
Sallins
Co. Kildare

British Library Cataloguing in Publication Data
An entry can be found on request

978-1-78537-006-9 (paper)
978-1-78537-007-6 (cloth)
978-1-78537-008-3 (PDF)

Library of Congress Cataloging in Publication Data
An entry can be found on request

Printed in Ireland by SPRINT-print Ltd.

CONTENTS

LIST OF PLATES

1. Joshua Jacob, Domhnall ua Buachalla's maternal grandfather, was a Quaker who converted to Catholicism. (*Photo: Dublin Friends Historical Library, Quaker House*)
2. The Maynooth cricket team c.1875, which includes two of Domhnall ua Buachalla's brothers. The names provided by him differ slightly from those which accompany the photo in the Maynooth Library. Back row: Con Ó Buachalla, Seán Ó hÉachám, Joseph Fulham, Seán Launders, Seán Ó Buachalla. Front row: James Phelan, Seosamh Ó Raghallaigh, Thomas Weafer, Thomas Carr, Michael Carr. (*Photo: O'Buachalla Collection*)
3. Sarah Buckley (née Jacob), Domhnall ua Buachalla's mother. (*Family photo*)
4. Cornelius Buckley, father of Domhnall ua Buachalla, c. 1895. (*Family photo*)
5. Sinéad (née Jane Walsh), Domhnall ua Buachalla's wife, c.1900. (*Family photo*)
6. The RIC receipt for a roll of material bought by Patrick Fitzsimons at auction for £1 in 1906 after Domhnall ua Buachalla refused to pay a fine for 'not having his name on his cart', the term used for having his name in Irish on his cart. The material was seized from ua Buachalla's shop – and duly returned to him by the sole bidder. (*Photo: Author's Collection*)
7. The ua Buachalla family at home in 'Gleann Ailighe' in Maynooth: Joe, Sinéad, Domhnall Óg, Síghle, Kevin, Domhnall, Bríghid; front: Séadna and Máirín, c. 1913. (*Family photo*)
8. Domhnall ua Buachalla, centre, front, with members of the Black Hand group in Frongoch in 1916. George Lyons is first left in the

back row; Charlie Murphy is on ua Buachalla's left. Also in the picture are Seán McMahon and Martin Ryan. *(Photo, O'Buachalla Collection)*

9. The mug used by Domhnall ua Buachalla in Frongoch and notes taken during Irish class on an official label. *(Photo: Author's Collection)*

10. On the right shoulder of Domhnall ua Buachalla's jacket a pencil protrudes where a bullet narrowly missed killing him as he sought a safe passage from the GPO in 1916. *(Family photo)*.

11. A child's rein made by Domhnall ua Buachalla in Frongoch. *(Photo: O'Buachalla Collection)*

12. Members of the First Dáil at their initial meeting in January 1919. Domhnall ua Buachalla is in the second row, third from left. *(Photo: O'Buachalla Collection)*

13. Domhnall ua Buachalla's shop in Maynooth, c. 1925. *(Family photo)*

14. Mick O'Neill, son-in-law of Domhnall ua Buachalla, on horseback at his brother's residence, Weston Park, Leixlip, c. 1926. *(Photo: Nóirín O'Neill)*

15. A poster used in the 1932 general election which saw voting power in Kildare transfer from Domhnall ua Buachalla to Tom Harris, who would hold the seat until 1957. *(Photo: O'Buachalla Collection)*

16. Domhnall ua Buachalla on the day he was sworn in as Governor–General at his brother's house in Booterstown in 1932 with his sister-in-law Mary Buckley, her daughter Máirín, his brother Michael (centre, back), Con Ó Laoghaire and Seán Ó Cuiv. *(Family photo)*

17. Gortleitreach, Monkstown, Co. Dublin, Domhnall ua Buachalla's residence during his term as Governor–General. *(Family photo)*

18. The *Evening Standard* delved into 'paddywhackery' when Domhnall ua Buachalla was appointed Governor–General, with a cartoon and caption which read: 'Arrah! It was an iligant cirimony, the swearing-in of the Governor–General. His Excellency took the oat' in his own private language (which no one but himself could understand at all at all) whoile the mimbers of the Government sang an Oirish version of the National Anthem – God Save the King from matters which don't consarm him. Despite the vigilance of the troops the proceedings were interrupted by a child coming to buy a penn'orth of acid drops for Mr. Twomey.'

19. The youngest of the ua Buachalla family, Séadna, c. 1935. *(Family photo)*

20. A historic moment for Domhnall ua Buachalla as he signs the Constitution (Amendment No. 27) Bill, 1936, abolishing the post of Governor–General. *(Family photo)*

21. With tongue in cheek, *Dublin Opinion* suggested that Domhnall ua Buachalla might have considered asking the Government for a 'farewell broadcast' before leaving office in 1936.
22. Domhnall ua Buachalla's son, Joe, receiving the Liffey District, L.D.F. flag at Maynooth College in March 1943 after it had been blessed by the Very Rev. Edward Kissane, President of the College, following a march of 600 members from the Presentation Convent. *(Photo: The Irish Press)*
23. Domhnall ua Buachalla chatting with the Very Rev. Edward Kissane and Major–General Hugo MacNeill after his son, Joe, Leader of the Liffey District, L.D.F. received the unit colour in Maynooth College in 1943. *(Family photo)*
24. Domhnall ua Buachalla with his sons, Joe and Kevin, his daughter Máirín and Kevin's wife, Peggy, in Rome for an audience with Pope Pius X11 in 1950. *(Family photo)*
25. Twelve of the fifteen Maynooth Volunteers who walked to the GPO in 1916 photographed many years later in Croke Park. Back row: Pat Weafer, Tom Byrne, Joe Ledwidge, Tom Mangan, Mathew Maguire. Front row: Pat Kirwan, Tom Harris, Jack Maguire, Patrick Colgan, Domhnall ua Buachalla, Tim Tyrrell, Liam O'Regan. *(Photo: The Sunday Press)*
26. Domhnall ua Buachalla's son, Joe, with his wife, Helen in 1960. *(Photo: Fintan Buckley)*
27. Cardinal Agaginian, Éamon de Valera, Domhnall ua Buachalla and his daughter, Máirín, at a Patrician Year garden party in 1961. *(Photo: The Irish Press)*
28. Éamon de Valera kneels in prayer at the bedside of Domhnall ua Buachalla in the Pembroke Nursing Home, Dublin on 30 October 1963. *(Photo: The Advocate, Australia)*
29. Éamon de Valera and Seán Lemass at Laraghbryan Cemetery, Maynooth where Domhnall ua Buachalla was laid to rest with full military honours. *(Photo: The Sunday Press)*
30. The monument in the Town Square which honours Maynooth's fifteen Volunteers who walked to the GPO for the Easter Rising in 1916. From top: Domhnall ua Buachalla, Tom Byrne, Patrick Colgan, Jack Graves, Tom Harris, Patrick Kirwan, Joe Ledwidge, Jack Maguire, Mathew Maguire, Tom Mangan, Ted O'Kelly, Liam O'Regan, Oliver Ryan, Tim Tyrrell and Pat Weafer. *(Photo: Author's Collection)*

LIST OF TABLES

ACKNOWLEDGEMENTS

The 1916 Rising, the War of Independence and the Civil War were not on the curriculum during my schooldays. The country needed more time to distance itself from those traumatic years. All of which should not suggest that I walked blind into this undertaking. My family background on both sides was strongly republican, so I was certainly acquainted with one side of the story. I also had Domhnall ua Buachalla's copy of *The Irish Republic* in which Dorothy Macardle fortified the republican line, as did the arrival of *The Irish Press* in 1931 which I turned to as a reference on many occasions.

The need for balance came from people I spoke to in hours of need, from a variety of books, and in particular from *The Irish Times*, the *Irish Independent*, the *Kildare Observer* and almost any newspaper that crossed the Irish Sea.

A graduate of University College, Galway in modern history and author of *Ireland and the Crown 1922–1936*, Brendan Sexton was a mainstay for me, always available to offer encouragement and keep me on the right path. Maynooth historian, Séamus Cullen, was equally enthusiastic and a wonderful authority on his native county. Author James Durney came from the same mould and both he and Mario Corrigan guided me through the Kildare County Council Library archives in Newbridge for many weeks. Another Kildare historian, John Colgan, was most enlightening when we met at his delightful riverside home in Leixlip. Further west in Kilcock, Thomas O'Keeffe, the publican, and Thomas O'Keeffe, historian, were most helpful. Former journalistic colleague Eoghan Corry provided impetus and expertise in the early days and his wife, Ida Milne, welcome assistance in the latter stages.

Author of *Comrades* and *Witnesses,* Annie Ryan, a daughter of Tom Harris, lifted my spirits when I approached her at the outset and was helpful in many ways. Further assistance came from Fergus White, Terry Nealon and Brendan Coffey in Maynooth; also Jim Doyle in Celbridge. In the Pearse Museum in Rathfarnham Brian Crowley and his staff were most accommodating, as was Elizabeth McEvoy in the National Archives in Bishop Street, while the staff in the National Library of Ireland responded to a litany of requests with good humour. In the Military Archives in Cathal Brugha Barracks, Noelle Grothier set me on the right path and visits to Belfield and the UCD Archives were always facilitated by kindly staff.

It was Anne-Marie Ryan who got the ball rolling in Kilmainham Gaol Museum when she catalogued the O'Buachalla Collection to the highest standard. Amy Hughes, in the Royal Irish Academy, came to my aid with information about John Buckley and colourful elaboration was at hand when I met his granddaughter, Helen, in Sandyford.

Camilla McAleese, in Dublin, and her sister, Sarah Gallivan, in Cambridge, Massachusetts, kindly provided a background to the Gallivan family who lived in Leixlip. Fr Tom Murray, Diocesan Archivist in St Mel's College, was equally helpful on Longford matters. Professor Cathal Brugha gave me sound advice when I spoke to him about his grandfather's death, while Eanna Burke was invaluable in putting shape to his father Frank's life. With my school Irish inadequate to meet the needs of the book, I turned to Galway-native, Pádraic Ó Gaora, the former RTE newscaster, and also the mother and daughter team of Maura and Niamh Oman.

While searching for information on the history of the Buckley family and their origins in Cork, a hint of desperation was creeping into my research in the Mallow area when I was pointed in the direction of Bobby Buckley in Churchtown, Dublin 14, who shone a bright light into the family background, while mentioning that it was his mother's detailed records that made it possible.

There was great enthusiasm within Domhnall ua Buachalla's extended family to have his story recorded for posterity and without their contribution it would never have been completed. Nóirín, a granddaughter of Domhnall and daughter of Mick O'Neill, together with her husband Aiden and family in Belfast, responded to every call for assistance. Similarly, her brother, Eoghan, his wife, Terry, and son, Shane, were generous with their time and responses when I called to a restful, sun-lit, seaside cottage in Kilbrittan. Always good-humoured and gracious to many appeals was Fintan Buckley, a grandson of Domhnall's and son of

Joe, and his wife, Betty. I was also facilitated by the last of the family to run the business in Maynooth, Joe, and his wife Carmel. And on the Kilcock side of the family, Aidan and Rita Byrne were very helpful.

In tracing Domhnall ua Buachalla's maternal antecedents, I received great attention at the Dublin Friends Historical Library in Quaker House, Rathfarnham. And on cricketing matters in Kildare, Ger Siggins and Pat Bell were invaluable.

My brothers and sisters, their husbands and wives – Domhnall and Josephine; Sinéad and David; Eoghan and Ann; Bridín and Greg as well as Janet – answered calls for every scrap of information they had accumulated over the years, and offered welcome assistance and words of encouragement throughout the project.

When a little desperation crept in, or the day was dark, it was to my own family I turned for a shoulder. Encouragement and advice was always available; particularly when the computer refused to accept my instructions, or hid the text, or made it disappear, or raised my blood pressure. In those moments Sharon arrived with a cool head and calming influence. John came to my aid when professional assistance was required, while their spouses, Seán and Michelle, added to my store of ideas. Occasional visits to the room in which I worked from five lively grandsons – Mikey, Conor, Seán, Cian and Eoghan – to see if I was still alive, provided welcome light relief.

However, without the support, patience, understanding and love of my wife, Jacqueline, the book might still be a notional plan.

Finally, my thanks to Conor Graham, M.D. of Irish Academic Press, who responded so positively to my appeal to publish the book, and Lisa Hyde, the Editorial Manager, whose temperament – under constant pressure from me during my learning curve – was always gracious.

To everyone who played a part, and I'll have to live with the fear of omission, *míle buidheachas*.

NOTE ON NAMES

Born Daniel Richard Buckley in 1866, the Maynooth merchant was using the Irish form of his name – Domhnall ua Buachalla – from 1901, having joined the Gaelic League in 1893, and that form is adhered to throughout the book. He has also been referred to in print as Dan Buckley, Donal Buckley, Donald Buckley, Donal Ó Buachalla and Domhnall Ó Buachalla: where passages from books, newspapers and periodicals are reproduced, the printed word has been followed. Many of the extended family used the English form of the name, or were referred to as Buckley.

INTRODUCTION

A few words spoken while I was being driven home from a friend's house in the summer of 1952 have stayed with me since I was 11 years old. We were passing an attractive residence in which Domhnall ua Buachalla had previously lived when the driver drew attention to it, remarking that the man who had lived there retired with a big pension, having been paid a considerable salary when employed as Governor-General, but did little to earn it.

I knew the truth, but I also knew my place. In the early fifties you did not dare question or attempt to correct an elder, and being a timid youngster, there was little chance that I would have done so. My mother had told me that her father accepted the position because Éamon de Valera was anxious that he do so, and that the purpose of the appointment was to abolish the Oath of Allegiance and the position of Governor-General. Pledging loyalty to the king was totally alien to ua Buachalla's beliefs; the fact that he did so personified a compelling need to see British rule in Ireland terminated. He chose to take a fraction of the salary his predecessors received, and the pension granted at the age of 71 was £500 annually. Yet, it bothered me that I sat in silence as my grandfather's integrity was questioned.

In subsequent years, I heard occasional stories at home about his remarkable life. They were generally about the Black and Tans raiding his shop in Maynooth, how guns were hidden in strange and secret places, and the fear that they would be discovered; about walking to the GPO with the Maynooth contingent in 1916; the subsequent months as a prisoner in Frongoch and about his refusal to live in the Viceregal Lodge in the Phoenix Park when appointed Governor-General (which disappointed me as an impressionable boy). Even a week's holiday in Maynooth in my early teens, enjoying the hospitality of Uncle Joe, Aunty Helen, my cousins and their friends, did not add greatly to my store of knowledge.

When *Seanpa*, as all his grandchildren knew him, died in 1963, I was 22. He was a regular visitor to our house, particularly on Sundays, generally for tea and always for a game of Solo later in the evening. If he came early in the afternoon, he might kick a football with us in the back garden. On one occasion he accompanied us to Kerry for a week's holiday – but in all that time I cannot recall him mentioning his involvement in the 1916 Rising, the War of Independence or the Civil War. He never spoke about his days as a *Teachta Dála* or as Governor-General. In fact, most of his life was virtually a mystery to me and my siblings. Yet he was warm, if not voluble, enjoyed a joke, had an endearing smile, puffed a cigarette, and would occasionally drink a bottle of stout, or a whiskey. More importantly, his day would be enhanced if any of his grandchildren spoke to him *as Gaeilge.*

As the years passed, I came across references to him, some laudatory, others far from it. Éamon de Valera and Pádraig Pearse spoke very highly of him; Daniel O'Leary referred to his pension in a Dáil debate as 'the greatest piece of corruption that has ever happened in this country'. Rather than be referred to as Governor-General, ua Buachalla used the Irish term for the position, *Seanascal*, though some wiseacres thought that *Seanasal* [old donkey] was preferable.

Having donated many items to the National Museum in 1936, which included a bullet-pierced coat, a pike, macramé bags, belts made in Frongoch, and later a gun, his daughter Máirín subsequently indicated in her will that his papers should go to the Kilmainham Gaol Museum, a wish that was implemented in recent years.

As those papers changed hands, and opinions on the 1916 Rising and the troubled times ua Buachalla lived through – and occasionally influenced – proliferated and diverged, it became increasingly apparent that his contribution to the nation could go unrecorded; that fact laced with fiction might give a lie to his life. And so, a little over sixty years after failing to raise my voice in the back of a car, I felt it was time to make up for an opportunity lost.

CHAPTER 1

'Heathen Language'

It was a Saturday in March 1905, just weeks after Domhnall ua Buachalla had his name painted in Irish on a delivery cart, in defiance of the law. Well stacked with orders, the sturdy vehicle moved away from his premises on the main street towards Maynooth College, turned right before the castle and continued out the Meath road to deliver goods that would complete the week's work for a busy grocer and hardware merchant.

Just beyond the picturesque All Saints Church and its landmark spire on the rich plains of north Kildare, driver and horse took their customary right turn into Moyglare House, home of the Tuthills. They proceeded up the avenue to the imposing residence before being called to a halt by the patriarch of a family that farmed almost 300 acres.

'Who owns that cart?' he asked the driver in an irritable manner.

'Mr Buckley', came the response.

'Well, tell him to take that heathen language off the cart or he can consider our business dealings at an end.'[1]

When the words were relayed later in the day outside the shop in Maynooth, ua Buachalla's eldest child, Joe, although only 7 at the time, observed his father's reaction and recalled the moment many years later. 'Father said nothing, but walked in a vexed manner into the shop, got out the ledger with the accounts in it, and looked at it for a few minutes. He then remarked to nobody in particular, "Yes, this is the end of the account".'[2] A few days later a curt letter arrived from Moyglare House:

> Dear Mr Buckley,
>
> The English language is quite good enough for me. The next time I receive any communication from you in a heathen language of the past, I deal elsewhere.
>
> Captain Tuthill.
>
> No answer is required.[3]

Although taken aback at the thought of losing such a wealthy client whose purchasing power would have been considerable, ua Buachalla was in no hurry to respond and it was not until April that he put pen to paper:

> Sir,
>
> Your letter of the 11th ult.
>
> A reference to the use of 'heathen language of the past' reached me duly. I am an Irishman. I love my country and my country's language. It is not a heathen language of the past; and, in the opinion of those competent to judge, it is going to be very much in evidence in the future.
>
> Had you made known to me in a rational manner your antipathy thereto, there would have been an end to the matter at once. It is therefore not for the purpose of giving you annoyance, but solely to resent your insult and assert my right to sign my name in my own language that I now repeat my former action.
>
> Presuming that our business intercourse is now at an end, I beg to enclose herewith statement of a/c to date.

I appreciate highly the patronage of each individual customer of mine and can ill afford to lose the goodwill of each one. In this case, however, there is too great a sacrifice of self-respect demanded.

Thanking you for past favours,

I remain,

Respectfully yours,

Domhnall ua Buachalla.[4]

This cameo reflects a strength of character that served ua Buachalla well through a life that spanned ninety-seven years. An extract from an essay Pádraig Pearse wrote in January 1914 under the title 'Psychology of a Volunteer' reveals why these two nationalists would develop a strong relationship in the years leading up to the 1916 Rising. It was a relationship based on mutual respect and a shared, all-consuming vision.

I do not know who among the Gaelic Leaguers that have joined the Volunteers has been foolish enough to suggest that he 'cares for the language merely as a sort of stimulant in the fight for nationhood.' Certainly not I: I have spent the best fifteen years of my life teaching and working for the idea that the language is an essential part of the nation. I have not modified my attitude in anything that I have recently said or written; I have only confessed (and not for the first time) that in the Gaelic League I have all along been working not for the language merely, but for the nation.

I now go further, and say that anyone who has been working for the language merely (if there be any such) has never had the true Gaelic League spirit at all, and though in the Gaelic League, has never really been [part] of it. I protest that it was not philology, not folklore, not literature we went into the Gaelic League to serve, but: Ireland a Nation.[5]

CHAPTER 2

A Deep Well of Hatred

In Annakissa, Co. Cork, Cornelius Buckley was born in 1828. He was well acquainted with the Fenian movement, would have known Fenian men personally, heard stories of their valour as he grew into manhood and been a conduit for these tales to his offspring in later years, one of whom was christened Daniel Richard Buckley. At the start of the twentieth century, that name would be replaced with the Gaelic form, Domhnall ua Buachalla.

To better understand ua Buachalla's nationalism, it is instructive to go back a little further in his family history. His great-grandfather, John, born in 1742, lived in Annakissa and married Mary Nagle from Lacknamona, near Carrick. Family history[1] indicates she was a member of the wider Nagle family of which Sir Richard Nagle, born in 1636, was an Irish politician and lawyer. He was elected Speaker by the Irish House of Commons in 1689, to a parliament known as the Patriot Parliament and he opposed the Act of Settlement, which punished royalists and Catholics who had fought against Parliament in the Civil Wars and unsuccessfully advocated its repeal.

In the Blackwater Valley between Fermoy and Mallow, with views of the Nagle Mountains, the family were wealthy landowners, but their loyalty to the Catholic King and the Catholic faith diminished their holding. However, when Garret Nagle married Ann Mathews, the family still owned extensive property at Ballygriffin and Killavullen. It was here in 1728 that Ann Nagle welcomed their first daughter and the eldest of seven children, Honora, who would later be better known to the wider world as Nano Nagle, founder of the Sisters of the Presentation of the Blessed Virgin Mary.[2]

In the maternal line, the Nagle family also gave the country the outstanding political philosopher, Edmund Burke. Edmund passed his childhood in Ballyduff, the seat of his maternal grandfather. He spent about five years there and received his early schooling in a ruined castle in which a hedge school of sorts was held. So when John Buckley, Domhnall ua Buachalla's great grandfather, sought the hand of Mary Nagle in the latter half of the eighteenth century, he was marrying into a clan which had served Cork – and later the wider world – with distinction. The couple were blessed with three sons: John, Michael and Conor (ua Buachalla's grandfather). In the early 1820s, Conor settled into married life with Johanna O'Reilly of Droumsligga, Mallow.

The driving force in this marriage was Johanna, which proved a blessing, as her husband was to die a young man, just twelve months before the Great Famine of 1845 wreaked havoc and desolation throughout the island. A primary valuation of tenements shows that the family rented two tracts of land from Pierce Nagle: one at Annakissa for £33.5s and another at Cooldurragha (including house and offices) for £71.5s, a holding of just over 120 acres, which was sizeable at that time.

It was said of the Buckleys that 'they always had a way with cattle', and for that reason the fact that Johanna brought five boys – John, Michael, Cornelius (Domhnall's father), Daniel and James – into the world would have made farm work more manageable after the premature passing of their father. At that time, there were two schools in Annakissa, one a mud cabin with an attendance of around sixty children and the other founded by Nano Nagle, which consisted of a large stone-built out-office of around seventy pupils. It is likely that the boys initially attended the latter school, but an obituary that marked the death of John in 1915 at the age of 91 revealed that he also went to school in Castletownroche, and so it would be reasonable to assume that the others boys did likewise. The obituary[3] also clearly indicated that they were the recipients of historical fireside stories from their mother, which instilled in them a strong sense of their nation's history and struggle.

The obituary also recalled the Famine. 'John's recollections of the Famine were vivid and left such an anti-British impression on him that when the Boer War was at its height, his fervent wishes were that the peaceful Boers would obtain the victory. His feelings remained unchanged to the end.'[4] It also mentioned that 'he was a fluent Irish speaker and practically the only person living in his locality who used that tongue'.[5] The obituary is a powerful indication of the legacy handed on by John's parents, particularly his mother, and also the deep well of hatred for a country that had subjugated them for so long. It is inconceivable that his brother, Cornelius, would have harboured anything but similar feelings.

The effects of the Famine spread far and wide. The population of Kilavullen and Annakissa in 1821 was 1,085 and had increased to 1,348 by 1841, before the Famine took its toll. By 1852, the figure had dropped to 793 as the country lost over a million to starvation and disease – and a similar number to emigration. One of the leading political writers at that time, John Mitchel, summed it up thus:

> The English, indeed, call the Famine a 'dispensation of Providence' and ascribe it entirely to the blight of the potatoes. But potatoes failed in like manner all over Europe; yet there was no famine save in Ireland. The British account of the matter, then, is first, a fraud – second a blasphemy. The Almighty indeed sent the potato blight, but the English created the Famine.[6]

In the midst of the desolation that followed 1845, Cornelius, third eldest in the Buckley family, made the decision that his future would not depend on the green fields of Cork and headed for pastures new. Whether by design or chance, he settled inside the Pale, in Maynooth, County Kildare.

Persecution and Intolerance

If the male line of ua Buachalla's antecedents was grounded in Catholicism, nationalism and a strong antipathy to all things British, the female line was spectacularly different. His mother, Sarah, was a direct descendent of William Edmundson, who joined the Parliamentary Army in the English Civil War and served in the Scottish campaign under Oliver Cromwell in 1650. The following year he wrote in his journal that he moved to Derbyshire where people called Quakers were much discussed. 'Various reports went abroad concerning them, some for good and many for evil, but my heart was drawn towards them for good.'[7]

Edmundson married Margaret Stanford on his release from the army in 1652 and influenced by his brother John, a soldier serving in Waterford at the time, he sailed into Dublin with a view to travelling south. He later settled in Mountmellick and put his life at risk during the Williamite Wars to defend the rights and lives of both his Roman Catholic and Protestant neighbours. After the death of his first wife, he married Mary Strangman in 1697 and died in 1712, aged 85, the first 'Apostle' of Irish Quakers.

William's daughter, Mary, married a son of Richard Fayle, also called William, and this line of endogamous marriages continued with two further William Fayles marrying Ellen Barcroft and Mary Higginson. Samuel Fayle, one of thirteen children, continued the dynasty when he married Mary Manliffe in Edenderry in 1796 and their daughter, Sarah, born in 1798, married Joshua Jacob in 1829.

Joshua (ua Buachalla's maternal grandfather) was the second son of Samuel Watson Jacob, who lived in Clonmel. While William Edmondson will be remembered for his heroic efforts in establishing Quakerism in Ireland, Joshua Jacob was to leave a more controversial legacy. Educated at Leeds in Yorkshire and Ballitore in County Kildare, he was employed in Dublin by Adam Calvert, Grocers and Candlewick Manufacturers, at No. 38 Thomas Street.

Joshua set up his own grocery business around the corner at No. 36 Nicholas Street under his sign of the Golden Teapot. He would, according to Gogarty, 'weigh an ounce or less of the finest Congou for the humblest room-keeper with the same urbanity that he did a hundred chests of tea for the merchant in the market'.[8] Prosperity, and the annual arrival of a new baby to the Jacob household, reflected a house of bliss. However, historian Lena Boylan's engaging essay on him reveals that 'he succumbed to the desire of the Jacobs' to be achievers. Their special characteristics were well assembled in Joshua.'[9] She quotes Isabel Grubb, M.A.: 'Kindly and benevolent to those who did not disagree with him ... he had two serious faults – a domineering spirit and a persecuting intolerance of those who opposed him.'[10] Joshua, and a few others with similar views, denounced those who differed from them:

> Joshua's revelations convinced him that too many in the society were indulging in extravagant living and that he was chosen to lead a Quaker reformation. His revelations were borne in on him from his surroundings in the Liberties, where there was extreme poverty ... As visual proof of his commitment and with his usual penchant for the dramatic, he smashed in the open street the mirrors which he had in his house; watches, clocks and bells he discarded ... he disposed of his valuable household furniture, replacing mahogany and walnut with plain white deal. In 1842 he arrayed himself completely in white.[11]

Joshua's followers decided to imitate his style of dress: 'They were commonly called "The White Quakers", but Joshua wished them to be known as "The Universal Community".'[12] Their establishments 'were extended to the towns where Joshua had strong connections. The Dublin centre was at No. 64 William Street from 1840–43.'[13] But in 1842 a decision was taken: any property that the members possessed or would acquire was to be held 'only in the will, counsel and direction of the Great Head of the Church'.[14] Lena Boylan explains the repercussions:

> Among the members of the sect of White Quakers were many of Joshua's relatives, including the widow of his late brother, Joseph of Clonmel, who left six children. Their property was assessed to be worth nine thousand pounds; this was duly realised and put into the common fund by their mother Anne. But Joseph Beale, the executor for the children, was not a White Quaker and took legal action against Joshua and Anne Jacob, Joseph's widow. Joshua was arrested on 10 January 1843 and brought before the Lord Chancellor in the Four Courts. He refused to recognise the court and denounced all judges, lawyers and newspapers and was consequently lodged in the Marshalsea, the old debtors' prison, where he was first regarded as a fanatic and an imposter, but his benevolence and rectitude of conduct in time won him respect.[15]

It would appear that Sarah Jacob was a quiet, home-loving wife who did not approve of her husband's later actions and this led to her being divorced. According to Mr Gogarty, 'she died in the Winter of 1845'.[16] It is conceivable that the divorce and relative poverty caused by the Famine contributed to her death, an event which would have damaged Joshua's standing in the community. It would also indicate why many of his supporters 'left him when he tried to convince them that a Divine revelation led him to making the decision'.[17] References to Sarah's circumstances after being divorced are very scarce, aside from the fact that she was buried in Glasnevin in a plot bought by Joshua for his family and friends. The Universal Community worked at weaving woolen cloth and helping the poor, but 'when they got possession of the estate of the late Judge Kilwarden at Newlands [later Newlands Golf Club] they branched into cultivation, with all activities being overseen by Joshua from the Marshalsea'.

Released in 1846, he recovered his health at Newlands, ably helped by Miss Abigail Beale of Mountmellick, and together with the community they performed heroics during the Famine years, including feeding everyone who came to the entrance gates.

> The good works of the White Quakers in the Clondalkin area restored Joshua's good name, but his critics renewed their attacks when, for lack of funds, he had to withdraw from Newlands with his community, and move to a place known as The Sabine Fields at Scholarstown, near Rathfarnham.[18]

In 1848, Joshua married a Roman Catholic widow, Catherine Devine, and in 1852 he leased a shop and farm in Celbridge and was received into the Catholic Church in 1859, as were all his children at a later date. He resumed his first occupation as grocer and extended his business interests to Leixlip and Maynooth. When he died in 1877 he left property in Leixlip and Lucan. His business in Maynooth passed to Cornelius Buckley, who had married his daughter Sarah Jacob, in 1860.

The wedding brought together two families from contrasting cultures who, nevertheless, were linked by a steely determination – and, in latter days – a common faith. Their fourth child was Daniel, born on 2 February 1866. His path through life would reflect many of the admirable qualities of his antecedents, but played out without any recourse to dramatics or flamboyance.

CHAPTER 3

A Family Rift

Although the Famine depleted the population of Kildare during the decade 1841–51 by approximately sixteen per cent, the barony of North Salt (Maynooth-Leixlip) increased, which made Cornelius Buckley's decision to settle there either fortuitous or inspired. Ua Buachalla's father certainly had the drive and ambition of a man who believed in his ability to successfully switch from farming to shop-keeping, and within a short time he leased No. 23 Main Street, consisting of a house, office and yard, from Christopher Murtagh and John Nelson. In 1853 he set himself up as a grocer and merchant at No. 25. It became a business that flourished as it diversified and kept the Buckley/ua Buachalla name over the shop for almost 150 years.

It was inevitable that his presence would come to the notice of Joshua Jacob, who was in the process of developing his business interests in Celbridge, Leixlip, Lucan and Maynooth. While a little rivalry might have been the anticipated consequence, what developed was the romance between Sarah, Joshua's daughter, and Cornelius. By 1860 they had married and when Joshua died in 1877, he passed on his business in Maynooth to his daughter and son-in-law. By this time, the Buckley household had been blessed with a daughter, Johanna, and five sons, Cornelius, John, Daniel, Michael and Richard.

The man who would be Ireland's third Governor-General received his primary education at the local national school. In a brief recollection of his early life dictated to Mary Cullen, a lecturer in Maynooth College, the eldest of the ua Buachalla boys, Joe, recalled his father talking about his schooldays: 'The national-school headmaster at that time, who lived next door to the school, was a great character, and a great teacher. He must have trusted my father because he used to keep a billycan in his desk and often gave my father 2d. and say, "Go up and get me a pint".'[1]

Patrick Colgan, who marched with ua Buachalla to the GPO in 1916, provided quite a graphic description of the town and its environs at the turn of the century in his witness statement to the Bureau of Military History.

> Maynooth was and is a poor little village. Mainly it was poor because all the land was held by a few. It was a happy hunting ground for the retired Colonels, Majors and Captains of the British Army. The few non-ex-military landed [people] in the area were graziers who aped 'their betters'. Outside the Duke of Leinster's estate and St. Patrick's College, there was little or no employment. Everything was taken from the Big Houses, except religion. To eke out an existence it was necessary to keep on the right side of the Big Houses.[2]

It would appear that Cornelius Buckley was comfortable in dealing with both sides of the divide and his business blossomed. In addition, he was busy renting, buying and selling property on and off the Main Street of the town. At different times between the early 1850s and his death in 1915, he had an interest in No's. 21, 22, 23, 25, 29 and 29a on Main Street; in Double Lane (now Buckley's Lane), he owned No's. 2, 3, 4, 5, 6 and 7, and in Back Lane, No's. 9, 10, 11 and 12. He also had five acres at Railpark.

Nevertheless, it was not a case of 'all work and no play' for Cornelius. He also dedicated much of his spare time to promoting Gaelic games. Although the Gaelic Athletic Association was founded in November 1884 in Hayes's Hotel, Thurles, Co. Tipperary, the games were played in Maynooth from 1875, at which stage cricket engaged the sporting attention of most towns and villages in the province.

In the mid-to-late 1800s there were in excess of 1,500 teams in the country, the majority of which benefitted from the patronage of the landed gentry. This is evidence of the spread of British customs and games across Irish life and culture. In his book on the history of cricket in Kildare, *Long Shies and Slow Twisters* (1993)[3] Pat Bell wrote that the first reported match played in the county was in 1838 and within forty years there were more than fifty district teams. He noted that while the growth of the Land

League in the 1880s may not have affected the sport directly, it would have affected the process whereby the game was beginning to develop a broader social base.

Although Bell has no record of a team in Maynooth, a photograph does exist of ten men dressed for cricket who appear strong and talented. A copy of it in the local library states that it is the Maynooth Cricket Team of 1870 and provides the names of all the players. A copy of it in ua Buachalla's papers[4] provides a list of names which differs slightly, and makes the point that it was taken at a time when 'the country's nationality was lost and before the arrival of Sinn Féin'.

It is likely, therefore, that there were sufficient enthusiasts in the town to take on some of the clubs in the neighbourhood, in friendly rivalry if not in serious competition. And, no doubt, much to the annoyance of ua Buachalla, if not his father, included in the side are two of his brothers, Cornelius and John. The other players, according to him, are Seán Ó hÉacham, Joseph Fulham, Seán Launders, James Phelan, Seosamh Ó Raghallaigh, Thomas Weafer and Thomas and Michael Carr. It is likely that the photograph was taken a little after 1870.

The Cultural Revival towards the end of the century, which was driven by blossoming nationalism and the Gaelic League, gave great impetus to the growth of national games; another factor which led to this growth was the absence of a team sport on Sunday, which was the young Catholic Irishman's day for recreation, whereas most cricket games took place on Saturday when the majority were working – and preference when selecting teams was entirely in the hands of the landed gentry. In addition, the Irish Republican Brotherhood (IRB) saw the benefit of large numbers gathering in the promotion of this sporting activity and soon their fields became readymade recruiting grounds. In fact, evidence from Royal Irish Constabulary (RIC) files in 1891 indicated that there was serious IRB membership at officer level in the GAA. Of the committee elected at the Kildare County Convention on 19 November 1890, eleven were listed by the RIC as IRB members. Among the names was Cornelius Buckley; some years later his son would also join the ranks.

Domhnall ua Buachalla was nine when *camáns* and *sliotars* were introduced to leisure activity, and by the time the Maynooth club team, *Crom Abú*, became involved in organised competition in 1884, he was an 18-year-old with a great game that demanded a place on the town's team. He devoted much of his time to the sport in subsequent years and in 1896, after Maynooth had won the County Championship, he was honoured with the captaincy of the county team for the Leinster Championship, but there was to be no glory attached as they capitulated in the first round.

The art of using a hurley would not have been influenced by his secondary education – those days were spent in the care of the Jesuits at Belvedere College in Dublin, beginning in 1876, with the date of departure unrecorded. His brother John attended Catholic University School (CUS) in Leeson Street and in a radio interview many years later, his son, also named John, mentioned that his Uncle Domhnall went to CUS, probably for his final year of education. It is ironic that he was followed into Belvedere in 1884 by James McNeill, who preceded him to the position of Governor-General, having held posts in the Raj Civil Service in Calcutta and as first High Commissioner (Ambassador) to London. When their paths crossed in 1932, it was Éamon de Valera who decided the immediate direction their lives would take.

With his schooldays completed, ua Buachalla turned his mind to the wider world and, surprisingly, it did not involve the family business. Joe recalled that he had decided to pursue a career in Customs and Excise, very much to the disappointment of his father, who thought 'he was mad',[5] but after a couple of years studying in Dublin, his ambitions were dashed when Cornelius took ill, leaving Domhnall with the responsibility of the family business. While he would probably have been happy to see one of his siblings take over instead of him, such an outcome was not realistic, as they had gone some way down their own life paths. The eldest, Johanna, had moved on to rearing a family after her marriage to Conn McLoughlin. His brother, Cornelius, who was five years older than Domhnall and married to Ann Manley from Edgeworthstown, was well ensconced in Kilcock as a merchant and publican.

The next in line, John, M.R.I.A., would have been the antithesis of your local shopkeeper, and almost certainly not suited to passing his days behind a counter. He started his career in the Land Commission, moved to Customs and Excise, before finally progressing to be Curator of the Art and Industries Section of the National Museum; in 1921 he was made Director. His contribution to Irish archaeological journals on art objects, and compilations of various guides to art collections, led to him becoming a member of the Royal Irish Academy. This was followed by his major work, a magnificent study of Irish Altar Plate. It deals with chalices and patens dating from the fourteenth century to the end of the seventeenth century that are now preserved in the National Museum and in a number of churches. He completed this study just before his death in 1939. It represents a lifetime of devotion and is probably the most complete work ever compiled on the subject.

Married to a Liverpudlian, Ellen Cronin, John lived in York Road, Rathgar, and dedicated himself to academic study and the arts. In the radio interview, his son mentioned that John's favourite brother was Domhnall. Yet despite this admission, he never communicated with Domhnall after leaving home; nor did he socialise in any way with his other siblings. Asked why, his son replied, 'John Redmond, he was a Redmondite. Need I say more?' But he did elaborate, briefly. Asked about Domhnall and the position of Governor-General, he said his father had the highest regard for James McNeill and felt that the decision of de Valera to dismiss him was a 'great insult'.

While Cornelius and Sarah had raised a tightly knit nationalist family, John was not totally at ease with their ideals and so disappeared from family life in Maynooth to raise a wonderfully talented family with Ellen. His son, Cornelius John, was an engineer who worked on the Shannon hydroelectric scheme, then took his talent to Mombasa and returned to finish his days as Chief Engineer of the Dublin Port and Docks Board. Eileen was a concert pianist, Eoghan an architect, and Jack studied zoology at University College Dublin, and later tropical medicine in London. Nuala worked in fine arts, particularly the embossing of fine leather, a subject on which her father wrote a paper for the Royal Irish Academy in 1916 – which contrasted dramatically with his brother's activities that same year.

But the Rathgar Buckleys did miss their relatives, a fact confirmed by granddaughter Helen Buckley, who spoke of being totally unacquainted with the extended Maynooth clan. However, her life was not short of excitement as she was capped twenty-seven times for Ireland at hockey, was later appointed a selector and coached the Triple Crown-winning team of 1977.

Michael, Domhnall's younger brother of three years, had also gone to CUS and from there to the Royal College of Science to study engineering. He married Mary Hooper, was Dublin City Chief Engineer on retiring, and would have a role in the early days of his brother's life as Governor-General. The youngest, Richard, pleased his parents greatly when taking up residence just a few hundred yards from home in Maynooth College where he studied for the priesthood. He sadly died at 19, before his ordination.

Thus, instead of pursuing a life in Dublin working for His Majesty, Daniel Richard Buckley accepted that his future would replicate his father's and focus on the family business, the people of Maynooth and its hinterland. The man who emerged from the enforced change was a cultural nationalist whose influence on the people of north Kildare – and further afield – would be memorable.

A Marriage Agreed – But No Dowry

While at school in Maynooth and Belvedere College, ua Buachalla maintained that he never learned anything about Irish history. 'I joined the Gaelic League on its inception and started an Irish class in Maynooth, and it was then I learned the history of my country, by reading.'[6] It would be reasonable to assume, therefore, that when the Gaelic League was formed on 31 July 1893 by Eoin MacNeill, it was an enquiring mind, probably stirred by the fireside stories of his father's and grandfather's life and times in north Cork, that fuelled ua Buachalla's need to know more about his country and learn the Irish language.

Ensconced in the life of the Gaelic Athletic Association, he was an ideal disciple for Douglas Hyde and Eoin MacNeill, the primary movers behind the formation of the League. An early advertisement issued from headquarters at No. 4 College Green stated that 'this Association has been founded solely to keep the Irish language spoken in Ireland. If you wish the Irish language to live on the lips of Irishmen, help this effort according to your ability.'

Hyde's father, Arthur, originally from Castlehyde near Mallow, County Cork, was Church of Ireland Rector of Kilmactranny, County Sligo. He was schooled at home by his father and an aunt due to a childhood illness, later went to Trinity College and became fluent in French, Latin, German, Greek and Hebrew. He married Lucy Cometina Kurtz in 1893 and had two daughters, Nuala and Una. It is interesting that after the Oath of Allegiance was abolished and ua Buachalla had stepped down from the position of Governor-General, de Valera appointed Hyde as Ireland's first President, and he subsequently brought life back to the residence that ua Buachalla had refused to occupy while in office, the Viceregal Lodge (now Áras an Uachtaráin).

Educated at St Malachy's College and Queen's College, Belfast, Eoin MacNeill had a deep interest in history and in 1908 was appointed a professor of early Irish history at University College Dublin. Later, through contact with other nationalists, he became chairman of the council that formed the Irish Volunteers and later Chief-of-Staff. He held this position up until the Easter Rising, but lacking the conviction that an armed rebellion was the best option at that juncture, his countermanding order on the eve of the Rising caused confusion in the ranks of the Volunteers – and forced ua Buachalla to cycle into Dublin on Easter Monday morning to find out whether the Rising was in fact under way.

Although ua Buachalla formed a branch of the Gaelic League in Maynooth shortly after the movement's inception, it failed to attract sufficient enthusiasts to make it a worthwhile exercise and he was soon forced to abandon the undertaking. This abandonment, however, was not permanent – at the turn of the century he made renewed efforts to great effect.

Now heading into his thirties, he was running the family business, playing hurling and travelling to Dublin regularly to talk to suppliers about weekly needs for the shop – a busy schedule, but one that was to provide him with an unexpected bonus. Early in 1896 he met Jane Walsh, who was one of a number of orphans in the care of John Conway and his wife, friends of the Buckley family. They lived in Gibraltar House, Dolphin's Barn, a large residence on its own land, which was demolished in the latter half of the twentieth century to make way for an industrial estate. Jane's father, Charles, had been a coach builder. By August 1896 the relationship had blossomed to the extent that ua Buachalla had written to John Conway, seeking Jane's hand in marriage. He was not to be disappointed.

Dolphin's Barn,

21 August 1896.

My dear Dan,

In reply to your letter of yesterday's date I hasten to assure you that I most cordially join with Aunt Mary and Uncle Michael in assenting to your becoming the future guardian and protector of our dear Janie, who has ever been a docile and dutiful child; always anxious to do what was right to the extent of her knowledge and ability.

We all have the most unreserved confidence in your honour, integrity and thoroughly upright intentions and feel that Janie is fortunate in becoming a member of the Buckley family, for each and all the members of which we entertain the greatest respect and admiration. In giving you Janie I would, if I could, gladly give you a dowry with her, but it was not the will of Divine Providence that any of us should be possessed of worldly goods and poor Janie must make up for them by the stock of Christian virtues which her Heavenly Father has endowed her.

Need I assure you that I shall ask the blessing of God on your undertaking?

In the words of the holy Church occurring in the Nuptial Mass, 'Thus shall be blessed every man who fears the Lord. May the Lord bless you from the height of Sion and grant you to see, all the days of your life, prosperity in Jerusalem. And may you see the children of your children and peace in Israel.'

Let me assure you we are not over-anxious for an immediate departure of dear Janie from our midst, and you must consult the wishes and arrangements of your good parents who have your best interests at heart.

Believe me,

My dear Dan,

Very faithfully yours,

John Conway.[7]

Cornelius and Sarah were happy to let their son and his fiancée get on with their plans for marriage and early in 1897 they decided that the wedding would be held on 3 June. To officiate, ua Buachalla turned to Fr Patrick Manley, whose sister Anne had married Domhnall's brother, Cornelius. Born in Edgeworthstown and educated at St. Mel's College, Fr Pat was later the Parish Priest in Killoe but had become acquainted with the Buckley family while studying in Maynooth College. However, accepting the invitation presented a problem for Fr Pat, as he explained in a letter on 15 May 1897.

My dear Dan,

I have received your letter. I feel deeply grateful to you and Miss Walsh for your kind thought of me in asking me to perform your marriage ceremony. But it is very hard to get a whole day at this time and the date and hour fixed for your ceremony would cost me a whole day.

Our examinations – the Intermediate – begin on the 15 June. I am not so cruel as to ask you to change by one moment the hour fixed for the important step you are about to take. I am not prepared to undertake the responsibility of asking you to postpone it, but will you kindly take it as an answer now that I shall take advantage of the privilege you have conferred on me; and I will send you a definite reply within the next few days.

Personally, I should feel highly honoured by having yours as one of the first marriage ceremonies I should ever have performed. May God bless you, Miss Walsh, and your undertaking.

Faithfully yours,

P. J. Manley.[8]

Despite the undertone of anxiety in the response from Fr Pat, whose obituary many years later described him as 'one of the most saintly, zealous and brilliant churchmen who ever adorned the Diocese of Ardagh and Clonmacnoise in which, for over thirty-seven years, he ministered with unflagging devotion to duty'[9], he was present early on the appointed June morning at Dolphin's Barn where the Church Register was signed by ua Buachalla's brother, Michael and Bridget Cooke. Afterwards, the guests gathered in Gibraltar House for breakfast before the couple set off for Cork. A letter to his sister, Johanna, three days later, indicated that the honeymoon couple were thoroughly enjoying themselves, despite the fact that Cork City had been a serious disappointment.

My dear Joe [Johanna],

Janie and I have been doing so much and enjoying ourselves so well since we left Gib., I didn't get time to drop a line to you until this evening. We've seen so much within the last two or three days that it appears more than a week since Thursday.

We were very much disappointed with Cork City, thinking it would be after the style of Dublin. But the two names should not be mentioned in the one day. Cork is a dirty, sleepy hole compared with Dublin. It looks fair at a distance – as one part of it is built on steep sloping ground. It looks well when seen from a particular point [of] about a mile or so. But don't come nearer to it.

Queenstown [Cobh] is a delightful place. On Friday morning we took the train to there, and after seeing the Cathedral – which licks Maynooth Chapel – we took a steamer to Crosshaven on the southern shore of the harbour, from whence a coach took us to a place called Weaverpoint, looking out on the Atlantic and near the entrance to the harbour. Here we enjoyed immensely a cup of tea and 'Hovis' bread and butter, and then went and sat on the rocks overlooking the herring-pond. We got back to Cork by steamer and train by a different route.

Yesterday we went to Blarney Castle (eight miles). We got up to the stone, had a good look at it, but didn't kiss it – it is much easier to look at it than to kiss it. Yesterday evening we left Cork for Glengariff [spelling on hotel notepaper] – via two and a half hours rail to Bantry and two hours coach from Bantry to Glengariff. Janie and I had a hotel boat for two hours to ourselves (and the rower) on the bay this evening. It is a heavenly spot. The fuchsia is far more plentiful in the hedges than the bush, and the rhododendrons are everywhere a mass of bloom.

We can see from our bedroom (in Roche's Royal Hotel) Bantry Bay and the Atlantic in the distance, and the grounds of the hotel go down to the shore of Glengariff Bay. Janie will be able to tell you about the remainder of the tour when she sees you. We expect to be home in Maynooth on Friday anyhow.

Love from Mrs Buckley [!] and self to all.

Your affectionate brother, Dan.

P.S. Tell Mother when you see her I got her letter here this morning.[10]

The letter certainly gives a strong indication that two very happy honeymooners returned to Maynooth in the summer of 1897, ready to settle into married life and buoyed by the expectation of raising a family. For both, the trip south was probably the first holiday of their young lives.

The Return to the Family Home

Before departing for Cork, father and son spoke about a home for the couple. Cornelius and Sarah had raised their family in a sizeable residence that included the shop and stores on Main Street, but at this stage it no longer echoed with the sound of youthful voices. As the newly married couple would be running the business, it made sense that they should move into the family home, which is best described by the official document drawn up when the property changed hands:

> Cornelius Buckley, gentleman, of Leinster Lodge, in consideration of the natural love and affection borne by the said Cornelius Buckley to the said Daniel Buckley, assigns all the dwelling house, shop and stores and the appurtenances thereto belonging with two cottages at the rear thereof situate at the north side of the Main Street, now in the possession of John Greaves, containing in front to said street thirty feet, in the rear a like number of feet, and from the front to rear 170 feet bounded on the east by a lane, on the west by Dr Pellessier's house together with all other if any the premises now held by Cornelius Buckley under said lease of May 1 1816 ...[11]

With that decision made, the choice of Leinster Lodge as a new home for Cornelius and Sarah ensured that they would not be greatly inconvenienced, being situated just a few hundred yards from the shop in Parson's Street, opposite the ruins of the Fitzgerald Castle and the entrance to Maynooth College. One of the most attractive houses in the town, Leinster Lodge [later changed to *Gleann Ailighe*] is still standing, but has been unoccupied for many years. A stream runs close to the front lawn and the land attached is sizeable; adjoining it on the Leinster Street side is a barracks, which was a focal point in the town during the War of Independence.

The choice of residence was, in one sense, ironic. In 1903 the ua Buachalla family could have invited the rulers of Britain and its Empire into their home for afternoon tea as they were passing within a few yards of the front door on their way into the College. It's more likely, though, that the blinds would have been drawn by Cornelius as the town feted the arrival of King Edward VII and Queen Alexandria, who were warmly greeted on the red carpet by Ireland's leading Catholic bishops. There was even less chance of an invitation when King George V came to the throne in 1911. Accompanied by Queen Mary,

> the Royal Party were driven by car from the Viceregal Lodge to Maynooth, where they were greeted by a massive crowd who lined the main street as the royal entourage passed. At the entrance to the College, the Royal Party was greeted by Cardinal Logue and virtually the entire aristocracy of the Catholic Church. The King and Queen were brought on a tour of the College ... however, the visit occurred during a period of national revival when nationalism in the country was at fever pitch and there was opposition in Maynooth to the visit.[12]

The opposition is best described by Patrick Colgan who was secretary to the St Mary's Brass and Reed Band. Their marching banner had the words 'Maynooth Band' on the front and 'Kildare Men Remember '98' on the back.

> A week or two before the visit was to take place I received a letter from Very Rev. Dr Mannix, President of St. Patrick's College, inviting the band to meet their Majesties at the entrance to the College, [and] to escort them to the reception room. I had a chat with Domhnall ua Buachalla about the letter; we felt the members of the band, who were all employed at the College, the Duke of Leinster's estate or at the Big Houses, might be afraid to reject the invitation. So it was decided to ignore the invitation.
>
> A few days before the arrival of the visitors, a College employee, John Nolan, came to my home saying Dr Mannix had asked him to enquire if I had any reply to his letter. I told Nolan to say I would give a reply [the] next day.
>
> I called a meeting of the band members that evening. It was unanimously agreed to refuse the invitation. The following evening

a demand was made on me for another meeting. The prime movers were members employed at the College and at the Duke of Leinster's estate. The voting at this meeting was seventeen for acceptance, fifteen against. The seventeen paraded, the fifteen resigned.

Within a week there was a change-over; the fifteen got control and fired the ring leaders of those who paraded. It is easy to excuse those fellows now; as they saw it, their only means of livelihood was threatened. It is worth mentioning that eight of the fifteen afterwards saw service in 1916. Of the seventeen, three or four of them were desirous of dying for Ireland as and from mid-July 1922.[13]

For those members of the band who refused to entertain royalty, ua Buachalla and his Gaelic League friends decided that it would be an appropriate day for an outing and so they headed off on an 'Irish Class Excursion' to the Hill of Monaigh in Westmeath.

CHAPTER 4

First Impressions

As the nineteenth century edged closer to its end, Domhnall ua Buachalla had good reason to be pleased with life. Although deprived of the opportunity of a career in Dublin, he was now in effect the master of a thriving business in the heart of Maynooth and well respected in a community that appreciated his contribution to its general welfare. Belatedly, he was also receiving a more positive response as he sought to encourage interest in the Irish language. To crown it all, Jane presented him with a son just two days before St Patrick's Day in 1898.

While there would be six additions by 1910, Joe was destined to play a significant role in his father's life over the next thirty years. The fact that he was a pupil in St Enda's College from the day it opened in 1908 until Easter of 1916 ensured there was constant communication between his father and Pádraig Pearse. The friendship began in 1900 when Pearse accepted an invitation to attend a Gaelic League class in Maynooth and then blossomed during a court case in which Pearse defended ua Buachalla in 1906. Ua Buachalla's determination to use the Gaelic form of his name surfaced publicly when he had it painted on his delivery carts in 1905. It would not have surprised him that challenging the law came to the attention of the local sergeant or that it would lead to a day in court, concluding with ua Buachalla refusing to pay a fine of 2s. 6p. Early the following year he was back in court with Pearse at his side for a 'Case Stated', which drew national attention, and which will be referred to in greater detail later.

Despite the friendship, ua Buachalla was not a dedicated enthusiast of Pearse's vision for Ireland at the outset, as Joe recalled. 'My father did not altogether agree with Pearse. Pearse wanted to free Ireland but my father said, "What can you do with a country the size of Britain over there?" My father hadn't developed at that stage, if you like.'[1] This view might have surprised his father, but the thrust of Joe's thinking was that as 'a wonderful friendship developed through the years'[2], his father could see that 'Pearse was not as mad as he first thought.'[3] All that would be in the future, but for now Joe's arrival had ensured the continuation of the ua Buachalla clan.

Despite the United Ireland League being organised in 1898 by William O'Brien and John Dillon, and in 1900 the Party being re-united under John Redmond, there continued to be an air of restlessness in Irish politics. Dorothy Macardle wrote about the period of Redmond's leadership being described as an 'English Tragedy' by those 'who believe that a timely grant of the subordinate Parliament which he demanded would have rendered the Irish people proud citizens of the Empire and loyal subjects of the Crown'.[4] She suggested that these

> are unsafe speculations: the reign of Edward VII covered a decade very deceptive to the superficial observer of Irish affairs. There were few of the Irish Members who did not become subdued by the atmosphere of the House of Commons; the Home Rule Party grew gradually parliamentary in language as well as method and the game of mingled chance and skill being played at Westminster diverted attention from the growth of potent, deep-rooted ideas on Irish soil.
>
> The spirit of liberty is not killed by kindness. A conquered people in whom the spirit still lives must be given justice or nothing; an alien government, which permits them to rise above hopeless destitution will be confronted with a nation in revolt.[5]

Although very much a cultural nationalist at this time, ua Buachalla's views grew more radical as the years of the new century slipped by and approaching 1916, the resolute militant within him was becoming increasingly evident.

With his father unable to work, the demands on ua Buachalla's time increased, but rather than taking on an experienced man to aid him, he decided to trust in youth and so sought a steady young Irish Irelander, about 14 years of age, to serve his time in the hardware, drapery and provision business. A letter to the editor of the *Leinster Leader* shortly after placing the advertisement reflected a satisfied customer.

> Dear Sir,
>
> Thanks to my advertisement in *The Leader* for an Irish-speaking apprentice, I have been successful in securing – through the National [School] teacher of Ring, Co. Waterford – Mr M. J. Foley – a boy who has spoken Irish from the cradle.
>
> *Go mairidh tú*!
>
> Domhnall ua Buachalla.[6]

The appointment of Liam O'Raogáin (or Liam O'Regan as he was better known in Maynooth) was inspired as he developed into an outstanding worker and a mainstay of the business for many years. He later lived in Climper Hall, Kells, Co. Meath, and married Florence Bolton in 1923 before subsequently moving to Wexford. Imbued with the nationalist spirit of his employer, he was one of the Maynooth contingent that marched to the GPO on Easter Monday.

Later, another O'Raogáin – Donnchadh – joined the staff at ua Buachalla's and with the appointment of Pádraig Ó Curráin and Seán Ó Griobhtháin, a Ring quartet was virtually running the business. (Ó Griobhtháin, was also from Ring in Co. Waterford, a parish within the Irish-speaking *Gaeltacht na nDéise*.) They lived in the quarters specifically for the shop boys and were looked after by a Maynooth woman, Mary Tyrrell, the *cailín aimsire*, who was probably the original Super Nanny. By 1910, she and Jane – who was now using the Gaelic form of her name, Sinéad – were looking after all the employees, and seven siblings under the age of 12. A brief recollection of his early life penned by the youngest of the family, Séadna, reveals that she was first out of bed every morning at 6 a.m. to get the milking done. They had land in Railpark for the animals and each morning a cow, or maybe two, would be brought to a shed in Coate's Lane where Mary started her working day. In later years, Joe's sons did some of this work, 'under supervision'.

Although in the Gaelic League since its inception, ua Buachalla was still a relatively raw student of the language, as well as a secretary/treasurer of *Craobh Magh Nuadahat* (the Maynooth Branch of a national movement which ran weekly classes for people who wished to learn the Irish language) when he received a letter from Fr Michael P. O'Hickey, D. D., Professor of Irish in Maynooth College, in October 1900:

> Maynooth College,
>
> 10 October 1900.
>
> Dear Mr Buckley,
>
> I am pleased and delighted to learn that you have been working so hard for the Language Fund. You are helping on a most patriotic work, and so are those who have responded so generously to the appeal you have made to them.
>
> As regards the College, I imagine it is best to leave the matter where it is. Many of the professors subscribe liberally every year to the Fund, and prefer to send in the subscriptions to the Gaelic League treasurer. Those who have not hitherto done so are unlikely to be influenced very much by a personal appeal. But I have every confidence that with a slight additional growth of the movement they too will come to recognise that this work is a patriotic one, and should appeal to their sympathy and support.
>
> You have done splendidly. I am quite overjoyed to find the movement so warmly supported, and in such a practical manner, in this neighbourhood. I am sure that to-morrow evening's meeting will be most successful. The lecturer's name and reputation are quite sufficient to see to that.
>
> Yours very sincerely,
>
> Michael P. O'Hickey, D.D.[7]

The letter suggests that ua Buachalla was attempting to get his hands on some of the riches within the walls of the College for his branch through the good offices of the class tutor, but was gently rebuffed with words of encouragement. In response to a letter from Fr Hickey in April 1901, details of membership are revealed:

Very Rev. and dear Father,

I beg to enclose [a] list of names as requested. I fear a few of those who have joined will scarcely hold in very long; but should we succeed in keeping the number up to forty or fifty permanently, it will be satisfactory work done.

I very much regret my inability to translate the contents of your post-card of the 3rd inst. but '*ní béid annso arís go ceann deich lá nó mar sin*' is, I think, 'will not be here again for ten days or so'. That means we shall not have your reverence on next Thursday evening. I am sorry; but we shall meet, at any rate, and try and do something.

Very respectfully yours,

Domhnall ua Buachalla.[8]

The struggle to stay financially afloat is reflected in a letter to Stephen Barrett in Head Office in Dublin a few days later on foot of a request for the affiliation fee. 'I beg to say it is impossible for us to send in same for a little while longer … there are no funds – in fact, we are a little in debt. However, we hope to be able to forward the fee in two or three weeks.'[9] The final sentence of the letter, 'are there any special rules for the guidance of classes?'[10] suggests that the undertaking was weighing a little heavily on him.

Plans Are Upset

Another letter, on 1 May 1901 to Fr O'Hickey, raised a problem far more serious than inadequate financial resources.

Rev. dear Father,

Unfortunately, there will be some sort of a west-British show in the town tomorrow (Thursday) night, and I fear a good many of the members of your Irish class are not yet sufficiently imbued with the proper Irish spirit necessary to enable them to withstand the temptation of attending the show in preference to the class. The committee think, therefore, it would be well to postpone the class until 8 p.m. (after Devotions) on Friday night, should it be convenient for your reverence to attend on the night. If you think it would not be wise to postpone the class, we shall be guided by your decision.

Domhnall ua Buachalla.[11]

Within a week though, a letter to *An Claidheamh Soluis* reflected more positive news from Maynooth. 'I have pleasure in enclosing herewith a cheque for £1.10s., 10s. affiliation fee and £1 for the Oireachtas Fund. Our class has a membership of over fifty. You will be glad to learn that the good Sisters of the Convent School have just begun the teaching of Irish also.'[12]

Up to that point, classes had been held in the Town Hall, but the offer of a room in the National School was deemed more convenient. In 1901, in an attempt to create a little more revenue, ua Buachalla drew on his friendships in Maynooth GAA circles, in particular a Richard O'Brien, to run a football tournament, which proved to be a great success. The report to Head Office stated that 'the games were well and quickly played, and the collection was good',[13] but the actual figure was not mentioned.

Ua Buachalla did include a cheque for £1 in response to another appeal for the Language Fund and reported that the class was now meeting twice a week 'with a constant attendance of thirty' and 'singing – at present Anglo-Irish – and step dancing are not neglected'.[14] The push for new recruits was stepped up 'with an excursion to Galway with the Colmcille [Dublin] Branch'[15] and finger-posts were erected throughout the county.

By 1903 the annual collection for the Language Fund had increased to £10.3s., donated by forty members, with four giving 10s., a sizeable sum. They were Patrick Canning, M.D., Martin Kelly, Concobhar ua Buachalla (Domhnall's brother) and the Presentation Convent. An annual raffle was later introduced with prizes ranging from a china tea set to a pair of boots and socks. On 8 April 1905 a letter to the editor of the *Leinster Leader*, accompanied by a cheque, referenced an incident which upset the Maynooth branch.

A Chara,

At a committee meeting of the above Branch it was unanimously decided – as a protest against the action of those responsible for the disgraceful incident of the Language Procession – to send through you the proceeds of this year's Language Procession. You will, therefore, kindly take charge of the enclosed cheque [for] £9.5s.4p. and list of names as appended.

Domhnall ua Buachalla.[16]

More uplifting publicity appeared in *The Irish Times* after the following year's procession:

The Gaelic League is a living and important force in Ireland. Nobody can deny the fact who watched its great annual procession pass yesterday through the streets of Dublin. For a full hour and a half the procession flowed past a given point, and its comprehensive elements included energies – educational, industrial, artistic, literary and athletic – which play a large part in the life of Ireland. The procession was a very great credit to the spirit and organising ability of the League. It was sober, earnest and well-disciplined.[17]

An Claidheamh Soluis, though, did not miss the opportunity to suggest that the roar of resurgent Ireland had at long last penetrated into the closely shuttered premises of Westmoreland Street.

Carts, Courts and Prams

Captain Tuthill's ultimatum concerning the 'heathen language' on ua Buachalla's cart in March 1905 would have gone unnoticed in Maynooth, with the exception of those who were aware that the delivery cart was no longer entering Moyglare House. But ua Buachalla's determination to defend his right to use the Irish language certainly did garner some attention on 12 December of the same year with the publication of a court report in the *Leinster Leader*. It appeared under the heading 'Prosecution in Celbridge' at the foot of an inside page.

At the Celbridge Petty Sessions on Monday before Mr W. T. Kirkpatrick, Captain Murray and R. McKenna, Mr Daniel Buckley, Maynooth, was summoned by Sergeant Finnegan, Maynooth, for having his name in Irish (only) on his carts.

Chairman: You are fined 2s. 6d. and 1s. 6d. costs.

Mr Buckley: I refuse to pay the fine.

Chairman: Then a warrant for a distraint must be issued.

Sergeant Finnegan: If there is any alternative to a distraint, I would prefer it, your Worship.

Mr R. McKenna: Why, has he not value enough to distrain for the amount?

Sergeant Finnegan: Oh, he has, but it is more troublesome. Perhaps he would like to go to jail himself.

Mr Buckley: *Is cuma lion, a mhico.* (It's all the same to me, my dear boy.)[18]

The following month, under the heading 'Irish Names on Carts', with a sub-heading, 'Case to be Stated', the *Freeman's Journal* reported from Celbridge:

In the Celbridge Petty Sessions today – Mr W. T. Kirkpatrick presiding – Mr Daniel Buckley, Maynooth, was again charged with allowing a cart, his property, to be used on the public streets without having his name and address painted in legible letters.

A few months since, Mr Buckley was fined for having the nameplate on his cart printed in Irish characters, and in this instance he was summonsed for having his name and address in Roman characters, which were equivalent to the same in the Irish language. Defendant was fined 5s. and costs, but on asking the magistrates to have a case stated, they agreed to do so.[19]

On 14 February, the *Freeman's Journal* made their report a page-topper with the headings, 'Irish Names on Carts' and 'Attorney-General's View':

In the King's Bench Division No. 1 (Crown Side), before the Lord Chief Justice, Mr Justice Andrews, and Mr Justice Wright, the case of Finnegan v. Buckley was a case stated by the magistrates at Celbridge Petty Sessions for the opinion of this Court. The

complainant, Sergeant Patrick Finnegan, of Maynooth RIC, charged
Donal Buckley of Maynooth, for that on the 23 December last at
Maynooth, the defendant allowed his cart to be used on the public
street without having his name and address painted thereon in
legible letters.

The evidence was that the name and address were printed in Irish,
though the letters which composed it were in Roman characters and
the complainant admitted this was on a conspicuous part of the cart,
and that the letters or characters were legible letters in the Roman
or English type; that the letters were at least an inch in length, and
that they were painted in white on a black [back] ground. The
magistrates convicted and fined the defendant 5s. and costs.

The defendant was represented by a solicitor, who contended that
all the requirements of Section 12 of the Act, Sub-Section 1, were
complied with. The magistrates held that the letters were not legible
to any person, not conversant with the Irish language and none
of the justices were able to decipher from the copy produced the
name or address. The magistrates presiding were – Messrs W. T.
Kirkpatrick, Bertram B. Barton, John Murray and W. G. Dease, and
they, at the instance of the defendant, stated the present case as to
whether they were right in their decision.

Mr James O'Connor and Mr Pearse (instructed by Mr Buckley and
Mr Gore) appeared for the defendant and addressed the court for
him.

Mr Pearse opened the arguments and read the case stated.

The Lord Chief Justice: Has not this been recently decided?

Mr Pearse: There is a point in this not decided by that case.

Counsel proceeded to cite the cases referred to, and argued that
this case was not on all fours with the case recently decided.

Mr Dudley White appeared on behalf of the Attorney-General
(instructed by Mr Malachy Kelly, Chief Crown Solicitor) and stated

that in the opinion of the Attorney-General, there was not an offence shown within the four walls of the case as stated by the justices. They seemed expressly to find that both the names and the address were printed in Roman characters. Counsel himself thought that in fact they were not in Roman characters, because, that though the letters were, in fact, Roman, there were Gaelic aspirant marks above some of them, which in the Gaelic language completely qualified their ordinary force as Roman letters.

In addition, the magistrates did not expressly find that the defendant was known by the English name of Buckley and not the Irish equivalent thereof. Therefore, so far as the name was concerned, it was quite consistent with the case, as stated, that the defendant's name in fact was an Irish name, and that he had complied with the recent King's Bench Division Court's decision in MacBride v. McGovern by painting that which was his name in fact in Roman characters.

Counsel stated that now, for the first time, he saw the actual label which was on the cart, and by it, the address was not the word 'Maynooth' as residence of the defendant in any characters whatever, but was a different residence altogether alleged to be the equivalent of his address. Seeing the name of the residence given in that manner, counsel thought it was unarguable that to paint the address in that manner was in fact compliant with the Act. But the case, as stated by the magistrate, had not shown what was on the label as the residence of the defendant.

Mr James O'Connor addressed the Court at length, and said that the people in Wales were mostly known by the old Welsh names. He submitted that the magistrates had not decided the question of fact, and that, therefore, their order should be discharged and that they were wrong in their decision.

The Lord Chief Justice said the Court was unanimously of the opinion that there was nothing in the case to be argued, and that the Magistrates were right. It was admitted that [the word] 'Maynooth' was well known in the town and neighbourhood, and that Buckley's name was well known also. It was distinctly a violation of the Act of Parliament to do what the defendant had done. The magistrates said they could not decipher the description. 'We consider the Act quite plain. We make no order as to costs, owing to the views of the Attorney-General, expressed by Mr White.'

Mr Justice Andrews concurred, and said the case of Macbride v. McGovern governed this case. This was an English Act, and it is not in compliance with that Act to use Irish. This man was known as Daniel Buckley, of Maynooth, in the English language. The magistrates were right in their decision.

Mr Justice Wright concurred with the decision ... this Act was passed not merely that policemen might be able to read the name and address, but for the protection of the public at large.[20]

An Irritating Policy of Pinpricks

An editorial in the *Freeman's Journal* was critical of the decision:

> The Lord Chief Justice, with Judge Andrews and Judge Wright, gave an extraordinary decision in the King's Bench yesterday. The question was with reference to a name upon a cart. Some time previously this same Court held that for a man to have his name painted on his cart in Gaelic letters was an offence, as the letters were not 'legible'. It appears from that decision that in order for letters to be 'legible', they should be in Roman characters. The magistrates stated a case for the King's Bench.
>
> The prosecution had, of course, been started during the Tory regime, but when the Attorney-General came to consider the question he saw that it was absurd, and instructed his counsel to go into court yesterday, which they did, and state that in his opinion the prosecution could not be supported.
>
> But Lord O'Brien and the two colleagues were not going to let a Gaelic Leaguer escape so easily. Where the Attorney-General laid down the prosecution, Lord O'Brien took it up, and he and Justice Wright proceeded to a conviction with all the ardour of their early career as prosecutors.[21]

The *Cork Constitution* also referred to the case:

> It is really too bad that with a Liberal and sympathetic Government in office, Irishmen should still be subject to the indignity of having to use a 'foreign' language when affixing their names and addresses to their vehicles. The Gaelic League had just been congratulating themselves that with the advent of a radical government this 'irritating policy of pinpricks' would be abandoned. But it appears they will have to fight on for some time longer if they are to bring about the removal of this tremendous obstacle in the way of the country's progress.[22]

The *Irish Law Times and Solicitors' Journal* also referred to the case:

> Justices – The defendant was summoned under 14 & 15 Vict. C. 92, S. 12, S. 12, Sub. S. 1, for not having his name and address painted in legible letters on one of his carts. There was, on a conspicuous part of his cart, a name plate, on which the name and address were painted in the Irish form though the letters were in Roman characters.
>
> The magistrate found as a fact that though each letter was a legible character, they were collectively not legible by any person not conversant with the Irish language, and they, therefore, convicted the defendant. Held, that the conviction was right in point of law. The owner's address must be painted in the ordinary English form, and where he has a name in English, such name must also be painted in the English form.
>
> Buckley, appellant, v. Finnegan, respondent. Feb. 13. Counsel: Healy K. C., James O'Connor, Pearce [sic], Dudley White. Solicitors: John Gore; Malachy Kelly.[23]

While the negativity of the decision drew the ire of some editorial writers, Pádraig Pearse took a positive view of the proceedings in a summation in *An Claidheamh Soluis*, which he was editing at that time:

> The language movement has won yet another victory in the British courts of law. That is to say, it has forced a British tribunal to

pronounce the Irish language illegal – an excellent thing for the language movement. Henceforward, there can be no mistake. However lenient a 'sympathetic' British government may be, however gracious a British viceroy or even a British monarch, we of the Gaelic League are rebels and law-breakers; our organisation has an illegal propaganda; the meetings of the *Coiste Gnótha* are liable at any moment to be broken in on by soldiery. So says the law ... '*Tá breall ar an dlighe, adeirimid-ne*'. [The law is defective, we say.][24]

This was one of only two court cases that Pearse took as a barrister. The other involved Niall MacGiolla Bhríde, a Cresslough street-market trader and poet who wrote an autobiography dealing with the Land War in Donegal, the struggle for Tenant Rights, the Gweedore and Derryveigh evictions and the shooting of the Second Earl of Leitrim. He also displayed his name in Gaelic on his cart and was fined one shilling, or a week in Londonderry Gaol; Judge Nigel Huntingdon-Smythe stated that he would not tolerate native Irish people either speaking or writing their names in a 'foreign' language. The case was appealed with the help of *Conradh na Gaeilge* and Pearse to the High Court in Dublin.

Finality for ua Buachalla's case came with the issuing of a warrant for a distraint, which produced a heart-warming conclusion. A roll of material was taken from the Maynooth shop and was subsequently auctioned. When bids were sought, only one voice was heard. An elderly man who lived in the village handed one pound to Sergeant Finnegan on 14 April 1906. Patrick Fitzsimons then picked up the roll, took it to ua Buachalla's shop, put it on the counter with the RIC receipt – and walked home.

This did not end ua Buachalla's struggle to use the Irish form of his name on his carts and over the door of his shop. It did, however, continue to foster a relationship with Pearse which would develop through the Gaelic League and the schooling of Joe and the Volunteers. During this period, the Maynooth merchant appeared to become increasingly convinced that independence would only be achieved by force of arms.

Nevertheless, the social and political aspects of his life, as well as keeping his clients happy, had a balance in domestic affairs. His second son, Domhnall, was born in 1900, followed by his first daughter, Síghle, in 1902; Kevin arrived in 1904 and a second daughter, Bríghid, in 1906. Between carts, courts and prams, his days did not lack for action.

CHAPTER 5

'Since It's Yourself, £30 Will Do'

Despite fluctuations in Gaelic League membership numbers in Maynooth, Domhnall ua Buachalla's enthusiasm for the revival of the language never waned. By 1908 he was producing pamphlets with the names and donations of subscribers and words of encouragement to the League's members. He also ensured that the list of people who gave money would be published in the *Leinster Leader*, which was a great supporter of the Gaelic League.

His efforts were generously facilitated by the editor, Seumas O'Kelly, a Galway nationalist, playwright, poet and author who arrived in Naas in 1906, started a branch of the Gaelic League and joined Sinn Féin. A good friend of ua Buachalla, he directed the editorial line of the *Leader* until 1912 when he was appointed editor of the *Saturday Evening Post* in Dublin. There, he became involved in literary circles with such notables as James Stephens, Oliver Gogarty, Seán McDermott, Arthur Griffith and Thomas McDonagh. *The Shuiler's Child* (1909) was produced at the Abbey and his other plays included *Meadowsweet*, *The Matchmakers* and *The Parnellite*. Among his novels were *The Lady of Deer Park* and *Wet Clay*. Collections of short stories included *By The Stream Of Kilmeen* while *The Weaver's Grave* was a memorable novella. He also wrote the poem 'Bodenstown' as a tribute to Wolfe Tone.

He had promised Arthur Griffith he would take over editorship of *Nationality* should the need arise, and when it did he moved into Sinn Féin headquarters at No. 6 Harcourt Street. On Armistice Day, 11 November 1918, as the Union Jack flew from all principal buildings, the republican flag flew over No. 6, which provoked British soldiers and a mob to attack it. After three days of pressure with the Volunteers resisting, the office was entered and Seumas collapsed while defending himself with a walking stick. He died of a heart attack that night. In the week of his death his book of poems, *Ranns and Ballads*, was published; the title of the last poem in the collection, 'Slán Leat' ['Goodbye'], was particularly apt. His funeral was one of the biggest of its time.

Another friend of ua Buachalla with a great love of the Irish language was An tAthair Peadar Ó Laoghaire, a driving force in modern Irish literature who was ordained in Maynooth College in 1867. His most famous story was 'Séadna', written while he served as Parish Priest in Castlelyons, and well known to generations of Irish students. In May 1910, ua Buachalla received a letter from O'Laoghaire, thanking him for an offering of ten shillings and assuring him that he would say Mass, adding that he hoped God would grant him his wish to look after Sinéad, who had a heart complaint, and was about to give birth to her seventh child. Just days before the letter arrived, the last of ua Buachalla's children was born, a son. Appropriately, the name chosen for him was Séadna.

Seumas O'Kelly's successors in the *Leinster Leader* continued to facilitate ua Buachalla's efforts through his Gaelic League days and, later, during election campaigns. His pamphlet for 1908, which informed members that their total contribution to the Language Fund was £12.3s.6p., carried the following message beneath the list of subscribers:

> Whether or not Irish be made essential for entrance to the National University, the movement for its revival, which still continues to forge ahead, is deserving of our warmest support. The movement for the revival of Irish industries follows closely in the wake of the Language Revival. Should the latter fail through want of support from Irishmen and Irishwomen, the former will almost assuredly fail also; therefore, **Every Leaguer should Collect and every Gael should Subscribe.**[1]

In the list of subscribers was a section for Maynooth College, which suggests that Fr Hickey's earlier view that it was better to let them send their donations directly to head office had finally been circumvented by the secretary/treasurer, with a little help from a Christopher Slevin who worked there. And the name of Patrick Fitzsimons, purchaser of the roll of material following the court case, was listed as one of eight who contributed 6d.

Among other words of encouragement ua Buachalla passed on to the members were international views on the benefits of learning the language:

> What Latin has done for Europe, Gaelic may do as a training instrument for Ireland ... Gaelic provides ample exercise for mental training in its elaborate accidence, its beautiful phonetic system, its exquisite flexibility and its copious vocabulary ... the boy who has really mastered Irish has learned to use his brain. No other language will seem unconquerable to him – **Professor Stanley Lane-Poole, English Linguist in the Fortnightly Review, June 1907.**

> I know of no other modern language which, regarded purely as a language, possesses a higher educational value than modern Irish for a boy who knows English ... for through education and schooling of the mind, Irish stands, at the very least, on a level with the above-named languages [French and German]; in fact, it is in many respects superior to them – **Dr. H. Zimmer, Professor, University of Berlin.**[2]

Considering ua Buachalla's love for the language, he would have welcomed the letter that arrived in August 1908 from Pádraig Pearse, informing him that St Enda's College would be opening the following month. It was well laced with the benefits that awaited Joe, but the need for a 'hard sell' was unnecessary as the headmaster was preaching to the converted:

> *A Chara,*

> Many thanks for your letter. I enclose a copy of the School's programme, and I hope you like it. I needn't say that there will be great welcome for any student you send to our school, *Scoil Éanna.*

> Some amount of Irish is taught in many of the intermediate schools around the country, but we will give a truly Gaelic education to our students, we will make Irish speakers of the boys who come to us, something that no school or college other than a Gaelic school can

guarantee. I believe we can provide better education in English and in all other necessary subjects than any other college.

Firstly, we have acquired the best teachers in the country; secondly, we practise the best teaching methods; and thirdly, we'll only have a small band of boys compared with big colleges and we will be able to give special attention to each one.

Among the children already promised to be with us are the sons of Eoin MacNeill; the sons of Peadar Mac Fhionnlaoich; the son of Uilliam Bulfin (Editor of *Southern Cross*); a son of Dr C. Mac Murchadha; a son of Dr S. Ó Tuathaigh and a son of Eoin MacNeill's sister from Gleanneaíl, Co. Antrim. We also hope to have a son of Uilliam Uí Riain (the *Peasant* man) and the sons of Dáithí Ó Moráin (the *Leader* man). That's a great band of young Irish people and I am hoping that the sons of Domhnall Ó Buachalla will be among them. Also, do your level best to encourage your brothers here in Dublin to have their children sent to us.

Yours, expecting good news from you.

Your constant friend,

Pádraic Mac Piarais.[3]

Having received a letter confirming the good news, Pearse wrote again:

A Chara,

Many thanks for your letter. It is music to my ears to learn that your son will be a student of ours in *Scoil Éanna*. I promise you that I will do my best on his behalf, and I hope, please God, to direct him to be a good Catholic and a good Irish person. We expect the boarders on the 7th of the month. On the 8th of the month we expect the day students. Work will start in earnest on that day and your son should be in by then. I am very thankful to you for sending the programme to your brothers. One of them lives close to the school and he should send his children to our school.

Your constant friend,

Pádraic Mac Piarais.[4]

St Enda's, initially in Cullensford House on Oakley Road, Rathmines, proved to be a haven of culture and creativity in which Joe flourished. For the first two years he was a day pupil, living with the Conway family in Gibraltar House where his mother was looked after when orphaned. During the week he would cycle to school and take the train back to Maynooth at the weekends.

Pearse preferred his pupils to board at the school and got his wish two years later when the decision was made to move from Rathmines to The Hermitage. With Joe now 12, and a wonderful leafy setting opening up for the pupils in Rathfarnham, ua Buachalla wrote to Pearse to suggest his son would become a full-time scholar – if the price was right.

22 August 1910.

A Chara,

I received your letter today. I would not accept any other student for that money, but since it is yourself, I will take Seosamh for £30 a year without any extra. Let that be the bargain then. We will give his food the best of attention – he will have porridge, brown bread and eggs, and much of them. Will he need porridge and egg for every breakfast ... I wonder? The practice we have here is egg or porridge every morning and plenty [of] bread and butter. We will have hens in the new place [The Hermitage] and perhaps eggs will be scarce enough at times (because we will have sixty people to feed each day) and if you wish to send him eggs yourself, the better we would like it.

Your constant friend,

Pádraic Mac Piarais.[5]

Whether ua Buachalla ever got around to ensuring his son's breakfast needs were augmented by Maynooth eggs will never be known, but he did provide a much-appreciated gift shortly afterwards. As there was an abundance of wild life in the extensive estate, pupils had been warned by the teachers, and in particular by Pearse, that animals 'were put on this earth to live, not to be killed'. In fact, Pearse himself took the classes dealing with fauna and flora and in a report on the first term's activities in 1910, there was a note of thanks to ua Buachalla 'for a gift of his valuable collection of Irish birds' eggs', which were prominently displayed.

Two years later, when Pearse found a duck that had gone to the great pond in the sky while out walking, and also discovered a catapult close to the scene of the crime which he proceeded to pull apart, the pupils expected recriminations, despite the fact that the matter was not mentioned at evening meal. Later that night, Joe recalled, the dormitory door opened:

> I was in a room with five others and he came in to put the light out. He might not come in every night, but I guessed he would come in that night, so I was over in a corner and I had my face to the wall. I was about 14 at the time. He came over and sat down on the bed and was talking to the others, and suddenly he gave me a bang on the back of the head and said 'You're not asleep, turn around here', or words to that effect.

> I was sulky of course and then he said, 'Where did you get that catapult?'

> 'I brought it from home, my father made it for me.'

> 'Oh', he said, 'that's another matter. Well now, you know you shouldn't have brought it back to school, whatever you might do at home with it.'

> He gave me a little lecture, and then took an orange from his pocket and handed it to me, saying 'there', and went off with himself.[6]

> Another day I was down at the lake with three other lads and we saw water hens and, of course, up with a stone, I was unlucky enough to kill one of the hens. It was found and brought up to the study hall.

> 'Who killed the water hen?' the gathering was asked.

I told him I did – and got six on the hand. He was very adamant about things like that. There was never corporal punishment for not knowing your lessons, but for other things – like that – you would get five or six. He didn't like doing it, but he would always come back at night, with a few sweets in his pocket or something. Either he, or Willie, administered the corporal punishment. He did not let anyone else do it.

If you did not do your lessons you were kept in after 3.30 p.m., or after dinner, but the funny thing is that there were lads in the school – three that I can recollect – who were expelled from other colleges in Ireland, but they're all good men now, and he made men of them. He had that – what I don't know – personality? I've heard people give lectures on Pearse, and my reaction to them was that they did not know what they were talking about, that they were never in St. Enda's and they had never met Pearse.

I don't think it is altogether right to call him a mystic – he wasn't – but I think his mind, when we really got to know him, was then drifting towards the Revolution ... I'd say that Pearse went out in the Rising knowing more than any man that he wasn't going to come back.[7]

Pearse edited a diary-like newsletter, *An Macaomh*, which revealed a great appreciation of the qualities of the students. In 1910, with a dateline of September 12, readers were informed that:

Some faces and figures we sorely miss; Maurice Fraher will never more turn a forlorn hope on the hurling field into a glorious victory for *Scoil Éanna* – his place henceforth is with the hurlers of his native *Déise*; if Conroy ever again quavers forth the songs of *sean-Mhaitias* or tells the famous tale of 'The Piper in the Snail's Castle' it will be to the little boys of *Tír Eoghain* to whom he has gone to teach his *Iar-Connacht* Irish. Nearer home Denis Gwynn is carrying the banner of Scoil Éanna into the National University ... on the western breeze comes a faint murmer of the possibility of the return of Frank Connolly, another of our undergraduates ... and Eamon Bulfin is here, of course, looking taller and more heroic than ever ... Dick Humphreys and Joseph Buckley, who were day boys at Cullenswood House, have come to us in Rathfarnham as boarders ...[8]

Dated September 16 is a report on a céilí: 'Donal O'Connor, Fred O'Doherty and Joseph Buckley sang with all their old blitheness. Frank Burke and Fred Holden discoursed most excellent music on the piano. Richard O'Connor played hauntingly on his violin old airs he had picked up in the gaedhealtacht of Munster . . .'[9]

Later in the year there is mention of a body of Fianna being formed. 'Mr Colbert has started a class in code-signalling . . . and he gave us our first lesson in military foot drill.'[10] In December 'the Headmaster retains the Commandership-In-Chief under the title of *Árd-Taoiseach* . . . our programme includes drill, gymnastics, shooting, fencing, boxing, wrestling, swimming, ambulance work, mountain marches, camping out and scouting'.[11]

Writing about Pearse's commitment to cultural nationalism at this time, historian Elaine Sisson suggests that his direction 'gained a more military and political edge after 1913, when he became a member of the IRB. From then on even his closest friends observed that his worship of military discipline became fanatical, and a private obsession with Napoleon was deemed to be excessive.'[12] She also points out that of the fourteen men who were executed in 1916, five – Patrick and Willie Pearse, Joseph Plunkett, Thomas McDonagh and Con Colbert – had taught in the school.[13]

While ua Buachalla would have been reassured with Pearse's style of education in Rathfarnham, and the political path he was taking, others were a little less enamoured. The book, *In The Footsteps of Big Jim: A Family Biography* (1966), reveals how Jim Larkin's family reacted to life there:

> Despite the Christianity shown by the Pearse brothers, I can say with certainty that my father and his two brothers disliked St. Enda's intensely. The regime in the school was strict, the living conditions were spartan and the food was scarce. During the winter, heating was kept at a minimum and there was a great belief in much physical exercise to keep oneself warm.[14]

As a final-year student in the college in 1916, Joe's plan was that he should be handed a rifle by Pearse and given the opportunity to follow him into O'Connell Street with others from St Enda's. It would meet with rejection, though not because Pearse thought Joe was too young.

The Fools, the Fools, the Fools

An article in *An Claidheamh Soluis* in November 1913, 'The North Began', advocated the formation of a national volunteer force, similar to that which existed in the North.[15] The author was Eoin MacNeill and the idea appealed to the IRB. The O'Rahilly had a lengthy meeting with him and a provisional committee was formed under MacNeill's chairmanship. It included Pádraig Pearse, Éamonn Ceannt, Seán MacDermott, Bulmer Hobson, Piaras Béaslaí, W. J. Ryan, Colm Ó Lochlainn, Seumas O'Connor, Seán Fitzgibbon, J. A. Deakin, The O'Rahilly and Joseph Campbell.

The inaugural meeting took place at the Rotunda on 25 November 1913. Few parliamentarians attended. Originally the concert room was booked by Bulmer Hobson, but the general response was overwhelming and the venue was switched to the Rotunda Rink, the biggest hall in Dublin at that time. In addition to the 4,000 inside, 3,000 were outside, unable to gain admission. Part of the Volunteers' manifesto, which was written by MacNeill, read:

> To drill, to learn the use of arms, to acquire the habit of concerted and disciplined action, to form a citizen army from a population now at the mercy of almost any organised aggression – this, beyond all doubt, is a programme that appeals to all Ireland, but especially to young Ireland. We begin at once in Dublin, and are confident that the movement will be taken up without delay all over the country. Public opinion has already and quite spontaneously formed itself into an eager desire for the establishment of the Irish Volunteers.[16]

It concluded with the words: 'We appeal to our countrymen to recognise and accept without hesitation the opportunity that has been granted them to join the ranks of the Irish Volunteers, and to make the movement now begun not unworthy of the historic title which it has adopted.'[17] Among the 3,000 who enrolled that night was a young professor of mathematics and an enthusiastic member of the Gaelic League, Éamon de Valera. Macardle wrote of that period:

> The sudden change that comes over a conquered people at the first motion to resist in arms swept over Ireland now. The Parliamentarian leaders were slow in recognising it, but they were to recognise it later. Irish men and women who had despaired of independence

and had numbered themselves among the suppliants for a measure of Home Rule became filled with a larger aspiration and with the courage to strive for it. The Fenian spirit, dormant in the old people and latent in the young, quickened into life.[18]

These words would have resonated with Patrick Colgan, a neighbour and close friend of ua Buachalla. Both Colgan and ua Buachalla were willing to advance the cause of freedom in whatever manner they could, but unfortunately they had drifted apart in 1913, a situation recalled by Colgan:

> One thing that helped me along the right lines was the fight put up by the Dublin workers in 1913. It was the first time I commenced thinking along physical-force lines. It was the only time that bad feelings came between ua Buachalla and me. He was at that time an active member of the Ancient Order of Hibernians and anti-Larkin. We were not on speaking terms.[19]

The Ancient Order of Hibernians was a right-wing, popular, working-class and farmers' organisation for communal defence and welfare that, up to 1904, came under an ecclesiastical ban as an oath-bound society.[20] Tom Garvin pointed out that 'many prominent leaders of the 1916–23 period, among them Seán MacDermott and Rory O'Connor, were members ... but it had always been a threat to the Gaelic League and to the new Sinn Féin'.[21] Ua Buachalla did not have to deal with organised labour in his business, but a short news-story in the *Leinster Leader* revealed how he faced up to such problems:

> Last week two employees of Mr Daniel Buckley, general trader, Maynooth, refused to handle a wagon-load of flour which had arrived at the Railway Station from Messrs. Shackleton's mill, Lucan. After receiving twenty-four hours to consider their action, the men – who belonged to no trade union – were dismissed, and up to the time of writing, Mr Buckley has not sought to replace them, their duties being performed by himself and his shop assistants.[22]

It came as a surprise to Colgan, therefore, that ua Buachalla should call to his house early in 1914 to ask him if he would help organise the Volunteers in Maynooth. Harmony was instantly restored and the two men set up a

meeting, ironically, in the AOH Hall in Maynooth on 30 May 1914, which
was addressed by Laurence Kettle, Michael Buckley (Domhnall's brother)
and Art O'Connor, the Kildare District Council Engineer. In early June,
Irish Volunteer companies had been formed in Maynooth, Celbridge
and Newbridge; Colgan reckoned Maynooth had 180 members but ua
Buachalla's estimation was decidedly smaller. On 7 June over 7,000 people
gathered on the Curragh for a meeting.

From the outset, initiation was somewhat haphazard. 'On joining we
took no oath', ua Buachalla recalled. 'I cannot remember if I signed
a register or was issued with a membership card. We paid a weekly
subscription of a few pence towards expenses and the purchase of arms
and equipment. We had no arms of any sort.'[23] A receipt from the offices
in No. 41 Kildare Street, Dublin for February and March 1915 indicated
that he had paid five shillings for those two months. In Maynooth they
appointed as Company Captain a reservist of the Dublin Fusiliers called
O'Toole. When the First World War broke out in August 1914 he returned
to his regiment. 'He acted as a Recruiting Sergeant during the day and a
Volunteer Company Captain in his spare time',[24] Colgan recalled.

> We drilled with broom handles during the summer. I was appointed
> Section Leader. I was totally unfit for the appointment. To make
> matters worse, I had a fair sprinkling of ex-militia men in my Section;
> their comments on my right to be their leader often caused me
> embarrassment. After the outbreak of war it was noticeable that the
> colonels, majors and captains who were still with us showed an interest
> in what we were doing; often they visited just to say we were fine fellows.
> Once our company captain ordered us to parade; to be inspected by
> one Major Montgomery. I refused to parade my Section; I was fired
> immediately. However, I was reinstated within a short time.[25]

Colgan's action would have reflected the view of some of his fellow
Volunteers, but not the majority, and this was to become apparent almost
immediately. On his way home to Aughavannagh from London after seeing
the Home Rule bill passed, John Redmond stopped off in Woodenbridge,
Co. Wicklow on 20 September 1914 and made a speech which caused the
final split in the ranks of the Volunteers.

> I say to you, therefore, your duty is twofold. I am glad to see such
> magnificent material for soldiers around me ... go on drilling

and make yourselves efficient for the work, and then account for yourselves as men, not only in Ireland itself, but wherever the fighting line extends, in defence of rights, freedom and religion in this war.[26]

On 5 October, a letter in the *Irish Independent* written by Sir Roger Casement stated: 'Ireland has no blood to give to any land, to any cause, but that of Ireland'.[27]

Redmond was driven by the need to see the enactment of the Home Rule Act of 1914, and to this end he worked relentlessly in encouraging the National Volunteers to join in Britain's commitment to the First World War. He saw it as an opportunity that would be good for the future welfare and integrity of Ireland, and believed that Britain would not renege on its commitment to the nation. He even suggested in the House of Commons that Britain could take their troops out of Ireland during the First World War and that the Irish Volunteers in the south, with the help of their Ulster counterparts, would defend our coasts.

Adding appeal to his views was the expectation that the First World War could be a short-lived confrontation. Also, as there was widespread unemployment in Ireland, particularly in Dublin, an opportunity was being presented that would put food on the table for thousands of starving families who would later welcome their heroes back to a country that was about to be given Home Rule. For many, it was an attractive scenario.

It was, however, utterly at variance with the views of members of the IRB, who saw the Volunteers as a vehicle to gain independence, and to whom the idea of aiding the British War Effort was alien. But when it came to a national vote, the vast majority of the country's estimated 185,000 Volunteers backed Redmond and took the name 'National Volunteers'; about 12,000 sided with MacNeill and remained 'Irish Volunteers'.

As soon as the War began, the IRB took action. At a meeting in No. 25, Parnell Square, it was decided that Ireland would use the War to rebel against England.

In Maynooth, no more than twelve sided with ua Buachalla and Colgan in taking the anti-Redmond side, the vast majority going with the Wexford man, including the instructor. Nevertheless, ua Buachalla recalled how comfortable the men were despite their differing views. 'We had the use of a hall for drilling and after the split, both Volunteer units shared it, but the Redmond Volunteers faded out after a while. A man named Saults, also an ex-British army man, was now our instructor. I think he gave his services free.'[28]

At that stage, ua Buachalla's mind was very much on a rebellion, with planning and preparation uppermost in his mind. In a conversation with Pearse, he suggested that dealing with British cavalry could present a problem, but that he had a plan. Joe recalled that he went to Henshaw's, a hardware store with a factory in Clonsilla, where he put in an order for a few dozen pikes which his 'customers' required for throwing sheaves of corn onto a reek. When the delivery arrived he put on the handles and stored most of them. Word of mouth, though, must have informed Seamus Kenny of Emmet Road, Inchicore, who was Quartermaster to the Battalion Council and Commandant to Eamonn Ceannt, of their availability. He wrote in his Military Statement that he often had £200 or £300 given to him in Bank of England five pound notes 'to buy stuff. I bought guns wherever I could get them, and pikes from Domhnall ua Buachalla in Maynooth'.[29]

Besides pikes, Joe remembers his father purchasing – over a period of time – twenty four shotguns and he also got his hands on an Epic, which was the 'acme of good weapons at that time',[30] and one of the reasons why ua Buachalla was considered one of the best marksmen available to the leaders during the Rising.

As the two Volunteer bodies were going their separate ways, Colgan paid close attention to where the company's diligently collected money would find a resting place. 'We had funds amounting to about £80. The treasurer came with us and I advocated holding on to the money.'[31] The money was eventually split fifty-fifty, which was a reasonable outcome for him considering the numerical split, and reflective of the harmony between the groups. 'The Redmondites spent their share on caps and haversacks; we spent our money on arms and ammunition.'[32]

At this time, Sir Roger Casement's efforts in America and Germany were coming to fruition: on 27 December an undertaking was signed in Berlin that an Irish Brigade would be formed from the prisoners-of-war to serve Ireland solely. It was to be furnished and equipped by the German Imperial Government. At the same time, Home Rule was suspended, Ulster was set on partitioning the country, Redmond was recruiting for the British Army, the IRB preparing for a Rising – and the term 'Sinn Féin Volunteers' – to distinguish the republicans from Redmond's force – was gaining traction.

In July 1915 came further inspiration at the funeral of the Fenian, Jeremiah O'Donovan Rossa. Having lived through the Famine and imprisonment for activities associated with an emerging IRB from 1865 to 1871, he went to America, raised money through a 'skirmishing fund', which was used in the 'Dynamite War', the first Republican bombing campaign in London. When he died, his body was brought back from New York to a hero's welcome. On 1 August 1915, marshalled by Volunteers in green uniforms, thousands walked to Glasnevin Cemetary behind the coffin. With them, dressed in his Volunteer's uniform and his hands resting on his sword-hilt, Pearse concluded his oration with the words:

> The Defenders of this Realm have worked well in secret and in the open. They think that they have pacified Ireland. They think that they have purchased half of us and intimidated the other half. They think that they have foreseen everything, think that they have provided against everything; but, the fools, the fools, the fools! – they have left us our Fenian dead, and while Ireland holds these graves, Ireland unfree shall never be at peace.[33]

Another funeral, on 20 April 1915, had far greater significance for ua Buachalla. His father passed away after a lengthy illness at the age of 88. Cornelius had lived through harrowing times, most notably the Famine, which prompted him to move from Cork farmland closer to Dublin. He had observed Home Rule machinations from 1868; he saw the founding of the Land League and the Land War; he observed Charles Stewart Parnell's push for Home Rule and his role in the formation of the Irish National League; and then there was the Ulster Question, which started with the First Home Rule Bill (The Government of Ireland Bill) in 1886. He would have been aware of his son's increasing activity in cultural and political matters, but could never have envisaged the road he would travel, or the ultimate destination.

In addition to losing his father, ua Buachalla's mother, Sarah, was also failing at this time and in need of constant attention while Sinéad, who had completed the family with the births of Máirín in 1908 and Séadna in 1910, was not enjoying good health. But even with these problems, his commitment to the Gaelic League and the Maynooth Volunteers never wavered. 'We had drills and route marches on Sundays and weeknights. I had a .22 rifle and we had firing practice with this in the hall. There were a couple of other .22 rifles. I supplied the ammunition for firing practice ... and we never had any visits from the officers at Volunteer Headquarters.'[34]

Although the Volunteers had difficulty getting their hands on guns, the Maynooth merchant had other avenues open to him, but some of the guns he acquired were purchased in the line of business for 'sporting purposes' and he needed official approval. Among some papers discovered by a grandson in recent years is a document headed 'Permit for Sale of Arms, Ammunition, or Explosives'. With the stamp of 'Major General L. B. Friend, Commanding Troops in Ireland', and signed by a district inspector, it lists the names of six people who had been given permission to buy a gun through ua Buachalla's business.

Guns for the College Students

The first batch received approval on 27 December 1915. All the recipients were attached to Maynooth College. The names and addresses were: Rev. John Kelly, Castlebar, Co. Mayo; Rev. Myles Allman, Beaufort, Co. Kerry; Rev. Timothy Donovan, Curraheen, Kinsale, Co. Cork; Rev. P. J. Durcan, Main Street, Tubbercurry, Co. Sligo; Rev. J. Kennedy and Rev. J. McCaffrey, Maynooth College, Co. Dublin. A day later, permission was given for another gun for C. J. Dillon, of No. 192 Great Brunswick Street, Dublin, but there is no indication that he was a resident in the college. The approval dates suggest that none would have been available as they had departed for their Christmas holidays.

A shotgun, also known as a scattergun and peppergun, was historically referred to as a fowling gun, a firearm which uses the energy of a fixed shell to fire 'shot', or a solid projectile called 'slug'. Very popular for bird hunting, it was also used for more general forms of hunting, especially in semi-populated areas where the range of the rifle-bullet posed a hazard. They were in common use during the Rising and the War of Independence. The text of the letters were similar:

Dear Mr Buckley,

Please supply one fowling piece, same as you supplied to Mr O'Connor (Kerry) last year. Send to Broadstone Station on Thursday next, 2.30 train. Send in bill to me in the meantime. I will let you have the cash before Thursday.

Myles Allman, St. Mary's.

A Chara,

Kindly obtain for me as soon as possible a single-barrel fowling piece
– see that it is a reliable make and British stamped. If you supply me
with ammunition I should be much obliged as it is difficult to get in
my native village. If possible send me the gun before going home –
otherwise I will send you my home address.

Timothy Donovan.

Dear Mr Buckley,

Now that the Xmas holidays are at hand I would like to have a gun
for sporting purposes. The students say that you keep a good stock
so I hope you will be able to supply a good one. You must have it
delivered before Dec. 23 as we are leaving for holidays that day. I am
sure you won't disappoint either as regards quality or terms. I would
also like to know your prices for ammunition for sporting rifles.

J. Kennedy.[35]

It is possible that ua Buachalla was in a position to purchase some ammunition
from his suppliers for the Volunteers without the Major General's approval,
and to this end he ran a raffle 'in aid of the equipment fund for the local
corps of the Volunteers' at 3d. a ticket with three prizes: the first prize was
an excellent gold watch; the second a beautiful china tea set; the third a
sovereign, and there was a consolation prize of 'No Conscription!'

His youngest son, Séadna, in notes written later in life, mentioned
that his father would go out into the countryside late at night with Liam
O'Regan, both wearing masks and on bicycles, and bring home what arms
and ammunition they could 'confiscate'.[36] If they succeeded in getting
a gun, it was immediately cleaned, oiled and then hidden. In the year
leading up to the Rising, he became a master at creating space in the
attic, stores and other rooms with false fronts, behind which he secured
the guns and ammunition.

Eventually his sources began to dry up and as Secretary of the Maynooth
Volunteers, he was forced to go down another avenue for ammunition,

which Séadna also mentioned. His father asked Sinéad to make a few bandoliers and put extra pockets on the inside of his long, heavy coat; while that was being done, he went into Dublin to talk to his suppliers, Keegan Brothers, a gunsmith firm near the Four Courts, about the availability of ammunition in Manchester and where he might source it.

His next stop was the home of Diarmuid O'Neill, a young and enthusiastic member of the Volunteers and an ideal accomplice for ua Buachalla. The pair headed for the Mail Boat and from Holyhead they took a train to Manchester. Having completed their business and secreted the ammunition as best they could, they took their seats on the train back to Holyhead, happy that their undertaking had been a success. And it was, until one pocket failed to retain the ammunition it was holding and the two men watched as bullets dropped to the floor of the carriage and gently rolled from side-to-side before finally being recovered. Whether fellow passengers were afraid to remark on the incident unfolding in front of them, or were not aware of the significance of the ammunition, the goods arrived back in Maynooth – and ensured that additional recesses would have to be created in the house.

Ua Buachalla's friendship with Diarmuid blossomed, as it did with his younger brother, Mick, who had moved up from Kenmare to live with Diarmuid and study veterinary medicine. The association of the O'Neill and ua Buachalla families would later bring great joy to both, as well as devastating sadness much later in life.

CHAPTER 6

The *Aud* Debacle

In October 1915 a young student in the Agricultural College at Ballyhaise, Co. Cavan returned home to Prosperous in Kildare. A member of the Gaelic League from 1913, Tom Harris had developed a rapport with his teacher, Seán O'Connor, who lived in Celbridge, and took a great interest in *Irish Freedom* and other national papers, which were read and discussed during classes. Both were enthusiastic supporters of the IRB, O'Connor in particular taking direction from Pádraig Pearse, and together they made trips to headquarters in Dublin where they also became acquainted with Liam Mellows.

Although O'Connor subsequently went to live in Dublin, Harris became deeply involved with the Volunteers, particularly Tom Clarke, whom he would seek out when in Dublin. Clarke told him that Ted O'Kelly was trying to organise Kildare and would call on him, which he did. Harris recalled attending a meeting at Dawson Street in Dublin and met O'Kelly again. Seán Boylan from Dunboyne, Jack Fitzgerald from Newbridge and Domhnall ua Buachalla were also present:

> There was a kind of preliminary meeting in the Kildare district with a view to seeing what could be done to build up the organisation. Arrangements were made to hold a further meeting in Naas ... O'Kelly gave instructions on a few occasions to the Prosperous Company and I tried giving it as best I could. I attended a few parades in Maynooth and Leixlip and O'Kelly gave drill instruction

there. This was around the end of 1915 and early 1916. At that time I had a .32 automatic. I think O'Kelly had a gun of some sort ...

On Spy Wednesday in 1916 a young fellow named Sweeney came out from Naas with a dispatch to tell me to go to Newbridge, that O'Kelly wanted to see me ... that was the first time I met Tom Byrne. He had been sent down because he had a good knowledge in the use of explosives. His task was to blow up the railway lines and cut off communication with the Curragh. We were to mobilise around Bodenstown and to cut the railway line there and then go into Dublin and join up with the insurgents there. We got nothing in the way of arms from Dublin that week.

Byrne and O'Kelly informed us that the Rising would take place anytime within the next week and that arms were on their way from Germany. They said the arms would be landed in the south, off the Kerry coast, and that the Rising would take place in Dublin first.[1]

There is a remarkable family connection between ua Buachalla and the people on the periphery of the failed attempt by Sir Roger Casement to land arms, when the *Aud* was intercepted in Tralee Bay by British cruisers and scuttled by the German crew as it was being escorted into Queenstown [Cobh].

On Good Friday morning six men, led by Denis Daly, left Dublin by train for Killarney. Their destination was Cahersiveen, where they were to seize a wireless transmitting set and bring it to Ballyard in Tralee, there to be erected under the supervision of Austin Stack and used to mislead the British authorities as well as broadcast news of the Rising. They were met by two cars, the second of which was owned by Tommy MacInerney of Limerick. He took three men, one of them being Con Keating, a wireless expert from Cahersiveen, who sat beside the driver. His orders were to keep the tail-light of the first car in view, but as this car had to stop twice – once to respond to questions from an RIC constable – he was unable to do so.

Heading into Killorglin they decided it would be safer not to pass the police barracks at the top of the hill, so they took a detour to the right of the church, which would circumvent the town and later take them back onto the Cahersiveen road. It also led to Ballykissane Pier. As the road deteriorated, and within seconds of MacInerney asking the driver whether they were on the right road, the car's lights flashed on water. The brakes were jammed on and the car stopped with the front wheels facing down into the Laune Estuary. It then toppled into sixteen feet of water; James Monahan of Dublin, Donal Sheehan of Monagea, West Limerick and Keating were drowned.

Killorglin-born Máirín Cregan got her first job teaching in Goresbridge, County Kilkenny and moved to Dublin in 1914 to study music under Madame Coslett Heller. Her friends were members of Sinn Féin, the Gaelic League and the Volunteers. Late on Holy Thursday night Seán MacDermott arrived at her digs in No. 82 Grove Park and told her to go to Fr Joe Breen in Tralee – he would put her in touch with Austin Stack and Paddy Cahill. She was to give them automatics, ammunition and letters which had been delivered earlier in the evening by a young man named Cullen. This she did, having carried the guns and ammunition in her violin case, and then headed for the family home in Killorglin.

As she prepared for bed, word arrived that a car had gone over the quay in Ballykissane. With her sister she went there and managed to get hold of Tommy MacInerney. 'Only for the presence of mind of Patrick Begley, Ballykissane, my former Irish teacher, who took MacInerney's revolver and hid it, he would have been arrested much sooner than he was.'[2] Grasping the significance of the event, Cregan set about limiting the damage to the whole project, which would follow with police questioning, by bringing MacInerney to a safe house in Killorglin. 'He remained up all night, dosing occasionally and rather shocked, but on the whole bluffing his way through police inquiries very well.'[3]

Máirín Cregan continued to play a very active role during the ensuing years and married Dr Jim Ryan, later to serve as Minister for Agriculture (1932–47), Minister for Health and Social Welfare (1947–48 and 1951–54) and Minister for Finance (1957–65). Her sister, Eilie, married a local man, James O'Sullivan, and their son, Séamus, having moved to Dublin in the mid-thirties, married Bríghid, ua Buachalla's second daughter.

There was a heart-warming postscript to Máirín Cregan's trip to Kerry. A couple of hours before his execution, Seán MacDermott asked Min Ryan, who was visiting him, to take a memento from him to Máirín as she was a 'good girl' and had carried out the mission in accordance with his instructions. 'He took a penny out of his pocket and asked one of the two soldiers on guard for a penknife. Seán quickly appreciated the soldier's refusal and scratched his initials and the date with a pin on the coin ... it was an indication of the thoughtful person he was, as well as encouragement to carry on.'[4]

For Austin Stack, the bungled Banna Strand landing, loss of the *Aud's* cargo and arrest of Roger Casement was a serious blow. To add to his misery, Stack was arrested when he returned to Tralee and sent to Spike Island, the first of many incarcerations. In 1917 he led the hunger strike in Mountjoy Jail, which resulted in Thomas Ashe's death from forcible feeding. Subsequently he spent time in Dundalk Jail and Strangeways in Manchester – and was back in Mountjoy in 1923 after being captured near *Sliabh na mBán*. Again he went on a hunger strike that lasted for forty-one days, during which he received a letter from his goddaughter, Ballybunion-born Peggy Clarke, and replied thus:

Mountjoy Prison,

Dublin,

28 August 1923.

My dear Daughter,

I got your lovely letter on Saturday last and was very glad to have it. You were a good little girl – or should I say, big girl – to think of me. And so you are a whole thirteen years. Oh, my! You will be a finished young lady soon. And you did not go back to Ring. But I am sure you can speak Irish now better than English. You must write to me in Irish next time – and be sure to write soon.

Are you going to any school at all now? Are you too good at everything? No matter how good you consider yourself, one has always lots more to learn. Do study hard and be a great scholar. Won't you?

I have been considering how you all have been getting on since I saw your (other) father last. How is he? And is he at home often? And your aunt? She is well I hope. And your new little brother, Seumas? I suppose Tommy is home from Rockwell these days – fit and big and strong, I'm sure. And Maire, Sheila and Páid. Give them my love.

And little Rosie. She must be a great young lady by this time. Tell me about them all when you write.

We have Bertie Hawney here with us. He is a good lad and very popular. We are getting along, everything considered, so don't worry. We can put up with the worst conditions – or the best. Still, it would be nice to be out, seeing one's friends and doing work. I am in pretty good form, thank God.

My love now to all the family – and particularly to your good self. Do not fail to remember me to my Ballybunion friends. Good luck to Ballybunion and the Clarkes.

Your affectionate godfather,

Austin Stack.[5]

Stack died in 1929 due to poor health brought on by his hunger strikes. Many years later, Peggy Clarke married Kevin, ua Buachalla's third son.

A Tale of Bravery

Tom Byrne's arrival was welcomed in Kildare. He was born in Carrickmacross in 1877 and five years later the family moved to Dublin. In his Witness Statement he recounts travelling to Johannesburg at the age of 19, where he joined a branch of the Irish National Foresters. Seán McBride was also a member. When the Second Boer War was declared in 1899, Byrne was part of mounted group, organised on a commando basis, which was led by an American, Colonel Blake, with McBride as their Major.

Their story is an amazing tale of bravery, which eventually ended in captivity. An early release and financial assistance from the Boer Government gave Byrne the opportunity to head for America, via Germany. He worked in mines in Montana, Nevada, Colorado and other places for twelve years, then returned to Ireland and attended the Rotunda meeting. He became a member of B Company, 1st Battalion and was involved in the landing of guns in Howth and Kilcoole. Two weeks before the Rising, Byrne attended an all-night Volunteer dance in Parnell Square:

At about 4 or 5 a.m. a message arrived for me from Pearse, asking me out to St. Enda's, Rathfarnham. I went immediately and Pearse told me that he wanted me to go down and take charge of County Kildare. He gave me a note to show that I was in charge, because I was to take over from Ted O'Kelly. [The RIC had been monitoring O'Kelly's activities from 1915, which worried Pearse.]

Pearse said he was going to recall O'Kelly, and I asked him would he not let him stay down there as my second-in-command, as he was familiar with the locality, to which he agreed. Pearse gave me no definite word that the Rising was to take place. I was not to travel by train to Kildare but to cycle down as I might be spotted by the police at the station. I had a few hours' sleep in St. Enda's before leaving for Kildare.[6]

Byrne's first place of call was ua Buachalla's home. He recalled showing his credentials and explaining what his role was and then proceeded to Prosperous and Newbridge, where he stayed in the Prince of Wales Hotel. There he met O'Kelly and with a 'very keen'[7] Tom Harris they called to several companies over the next few days. Colgan, who was with ua Buachalla when Byrne arrived in Maynooth, recalled that Byrne told them they would march to Bodenstown to link up with other units:

Our arms consisted of one .45 revolver with ten rounds of ammunition; fifteen .22 revolvers with thirty rounds of ammunition each; one Lee Enfield rifle with fifty rounds of ammunition; twenty American single barrel shot guns with approximately fifty rounds each, buckshot made by ourselves during the winter of 1915 and spring of 1916 [in ua Buachalla's house]; and three pikes seven feet long.

Our job when we met at Bodenstown, with the Dublin Volunteers on our left and the Meath and Midland Volunteers on our right, was to prevent military from the Curragh entering Dublin and to destroy telegraph and telephone lines and railway tracks. It was necessary to keep the news within a small circle.

However, on Easter Saturday all Volunteers were notified to get confession that night and (to be less conspicuous) to travel to outlying districts for Communion on Sunday morning. The hour of mobilisation was 10.15 on Sunday morning, the centre, ua Buachalla's store. The following Volunteers mobilised on Sunday: ua Buachalla, Liam O'Regan, Jack Graves, Patrick Kearney, John Kenny, Edward Kenny, Patrick Ledwidge, Joseph Ledwidge, Mathew Maguire, John Maguire, Timothy Tyrrell, Thomas Mangan, Thomas Magee, Patrick Kirwan and Patrick Colgan.

I wanted to give the honour of announcing the starting of the Rebellion to ua Buachalla. His example and his patriotism had kept us together. He was always a self-effacing man. He insisted that I would make the announcement.

I cannot recall what I said, but it was something about going out in a rebellion. I emphasised the seriousness of what we were about to do and I remember well saying that if any member wished to withdraw, no hard feelings would be held. No Volunteer withdrew. We were about to issue the guns, ammunition and pikes when a messenger on a motor cycle arrived with word from Eoin MacNeill, addressed to ua Buachalla, cancelling any movement of Volunteers. We hung around discussing the matter. Before we dispersed a further message to ua Buachalla from P. H. Pearse ordered us not to leave our district, but to await further orders.[8]

Tom Byrne received instructions in a dispatch from Pearse, probably on Easter Thursday, that the Rebellion was to start on Easter Sunday:

I was to mobilise all the Companies in Kildare and they were to march in full kit to Bodenstown churchyard. At 4.00 p.m. I was to address them and tell them that the fight was on, that those who wished to fight could follow me, and that those who did not wish to fight could go home. I visited all the Companies and sent word around. There was promise of a big response. On Easter Sunday morning we read the countermanding order in the *Sunday Independent*.

[Owing to the very critical position, all orders given to Irish Volunteers for tomorrow, Easter Sunday, are hereby rescinded, and no parades, marches, or other movements of Irish Volunteers will take place. Each individual Volunteer will obey this order strictly in every particular – Eoin MacNeill.]

We were in a muddle because I had received no countermanding order. Kelly, Harris and myself decided to cycle into Naas ... As we were standing on a sidewalk, a motor cycle came tearing through the town. The rider was Dick Stokes and he brought me a dispatch, which read, 'postponed until 12.00 tomorrow'. It was signed by Pearse ...

On Easter Monday, Harris, Kelly and myself left Newbridge (carrying gelignite, which had been collected from a sympathetic Fr McCluskey in the Dominican College) for Bodenstown ... Having examined the bridges near Bodenstown and Sallins, I could not see any place that would be suitable to use it. Being a miner, I knew we had no time to do a good job. There was an ordinary passenger train going back and forth along the line. The Rising had already started and the train could not get into the city, and we did not want to do any damage to it. I eventually decided that blowing up a bridge like that would not delay the British five minutes.[9]

After the meeting with Stokes, Tom Harris recalled that Byrne, O'Kelly and himself decided to cover the whole area, stressing that all Volunteers had to be ready next day at midday in Bodenstown.

Byrne took Athgarvan, Newbridge and Ballysax. O'Kelly and myself did Naas, Prosperous and Rathangan, arranging that we would all meet in Newbridge that night. At this time we were not thinking of Maynooth. We did our tour and saw our men in the different places but most of them had some excuse that they would not be able to turn up. We told them the plain truth, that the fight was starting in Dublin and that we were joining in it ...

We called at Kenny's in Rathangan that evening. Kit was there ... and we had tea. There were sixteen Lee Enfield rifles in the possession of T. J. Murphy, who had bought them for the Rathangan Volunteers. O'Kelly told Kenny to get hold of them ...

Next morning O'Kelly sent me down to Jack Fitzgerald who had not got word, to tell him to be ready to come with us. When I got there his sister told me he was in bed; he came down and told me to tell O'Kelly that he wouldn't turn out until the bungle of yesterday was set right. O'Kelly sent me back to get his revolver and to tell him that the first duty of a soldier was obedience. Jack said that he had not got his gun ...

On arriving at Bodenstown there was no one else there ... In order that there would be no mistake, O'Kelly and Byrne went in one direction and I went towards the Clane road ... we waited until about 1.30 [p.m.] ... no one turned up. We headed for Maynooth.[10]

In Maynooth, Colgan sent Jack Maguire to mobilise the Dunboyne Company. 'He spoke with Seán Boylan and arranged to have the Dunboyne men meet us at Leixlip Railway Station at 8.00 p.m.... . about thirty left to keep the appointment before Maguire left Dunboyne. It appears they went about a mile on the journey and then returned home.'[11]

The Celbridge Company was the best-equipped unit in north Kildare. Their O. C., Art O'Connor, did not mobilise his men. 'A sister of mine living in the Celbridge district, having heard [that] the Maynooth Volunteers had gone out, called on Art O'Connor ... she afterwards told me she met Art, Seamus O'Connor, solicitor, Dublin, and Eamon Moran, Ballysax, at O'Connor's house, and that Art said the Rebellion was a foolish step and he was not taking part.'[12]

On Easter Monday morning, ua Buachalla learned from a bread van driver that fighting was taking place in Dublin and immediately got up on his bike.

I proceeded to Dublin to get instructions, to find out what we were to do. On approaching the Phoenix Park I heard firing, I think it was from the Magazine Fort in the Park. I proceeded down the northern quays. At the Mendicity Institute there were British soldiers taking cover under the Liffey wall on the north side of the river and avoiding the firing, which was coming from the Institute. They did not stop me and I passed through.

Further down the quays near the Four Courts, the Volunteers had a barricade across the street. I was halted there. I told the officer who was in command who I was and where I was going. He let me through. I proceeded to the headquarters of the Volunteers, but found the place locked up. I started back for home and travelled via the North Circular Road. The British had a barricade between

Doyle's Corner and Phibsboro Church. I was allowed through and cycled back to Maynooth.[13]

When Colgan met Fr Malachy Eaton, the Junior Dean of Maynooth College, in the town on Monday afternoon, he heard for the first time that the Volunteers were active in Dublin.

> I rushed to ua Buachalla's shop to find the shutters down on the windows and the shop closed and Domhnall busily engaged filling school bags with buckshot, and the guns and pikes withdrawn from their hiding place, ready for issue. With the exception of Tyrrell, the Maguire brothers, the O'Neill brothers from Celbridge and the Ledwidge brothers, the remainder of us lived in the village and word was sent to all except Patrick Kirwan ... I decided not to mobilise Kirwan, as he was a married man with five small children; without his small earnings they had nothing to live on.

> All the party had not reported before I was called to the store door where I found Kirwan in a towering rage due to my omission to call him. I tried to reason with him about his helpless family, all to no avail. He argued [that] 'he had lived to fight for Ireland'. I admitted him and he proved himself during the week in Dublin to be a very courageous fellow.[14]

A few of the Maynooth Volunteers who were due to march dropped out in the final two days for various reasons, while Patrick Weafer came late to the group. He was a prominent member of the Ancient Order of Hibernians and also a captain of the Maynooth Redmondite Volunteers.

Go Home – Or Be Slaughtered

The culmination of fifty years in a nationalist environment, which increasingly stiffened his resolve to live in a country 'no longer tugging at the chains that bind us', had finally led ua Buachalla to the point where there was no turning back. Standing in the yard of his house on Easter Monday, Mauser rifle in hand, he was ready to put his life on the line, comfortable in the company of thirteen like-minded Volunteers. They were Liam O'Regan and Jack Graves who worked for him in the shop; Boer War veteran Tom Byrne and Ted O'Kelly who was studying medicine;

the youthful Tom Harris; Patrick Colgan of Leinster Cottages; Matthew and Jack Maguire, Pat Kirwan, Tom Mangan, Patrick Weafer, Joe Ledwidge and Tim Tyrrell.

More pertinently, following the death of his father the previous year, he was willing to walk into the unknown, leaving behind Sinéad and their seven children. And while his wife would have been aware that a day like this was the inevitable outcome of two years panelling the walls of their home to hide guns and ammunition, and of weekly drilling in the yard and further afield, parting had to have been charged with great emotion.

The anxiety of the evening for each of the Volunteers was added to by the fact that the Grand Plan had failed to materialise. The dream of the three Companies coming together at Bodenstown to stand proudly together as Tom Byrne exhorted them in the name of Ireland free had disappeared. Nevertheless, the platoon formed at the back of ua Buachalla's shop and marched in double file down the main street to Maynooth College. They were viewed with a certain curiosity by a gathering of locals and by those returning from the Fairyhouse races, but more seriously by two unarmed RIC men – Sergeant Peter Cleary and Constable Michael Nolan. As they reached the gates, Ted O'Kelly drew his revolver and told them that if they came any closer, he would let them have the contents.[15] They took the easier option.

Moving into the College, the group attracted the attention of many students who let them know they were favourably disposed to their activities. So enthused was one of the employees of the College, Oliver Ryan, at the sight of these armed men, that he decided he would march with them to Dublin, and was welcomed into a group which now numbered fifteen. For ua Buachalla, Ryan's decision to join would not have been totally unexpected as he knew him as early as 1911, when Ryan first contributed to the Gaelic League through a collection made by Christopher Slevin among the employees in the College. The collection was then passed on to the Maynooth branch. The President, Monsignor J. Hogan, didn't have the same lofty regard for the group of fifteen, and appealed to ua Buachalla to abandon plans and get the men to return to their homes, because the 'poor fools were going to be slaughtered'.[16] When the plea fell on deaf ears, however, the Monsignor said 'if you kneel, I'll give you my blessing'.[17]

Whether Monsignor Hogan was aware of it or not, the Executive of the Volunteers had already made provisions with the Catholic Church by sending Count Plunkett George Noble to Rome in advance of the insurrection to explain what was about to happen. In 1933 he revealed the details:

> I was received in private audience by His Holiness (Benedict XV); for nigh two hours we discussed fully the question of the coming struggle for Irish Independence. The Pope was much moved when I disclosed the fact that the date of the Rising was fixed and the reasons for that decision. Finally, I stated that the Volunteer Executive pledged the Irish Republic to fidelity to the Holy See and the interests of religion. Then the Pope conferred His Apostolic Benediction on the men who were facing death for Ireland's liberty.[18]

It was late evening when the Maynooth men left the College by the back gate and headed for the canal. About a mile out, at Pike Bridge, they switched to the railway line. Colgan and Mangan were detailed by Byrne to walk about 800 yards in advance of the party to check if the railway bridges were occupied and to report back from each bridge. It was dark when they reached Lucan and a heavy drizzle had set in as they passed through Clonsilla and Blanchardstown. Byrne then took them across the countryside, insisting on silence as they travelled.

The peace was broken at one stage by a loud explosion, which Byrne suggested came from Dublin. Movement was becoming more difficult as high walls and thick hedges had to be cleared. At one stage Byrne ordered Mathew Maguire up a wall; he, in turn, pulled another fellow up and so on until they were all on the wall. He then told Maguire to jump – noiselessly.

> Maguire, armed with a pike, jumped and landed in a heap of empty tin cans. I believe it was the dumping place for Ashtown Racecourse. We thought the whole British Army had attacked us ... Shortly after, we headed back to the canal banks and soon got our first rest and a smoke. Even though it was raining and the ground wet, we enjoyed the rest.[19]

A Strange Resting Place

Dawn was breaking as they passed Finglas Golf Links and shortly afterwards they waded across the Tolka River and entered Glasnevin Cemetery, near one of the water towers. They found a dry cistern in which to hide their guns and settled down for a rest. Early on Tuesday morning Byrne said to the men:

> 'It is near daylight. The grave-diggers will be here early and you must all scatter around. I am going into the city to see how things are'. I made my way to the GPO first, without trouble, and I told them that I had some men on the outskirts of the city. I forget who I saw there. There was nothing to bar my way to and from the GPO. On my way back to the cemetery, I decided to call to the house where I lodged and put on my captain's uniform, which I had left there when proceeding to Kildare. When I went in I found that the Sheehans had disposed of it.
>
> I left the house and proceeded towards Doyle's Corner, just in time to see my men marching along in the direction of the GPO ... they had decided not to wait for me. I had been gone from them for a considerable time.[20]

At this stage, Maguire was again moving ahead of the column, alone, with instructions to report if there was any trouble. Having turned at Doyle's Corner, he quickly reappeared in some confusion, and as the group dropped to their knees close to the houses, as instructed, he revealed 'that he had come face-to-face with his boss, William Chamberlaine of Crew Hill in Maynooth, and he couldn't face him!'[21]

They moved on by Cross Guns Bridge, down Berkeley Road and into Blessington Street, where they saw a few other Volunteers, as well as people gathering on the streets and many more watching from their windows. Colgan recalled the conclusion to their journey:

> Some of the residents advised us to go home or we would be slaughtered; others cheered us on. When we reached the Parnell Monument a rifle fire barrage greeted us. We thought we were being attacked and we all raced for the shelter of the monument. It turned out to be a volley of rifle shots from the occupants of the GPO to welcome us ... Comdt. James Connolly was at the door. He shook each of us by the hand and smiled his welcome. Connolly was one of my heroes. I had never before met him. I felt all excited that he would show such an interest in us.[22]

While Colgan was elated with the reception, a more composed Harris was less so when Connolly told the group that 'it didn't matter a damn if we were wiped out, as we had justified ourselves'. Harris thought this 'a bit rugged'.[23]

The group was marched into the main hall of the building where they were greeted by the Kildare men who were members of the garrison, among them Frank Burke, Miceál Cowley, Tom Brien, Mick Croke and Paddy Byrne. They got tea and buns from Brian O'Higgins and when finished, 'Pádraig Pearse spoke to us. His words have remained with me since. I think of them with great pride. He told us how glad he was to have us with them in the fight; that our action in marching from Kildare, even if we did no more in the Rebellion, would gain us a place in history.'[24]

Pearse then outlined the position to them: 'He did not expect any action in the GPO for days. The Citizen Army at St. Stephen's Green was hard pressed and had not sufficient men ... and a group were cut off at Dublin City Hall and the *Evening Mail* office. He gave us the privilege of selecting our own post. He added that "the opinion is [that] a rescue party at the City Hall would have little chance of surviving".'[25] The Kildare men chose the City Hall.

For ua Buachalla it had been a physically exhausting thirty-six hours. Monday morning's cycle to Dublin and back followed by words of reassurance for Sinéad and the children, and then a long slog through the evening, night and morning would have left him seriously drained. And that episode was a mere prelude to the business of rebelling against an Empire.

As the Maynooth Volunteers were making their way to the GPO, Ivor Churchill Guest and Baron Wimborne, the Lord Lieutenant-General, had issued the following proclamation:

> WHEREAS in the City of Dublin and County of Dublin certain evilly disposed persons and associations, with the intent to subvert the supremacy of the Crown in Ireland, have committed diverse acts of violence, and have with deadly weapons attacked the Forces of the Crown, and have resisted by armed force the lawful Authority of His Majesty's Police and Military Forces. AND whereas by reason thereof several of His Majesty's liege Subjects have been killed and many others severely injured, and much damage to property has been caused.
>
> AND whereas such armed resistance to His Majesty's authority still continues. NOW, I, Ivor Churchill, Baron Wimborne, Lord-

Lieutenant and Governor-General of Ireland, by virtue of all the powers in me thereunto enabling DO HEREBY PROCLAIM that from and after the date of this Proclamation and for the period of One Month thereafter (unless otherwise ordered), the CITY OF DUBLIN and COUNTY OF DUBLIN are under and subject to

MARTIAL LAW

AND I do hereby call on all Loyal and well affected Subjects of the Crown to aid in upholding and maintaining the peace of the Crown and the supremacy and authority of the Crown. AND I warn all peaceable and law-abiding Subjects within such area of the danger of frequenting or being in any place in or in the vicinity of which His Majesty's Forces are engaged in the suppression of disorder.

AND I do hereby enjoin upon such Subjects the duty and necessity, so far as practicable, of remaining within their homes so long as these dangerous conditions prevail. And I do hereby declare that all persons found carrying Arms without lawful authority are liable to be dealt with by virtue of the Proclamation.[26]

With those posters as a backdrop, the Maynooth contingent prepared for their first engagement:

We were marched to the GPO magazine [the area where arms and ammunition were stored during the Rising] and had further cause for pride in learning the Volunteer in charge was Jim O'Neill from Leixlip. I handed over the powder I had brought from Maynooth. O'Neill made me feel I had saved the Rebellion by the contribution ... From the magazine, each of us was issued with a home-made bomb, about one foot long, cylindrical in shape with a sulphur fuse sticking out through a hole at the top. The instructions on the manipulation of the bomb were 'to strike a match, light the fuse, count three, then throw' ... we were reinforced with Sean Milroy, who wore an officer's uniform, J. J. Scollan of the Hibernian Rifles and two engineers, Edward Walsh and his son from Dominick Street, both of whom had a sledge hammer and a crowbar.[27]

CHAPTER 7

An Axe Spiralled,
A Soldier Dead

Departing the GPO by a wicket gate that led to Abbey Street, the Maynooth Volunteers moved on to the quays and crossed the River Liffey at the Metal Bridge, using a gun to convince the toll-keeper that they would not be paying the halfpenny charge. Tom Byrne said he was not instructed to take over any particular building, that their primary objective was to relieve the Citizen Army volunteers who were surrounded in the *Evening Mail* office.

On a side street close to their objective, they broke into a premises that belonged to Sir Patrick Shortall, a member of Dublin Corporation, and having gone upstairs, hammered their way into the Exchange Hotel. Patrick Colgan recalled following Byrne into the building:

> He rushed upstairs, I followed; he ran into a room, I ran into another where I found two fat men. They turned out to be two jugglers who were due to open at the Coliseum Theatre that night. They were English. In my most authoritative voice I ordered them out, advised them to go home to England and not to speak to anyone as we had all the houses occupied between Dublin and Dun Laoghaire. They were glad to scram. Byrne then ordered Harris, Kirwan, Milroy, Scollan, Weafer, Graves, Tyrrell and the younger Walsh to defend the ground floor. The remainder were taken upstairs.[1]

From the roof, they had a good view of Parliament Street, but were on view themselves and within minutes a bullet ricocheted from a chimney and struck Edward Walsh in the groin. Byrne sent word to the GPO while the medical student, Ted O'Kelly, did what he could to prevent loss of blood. A Dr McKee organised a party to bring Walsh back to base, but before the night was out he had died in Jervis Street Hospital. Because Walsh's injury was serious, Byrne told his son that he should return to the family home, which he did. Later in life, Tom Byrne was appointed Captain of the Guard at Leinster House, with Walsh employed in the same building as an usher.[2]

Those on the roof decided it was time to bring their bombs into play. 'Mathew Maguire lit and handed me the bombs. We carried out our instructions about lighting and counting to three ... but nothing happened, no explosion. I pitched about six of them. Maguire relieved me and he had similar results.'[3] Byrne withdrew all personnel from the roof with the exception of ua Buachalla and Colgan, but they had to follow almost immediately when a rifle grenade exploded close to them.

Later, with the windows well manned, ua Buachalla and Colgan took the best positions available, just as an attack was made on the *Evening Mail* office. Many years later, ua Buachalla spoke of this moment in the company of his daughter Bríghid, her husband Séamus and their brother-in-law, Lieutenant-Colonel Matt Feehan, then editor of *The Sunday Press*, who took notes as the conversation developed:

> A very courageous British officer emerged from the Castle armed with a fireman's double-edged axe, and proceeded to batter down the front door of the office. With admiration for this man's courage, ua Buachalla reasoned that if he permitted the soldiers to gain entrance to the ground floor, the position of the Volunteers on the roof would soon be untenable. So he took aim, fired and the axe spiralled in an arc before hitting the stone 'sets', kicking up sparks on impact. The Sergeant-Major lay dead at the door.[4]

Ua Buachalla recalled that 'the man next to him also fell', later disclosing that he also died:

> The rest of our boys opened up with the sporting guns and in a few seconds at least a dozen soldiers were lying on the street. An amazing thing was [that] a priest appeared on the scene and attended to

the soldiers who were wounded or dead. We went back to the roof to see if we could engage the soldiers in the Castle. The roof was heavily under fire from the Castle and the enemy had a party in the drapery establishment at the corner and junction of Dame Street and Parliament Street and opposite the *Evening Mail* office. Shortly after this we got orders from Byrne to go back to the GPO.[5]

The retreat, like many incidents during the week, is described in Witness Statements in slightly contradictory terms. Colgan's appears to be the most comprehensive, encapsulating much of what was recalled by others:

We were allocated our places in Shortall's when a terrific outburst of gunfire was laid down. None of us ever heard anything like it. It was machine-gun fire. Harris, Ledwidge and I were posted inside the front door. Our orders were to engage the soldiers if they attempted to get through the outer door. Harris had a .45 revolver, Ledwidge and I a shotgun and bomb. The remainder of the party was spread throughout the other two landings.

The firing became more intense and closer. The soldiers from City Hall, with reinforcements from Ship Street, had entered the Exchange Hotel and riddled the lower ceilings with machine gun fire. From our place at the front door we could see the lower portion of the soldiers' legs through Shortall's window. Harris asked me if he would fire and I advised against it. After a time the soldiers withdrew; it was a narrow shave for us; we hadn't a chance of survival. Judging by the madness we displayed in the Exchange Hotel, we would have been a danger to ourselves, as much maybe as to our enemy.

Byrne, who had gone out to scout around, announced there was a chance we might be able to evacuate. We were to go out singly by the back door; we were to keep close to the houses; we were to fight it out if attacked. We started out, everyone for himself. I was last out. I was first to the Metal Bridge. The toll collector was absent. Crowds lined the quay footpath (northern side). I ordered them to move to the edge of the footpath to give us cover. They all did except one old man who wore a topper; he refused to make way. I regret to say I pushed him on to the roadway. We reached the GPO to be received as heroes.

> We were told we would be mentioned in dispatches in *War News* the
> next day. I was terribly disappointed the *War News* was not published,
> but I was very glad that fate had been so kind during the time the
> courts martial were being held after the surrender.[6]

The thought that immediately struck ua Buachalla on returning was how
quiet and well organised everything in the GPO was, with everyone going
about their duties in a purposeful and efficient manner. It would certainly
have contrasted with the hours spent in Parliament Street and the stark
realisation that the undertaking of the men from Maynooth would be a
matter of kill-or-be-killed.

Brigadier-General Lowe had arrived in Dublin to take command of the
British forces. He had 2,300 troops of the Dublin garrison at his disposal,
'1,500 men from the Curragh and 840 men from the Irish Reserve Infantry
Brigade. These were reinforced by the Dublin Fusiliers from Templemore,
a composite battalion from Belfast and a battery of four eighteen-pounders
from Athlone.'[7] Lowe had completed his first objective of establishing a
line of posts from Kingsbridge to the Castle and on to Trinity College,
cutting off the southern Volunteer positions from headquarters in the
GPO. 'Every step of the way had cost him men. Now he was tightening
a cordon around the north side of the city from Parkgate Street along
North Circular Road to the North Wall, having used artillery to smash a
barricade at Phibsboro.'[8]

After having something to eat and a short rest, ua Buachalla was
detailed to go to Arnott's in Henry Street with a man he did not know
to take up a position in the dome. Provided with good field glasses, the
instruction was to try and keep the sniping from the far side of the quays
under control. They immediately used bales of cloth to barricade the
windows in an effort to make them bullet-proof, but had great difficulty
locating the sniper.

> After some time, I noticed one of the upper windows of McBirney's
> drapery establishment on Aston Quay was open, the rest being
> closed. I could see a waitress in uniform carrying a tray past the
> window. It occurred to me that it was strange for a waitress to be
> on duty when the premises was closed, being right in the centre of
> the area where the fighting was taking place. I got my glasses on to
> the window and, as I suspected, I observed a soldier in a stooped
> position on the far side of the room holding a rifle. I took aim at the

window and fired. The first shot was high, hitting over the window. My second shot went through the pane and my third went into the room. No firing took place afterwards.[9]

Ua Buachalla also told Feehan that he was 'detailed by Connolly to try to kill a sniper in the dome of Todd Burn's, a department store in Mary Street, who had killed several Volunteers positioned on the roof of the GPO'.[10]

Snatched rest was welcomed when possible and scanty food rations when available. On the Wednesday morning, ua Buachalla was allotted a loop-hole window on a landing in the GPO. Outside, O'Connell Street was a desolate thoroughfare. A few steps below him on the stairs a Volunteer looked about vacantly, a shotgun in his hands with which he was continually fiddling. Suddenly the gun went off and the shot lodged in the books barricading the window at which ua Buacalla was keeping post. He jumped down, took the gun from the frightened young man and dumped it in a big wastepaper basket. When the retreat from the GPO was under way later in the week, he was to come across the half-crazed young man again, this time in Henry Street, with the butt of the gun on the ground. A shot went off. Ua Buachalla recalled that 'the poor fellow got the complete contents in his throat and died immediately'.[11]

The Rosary

As dusk was falling on Wednesday, he was sent across to the Dublin Bread Company on O'Connell Street, better known to generations as the DBC restaurant, which was occupied by the Volunteers. 'They had been having serious trouble with sniping from Trinity College and I was sent there to try and deal with it. I engaged some soldiers on the roof and, while drawing back from the loophole in the barricaded window from which I was firing, a bullet came through and grazed my hair.'[12] With a view of Liberty Hall from the window, he observed the effect of the shelling by a British war vessel, the *Helga*.

The narrow escape from death, allied to the sight of Dublin City Centre beginning to crumble, would have heightened any feelings of insecurity ua Buachalla might have had. Biscuits and confectionary were devoured in one room and another was taken up with equipment for a radio transmitter that had been broadcasting news of the Rising. Throughout the night the bombardment continued and the next morning the city was covered by a cloud of smoke. In the DBC, 'the *Cumann na mBan* girls began the Rosary, the men at the loopholes joined in'.[13] Instructions were given to return to the GPO and to bring the wireless apparatus.

Ua Buachalla brought a heavy battery with him down the stairs. They began moving through buildings until they reached a chemist's shop on the corner of Earl Street. Here he met Liam Pedlar, who had come home from America to fight in the Rising. There were other Volunteers in the building, some of them said to be 'on the verge of hysteria'.[14] As more buildings crumbled, Pedlar and ua Buachalla eventually decided to make a dash, and legs that had little to give carried them across O'Connell Street to the relative safety of the GPO.

On Thursday evening they got word that James Connolly had been injured while establishing outposts close to the GPO, taking two bullets to the leg. He had been initially looked after by Dr Jim Ryan and an operation was later performed by a British Army doctor who was being held in the post office. Ua Buachalla caught glimpses of some of his comrades from Maynooth as he moved through the building. O'Regan was at one of the barricaded windows while Harris had spent his time shooting from different points of the building, including the roof.

With much of the building destroyed by Friday, the garrison was ordered to prepare to evacuate. Pearse's intention was that they would depart by the side door, cross Henry Street into the lane opposite which turned into Moore Street, make their way into Parnell Street, occupy the Williams' & Wood's Jam Factory and establish communication with the Four Courts. 'Little did he know that such an undertaking was impossible. At dusk the evacuation was not complete and Pearse went back to make sure everyone was out. He was one of the last to leave.'[15]

Volunteers spent Friday night trying to work their way up to Parnell Street by breaking through the partition walls in the houses of Moore Street, but a mound of debris frustrated their efforts. On Saturday morning they saw flames consuming the GPO and surrounding buildings, while the British Artillery bombarded the centre of Dublin. Pearse finally decided to end the bloodshed as the lives of innocent civilians had to be safeguarded. Gathered close to Connolly's bed, the leaders made the decision to surrender.

Approaching midday, Elizabeth O'Farrell was entrusted with the message: 'The Commandant-General of the Irish Republican Army wishes to treat with the Commandant-General of the British Forces in Ireland.'[16] Carrying a white flag, she walked to the British barricade in Parnell Street.

Unconditional surrender was sought. About mid-afternoon, Pearse, with O'Farrell beside him, surrendered his sword in Parnell Street to Brigadier-General Lowe.

Ua Buachalla had moved out of the GPO on Friday night with the main body of men into Henry Street and then entered Moore Lane. While there he was asked to undertake a mission with three other men:

> I can remember running down Henry Street towards Mary Street; the enemy had a barricade across the street at Williams' shop. We were under fire all the time. When half-way from Moore Lane to this barricade, the man in front of me dropped, having been hit. Almost immediately the man behind was also hit. I dropped down in the channel on the side of the street. I saw [that] a large window of Williams' shop was devoid of glass, apparently having come under the notice of the looters. I got up and jumped in through the window, leaving my rifle on the path.
>
> When inside, it struck me that there might be a shop hook and I searched around in the dark for it. I found one. With this I hooked in my rifle. There was a big number of young men inside, apparently after loot, and making an awful amount of noise. I asked them to keep quite but it was to no avail, so I decided I was getting out. I took off my boots and after discarding my rifle, tried to get out through the back. The place was a mass of broken glass, jam, treacle, etc.[17]

'D'ya want a pair of boots, mister?'

His recollection of his movements after that was a little sketchy and his Military Statement relatively short, but following lengthy interviews with Michael O'Halloran for *The Sunday Press* many years later, much of what happened was recounted by the journalist:

> Domhnall came to a door that opened out into a laneway. As he stepped through, a *Sassanach* voice snarled in the darkness, 'Halt, or I fire.' He jumped sideways [and] flung himself around a corner without feeling the impact of a bullet. He hurried through strange laneways and streets, striving to maintain a northwards course, until

weariness slowed him … and a light beckoned from a basement window. He thought he must be somewhere in the Parnell Square area. Iron railings interposed between him and the window and he climbed them … there was a woman inside. He attracted her attention and asked if he could stay the night.

Her face hardened and she shook her head. 'The soldiers are above', she said, looking towards the ceiling. He turned and walked through the dark streets again, the chill of the pavement biting through his tattered socks. A dark doorway yawned. He entered and climbed the stairs. He was in a tenement. On the first landing there was an old mat before a doorway … and in a moment he was asleep.

Slowly he became conscious of gloomy walls and thin daylight. He looked about him. There was a pair of feet beside his head. A door was open and a woman stood over him, he looked at her and she closed the door. He sat up painfully, he strove to give order to the chaotic impressions of the hours before he slept.

The door opened and the woman stood there again. In one hand she held a steaming mug of tea, in the other a couple of slices of bread and butter. He drank gratefully and the hot tea eased the chill in the bones. The bread reminded him that he had eaten nothing since the biscuits in the DBC. [He later revealed that the woman's husband was serving abroad with the British Army.]

The children in the tenement gathered around, cautiously at first, eyeing his dishevelled clothes and unkempt hair and beard. One youth approached, gazing at his torn socks. 'D'ya want a pair of boots, mister?' Ua Buachalla nodded to him and the lad disappeared to return with six brand-new pairs. They had been looted from the O'Connell Street shops. He found one pair that fitted him well and took them, giving the boy what money he had in his pocket.

Then he remembered the gold badge inscribed with the words '*Connradh na Gaeilge*'which he wore on his lapel. It had been specially made and presented to him. The future was highly uncertain and he felt the badge might lead to a lot of questions if he were taken prisoner. He took it off and gave it to the lad with his name and address, asking him to keep it safe for him. Many eventful years afterwards, in 1934, it was returned to him by a young man who was then a soldier in the Curragh.

Outside the grimy tenement with its homely people was a city cluttered with the wreckage of a dream. Ua Buachalla could hear gunfire still. A laneway led from the tenement and he walked on, sagging from weariness. There were odd shots and the sounds of military activity beyond the lane. When he reached the end he raised his hands wearily and stepped out. There were shots immediately and he felt the breath of bullets. Instinctively, he pulled back. But then nothing seemed to matter any more, except that he was deadly tired. He raised his hands and walked out again. No shots came.

[Some weeks later in Frongoch Jail, a Volunteer confronted him and prodded the shoulder of his coat with a pencil. It passed through the material where a bullet had drilled a clean hole. Ua Buachalla saw it for the first time and remembered the bullet that had fanned him when he stepped out of the laneway. The difference between the entry and exit hole showed that the bullet had penetrated from the front and he laughingly displayed it as evidence that he had not been shot at while running away. He later gave the coat to the National Museum.]

He saw a barricade manned by soldiers in khaki. It was a check-point where people were being questioned before being let through. He went towards it.

'Were you involved in this blasted business?' an officer demanded.

'No, I wasn't', said ua Buachalla.

'Then get the hell out of here and consider yourself lucky'.

Shortly after he saw a queue of people lining up for passes to leave the city and on an impulse he joined them. Then, before he reached the head of the queue he changed his mind and walked away. His wandering was aimless and his brain empty except for one benumbing thought – all was lost.[18]

His meandering eventually brought him to Broadstone Station where he hoped to get on a goods train that might take him to Maynooth, but he was doomed to disappointment. 'When I reached the station there was a guard of British soldiers on the gate ... I was brought in and placed under guard in the ticket office. There were a few prisoners already there whom I did not know. We got no food or refreshments.'[19]

The following morning he was brought with what was now a large contingent of prisoners to Richmond Barracks and placed in the gymnasium:

> The police and detectives and military officers were moving along the lined-up prisoners and picking out the leaders. I saw Eamonn Ceannt in the corner, having been one of the men picked out. We were given some bully beef and dog biscuits. We were kept in the barracks that night and on Monday, together with some hundred other prisoners, we were marched via Kilmainham and Kingsbridge to the North Wall and put on a cattle boat. We were placed in the cattle pens, packed like sardines. I cannot remember if we got anything to eat. I don't think we did.

> We sailed to Liverpool and from there we travelled by rail to Knutsford Goal where we were placed in single cells. Food was very poor and very scarce. We got a mattress and a couple of blankets. After a time we were allowed to associate and talk with one another. The food improved and we were allowed to receive parcels, and the White Cross also sent parcels of food.[20]

The fact that they were close to Manchester ensured that a number of Irish emigrants visited whenever they could and never arrived empty-handed. It made life a little more acceptable for the prisoners, but was short lived. Soon word reached the camp that they were to prepare to move on to Frongoch. A Wexford man, Adjutant W. J. Brennan Whitmore, who had previously served with the British Army, recalled in *With The Irish in Frongoch* that he arrived in Knutsford with nothing and left the prison with five parcels of books, clothing, fruit, biscuits, cigarettes, tobacco and writing material. Creature comforts were not as plentiful in north Wales, but in the long term it proved to be a camp that benefitted all its residents in their desire to see their country free.

Two of the trio who had been serious collaborators with ua Buachalla in the final weeks before leaving Maynooth for Dublin, Tom Harris and Patrick Colgan also ended up in Frongoch. As the GPO was being evacuated, Harris was asked to help with the distribution of rations to each man, but as he was doing so 'some fellow let off a shot and I got most of it and it put me out of action. I was carried out on a stretcher … to Moore Lane for that night … and later to the Castle Hospital'.[21] After an operation, he was detained for three months, moved on to Frongoch and released in mid-August.

The fate of the rest of the Maynooth men provided a variety of tales. Colgan's route from the GPO was dramatic as he was sent by Tom Clarke to the Coliseum Theatre to inspect the strength of the roof, in the knowledge that an officer would follow later and report back to the GPO. He took Tom Mangan, Jack and Mathew Maguire and Joe Ledwidge with him but they were unable to access the roof. At that stage Colgan noticed that Mathew Maguire 'had become a bit hysterical … for want of sleep. He got the idea that I had taken him away from the GPO to shoot him. He was still in possession of a pike. The other fellows tried to reason with him to no avail, so I suggested to his brother to take him to the top of the building and let him have a sleep.'[22]

As no officer followed from the GPO, they managed to get Ledwidge back into the building, but it was deserted, so they returned to the Coliseum. A shaft of light under a door caught their attention and with some trepidation Mangan moved to find out what was happening on the other side, 'when it was opened by a priest from the inside. The priest was Fr O'Flanagan C.C., of Marlborough Street … there were twenty to thirty people in the room, [including] wounded men, *Cumann nn mBan* members, Ted O'Kelly, who had a foot damaged in the GPO at the same time as Harris [and] Desmond Fitzgerald and Frank Sheridan. The only lady I knew was Miss Louise Gavan-Duffy.'[23] Colgan was instructed by O'Kelly that it was their duty to get the wounded to hospital, which he reluctantly agreed to. Fr O'Flanagan also insisted they lay down all arms, which were thrown into the GPO. 'He asked us individually if we had any other arms; I then had to surrender my valuable .22 revolver.'[24]

Sharing the Cigarettes

Inevitably, surrender ensued for Colgan, and a stay in Richmond Barracks, where he saw Pádraig and Willie Pearse, Major John MacBride and Tom Clarke, before marched to the cattle boat and on to Stafford Prison, where he had Tom Mangan for company. They were transferred to

Frongoch on 29 June. Colgan was in Hut 7 with Michael Collins, a man he found to be good company, humorous and, importantly, 'willing to share his cigarettes'.[25]

Tom Byrne took a circuitous route from the GPO to his mother's house in Eccles Street. With the good suit on, he moved to the Athlone Hotel nearby, and then over a period of months to Baldoyle, Balbriggan, Stamullen, Magheracloone (near Carrickmacross) and a few more safe houses before finally arriving in Derry. Later he travelled on to Belfast, and then returned to Dublin before Christmas where he became Vice-Commandant of the 1st Battalion, and later Commandant. He married in 1919, and in 1920 was arrested in the middle of the night in his Eccles Street home and sent to Wormwood Scrubbs and then Brixton Prison. Later released and re-arrested, he was interned in Rath Camp at the Curragh from which he tunnelled to freedom with about forty others during the Truce.

Patrick Weafer and Jack Graves returned early to Maynooth from the GPO and were arrested, court-martialled and sentenced to two years in prison with eighteen months remittance. Joe Ledwidge made a successful escape after the surrender but was also arrested when he returned to Maynooth and received a similar sentence to Weafer and Graves. Tim Tyrrell, Oliver Ryan, Liam O'Regan, Pat Kirwan and Jack and Mathew Maguire all ended up in Frongoch. When his injuries healed, Ted O'Kelly escaped from Jervis Street Hospital, assisted by his aunt who was a nun and a member of staff there. She was a member of the Cullen family from Greenfield, Maynooth.

For a cultural nationalist and devout Catholic, ua Buachalla's willingness to espouse the use of force to the point of killing, to arm his neighbours, to ensure they were drilled for active service, to put his – and their – lives at risk and to hand them over to Tom Byrne in his back yard on Easter Monday reflected a rebellious trait that would not have been as obvious in earlier years. Pearse's prescience in referring to him as 'the most determined man' was becoming more apparent.

CHAPTER 8

A University of Revolution

Originally a distillery for Welsh Whiskey and later an internment camp for German prisoners during the first two years of the First World War, Frongoch was in the Welsh-speaking area of Merionetshire. It had two camps – North and South – which were divided by a side-road running to a railway station. The South Camp, set in a depression, took the early prisoners, and when it reached its capacity of approximately 1,100, the North Camp, on more elevated ground, received the remainder. Hansard's official total for the camp was 1,863, a number that was probably close to the number of rats that infested the compound.

In the first few weeks, Domhnall ua Buachalla was part of a Civil Government that ran affairs, but it was quickly superseded by the military arm of the internees who turned it into what was in effect a Military Academy or 'University of Revolution'. British Army veteran W. J. Brennan-Whitmore, who was second-in-command to Commandant J. J. O'Connell in the South Camp, explained the relevance of their intentions:

> What Sandhurst was doing for the British Army, Frongoch Camp was bidding fair to do for the Irish Republican Army. Before the Irish Volunteers had been many months in existence, it was evident to those in control that if it was ever to be raised into a really efficient military arm, training camps would have to be established all over the country. During the last year of their existence, the General Staff of the Irish Volunteers had carried through with immense success a scheme of temporary training camps in various parts of Ireland.

But a great deal remained to be done. Now, however, the British Government had swept up the cream of the Irish Volunteers and dumped them all down in a huge training camp in North Wales. We had *carte blanche* in the matter of drilling and military lectures.[1]

Ua Buachalla was a very willing student at these classes, among other such dedicated nationalists as Michael Collins, Richard Mulcahy, Tomás MacCurtáin, Terence McSwiney, Seán T. O'Kelly and a host of others who would resume their struggle in early 1917. Brennan-Whitmore was convinced that they would be kept in internment until after the War:

> We were certain that by the time we would be released the nucleus of a magnificent military machine would be presented to Ireland. That was the objective we had mostly in mind when we decided to assume responsibility for the control of the camp. Our plans did not fully materialise, inasmuch as we were all released after seven months. But who can attempt to measure the amount of military gain achieved by willing hearts for Ireland in those seven months of incarceration?[2]

Accord, however, was not always in evidence, primarily because the authorities refused to keep their undertaking to recognise and treat the Irish as prisoners-of-war at all times; also because of the determination of the internees to prevent the conscription of their fellow prisoners who were liable under the Military Services Act. Up to early 1916 the British Army relied on voluntary enlistment, and later a form of moral conscription called the Derby Scheme. The Act, signed by Prime Minister H. H. Asquith on 2 March 1916, made conscription mandatory, specifying that men from 18 to 41 years old were liable to be called up. For political considerations, the Act did not extend to Ireland, but the authorities attempted to enforce it for prisoners in Frongoch who were normally resident in England and therefore liable for Military Service. It was resisted, though, principally by the prisoners making identification impossible; it became known as the 'No Names, No Numbers Strike'.

Colgan wrote that 'the lead was given to us by two of the oldest members in the camp who had the honour of being the first to refuse to identify themselves – Domhnall ua Buachalla and William Sears'.[3] He also mentioned the character shown by Tom Daly 'when he received word his wife had died in Dublin and that parole would be granted him if he would only answer his name and number. A similar stand was made by Martin Murphy, Four Courts Garrison, on the death of his mother.'[4]

The stand-off resulted in deprivation, confinement to huts, solitary confinement, courts martial and terms of imprisonment combined with hard labour. It took a hunger strike to get privileges restored, one of the principal players in this act of defiance being Michael Collins, who also came to the aid of Patrick Kirwan's family in Maynooth.

Colgan had made a valiant effort to prevent Kirwan heading to the GPO on Easter Monday, to no avail, but word obviously reached Wales of the family's growing predicament now that he was incarcerated in Frongoch. In one of a number of letters exchanged with Susan Killeen, a girlfriend since 1914, Collins asked her could she 'get in touch with some of the *CmBan* [Cumann na mBan] people and ask them to look up Mrs Kirwan of Maynooth, whose husband is here. They have five or six children who are not, I am afraid, being attended [to] at all.'[5] The intermediary was probably Colgan.

Despite many deprivations, numerous activities were organised, which kept spirits up, and by mid-August the educational system provided for drama, choral, debates in Irish and English, book-keeping, maths, shorthand, Irish language and history, dancing, Spanish, and private classes in German and French. This was backboned by a considerable number of highly qualified teachers in the ranks. Dearest to ua Buachalla's heart was the Irish language. A factor that strengthened his resolve to see it flourish throughout the country, he recalled later in life, was the fact that the majority of men executed after the Rising spoke of their great love of it and how it had awakened their spirit of nationalism.

He was central to organising classes, and among possessions he brought home was a parcel-label with the letters 'O.H.M.S' at the top, 'Commandant' in the middle and 'Frongoch' at the bottom-right. With writing material scarce, he had obviously taken the liberty of 'borrowing' sufficient labels to take notes at classes. One of the phrases still legible reads '*Carbad trí seacht gcumhal*' – 'A chariot worth thrice seven young female slaves'. He also included a little German – '*England's verlegenheit ist Ireland's gelegenheit*' – 'England's difficulty is Ireland's opportunity'. He also availed of facilities for shoemaking and an artists' shed – a workshop for engineers.

During the seven months of internment, no opportunity was overlooked when the prospect of embarrassing the enemy presented itself. Michael O'Halloran recalled one such episode:

The men slept in large dormitories and over each bunk there was a shelf to hold their possessions. Domhnall kept some personal effects in a biscuit tin, and one night the biscuit tin fell.

'A *thiarcais*, who hit you?' a friend asked in the morning.

Domhnall told him what had happened.

'Don't be absurd, man! Weren't you bitten by a big rat?'

Domhnall grasped the idea immediately and made a bee-line for the medical hut. There were two doctors attached to the camp, an elderly man and a young doctor, and they listened gravely to Domhnall's complaint that he had been bitten. They examined the wound closely. Then the elderly man gave his decision – it *could* be a rat bite. The young man ridiculed the suggestion. At this, Domhnall jumped up and stormed out.

The story that prisoners were being bitten by rats in their sleep got back to Ireland. The matter snowballed into an outcry about bad conditions in Frongoch, which proved highly embarrassing to the camp authorities. Domhnall received sympathetic letters from friends in Ireland.

Soon afterwards the elderly doctor was found drowned in a stream near the camp. The prisoners were paraded and accused of driving him to suicide. They shouted angry denials. It was a rule that they should parade with bare heads and [the] next day they defied the rule by parading with headgear. When they were ordered to take off their hats they refused. And with that, the matter ended.[6]

Naturally enough, with a sizeable number of internees from GAA clubs throughout Ireland, football became the focal point of their recreation, particularly as the camp authorities would not countenance the idea of hurling being played.

The pitch in Frongoch was called Croke Park ... there was a fine crop of footballers and hurlers among the prisoners and the games were physical – a means for the players to exercise and release tension. In fact, the games were so rough one of the guards was heard to remark, 'if that's what they are like at play, they must be bloody awful in a fight'.[7]

A prime mover in organising the teams and coaching was one of Kerry's greatest exponents of the game, Dick Fitzgerald, after whom the stadium in Killarney is named. He had togs made from flour bags, but as the material resisted the most strenuous efforts of the laundry to remove the name of the brand of a well-known flour, it could be said that Frongoch was the first venue to see the introduction of advertising in the history of the sport.

Another outlet for prisoners was home crafts and ua Buachalla busied himself making *macramé* bags and reins for children which he brought home to Maynooth. In 1936 he donated them to the National Museum, as well as the coat he wore during the 1916 Rising. In addition, he donated a pike that had been given to him by Eamonn Ceannt in 1915 which was used as a template for those forged in Clonshaugh leading up to the Rising.

Bloody Maxwell

His days in Frongoch also provided him with a picture of a dozen internees displaying a flag with the words 'Black Hand – Frongoch'. He is the central figure, which might suggest that it was his influence that brought them together. At that time there was a secret society devoted to Serbian unification, unofficially known as the 'Black Hand'. By 1914 there were as many as 2,500 members, many of them Serbian army officers. The professed goal of the group was the creation of a Greater Serbia, by use of violence if necessary. The Black Hand trained guerrillas and saboteurs and planned political murders. A point was eventually reached where saying 'no' to the Black Hand was a dangerous act. Crown Prince Alexander was an enthusiastic financial supporter. Through its purported connections to the June 1914 assassination of Archduke Franz Ferdinand in Sarajevo, the Black Hand may have been one of the catalysts for the start of the First World War; Gavrilo Princip, who assassinated the Archduke, was also one of several members of the Black Hand.

Other underground groups with the name 'Black Hand' included the *Camorra* and Mafia extortionists in Italy and the United States, while there was also *La Mano Negra*, a secret and violent anarchist organisation in Spain at the end of the nineteenth century. Thus, in terms of having a variety of international terrorists to learn from, the Frongoch group was not short on case studies. As the months passed, so the Academy blossomed and the ingenuity of the Irish prisoners continued to frustrate attempts to impose prison discipline.

Meanwhile, in London, the Irish Parliamentary Party was demanding the recall of General Maxwell, the cessation of Martial Law, political treatment for convicted insurgents – and the release of the internees in England. In November, they succeeded on one front when Maxwell was brought home. A much despised figure during his stay in Ireland, he was regularly referred to as 'The Butcher' and 'Bloody Maxwell'. In May 1916 he visited Maynooth College to reprimand the President for giving his blessing to the men of Maynooth as they set forth for Dublin on Easter Monday. He had also previously called on Dr Walsh, Archbishop of Dublin, asking him to punish priests for attending to wounded and dying soldiers.[8]

The following month, in June 1916, with the Government under pressure, Prime Mininter Herbert Asquith resigned and Lloyd George replaced him while Andrew Bonar Law was appointed Chancellor of the Exchequer and Leader of the House of Commons. And then, on 21 December, in reply to questions from John Dillon, Henry Duke, the Chief Secretary for Ireland, stated that 'the time had come when the liberating of the internees would be less than the risks which might follow detaining them longer'.[9] The first Irishman to hear that Frongoch was being evacuated was Brennan-Whitmore, who was called to the Adjutant's compound:

> 'Well, Whitmore,' he said. 'I have just received the order to release you all. I've just got a telegram from the Home Office.'

> 'Do you mean an unconditional release of everybody?' I queried, not yet able to grasp the full significance of his remarks.

> 'The telegram simply says that I am to have the camps cleared of all Irish prisoners by eight o'clock on Saturday night. No mention is made of any condition, or reservation whatever. The idea is to have you all home for Christmas. Men from the north, west and south of Ireland will leave the Camp at 5 a.m. tomorrow, those for Dublin and the midlands will leave at 8 p.m. Now, I will have to telegraph the name and address of every prisoner to the Home Office and Dublin Castle before he leaves the camp. It will be an all-night job for me, and unless you help me I will not be able to get through it in time.'

'Well,' I replied, 'since it's an unconditional release all round I will help you.'[10]

When word reached the dormitories, Brennan-Whitmore recalled that 'there was simply an orgy of feasting, singing, packing, and writing in autograph albums'.[11] The barbers were kept going all night haircutting and shaving. And although there was a delay in leaving the next day, the gates were eventually opened, with uninterrupted passage permitted between the camps and along the roads, except the one leading to Bala. Men spoke later of the 'intoxication' of going about the roads without escort or restraint. The only disappointment was for the sentenced prisoners in Britain who would not be freed for another six months.

The most cherished possession brought back by ua Buachalla was a small album filled with thoughts, poems and drawings contributed by his fellow internees, reflecting a variety of moods in the camp and expressing the hopes for the future. J. M. Stanley of *The Gaelic Press* quoted a few lines from William Rooney's 'Ceann Dubh Dílis':

O Dear Dark Head, let not thy waiting daunt thee,

The future if thou wiliest can be thine;

The past can summon up no shades to haunt thee,

Of perjured faith or desecrated shrine.

Míceál Mac Stáin wrote:

The wind that blows its dew-filled bristle

Across those foreign green-clad hills,

Brings memories of love and death –

A scene again my spirit thrills

I see our dear flag floating free,

Its folds caressed by every wind,

Singing its message o'er land and sea

'Here freedom is once more cushioned'

And still that flag defies the rain

Of shot and shell and treachery,

For still it cries the old refrain

'I am, I will, I must be free'.

P. ua Braonáin of Meelick Cross, Limerick was more succinct:

Nil Desperandum

Pádraig Maelpait, of No. 55 Belgrave Dr., Rathmines, Dublin wrote:

In good or ill

Or where you will,

Our country's freedom

Is our duty still

The fight is long

It may be still,

But our country's duty

We shall fulfil.

With one exception, all the contributions to the album were written during internment in Frongoch. The exception was penned on 1 January 1917 in St Enda's College in Rathfarnham, which was probably ua Buachalla's first time to leave home after his return from Wales. The executions of Pádraig and Willie Pearse would have weighed heavily on him in Frongoch, and it was to Margaret Pearse that he headed on New Year's Day to sympathise; not only did she lose her sons, but many others who had taught with her, or were pupils, in St Enda's. With him, ua Buachalla brought the album which had words that were written by many people she would have known, and before leaving he asked her to contribute. She was also succinct:

No Cross,

No Crown.

As Frongoch released the exuberant internees, the first 500 were taken by train to Holyhead, and 130 were immediately transported to Dun Laoghaire, arriving on the morning of 23 December. The remainder followed in good time to celebrate Christmas with their families.

Ua Buachalla's lasting memory of his return to Dublin was how dramatically it contrasted with the departure. 'When we were being escorted to the boat for internment, the people of Dublin were inclined to be hostile to us, particularly in the Richmond Barracks area where they were mostly British soldiers' wives.'[12] What he returned to was a tumultuous welcome in Dublin, which was mirrored throughout the countryside with the addition of bonfires lighting the night sky. He felt there was a new heart in Ireland. The guns in O'Connell Street had reverberated throughout the nation. Kilmainham's firing squads had stilled some hearts, but for others it generated renewed commitment.

Despite surviving a torrid week at Easter and for the remainder of the year being locked up in a detention camp, ua Buachalla sat in a car he had hired in Dublin with a few fellow Maynooth Volunteers and took the western road in the knowledge that 1916, despite the tragic loss of some of his closest friends, was a step in the right direction. His Christmas blessing was the comfort of home and the joy of a family reunited.

'God Almighty Looked After Us'

Described as 'a Government man, one we would call a west-Britain' by ua Buachalla's son Joe, Pat Grehan was a good friend of his father, willing to pay an annual subscription to the Maynooth Gaelic League fund, but totally opposed to an armed insurrection. In vain, he tried to change ua Buachalla's stance in the months leading up to the Rising.

An ex-lighthouse keeper, he lived in Celbridge, and had the reputation of knowing many influential people. Having discovered that ua Buachalla had been captured in Dublin and imprisoned in Britain, he took the boat to Holyhead and eventually made contact, bringing ua Buachalla up to date on how things were in Maynooth and assuring him that the family was in good health. When Grehan returned home, Joe recalled him dismounting from his bike in Maynooth and coming into the house to tell Sinéad about her husband's exploits since Easter Monday, and letting her know that he had not sustained any injuries during the Rising. It was an act of kindness that would not have been expected from someone who held diametrically opposed views, but was never forgotten by the beneficiaries.[13]

In his recall of Easter Monday when the Maynooth Volunteers marched to the GPO, Joe explained how he never had the opportunity to say goodbye to his father:

> I knew that something was in the offing at that time, as did my father, but I didn't know when, so I went off to Fairyhouse on Easter Monday and when I came back father was gone. Now he did say to me before going 'what do you want to go to Fairyhouse for?', but he didn't say anything else and I told him I'd never been to Fairyhouse and I would like to go. I suppose he wanted me to stay with my mother that day.[14]

In the ensuing months, there was no time in the ua Buachalla household for Fairyhouse or Punchestown, as the three mainstays of the business – Liam O'Regan, Jack Graves and Patrick Kirwan – were also in prison. Joe had serious work thrust upon him and together with the shop boys and older children, they kept the customers satisfied. 'We were all too young', Joe recalled, 'but God Almighty looked after us.'[15] And while he admitted that he didn't worry too much about his father – 'one doesn't at that age'[16] – his mother most certainly did, as she had health problems to deal with at that time also.

Allied to the serious workload, Joe recalled that there was a feeling among some people in the town immediately after the Rising that his father was responsible for the fact that a number of men from the Maynooth area were now in British prisons. The cry was 'Where is my husband?' and 'Is Buckley going to feed us now?'[17] Later, though, that mantra began to change to 'There's that government over there keeping our people in jail.'[18] Long term, it had a profoundly beneficial effect on ua Buachalla's standing in the community, which would be seen in the polls two years later.

Of greater concern to him was Joe's immediate future. Pearse had written to him in August 1915, informing him that he had passed his exams and hoping that he would be returning for his final year. This he did, and as he prepared to head home for the Easter holidays in 1916, he had notions of being involved in the Rising.

> I knew something was going to happen. The older boys who were staying in the school, university students, were all in a core of Volunteers and they had all managed to get rifles from Pearse, and I couldn't see why I could not get one, as I was old enough to carry one.

> But a day or so before I came home, Pearse sent for me to go to his study. 'I know the whole circumstances of your family', he said. 'You are the eldest and I presume that from talking to your father you have a kind of idea that things will not be running so smoothly later on'. I said I see a lot of rifles around and it has put me thinking. He replied: 'I am going to ask you to do something for me, and I won't take a refusal. I know your mother is not too robust and your father will be leaving home one of these days, and I want you to promise me that when your father leaves home, you will stay until he comes home again, if he comes home.'

> I said I was disappointed, but alright. That was the thing about him; you couldn't refuse him. I mean if he wanted me to do anything, no matter what it was, I'd have done it. That was the end of the rifle and the Rising as far as I was concerned. All the other lads were older than me: Frank Burke, Eamon Bulfin, Desmond Ryan, Fintan Murphy ...

> My father took me aside when I came home at Easter and said practically what Pearse had ... 'I want you to look after your mother and the rest of the family.' That was that.[19]

From that day, schooling had finished for Joe. Within a week he was totally engrossed in running the business and there was no possibility of him returning to St Enda's in September. In late January 1917, after a period of recuperation, Domhnall got down to discussing Joe's future with him – and that took a little time as Joe admitted he had no idea what he wanted to do. His father eventually suggested engineering, which appealed. The Dodge agent in Ireland was John O'Neill, a good friend of the family, who readily agreed to give Joe a start – but initially the work had nothing to do with motor cars:

> At that time, O'Neill was doing war work for the Government, which included [making] bombs for the Air Force. So I started off as an apprentice making the part that took the charge. It was called a 'gain'. I was being paid five shillings a week, and twenty five shillings a week war bonus. I enjoyed the job and got to know a lot of fellows, about twelve of whom were IRA men, including myself.
>
> When my brother-in-law to be, Frank Burke, came home from Frongoch, he told me that he was going to join up with the Rathfarnham Company and that I should do so too. The fact that a group of us were involved did not go unnoticed at work and one day O'Neill read the riot act to me. 'I know what you're at', he said. 'I suppose you wouldn't be a son of your father if you weren't. Now, I'm not asking you to stop anything, but I'm telling you this, I don't think you're right in what you're doing.'
>
> He insisted on me going to tech. I did the London City and Guild exams in engineering in Bolton Street. I was in digs in Rathmines and there was a curfew in 1919 and 1920 and it was a terrible job getting from Bolton Street to Rathmines. They let us out at half-nine and you would have to be up in Rathmines and in the digs before ten o'clock. The soldiers used to wear rubber-soled boots and you could hear nothing when they came out from the barracks in the middle of Rathmines Road, but suddenly there would be a fusillade of shots up the road, and I tell you, you would run.
>
> There were times when a fellow might go missing from work, he might be out on a job with the IRA, and O'Neill would come to me and say 'where is that fellow?' I'd always just say 'I don't know' and his response would always be 'damn well you know'. He knew what was going on, but as long as fellows turned up for work in the morning he was happy.[20]

Joe's move to Dublin saw him return to Cullenswood House. When St Enda's re-opened after the Rising, the British Army had occupied the Hermitage in Rathfarnham and so all school activities had returned to Rathmines. It was here that he resided, in the company of Frank Burke, who was now teaching in the school, and a few other former pupils. More importantly, it was Michael Collins' headquarters for a while and, in time, Joe would be required to do some work for him.

Count Plunkett shocks Dublin Castle

More immediately, there was the pending by-election in Roscommon in which the Nationalists decided to challenge the Redmondites, putting forward Count Plunkett, father of the executed Joseph, to contest the seat. Father O'Flanagan harnessed the power of the Volunteers and Sinn Féin to engineer an emphatic victory by over 1,300 votes. Shocked at the outcome, Dublin Castle took heavy-handed action, imprisoning at will – amongst them Terence McSwiney, Thomas MacCurtain and Seán T. O'Kelly – and deporting many.

On the first anniversary of the Rising, an estimated 20,000 defied a ban by gathering in Sackville Street to commemorate the declaration of an Irish Republic. Even though there was a strong police presence, the Tricolour was raised over the ruins of the GPO at half-mast, people wore armbands with the Tricolour and the Republican Proclamation was posted on many walls. The South Longford by-election in May, which returned Joseph McGuinness, provided a narrow thirty-seven-vote success for Sinn Féin.

While the Volunteers re-grouped after their return from British prisons and followed instructions to resist any attempts at conscription, and Bonar Law released Irish prisoners from Portland, Maidstone and Parkhurst to return as heroes to Dublin on 17 June 1917, it was the Clare election of 11 July that concentrated the minds of British politicians. The Redmondite candidate was Patrick Lynch, K. C., well known and popular; his opponent, Éamon de Valera, a relative stranger who had taken part in the Rising. The Banner County elected Dev. with a majority of 2,975, a margin that was seen as a tidal wave.

With well over a thousand clubs in the country, Sinn Féin gathered on 25 October and unanimously agreed to a new Constitution, which declared in the Preamble that the organisation 'shall, in the name of the Sovereign Irish people, (a) deny the right and oppose the will of the

British Parliament and British Crown or any other foreign government to legislate for Ireland; (b) make use of any and every means available to render impotent the power of England to hold Ireland in subjection by military force or otherwise.'[21]

In selecting a leader, Arthur Griffith and Count Plunkett withdrew their candidature in favour of de Valera. And with the enthusiastic backing of the new President, Eoin MacNeill was elected to the Executive of twenty four members – which also included Michael Collins. At its Convention on 27 October, the Irish Volunteers Organisation (which remained independent of Sinn Féin) also elected de Valera as President. Michael Collins became Director of Organisation. Despite the subjugation of the nation, there would have been a general feeling of strong and decisive leadership as 1918 dawned, while Britain was struggling with Russia's departure from the War and an American army not yet in place.

For Domhnall ua Buachalla, the year would bring great sadness, and a role in the nation's political life which he never aspired to.

CHAPTER 9

Death Strikes Twice

As winter turned to spring in 1918, Sinn Féin blossomed. Their drive to have a *cumann* in every town received an enthusiastic response and the logical progression to having a *Comhairle Ceanntair* in each electoral constituency was creating a platform for future elections. The necessity to continue acquiring guns is reflected in Patrick Colgan's Witness Statement, which pointed out that north Kildare had fewer arms towards the end of 1917 than they had gathered for the Rising. In nearby Kilcock, though, an account of Patrick O'Keeffe's days in the Volunteers revealed that they were managing quite well, having relieved the National Volunteers of over thirty rifles.[1]

While the stockpiling of firearms and ammunition was important, the Volunteers were under orders to refrain from using their guns, irrespective of provocation. Macardle wrote of the attitude at that time: 'The movement, in short, was given the character of a consistent, non-violent resistance to English rule. A very high standard of discipline was demanded within its ranks, both military and civilian, and was maintained.'[2]

After many months of bad health, John Redmond died on 6 March 1918. Denis Gwynn, a pupil of Pearse in St Enda's when the school opened and later professor of modern Irish history at University College Cork, wrote: 'His life will stand forever as a symbolic tragedy of a greatly gifted and disinterested statesman, who trusted overmuch in the efficacy of parliamentary agitation.'[3] This contrasts with a formidable defence of Redmond's achievements by former Taoiseach John Bruton in 2014. Political journalist Stephen Collins summarised Bruton's thesis thus:

'Full independence could have been achieved without resort to violence and all the death and destruction that followed from the Rising right down to today.'[4] Collins continued: 'It is an arguable point. We will never know.'[5]

In April, a major threat to England developed as German efforts to conclude the First World War threatened the channel ports. The Army was dangerously short of troops for the Western Front. In the German Spring Offensive, troops broke through the Allied lines in several sectors of the front in France, with local advantage in numbers of four to one. One of Lloyd George's reactions was a declaration that Irishmen would be conscripted; on 16 April it was passed in the House of Commons by 301 votes to 103.

Two days later, a gathering at the Mansion House called by Lord Mayor Laurence O'Neill united Irish resistance. Parliamentarians John Dillon and Joseph Devlin attended, as did Sinn Féin's Arthur Griffith and Éamon de Valera; also three Labour representatives – William O'Brien, Michael Egan and Thomas Johnson. Cork MP William O'Brien represented his 'All For Ireland League'; T. M. Healy was looking after independent interests. The outcome was the anti-Conscription Pledge, 'denying the right of the British Government to enforce compulsory service in this country'.[6] On the same evening in Maynooth College, a Bishops' Manifesto declared 'the Irish people have a right to resist by every means that are consonant with the law of God'.[7] On Sunday 21 April the pledge against Conscription was signed throughout nationalist Ireland; two days later a national strike brought the country, with the exception of Belfast, to a halt.

Taken aback by the sheer intensity of the opposition, a new Irish Executive at the Castle was put in place to devise some means by which they could appear to justify disrupting Sinn Féin's position. The result was the 'discovery' of the 'German Plot', hatched to suit their purpose. The result was that seventy-three prisoners were deported to England; among them Arthur Griffith, Éamon de Valera, Count Plunkett, Countess Markievecz and William Cosgrave. Not one was put on trial.

Domhnall ua Buachalla continued to work with Patrick Colgan, strengthening Sinn Féin's base in Maynooth and adding to the Volunteers' store of guns. On headed notepaper from Thomas Henshaw & Co. Ltd of Christchurch Place in Dublin, he received the following letter, dated 22 May 1918:

Dear Mr Buckley,

I had an order from Father Clavin for books sent herewith. He will send to you for them this week. The article for you is in good condition, a late edition, plenty of fittings on hands. Get wood case tightened up. I had not time except to put it together. By the way I enclose 2/- which you might send on to Father Clavin. I left him short when giving change. You might forward it to him and point out error.

Yours faithfully,

Frank H.[8]

An innocuous letter, one would presume, without seeing two changes made many years later by ua Buachalla; the word 'guns' was inserted in pencil under 'books', while the 'H.' was completed to reveal the name. Ua Buachalla would have been a good customer of Henshaw's, and obviously built up a relationship over the years with Frank Harding, who held similar political views. A delivery of guns arrived with the letter, and a more sophisticated weapon for ua Buachalla, which could well have been a replacement for the gun he had to abandon as he fled the GPO.

Of much greater concern to ua Buachalla at this time was the fact that Sinéad's health was deteriorating rapidly. As the months slipped by she had to spend an ever-increasing time resting, during which the children would go into a slightly darkened room to talk to her. On 24 July 1918 she passed away, aged 48.

Under the heading 'Certified Cause of Death and Duration of Illness' on the death certificate, the Registrar, Joe Caulfield, wrote 'Cardiac Disease – Twenty Years', which suggests that her problem must have been discovered shortly after she married and almost certainly prompted her husband's request to *An tAthair* Peadar Ó Laoghaire for Masses close to the delivery of their youngest child. Séadna recalled that his earliest recollection in life 'was my mother playing the piano and singing the song "Mother" and bringing me for walks down the avenue in Carton Demesne. In winter she always wore a fur muff. I was only 8 when she died, and I remember going into her bedroom and looking at her in bed and not understanding why she would not waken up'.[9]

Her children spoke of her as a very gentle and loving person. Strikingly good looking, she was devoted to her husband and his ideals, which demanded that the country took precedence, even to the extent of leaving her without a husband, and the children without a father, if the necessity arose. Séadna also mentioned his father's Easter Monday departure for the GPO and his mother 'going into the parlour and breaking down in tears, and cousin Bridie going in to comfort her'.[10]

While a weak heart had threatened Sinéad's life for many years, it is also possible that she might have been affected by the Spanish Flu. In an article in the *Irish Daily Mail*, Ida Milne recalled those dark days:

> The earliest report of the misery and death that was to come was printed in June 1918 and referred to as a 'mystery malady' killing people in Leinster – and by the time the disease finally abated in mid-1919, the official death-toll on the island of Ireland was 20,057 people. By 21 October the *Evening Herald* said that 'the new influenza is sweeping through with whirlwind effect. The death rate in Dublin has reached an alarming figure. Burials at Glasnevin have increased to three to four times [the] normal levels. Most Dublin schools are closed, several teachers have died from pneumonia. Hospitals are crowded.'[11]

Within months, death had knocked on their door again. This time it was for ua Buachalla's mother, Sarah on 20 October, with family records showing the cause was 'influenza/bronchitis'. She had been ill for some time and went to live in Dublin at Castlewood Park, Rathmines with Domhnall's sister, Johanna, and her husband, Conn McLoughlin. So within the space of four months, the ua Buachalla family made the journey from St Mary's Church in Maynooth to the cemetery at Laraghbryan twice. For the children it was a case of Grandmother following Mother to the grave; for Domhnall, a distressing farewell to the two great loves of his life.

In the days following the second burial, ua Buachalla might well have pondered on his life, and the fifty-two hectic years that had brought him to the point where he was now a widower with seven children to raise, ranging from 8 to 20, with a business that demanded six long days every week, and his eldest son now resident and working in Dublin. Was his desire sufficiently strong to continue being the dedicated Volunteer with all the attendant pressures of sourcing guns and ammunition? Did he still yearn for an Irish-speaking country to the extent that he would continue to attend classes and raise money and deal with the Gaelic League? As a widower, could he continue to depend on Mary Tyrrell in the house and

Liam O'Regan in the shop to accommodate his cultural and politicial life? Whatever his thoughts, little did he know that life was about to make yet another serious demand on his time.

In October, the Irish Electoral Register was revised and women over 30 secured the franchise. On 25 November, the British Parliament was dissolved: polling day would be 14 December. Despite Sinn Féin having more than a hundred of its leaders in prison and much of the country under military rule, an Election Manifesto was issued, stating that it stood for Sovereign Independence and an Irish Republic. The convention to select a candidate for North Kildare was held in Prosperous. Patrick Colgan, a major player in the selection process, recalled the meeting:

> Two candidates were put forward. I nominated Eamon (Ted) O'Kelly. I had the support of the Volunteers. Art O'Connor was put forward by the Sinn Féin element. I had two reasons for pressing O'Kelly's candidature. He had been with us in 1916. He had been an organiser for the Volunteers in [the] pre-Easter Week days. O'Kelly sprung from the 'next door to the Big House' class. His father had been the local Medical Officer to Maynooth College. His grandfather had held the same position. His relatives in north Kildare and County Meath were the big graziers. Cardinal Cullen was his great grand-uncle. He had broken traditions, and from his set, in becoming a Volunteer. He had earned their intense dislike.
>
> Art O'Connor was a good Irishman too; he worked hard to build up the Volunteers in Easter Week. In spite of hard feelings over his non-participation in the Rebellion, particularly amongst the Maynooth fellows who had taken part, he was one of the first men I had approached when I commenced to organise in 1917. I had selected him as my adjutant and, whilst I realised Art's leanings were more to the political than the military side, I had a respect for him.
>
> The date for the selection of the Sinn Féin candidate in North Kildare was publicised. Two days before the selection took place, Art was arrested in County Galway, and the plea was made at our Convention that we should select a prisoner 'to put him in to get him out'.[12]

At this stage, O'Connor had overwhelming support to get the nomination for South Kildare, but there was serious disagreement about who should fill the role for North Kildare. While Colgan made a very valid case for O'Kelly, it would appear that there was serious opposition, and though he was not present, nor had he sought the nomination, ua Buachalla had many advocates in the room. Colgan summed up the final moments:

> Seamus O'Kelly presided at the meeting. Like Art, he was more politically minded than military minded. He advocated Art's candidature. Finally, the opposing sections at the Convention agreed unanimously on my proposal to select Domhnall ua Buachalla. I had the job of breaking the news to Domhnall, who accepted only because it was his duty to do so. O'Connor was selected to contest South Kildare.[13]

Once chosen, the self-effacing Maynooth candidate displayed the drive and commitment he brought to all his undertakings in life. On 25 November he opened his campaign with a lengthy article in the *Leinster Leader*, pointing out to the people of north Kildare that their choice in the election was a simple one – liberty or slavery.

'We Alone Have a Chance of Winning'

> Sinn Féin has chosen me as its representative for North Kildare, and as such I appeal to you for your support, not for any considerations personal to myself, but for the Cause for which I stand. Never in the seven centuries of our struggle for liberty and tugging on the chains that bind us has such an occasion arisen as the present. God grant that we may read aright the sign of the times, and prove ourselves worthy of our great cause. Poles, Jugo-Slavs, Czecho-Slovaks, Ruthenes, Slovenes and Croats are free – the liberty for which they longed, but for centuries appeared as distant as the rainbow and unreal as a mirage, is theirs today.
>
> What then of this our nation, one of the oldest in the world, which was a beacon of light, of learning and sanctity to all Europe while England was still plunged in paganism and barbarianism – is it to hug its chains, or will we have the courage to demand the liberty which even hitherto obscure states now enjoy? Are we going to brand ourselves as less than [the] Croats, the Ruthenes and the

Slovenes? If so, we deserve the slavery to which we doom ourselves; we betray the sacred trust handed down to us by our Fathers in blood and in tears; we forfeit the right to call Irish history our own, for its every page will sneer at us as degenerates and cowards; and to be consistent in our slavery we should never again mention the name of Emmet, and should remove the image of every Irish patriot from our homes.

We rub our eyes in amazement and ask ourselves, can it be possible at this unique, this supreme moment in the destiny of Europe, with the President of the United States pledging himself and his country that small nations shall have self-determination – can it be possible that there are some calling themselves Irishmen who scoff at the demand of freedom for Ireland as an idle dream?

Electors, the two policies are before you, and it is for you to choose. Sinn Féin stands for freedom. Parliamentarianism still hugs its chains, being content with the cowardly request of a little loosening of their iron grip. The slave makes the tyrant, and he who asks not for liberty does not deserve to be free ...

The Rising of Easter Week has been described as madness. Let me here state, in the words of our President, that one Easter Week is sufficient, and that the Easter Week was necessary to lift up our cause from the status of a mere domestic question, and to prove to the world that we are a distinct nation.

Had there been no Easter Week, what would be the cry of England today? It would have been a repetition of the sneering retort made in the House of Commons after the Boer War – 'the Boers have fought for liberty; what have you done?' Thanks to Easter Week we are saved that sneer, and what was once regarded in certain quarters as foolishness is today our greatest asset in our appeal to the world ...

A test: O'Connell once said that if the London *Times* had praised, him, he would examine his conscience to find out what he had done against his country. Quite recently, aeroplanes flew over this district and dropped leaflets advising the people to vote for the Parliamentary policy. If O'Connell were alive today and knew nothing further of the merits of the two causes, what conclusion would be drawn?

Fellow-countrymen, we Sinn Féiners do not claim a monopoly of wisdom. All we claim is that the alternative policy having failed and having, with its partition scheme, been repudiated by the country, we alone have a chance of winning. Certain it is that the country is unmistakeably on our side. Is it not wisdom then, in view of England's coalition of Tories and Liberals, to close our ranks and ban the demon of discord, at least while we stand before the bar of the world? We can settle our individual differences afterwards . . .

For the love we bear our dear country, let us, in this critical hour, when the eyes of the world are upon us, close our ranks . . . if not, Irish history has been read in vain: it will be the old sad story that runs through our annals – the curse of disunion. And how bitter will be the reproaches of our children, and our children's children if ever they read with brow of hatred and shame that the greatest opportunity in our country's destiny was lost . . .[14]

The same edition of the paper also reported that Donal Buckley would appear to be best equipped in the matter of organisation:

The high degree of efficiency which has characterised Sinn Féin activities in previous elections is at work in north Kildare . . . our representative questioned Mr Buckley and some of his prominent supporters regarding the probable result of the contest, and found the utmost confidence prevailing. 'The reports of our canvassers', Mr Buckley said, 'are excellent all round and much better in many districts than we anticipated. We are quite confident of the result, but we want to get the largest majority we can and poll every possible vote for our cause.'[15]

It was in the Town Hall in Naas on 25 November that John O'Connor got the backing of the Parliamentary Party to run again. Forty years in politics, he had represented the constituency in the House of Commons for fourteen years. Towards the end of a lengthy address he spoke of 'what was possible – between Home Rule and the constitutional means of getting

Home Rule – and Sinn Féin, which meant struggling for some vague Irish Republic, a problematical appeal to the Peace Conference, the adoption of means which have been tried and failed, and the abandonment of means, which have been proved successful'.[16]

Earlier, in proposing O'Connor, John Healy, J. P. [Justice of the Peace], said 'Mr Buckley was a man he knew, and for whom he had great respect as a straightforward and honest man, but to adopt his policy would be political suicide.'[17] A week later, O'Connor stated his case for election in print:

> Because you (men and women of Kildare) know me so long and so well, I have only to say that I stand today where I stood all my life. I took my place beside Parnell, Biggar and Davitt when we put before ourselves the task of gaining the land for the people, houses and land for labourers, equality of opportunity for all in education and, above all, self-government for the Irish nation. How well we accomplish our task you are witnesses.[18]

And in a pithy reference to ua Buachalla's article, he wrote: 'I do not address you in the language of poetical nonsense – I leave that to my opponent in this contest. I am a plain, practical man who tries to do practical things, and sometimes succeeds.'[19]

A sharper edge entered the field of play when ua Buachalla was concluding a speech in Kilcock. 'Mr Buckley said he did not desire to refer personally to Mr O'Connor, but he could not remain silent regarding one action of his. John O'Connor had gone to Maynooth College and tried to have the students prevented from voting. This was a contemptible action and unworthy of an honourable man, and he (Mr Buckley) could not find language too strong to condemn it.'[20] The following week O'Connor refuted ua Buachalla's accusation at a meeting in Kilcock:

> What happened was that the late President of the College and he were personal friends for the last twenty years. They had heard that the late President was stricken down with a malady not long ago. Being in Maynooth, the promptings of a long friendship urged him [Mr O'Connor] to call to see his friend in the time of his trial. He was admitted to see him, and did they think he should be guilty of such bad taste in the day of his friend's distress to trouble him with anything about the miserable squabbles of the outside world? He did nothing of the kind.[21]

Shortly after O'Connor had concluded, Cornelius Buckley, Domhnall's brother, presided at a meeting in the same town where

> he noticed a distinctive feature in connection with the other meeting which was being held down the street. The military had sent representatives. The presence of British soldiers and their obvious object being to protect the platform of Mr O'Connor furnished sufficient proof that they [Sinn Féiners] were on the right track.

Another speaker, Séamus O'Keeffe, addressed a few questions to his audience:

> Who came to Kilcock three years ago as a recruiting sergeant for the British Army? Who said that the place for every man in Ireland was on the plains of Flanders and on the hills of Gallipoli? Who refused to support Mr Tim Healy in the House of Commons on his motion for an inquiry into the treatment of Irish prisoners in Belfast ... and last, but not least, who is Crown Prosecutor in Bristol? Is this the man they were going to have representing them in future?[22]

The following week at Ballagh Cross, with the Timahoe Fife and Drum band in attendance, the *Leinster Leader* reported that

> Mr Buckley came to the platform last ... he said he wished to repeat in public the statement made by him at Kilcock at the start of the campaign, namely, that Mr O'Connor went to Maynooth College with the deliberate intention of having the students there prevented from exercising the franchise. Mr O'Connor that day at Clane had called him (Mr Buckley) a liar. He repeated the statement now, and Mr O'Connor had the remedy in his own hands.[23]

Another factor which influenced the election was the national influenza epidemic which was particularly severe in the latter months of 1918, with water and power shortages in Naas adding to the severity in north Kildare. In Maynooth it forced the College authorities to send the students home to their dioceses, a move that was expected to curtail the Sinn Féin vote. Thomas P. Nelson wrote that it was claimed that practically all the students and about one half of the professors were Sinn Féiners and the party 'was concerned enough to issue a specific election notice in the national press. The following appeared in the *Irish Independent* on the day before polling':[24] 'All Maynooth students are earnestly requested to travel to Maynooth on Saturday next and record their votes for Donal Buckley, the Sinn Féin candidate. Proxy voting does not apply in these cases. Personal attendance is therefore absolutely necessary. Owing to a misunderstanding it was stated that the college would be open for the accommodation of the students, and it has been found impossible. All arrangements have been made for the reception of the students. Every vote will be required to ensure the return of the Sinn Féin nominee, and every student is appealed to to record his vote in Maynooth on Saturday next.' It was signed by Tomás Macliam, the Sinn Féin Constituency Director.[25]

The newspaper report on the day of voting noted that

> general good humour prevailed throughout the day ... and the closing hours of polling in Naas were marked by extreme activity on both sides. On the closing of the booths the Sinn Féin representatives placed a private seal on the boxes and a bodyguard of Volunteers accompanied the latter to the Courthouse, where the boxes were placed in a room specially prepared for the occasion. The Sinn Féin representatives sealed the windows and doors. A bodyguard of Volunteers took up duty outside.

> Mr Buckley, the Sinn Féin candidate, and his agent, Mr Reddin, were present with a large number of supporters, but Mr O'Connor, or any other of his supporters, did not put in an appearance. A large crowd had assembled outside the courthouse and in the outer hall, which greeted Mr Buckley's appearance with an outburst of cheering, which was renewed again and again. A rush was made for the Sinn Féin candidate, who was carried shoulder high from the Courthouse to the election rooms where insistent calls had to be responded to.

> In the course of his remarks, Mr Buckley said that victory was theirs that night, which was greeted with 'you are in' and 'up Buckley'. He advised those present to disperse quietly to their homes and by their example show that Sinn Féin was an organisation of order and discipline.[26]

A number of soldiers who were in a particularly boisterous condition 'smashed the glass of the headlights in a Sinn Féin motor car ... and also a fanlight over the shop of Mr John Grehan whilst attempts were made to pull down Sinn Féin flags. On the appearance of a number of Volunteers the soldiers made off ... and the town renewed its normal appearance by midnight'.[27]

A Victory for National Independence

Sinn Féin and its candidates' assumptions were vindicated at the count, even if the overwhelming margin of victory might have surprised a few. For the *Kildare Observer*, which would have delighted in Irish Parliamentary Party successes down the years, the outcome was unsettling:

> In Ireland we have passed through the opening stages of a revolution which even the oldest and most sagacious political thinker in this country could not have foreseen, even a year ago. The Irish Party, which has for generations gone to Westminster in varying degrees of strength, but with a substantial vote and mandate in all its stages, has been swept out of the country, leaving the merest shadow of its once powerful forces.

> A little over a month ago it left the House of Commons with a damaged reputation, but yet sixty eight strong. Today, its total strength is seven members, with Mr T. P. O'Connor, sitting for an English constituency (Liverpool), its oldest and most influential member.[28]

On 28 December, the results of the election in Ireland were declared: Sinn Féin won seventy-three seats, the Unionists twenty-six and the Irish Parliamentary Party six. The significance of the outcome appeared to bypass the writer in the *Kildare Observer*. 'It may yet come to pass that the Sinn Féin members will find their way, under one pretext or another, into the Parliament they have been decrying. But we believe that even the most rabid member of the Sinn Féin party no longer harbours the high hope of seeing a Republic established in Ireland.'[29] Far more accurate was the admission in the *Freeman's Journal:*

> The meaning of the Irish vote is as clear as it is emphatic. More than two-thirds of the electors throughout national Ireland have

endorsed the Sinn Féin programme ... they invited the people to join to the demand for a Republic as something immediately obtainable and practicable as well as desirable, the declaration that they would accept nothing else and nothing less.[30]

The Republicans were facilitated by Labour agreeing not to contest the election and the fact that the franchise had been extended by the Representation of the People Act, 1918, which granted voting rights to women over 30 for the first time, and gave all men over 21 and military servicemen over 19 a vote in parliamentary elections without property qualifications.

It was to the Agricultural Buildings attached to the Courthouse in Naas that ua Buachalla returned for the count after the previous night's celebration of anticipated success. There he met the Returning Officer, Charles Daly, Sub-Sheriff, and his legal assessor, Morgan Byrne, B. L., who had arrived from Dublin at 10.30 a.m. The actual counting did not start until 1.45 p.m. and fifteen minutes later proceedings were adjourned for lunch, during which the Volunteers continued to maintain their watching brief on the ballot boxes. At 5.00 p.m. Mr Daly announced that Donal Buckley had received 5,979 votes, John O'Connor 2,772. The spoiled votes totalled 104. Following a few formal words from the candidates and Mr Daly, the new M.P., who had triumphed by the greatest majority ever in the North Kildare constituency, walked out into the main street of Naas to prolonged roars of approval and was carried shoulder high to the Royal Hotel where he thanked his supporters from a window.

He referred to it as 'a victory for national independence' and told the party members that 'they would shortly have elections for local councils and must ensure that only men pledged to sovereign independence were elected to represent them, and with the help of God, they would see the achievement of their greatest and highest ambitions, a sovereign, independent Irish Republic'.[31]

FIRST DÁIL KILDARE NORTH 1918	SEATS 1 POLL 8,701
CANDIDATES	
Donal Buckley (Sinn Féin)	5,979
John O'Connor (Nationalist)	2,722

Irish Independent

Donal O'Connor, a brother of Art who took the South Kildare seat by a majority of 5,559 votes whilst still in jail in England at the time, also spoke, as did J. J. Fitzgerald, a political activist and Chairman of the Kildare GAA County Board. Later that night a tar barrel was lit on the Abbey Bridge in Naas to celebrate ua Buachalla's win and on Sunday several tar barrels were ablaze in the town. The *Kildare Observer* reported 'that there was no unseemly incident beyond the fact that a Sinn Féin supporter – Mr Domican of Kill – was, it is alleged, struck on the head by a stone thrown by a woman while the crowd was being addressed on behalf of Mr Buckley from the window of the Royal Hotel.'[32] The *Leinster Leader* was more specific about 'the severe blow to the head', stating it had come from 'a dark corner where a group of soldiers' relatives were congregated'.[33]

The *Observer's* reporter also noted 'that a number of children were gleefully shouting a ditty with a catchy air that sounded to me something like this':

Inky, pinky, par lee voo

Inky, pinky, par lee voo,

O'Connor thought he was going to get in,

But Bucklee gave him a great suck in,

Inky, pinky, par lee voo.[34]

Speaking in Newbridge after the vote was announced, Sinn Féin organiser Tom McCarthy said the town was an Irish Republican one, and not a military town, 'and many a man behind that barrack wall might be as good a man as any in the crowd. Many a man behind that wall voted for Dan Buckley.'[35]

After nightfall, most of the houses were illuminated and a torchlight procession was formed and marched through the streets, headed by the Fife and Drum Band, 'whose sweet and inspiring music has so frequently enlivened nationalist gatherings in the county'.[36] It was hardly surprising that ua Buachalla did not make the evening parade – J. J. Fitzgerald announced that the Maynooth man would return within a few days to thank all his supporters.

The weeks of mourning and of coming to terms with the loss of his wife and mother within the space of four months followed by a hectic election campaign which required his presence at every crossroads in north Kildare, would have drained the most resilient of men. Nevertheless, the adrenaline rush that followed such a phenomenal performance – even if he was a reluctant hero – and the excitement in Gleann Ailighe when greeted by his children and neighbours, would have ensured much late-night chatter and excitement before the last light went out.

However, within days, he was back on a platform in Naas demanding the release of Irish prisoners in England. Tom Harris proposed the resolution 'that today the Irish people are assembled to voice a nation's demand for the release of Irish men and women who have been imprisoned by the military Government of England because they dared declare for Ireland the right that her people should self-determine the sovereignty under which they wished to live'.[37]

Greeted enthusiastically by a big crowd in inclement weather, North Kildare's new M. P. said that when the British Government wanted to upset the Sinn Féin organisation, they arrested the leaders and refused them a trial, and as an excuse for doing that they invented the German Plot. 'But the British Government do not know that even if they put a thousand Sinn Féin leaders in jail, there would be a thousand more to take their place.'[38] He emphasised that their work was only beginning and by their determination in this and other matters, the power of England could not prevail against them. Within days of this meeting he received a letter from Art O'Connor, M. P. for South Kildare, who was in Durham Prison.

Domhnall, my dear friend,

Isn't it about time I sent you a letter? Often I've said to myself during the past week that I should write, but didn't see my way to doing so. We are not allowed to send more than three letters a week and I had no writing material until today.

I praise you, dear friend, for the way you succeeded in Kildare North; that's a great win you had and there isn't a person in Ireland happier than myself at the result. I was always thinking that Kildare would be a problem, but in the end the opposite has happened and Kildare is as good as any county in Ireland.

I wonder will England ever move or will we ever be free? Nevertheless, I am not sad and I'm sound and healthy, thank God, and even though I'm far from home and the family, I wish you happiness and peace and Ireland's freedom during this year. I suppose there was enjoyment and merrymaking taking place last Saturday. Isn't it too bad I wasn't out to participate? It was necessary for me to make a speech, something I did not enjoy very much.

Remember me to all true friends in Maynooth, particularly Joe, and your family, and Dr Grogan. With all good wishes to yourself and the Irish people.

Your friend for ever,

Art Ó Conchubhair.

The Most Important Work

A meeting at the Mansion House in Dublin on 7 January 1919 prepared the way for the public opening of the Parliament of Ireland and a draft Constitution for the Dáil. On 21 January at 3.30 p.m., ua Buachalla took his seat as the first Dáil Éireann went into session. With both the President of Sinn Féin, Éamon de Valera, and Arthur Griffith in jail, Count Plunkett proposed that Cathal Brugha should preside. *Cumann na mBan* member and republican activist Máire Comerford, later a journalist with *The Irish Press*, recalled the day's events with a sense of excitement and brevity, having squeezed into a position half-hidden behind a statue:

> Cathal said that they were met to do the most important work that had been done in Ireland since the foreigners landed. The people of Ireland hoped and trusted in God, and for that reason they would humbly ask God to give them help in the work they had undertaken. He then asked 'the most faithful priest who had ever lived in Ireland', Fr Michael O'Flanagan, to ask the blessing of the Holy Spirit on their work. Then we saw Fr Michael's head and shoulders as he came forward, and our prayers went up with his.[39]

The Provisional Constitution of the Dáil was read and passed unanimously and was followed by the Declaration of Independence, read in Irish and English, stating:

Whereas the Irish people is by right a free people:

And whereas for seven hundred years the Irish people have never ceased to repudiate and has repeatedly protested in arms against foreign usurpation:

And whereas English rule in this country is, and always has been, based upon force and fraud and maintained by military occupation against the declared will of the people ...

When it came to the conclusion of the Declaration, Cathal Brugha said: 'Deputies, you understand from what is asserted in this Declaration that we are now done with England. Let the world know it and those who are concerned bear it in mind.'[40]

Máire Comerford wrote that 'some sixty-nine press men from home and overseas reported the proceedings. Outside, Dawson Street was thronged. Volunteers controlled the crowds, but reinforced Dublin Metropolitan Police kept the trams moving. Young people were perched at every point of vantage.'[41] She also recalled that an instruction went out from the Castle:

Press censor to all Irish newspapers: The Press are informed with reference to the Dáil Éireann Assembly that the following are not for publication:

1 The Democratic Programme.

2 The Declaration of Independence.

3 Speeches of the proposer and seconder of the Declaration of Independence.

However, 'secret printing presses all over the city pounded out the banned literature ... there was no difficulty in obtaining any document which the Dáil wanted to distribute. The material sold like hot cakes from under the counter everywhere.'[42]

The land policy of the First Dáil, which attempted to implement a fair and full redistribution of the vacant lands and ranches among the uneconomic holders and landless men, caused internal problems, and a committee appointed to look into the matter under the Land Department included ua Buachalla. And following the decision on 6 March by the House of Commons to release the Irish internees and convicted prisoners, Art O'Connor was appointed to a committee which would assist the Minister for Local Government, William Cosgrave, in preparing policy for his department. Any doubts O'Connor held prior to the election that Kildare would be a weak link in Sinn Féin's push for power had been dispelled.

On 3 February 1919, Éamon de Valera, with the help of Harry Boland and Michael Collins, escaped from Lincoln Prison. After spending some weeks concealed in English cities, he was back in Dublin for the second session of the Dáil on 1 April, which was held in private, and was elected *Príomh-Aire*, or President. On 8 April he was unanimously re-elected President of Sinn Féin at a public *Árd-fheis* and at another session two days later he said:

> There is in Ireland at this moment only one lawful authority and that authority is the elected Government of the Irish Republic. Of the other power claiming authority we can say, adapting the words of Cardinal Mercier: 'The authority of that power is no lawful authority. Therefore in soul and conscience the Irish people owe that authority neither respect nor attachment, nor obedience.'[43]

Macardle succinctly summed up the position nationally:

> Cathal Brugha's policy was militarily in advance of that which the Dáil as a whole would have initiated at this time, and Michael Collins favoured action, which even Cathal Brugha did not always approve [of]. Military councils were thus sometimes divided, and a good deal of initiative remained with the local companies of Volunteers. The Dáil refrained from interference, entrusting the military policy of the Republic to its very able Minister for Defence.[44]

☙

CHAPTER 10

Maynooth Sanctuary

As Irish eyes focused on the Mansion House on the morning of 21 January 1919, eight men hiding in a ditch a few miles from Tipperary Town heard the ninth member of their party shout, 'They're coming, they're coming!' Seán Treacy, Séamus Robinson, Seán Hogan, Tim Crowe, Patrick O'Dwyer of Hollyford, Michael Ryan of Grange (Donohill), Patrick McCormack, Jack O'Meara and Dan Breen had been waiting five days for this moment.

Frustrated at the general inactivity among the Volunteers, they had decided to move things along in Tipperary. Having had a visit from Dick Mulcahy from headquarters in Dublin in October, who had sanctioned the appointments of Séamus Robinson as Commandant (he was in jail at that time), Seán Treacy as Vice-Commandant and Dan Breen as Quartermaster, they planned their first operation. Their target was an RIC escort which accompanied consignments of explosives on the way to Soloheadbeg quarry, normally comprised of six men, but on this morning consisted of just two. The Volunteers needed explosives for grenades and demolition work in the area and Treacy believed that their operation would also have a salutary effect on morale throughout the country. Dan Breen recalled the moment:

> They were almost under the shadow of our revolvers when we shouted 'Hands up!' In answer to our challenge they raised their rifles, and with military precision held them at the ready. They were Irishmen, too, and would die rather than surrender. We renewed the demand for surrender. We would have preferred to avoid

bloodshed; but they were inflexible. It was a matter of our lives or theirs. We took aim. The two policemen fell, mortally wounded ...

Within an hour, hundreds of police and military would be scouring the countryside for us. From that moment we were outlaws with a price on our heads. We seized the rifles and equipment of the police, mounted the cart and drove away. The cart contained more than a hundredweight of gelignite. We had overlooked the seizure of the electric detonators. One week later we learned that Flynn, the County Council employee, had secreted thirty of them in his pockets ... Seán Hogan held the reins, Seán Treacy and I sat behind. The rest of the party had been ordered to make their escape in different directions.[1]

This was the first armed encounter in which RIC men were killed since the 1916 Rising. The War of Independence had, in effect, begun. The military authorities proclaimed County Tipperary a military area and a reward of £1,000 was offered for information that would lead to an arrest. The RIC conducted their efforts to trace the assailants by methods which caused intense resentment, yet the clergy, the public and the press had condemned the Tipperary men's actions.

After almost four months on the run, following a party in a house in Ballagh, Seán Hogan went out for breakfast to the Meagher family home at Annfield where he was captured and brought to Thurles barracks. Breen, Treacy and Robinson discovered that he would be brought by train to Cork and planned a daring hold-up at Knocklong which was successfully executed with help from the Galtee Battalion. One RIC man was killed and another mortally wounded. Breen took a bullet to his lung and arm, four of the Volunteers were injured, and as they departed the station, 18-year-old Hogan still remained handcuffed.

Having received the Last Sacraments, Breen was told that his chances of survival were slim. Nevertheless, he had to keep on the move and was royally treated in west Limerick before moving on to Knocknagoshel in Kerry, where his recuperation continued. Treacy had a problem also as he had been shot through the teeth and had great difficulty eating. Their journey took them back through Limerick and Clare as the quartet set their sights on Dublin. In north Tipperary they decided to split and having procured bicycles, Breen and Treacy moved on to Kilasally in Offaly and then sought a safe route to the capital.

Within a week of the Knocklong rescue, Patrick Colgan was called to Dublin by Dick Mulcahy. The Chief of Staff was in bed with the flu and the conversation took place in Cullenswood House, where he was residing. He explained to the Maynooth man that a decision had been made to form a Special Reserve.

> It was to be recruited from known and trusted personnel. Its duties were, if necessary, to travel to various centres as directed by GHQ to carry out operations. I was invited to join, and accepted. Mulcahy asked me if there were any other Kildare men who had taken part in the Rebellion whom I thought would be suitable. I nominated Tom Harris, Joe Ledwidge and Tim Tyrrell. I was instructed, without giving full details to the men mentioned, to sound them out. Harris and Ledwidge agreed to do whatever was required. We did a bit of secret training with revolvers and grenades, supplied by GHQ.

> Before going to see Mulcahy, I had met Mick Collins in his office on the ground floor of Cullenswood House and I went to the Farm Produce Store, Camden Street, for tea. I was anxious to get news of the Knocklong fight. I had a personal interest in it when he told me one of the participants was Séamus Robinson. My Volunteer area was the direct line of communication between [the] west and south of Ireland with GHQ ... It was not unusual to have three or four visits each day from both Joe O'Reilly and Dick O'Hegarty with dispatches. Rarely had they left when dispatches were received from Dublin.

> On the Tuesday following my visit to Mulcahy I noticed a fellow dismounting from a bicycle outside my office. Suspecting he was a dispatch carrier, I approached him to enquire [as to] who he wished to see. He wanted to see me. I asked him whom shall I say wanted to see him. He replied he was a friend of mine. I then identified myself. He in turn took a notebook from his pocket, opened it and showed a page with my name written on it. He asked me if I recognised the writing. I told him it was written by Mick Collins.

> He identified himself as Seán Treacy, a friend of Séamus Robinson. He told me the Knocklong boys were staying at Bulfin's near Birr; that Bulfin, while anxious to keep them, was having a bad time lest

they should be traced. Mick had sent him to me to settle them up for a few nights pending arrangements for finding quarters for them in Dublin. He wanted to move quickly from Birr, although I could not think of any place where they would be safe. I said to him to come along tomorrow. We arranged a meeting place beside Maynooth church for the following night.[2]

Having given the matter some thought, Colgan decided to call on the one man in the town who might help. Domhnall ua Buachalla readily agreed to look after them, once more making his decision on the basis of necessity and the national interest. He would also have been very aware that if caught harbouring the most wanted gunmen in the country, his own life would be on the line. In his book, Breen refers to the 'modest' Maynooth man and his exploits during the Rising and concluded: 'Donal proved as kind to us as we would have expected from his record. His house was put at our disposal for as long as we cared to remain as his guests, but we stayed only three or four days.'[3]

It is indicative of ua Buachalla's attitude to his involvement in events after the Rising that he did not make any reference to them in his Witness Statement. His personal story concluded with 'a royal reception on reaching Maynooth'[4] after release from Frongoch. His role in the War of Independence and the Civil War – and the attendant danger to his life and that of his family in the ensuing years – was a private matter; travails he had no need to share with the wider world.

The Tipperary men spent most of their days indoors, heading out in the evening for some exercise. Colgan recalls, much to his disappointment, that Robinson did not travel to Maynooth, but those who did arrive were Breen, Scannell, O'Brien and Treacy. 'Certain death awaited them if captured, yet a more cheery lot I had never met. It would not have been an easy matter to capture them. They were armed with revolvers and grenades ... Treacy, whilst as full of fun as anyone else, spent a lot of his time reading small arms manuals.'[5] For Domhnall's son, Joe, who was back home from his Dublin digs at that time, it was an introduction to a more violent type of Volunteer.

In the evening time I would go out for a walk with Breen, down the avenue [in Carton House]. The police also had a fashion of walking there too and one night I remember this figure coming towards us. It was a policeman and Dan had his hand in his pocket and if the policeman had said as much as 'goodnight', Dan would have shot him. It was a terrible way to live.

Breen set out to do a job that was to get rid of the British Army, and in that he was ruthless. If a soldier had to be shot, that was just too bad. But in other ways he was a lovely fellow. I have a letter he wrote to me when my father died. You can hardly read it as he was an invalid at the time. He typed most of his letters but he didn't type this one. It started, 'Dear Joe, You will have to excuse the writing but I wouldn't type a letter to anyone I thought anything of ... '

I didn't know Collins in the way that I knew Breen, even though I lived in the same house as Collins. But a man I did know was Liam Lynch, and Lynch, I'd say, was a more pure-souled patriot with a different outlook ... but it took all those fellows to make up the movement ...[6]

After four days in ua Buachalla's care, the Soloheadbeg men headed for Dublin and Phil Shanahan's pub. 'We made contact with Mick Collins, at that time Adjutant-General of the Irish Volunteers, and had a long and frank discussion with him', Breen wrote. 'Mick undertook to arrange that we should stay in Dublin if we so wished. With his assurance we re-mounted our bicycles and rode back to the country for Séamus Robinson and Seán Hogan.'[7]

I was dressed as a priest, not an uncommon disguise at that time. The Peelers [a British policing force set up by Sir Robert Peel in 1813 in Ireland to manage crime prevention] probably suspected that a good many of the men in clerical garb whom they saw travelling through the country knew more about guns than about theology ... but the old Peelers were staunch Catholics and gave the benefit of the doubt even to suspicious-looking clergy ...

When we reached Maynooth on the return journey, I discovered that my back tyre was punctured. I did not think it becoming [of] my clerical dignity to mend the puncture; I wheeled my machine to a mechanic's shop and asked him to repair it. He told me that he could not attend to the job for a few hours. I pointed out to him that I was going on urgent business ... to no avail. Finally, he advised me to go to the College where I would easily find someone to repair it ... I was afraid that the President and his staff might not be too pleased to find a gunman masquerading as a clergyman, so in a fit of bravado I turned towards the police barracks. At the door I met a policeman who raised his hat to me; with a show of dignity that would have done credit to even an archbishop, I acknowledged his token of respect.

I told him of my difficulties. Could he help me to repair the punctured tyre? 'To be sure, Father', he replied, 'in no time I can get you all that you want and, if your Reverence won't mind, I'll give you a hand with the job'. In two minutes the whole garrison were tripping over one another in their eagerness to get a solution and patches and the necessary equipment. When I entered the barracks I could see dozens of printed notices and official documents pasted all over the walls ... that night I reached the borders of Offaly and Tipperary and met Hogan and Robinson. A few days later we were all settled in Dublin.[8]

They left their spare revolvers, ammunition and grenades with Colgan in Maynooth and contacted him later to bring them to the city.

There were sufficient arms to fill two large portmanteaus. I made two journeys with a full portmanteau each time. I cycled from Maynooth to Lucan and took a tram to Parkgate Street, and a Dublin tram from there to O'Connell Bridge.

I had a vague idea where Corporation Street was. It took me quite a while to locate Shanahan's. I went to the counter and bought a bottle of lemonade. I had noticed a man talking to a woman who was drinking a pint. I asked the assistant who served me if Mr Shanahan was in. In a loud voice, he asked me 'Do you know Mr Shanahan?' I said I did. I heard a movement behind me, and was tempted to bolt with my portmanteau. I was soon assured I was in the right place: the man identified himself as Mr Shanahan. The portmanteau was taken over by the counter-hand and emptied. I enquired where the boys were, only to find that they had gone to Clontarf Baths for a swim. I couldn't get over the cheek of these fellows.

The following week I brought in the remainder of the stuff. They were again missing. That night I attended the Abbey, my first visit

there. I was in the gallery. When the lights went on at the conclusion
of the first act, I found that the fellow sitting on my right was Dan
Breen. I gave the Knocklong fellows up as being a set of loonies who
knew no fear.[9]

The Arbitration Courts

Because British law had become a weapon of suppression rather than
a vehicle for justice in Ireland, and with a view to undermining British
administration, Dáil Éireann introduced the National Arbitration Courts,
which were ratified at the Mansion House on 19 August 1919. The Report
of the Committee was adopted without discussion, and on the motion of
the Acting President it was decided that the Committee be given plenary
powers to complete their scheme.

Domhnall ua Buachalla was appointed a Justice for north Kildare with
Art O'Connor filling the role in the south of the county. Nevertheless,
it took almost a year before effective regulations began to operate
countrywide, with the establishment of the more ambitious Dáil Courts
not complete until June of 1920. The Dáil Courts generally looked after
local civil cases and land disputes. This system was based on: (1) Parish
Courts involving claims of not more than £10 and jurisdiction over many
of the areas previously under the British Petty Sessions Courts; having
ordinary and Petty Sessions Criminal jurisdiction, with power to deal
with civil claims under £10; (2) District Courts, the equivalent of County
Courts, having a civil jurisdiction of claims up to £100; (3) A Supreme
Court having unlimited original jurisdiction.

The creation of the Irish Republican Police in June of 1920, initiated
by Richard Mulcahy, then Chief of Staff of the IRA, and Cathal Brugha,
Minister of Defence, aided enforcement of decisions and protection for
the courts. It was handed over to the Minister for Home Affairs, Arthur
Griffith and later his successor, Austin Stack. Henry Hanna, K. C. explained
some of the reasons why the Dáil Courts took root:

> Though the Supreme and County Courts under the British regime
> were still functioning, the Petty Sessions Courts, which depended
> on the co-operation of the RIC, the Magistracy, and the British
> Executive, had collapsed. The RIC had been compelled to withdraw
> from the outlying districts and stations to the larger towns, and had

become an armed garrison rather than a civil police force. Many magistrates had resigned their Commissions of the Peace or had been removed. Hence, there was real work for these inferior Courts to do. The rival [Dáil] Courts were of a rough-and-ready character, and under much difficulty they decided the disputes of ordinary life more on the lines of common sense and neighbourliness than by strict law.[10]

The day after the ratification of the National Arbitration Courts, Cathal Brugha proposed a motion that every deputy, officer and clerk of the Dáil and every member of the Irish Volunteers must swear allegiance to the Irish Republic and to the Dáil. Terence MacSwiney seconded the motion but a few opposed it; the Dáil, on a division, carried Brugha's motion. It read:

> I, A. B., do solemnly swear (or affirm) that I do not and shall not yield a voluntary support to any pretended Government, authority or power within Ireland hostile and inimical thereto, and I do further swear (or affirm) that to the best of my knowledge and ability I will support and defend the Irish Republic and the Government of the Irish Republic, which is Dáil Éireann, against all enemies, foreign and domestic, and I will bear true faith and allegiance to the same, and that I take this obligation freely without any mental reservation or purpose of evasion, so help me God.[11]

This significant piece of legislation, wrote Macardle, agitated the Executive of the Volunteers for some months:

> Michael Collins and certain other members of the Army Executive who were members of the IRB opposed the pledge to the Dáil and maintained that the simple Volunteer oath to the Republic was enough. They argued that there were members of the Dáil whose loyalty had not been proved and that the Dáil might some day compromise the Republican case. They would have preferred that the army should continue to be controlled by its own executive and by the IRB.[12]

After agreeing that the Army Executive should remain in being and act as an advisory body with the Minister for Defence, Collins wrote to President de Valera on 25 August stating that 'the Volunteer affair is now fixed'.[13]

About that time, besides his involvement with the Courts, ua Buachalla had financial matters on his mind and was working on the North Kildare electorate to purchase bonds in the Republican Loan. He placed an order for 1,500 copies of a poster encouraging them to put their hands in their pockets.

TO THE PEOPLE OF NORTH KILDARE

In this, the most momentous crisis in the history of our country, it behoves every good Irishman to come forward and aid the movement for the uplifting of this country. At the elections in December last the vast majority of the people of Ireland voted in favour of an Irish Republic. Notwithstanding the fact that the newspapers give no information of its activities, yet a Republican Government is in being, and its ministers are in almost constant session, working practically day and night in Ireland's interests.

Without financial assistance, however, very little effective work can be done. We must, therefore, provide the necessary funds to meet the situation; and I can recommend no better means of so doing than by purchasing, each one according to his means, Republican Bonds. The money so invested will be used to promote Irish industries and foreign trade, and to counteract lying English propaganda.

Our friends in America are investing to the extent of 25,000,000 dollars, thereby showing to the world their faith in the ultimate success of the great ideal – Ireland a Nation, free and independent. Such being the case, surely it is up to us here in Ireland to prove also our unshakable fidelity to the cause of Irish Freedom.

The recent suppression of the nationalist papers of the country for having advertised the Republican Loan is sufficient proof of its value to the country's cause. Let that suppression be but a stimulus to our exertions.[14]

On the day after concluding the wording for the poster, 16 October 1919, ua Buachalla was to attend the 12th Annual Convention of Sinn Féin in the Mansion House, commencing at 10 a.m., but a subsequent telegram instructed him to travel the previous day. A few notes written by him on

1. Joshua Jacob, Domhnall ua Buachalla's maternal grandfather, was a Quaker who converted to Catholicism. (*Photo: Dublin Friends Historical Library, Quaker House*)

2. The Maynooth cricket team c.1875, which includes two of Domhnall ua Buachalla's brothers. The names provided by him differ slightly from those which accompany the photo in the Maynooth Library. Back row: Con Ó Buachalla, Seán Ó hÉachám, Joseph Fulham, Seán Launders, Seán Ó Buachalla. Front row: James Phelan, Seosamh Ó Raghallaigh, Thomas Weafer, Thomas Carr, Michael Carr. (*Photo: O'Buachalla Collection*)

3. Sarah Buckley (née Jacob), Domhnall ua Buachalla's mother. *(Family photo)*

4. Cornelius Buckley, father of Domhnall ua Buachalla, c. 1895. *(Family photo)*

5. Sinéad (née Jane Walsh), Domhnall ua Buachalla's wife, c.1900. *(Family photo)*

ROYAL IRISH CONSTABULARY.

RECEIPT for Amount levied on WARRANT

No. 69 against *Daniel Buckley*

for *not having his name on his Cart*

Date of Order *3 . 1 . 06.* Date of Warrant *20 Mar 06*

RECEIVED from *M. P. Fitzsimons*

of *Maynooth* the sum of *one* Pounds

—— Shillings and —— Pence, being the amount

levied on the above-mentioned Warrant.

Dated at *Maynooth* this *14* day of *April* 19 *06*

£ *1 : 0 : 0*

6. The RIC receipt for a roll of material bought by Patrick Fitzsimons at auction for £1 in 1906 after Domhnall ua Buachalla refused to pay a fine for 'not having his name on his cart', the term used for having his name in Irish on his cart. The material was seized from ua Buachalla's shop – and duly returned to him by the sole bidder. *(Photo: Author's Collection)*

7. The ua Buachalla family at home in 'Gleann Ailighe' in Maynooth: Joe, Sinéad, Domhnall Óg, Síghle, Kevin, Domhnall, Bríghid; front: Séadna and Máirín, c. 1913. (*Family photo*)

8. Domhnall ua Buachalla, centre, front, with members of the Black Hand group in Frongoch in 1916. George Lyons is first left in the back row; Charlie Murphy is on ua Buachalla's left. Also in the picture are Seán McMahon and Martin Ryan. (*Photo, O'Buachalla Collection*)

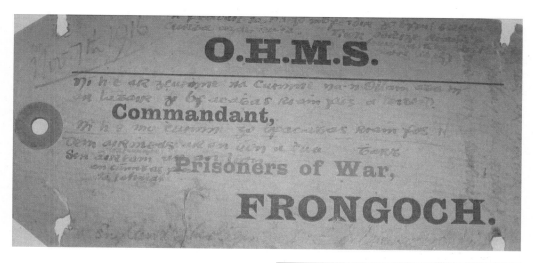

9. The mug used by Domhnall ua Buachalla in Frongoch and notes taken during Irish class on an official label. *(Photo: Author's Collection)*

10. On the right shoulder of Domhnall ua Buachalla's jacket a pencil protrudes where a bullet narrowly missed killing him as he sought a safe passage from the GPO in 1916. *(Family photo).*

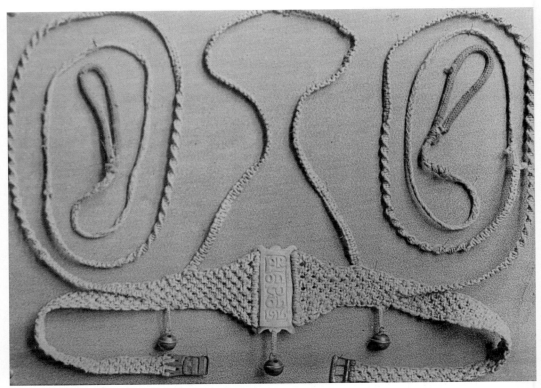

11. A child's rein made by Domhnall ua Buachalla in Frongoch. *(Photo: O'Buachalla Collection)*

12. Members of the First Dáil at their initial meeting in January 1919. Domhnall ua Buachalla is in the second row, third from left. *(Photo: O'Buachalla Collection)*

13. Domhnall ua Buachalla's shop in Maynooth, c. 1925. *(Family photo)*

14. Mick O'Neill, son-in-law of Domhnall ua Buachalla, on horseback at his brother's residence, Weston Park, Leixlip, c. 1926. *(Photo: Nóirín O'Neill)*

15. A poster used in the 1932 general election which saw voting power in Kildare transfer from Domhnall ua Buachalla to Tom Harris, who would hold the seat until 1957. *(Photo: O'Buachalla Collection)*

16. Domhnall ua Buachalla on the day he was sworn in as Governor–General at his brother's house in Booterstown in 1932 with his sister-in-law Mary Buckley, her daughter Máirín, his brother Michael (centre, back), Con Ó Laoghaire and Seán Ó Cuiv. *(Family photo)*

the original invitation revealed the reason for the change. The first is 'meeting suppressed'. This is followed by 'work had already been done the previous night' and finally, 'delegates retired in good order at No. 6 where Mr Griffith addressed us'.

Following the outbreak of the War of Independence, the British Government decided to suppress the Dáil and six days before the Convention in September, Dáil Éireann was declared a 'dangerous association' and was prohibited. That the edict failed to achieve its purpose is not surprising; the Dáil continued to meet in secret, and Ministers carried out their duties as best they could. In all, fourteen sittings were held in 1919, ten of them in private.

In response to a question in the House of Commons, Winston Churchill informed all present that there were 43,000 troops in Ireland in December at a monthly cost of £860,000. To all intents and purposes, war had been declared and what Macardle described as a 'reign of terror' was well under way as the year came to a close. What the British faced was described by the *Daily Mail* as 'a mature, determined, national, disciplined and, above all, intelligent revolt'.[15]

In January 1920, Churchill, then British Secretary of State for War, masterminded the formation of the reviled Black and Tans, advertising throughout Britain for recruits and providing as back-up to the RIC a collection of virtually unemployable individuals who were almost impossible to control and whose actions eventually alienated public opinion in Britain. In tandem with the Auxiliary Division, a counter-insurgency unit made up of former British officers also worked with the RIC.

The night of 7 February 1920 provided an example of how problems cropped up; a dance in aid of the local football and hurling club in Maynooth Town Hall attracted the attention of the Crown forces. The *Leinster Leader* reported that at midnight 'the building was surrounded by military and police who arrived in wagons, and young men entering or leaving the hall were held up at the point of bayonets and searched. These tactics continued until an advanced hour, when the forces were withdrawn. The concert programme consisted of items by the brass and reed band, songs, dances and recitations.'[16] The report listed the names of all the star attractions, including the 'Misses Buckley' – Síghle, 17 and Bríghid,13 – who, no doubt, would have performed early and been tucked up in bed long before the midnight hour.

More serious were the engagements of the Volunteers with the military and police. Patrick O'Keeffe of Kilcock, an extremely enthusiastic 21-year-old in 1920, recalled exploits he shared with ua Buachalla over a period of two years in notes he wrote in later life. 'One day Jim [his brother] and myself were doing a job at home when a dispatch arrived for Jim from Dan Buckley, Maynooth, with two revolvers and instructions to shoot the RIC man on his way back to Naas. The order came for the IRA command in Dublin.'[17] It appears that the constable did not go back to Naas on the anticipated road and the opportunity to carry out orders was frustrated.

There were other such days. 'An ambush was arranged on the Kilcock to Maynooth road. I was not called but I knew who was to take part – Jim O'Keeffe, Dan Buckley and Paddy Mullaney – and a few more whose names I have forgotten. But again there was disappointment as they did not pass. Soon after, another ambush was attempted on the Laragh to Maynooth road. Some three or four companies were involved but again there was disappointment.'[18]

Far more encouraging for them was the ratio of success in destroying buildings as there was a nationwide focus on barracks at the time. Ua Buachalla played an active part in the destruction of barracks and many bridges in north Kildare by embarking on night *sorties*, which he mentioned in his pension statement.[19] In early March 'the Maynooth barracks was ordered to be closed and the Constabulary and staff there are to be stationed at Celbridge. The Kilcock barracks was also to be closed and the men sent to Celbridge, which in future will be the headquarters station.'[20] Two weeks later the *Kildare Observer* noted that instructions were issued

> for the re-opening of the Maynooth barracks, arrangements being made that the men were to return there on Thursday last. It is stated that the Police Sergeant's wife, who continued to live on the premises with her family, was warned to leave, and told that no harm would come to her. She left the barracks and secured accommodation elsewhere in the village. The barracks was completely destroyed by fire on Monday night, all the contents being lost, including the furniture [and] the property of the Sergeant and his family.[21]

Within weeks, the paper reported that in tandem with the attacks on police barracks all over Ireland on the Saturday night,

> five barracks in Co. Kildare were destroyed by fire – Clane, Kilteel, Donadea, Ballinadrimna and Ballytore. People living close to the Clane police barracks heard the noise of a number of men actively

engaged in setting fire to the barracks [at] about 2.30 p.m. on Sunday morning. The building – a substantially built structure – was soon in flames, and was completely destroyed. Donadea, Ballytore and Kilteel barracks were also substantial buildings, and all were reduced to ruin, [with] only the walls remaining.[22]

The report also noted that 'in respect of the burning of Maynooth police barracks about a month ago, claims for £5,165 compensation have been lodged with the Kildare County Council. £4,020 was sought on behalf of the owner, the Duke of Leinster, and £1,000 by Sergeant Dunne for furniture and other property destroyed.'[23] On 22 May, the *Leinster Leader* reported that the Maynooth Town Hall and Courthouse had been blown up on the Friday morning at about 2.30 a.m., an incident

> that is one of the most sensational that has occurred yet in Co. Kildare. In a talk with a leading townsman, our representative was informed that a terrific explosion was heard which shook every house in the vicinity, blowing the ordinary glass out of the windows, while the plate glass in several shop fronts in the business houses was also in fragments. It will be remembered that the RIC, some two months ago, had evacuated their barracks at Maynooth, and it was immediately burned down.

> Since then rumours have been frequent to the effect that the Town Hall would soon be occupied as a kind of military outpost, but this, however, would not seem to have been treated very seriously by the people of the district generally.

> As far as the raid on the building is concerned, it would appear that a hole had been made in the dividing wall, and a bomb thrown in, blowing up some of the walls, with the result that a little time after the explosion was heard, flames were seen to burst forth, and in one instance a large portion of stone was blown completely out of the building, [and] through a shop window over thirty yards away, smashing the front and striking a corner of the inner wall, breaking a glass case and other articles.

> Two houses over fifty yards from the Town Hall were also struck with flying fragments. The walls of the Town Hall, which is the property

of the Duke of Leinster, were still smouldering at midday. It was a very fine building, and was used for the quarterly Council meetings; it contained a very fine ballroom, concert rooms, supper rooms, etc.[24]

A Strange Arrangement

The two principal activists behind the destruction of the town's landmark were ua Buachalla, whose shop was opposite the historic building, and Stephen O'Reilly, who lived at No. 16, O'Connell Avenue, Berkeley Road, Dublin, and worked as an 'inspector or instructor in transport'[25] throughout the country. Although associated with the Volunteers in South County Dublin from 1913, he was not a member, but attended occasional meetings. In 1916, while living in Stillorgan in south Dublin, he got word that something might be happening on Easter Monday and having walked to Blackrock that day, he met a man called Frank Gaskin who suggested he come into the city with him.

> We only got as far as Sandymount when we had to turn back again. I returned home on Monday night. On Tuesday morning I started off for the city with a .22 revolver. I got as far as Dawson Street without any trouble, but I could get no further. I went into the Automobile Club, where I was well known, thinking I might be able to wangle something or get some sort of a badge that I could use, but there was nothing doing. I stopped in town on Tuesday and Wednesday and returned home on Thursday … I returned to work on the following Monday.[26]

He joined C Company of the 3rd Battalion, was sent to the Engineers, later became involved in explosives, and on a date that he could not recall with any accuracy in his Witness Statement, he was sent to Maynooth to blow up the Town Hall, an assignment that had been planned by ua Buachalla.

> I brought 30 lb of gelignite with me. I went by train and arrived there at about three o'clock. I was to go and see Dónal Ó Buachalla, but he was out. There was a man in the shop who evidently knew or guessed who I was and he brought me in. Ó Buachalla arrived

home at about six o'clock and we had a chat. I was told I could get as many men as I wanted for the job.

We came out at about ten o'clock that night and went over to the Town Hall and forced the door open. Paddy Colgan was on that job. [Patrick O'Keeffe disclosed in his papers that he was also involved.] We got in, and I instructed a big hefty man to bore a hole in the centre main wall and to put some gelignite into it.

During that time, a runner came in and informed me that there were two men outside having an argument. We went out and saw a postman and some poor unfortunate civilian having an argument outside Pitt's public-house, where they had come from. One of the men was just going to light his pipe; he lit a match and as soon as he did I put the revolver up in front of him, and match, pipe and all went. The two men cleared off, and I was pleased to find later on that they had been taken prisoner by our guards who were holding up the roads leading into the town.

The gelignite exploded but did very little damage to the wall. We then got some paraffin oil and made short work of the building ... we went over to Mr Ó Buachalla's place where I enjoyed one of the best meals I ever had, after which I decided to get home. Mr Ó Buachalla informed me that I would have to pass five police stations on my way to Dublin if I cycled, but that it would be dangerous to drive a motor car. He said he would provide me with either a motor car or a bicycle, and I told him I would prefer the bicycle.

I left at about three or four o'clock in the morning and I cycled straight into Dunboyne and from there into the Phoenix Park. I had a good rest in the Phoenix Park, as curfew was until six in the morning and there was no use in my trying to get through. At about a quarter to seven I came along the North Circular Road, down into Goldsmith Street and into O'Connell Avenue. I delivered the bicycle later-on to O'Hanrahan's on the North Circular Road; I had arranged with Mr Ó Buachalla to leave it there. I went to Headquarters in the Plaza in Gardiner's Place that evening and reported that the job in Maynooth had been carried out satisfactorily.[27]

Ua Buachalla's involvement in active service during these months entailed much planning and implementation of destruction. One such event involved his own residence and was prompted by the arrival of the Black and Tans in Ireland. Whatever the provenance of it, ua Buachalla heard there was a possibility that the Tans would make his house their headquarters in the town. The location of the detached residence, on about half an acre, was ideal at that time, as it adjoined the police barracks at the College-end of the town. The very idea of his home being commandeered would have troubled him, and although such an eventuality was little more than rumour at that stage, he was leaving nothing to chance. Having discussed the matter with the IRA, a plan of action was agreed and a very brief description, written by Séadna many years after his father died, reveals how it unfolded:

> One evening we were invited to the Gallivan's who lived in Leixlip. On coming home late that night we noticed a very bright sky over Maynooth and wondered what the reason for it was. It transpired that it was our house – and that my father had ordered the IRA (the local body) to burn it while we were out, to ensure the Black and Tans could not occupy it when they arrived in town.[28]

The invitation to tea in the Gallivan home was extended at the behest of ua Buachalla, who had built up a good relationship with Daniel, a Kerryman born in Lixnaw. He left home at an early age and travelled the length of the country to take up a job in the prison service in Derry, but resigned in protest at the treatment of Fr James McFadden of Gweedore, Co. Donegal in 1888 for organising the boycott and non-payment of rents. This action led to the death of a Detective Inspector Martin in 1889 by locals on the steps of the priest's house. Martin had come to arrest Fr McFadden for encouraging further resistance to the evictions taking place.

Gallivan prospered in Derry, where he had a few pubs as well as a farm in east Donegal, before heading for a new life in Leixlip. He settled with his wife, Sarah Jane, in Hillford House, at the junction of Old Hill and Station Road, giving their name to Gallivan's Cross. His strong nationalistic outlook was shared by his offspring, some of whom were active in the Kildare/Meath area. He acquired business premises in Newbridge which became a base for men 'on the run' and which was regularly raided by Crown forces. His son Daniel later teamed up with ua Buachalla's son, Joe, in motor rally competitions in the thirties.

The decision to destroy his home epitomised the revulsion ua Buachalla felt for the despised Black and Tans. With the help of a local builder, Dick Bean, he restored the house and, ironically, got a grant of £100 towards the work, a fact that made its way into his Military Service Pension report.

The presence of the Tans in Maynooth made life a fearful period for the community, none more so than the ua Buachalla family, who received special attention at the shop with raids constantly made in search of guns and ammunition. Séadna recalls one such visit: 'An officer and two privates came into the shop and asked my father a question. He walked from the shop into the parlour, opened a safe and took out a revolver. When he returned to the shop the soldiers had left. They returned, and immediately *Athair* [Father] went over to where the bacon slicer and knives were and when he came back they were again gone.'[29]

A newspaper report under the heading 'Name in Irish, Armed Men Order its Removal' details another visit:

> Today a number of armed men visited the premises of Mr D. Buckley, T.D., at Maynooth. The premises were closed at the time, it being dinner-hour, but the door was smashed in. The name of the proprietor was in Irish on the doorstep, and the foreman of the shop got notice that if this was not removed the place would be blown up.
>
> There was no search made of the premises, but a pot of red paint was taken, with which the raiders painted the initials 'B.' and 'T.' on the front of the shop, and also the words 'God Save The King'. The man who ordered the foreman to have the Irish characters removed had a revolver in his hand.[30]

In *Cannonballs and Croziers*, John Drennan recalled the day 'the Tans ordered the foreman, Liam O'Regan, a veteran of 1916, to remove a sign in Irish. He refused and was only saved from being shot through the intervention of a daughter of Buckley's who ran over to the RIC barracks and got the sergeant to intervene.'[31]

On another occasion, when the Tans were searching the premises, a female customer who had just completed her shopping and taken her purchases out to her pony and trap was presented with an unexpected item – in full view of the busy forces of the Crown. It was a butter box which Joe put into the trap with her other messages and asked her to kindly deliver it to a specific customer whom he knew well. If opened, the butter was there for all to see, but it covered a large number of grenades.

Drennan also recalled a more lighthearted moment from those days. 'In Caulfield's bar, there is a shattered mirror which still has a bullet hole. Stories abound as to the cause of this. The most common one is that one night the Tans went on a massive drinking session in Caulfield's. They were leaving drunkenly when one of them, thinking that someone was going to shoot him, pulled out his gun and fired. He was somewhat disconcerted to find out he had shot his own reflection in the mirror; hence the bullet hole today.'[32]

CHAPTER 11

A Reluctant Chairman

While the British forces in Ireland grew significantly in the early months of 1920 and displayed a strong disregard for human life, they struggled to maintain control in the day-to-day running of the country. This weakness provided an opportunity for a republican police force, which was virtually unpaid, and without a uniform, to fill the vacuum. At a meeting of the Kildare County Council in late May of 1920, a letter from William Murray, Director of County and Rural District Elections in north Kildare, reflected the degree to which control had passed into the hands of the Volunteers, and complemented the efforts of the Dáil Courts and people like ua Buachalla in dispensing justice.

Dear Sir,

I have been instructed to apply to the Commandant in charge of the Irish Volunteers in Co. Kildare for the services of men to keep order in and at the different polling stations on the day of the [Kildare County Council] election [June 4]. I would feel obliged to you for the necessary forms of appointment (three men for each booth), so that their names and addresses may be given to you in time to have them supplied with forms of declaration of secrecy etc., and any instructions you consider necessary for the orderly conducting of the elections, and which may be compatible with the views of the commandant for the county. It is also intended to have [election] volunteers guard ballot boxes during the interval between the close of poll and counting of votes.[1]

A member of the County Council, Patrick Phelan suggested to the chairman that as 'we will have nobody else this year, I propose we accept the offer'.[2] Seconded by James O'Connor, the decision was carried unanimously. The following week a newspaper report revealed how justice was dispensed in the county:

> The Sinn Féin Executive in north Kildare are at present devoting themselves to tracing the perpetrators of larcenies. Complaints having recently been made in Newbridge in reference to the stealing of a large quantity of oats, arrests were made in the town on Friday night when three young men were held up and driven to a place a considerable distance away. They were kept in detention until Saturday evening, when they were formally charged with the larceny of the oats.
>
> The court was formed of officers of the Volunteers. Every detail of evidence was carefully sifted, while an officer was appointed for the defence. Several witnesses were examined, and at the close of the case the prisoners pleaded guilty. Heavy fines were inflicted, and the prisoners were also ordered to pay the full value of the oats, to be handed over to the manager of the firm from which the corn was stolen. A pledge was also given as to the future conduct of the prisoners, and they were warned that in the event of the repetition of any such offence, they would not be allowed to reside in the district.[3]

The outcome of an election that introduced proportional representation for the first time reaffirmed republican domination, with Sinn Féin taking total control of the administrative machinery in Kildare, as it did throughout the country. Despite all his obligations, ua Buachalla was persuaded to run for election, and his popularity in the Naas electoral area had increased – his tally of votes on the first count almost doubled the second-placed candidate. Sinn Féin ran six candidates and took four of the five seats, with the fifth going to the outgoing Independent candidate, Michael Fitzsimons.

There were 4,741 names on the register for the constituency of North Kildare, of which only 2,776 exercised the franchise. The number of spoiled votes was 140 and of these, many were lost due to the voter putting the figure 'one' before the name of more than one candidate. Despite it being a day of serious business, there were some light moments:

KILDARE COUNTY COUNCIL ELECTION 1920

CANDIDATES	FIRST COUNT	FINAL FIGURES
D Buckley (Maynooth) Sinn Féin	754	754
T Harris (Caragh) Sinn Féin	360	542
Jas O'Connor (Celbridge) Sinn Féin	396	490
M Carroll (Naas) Sinn Féin	170	441
M Fitzsimons (Naas) Independent, outgoing	301	436
N Travers (Portglorian, Kilcock) Sinn Féin	198	376
J Lawler (Halverstown) Sinn Féin	210	260
JJ Flanagan (Osberstown) Labour	147	165
E Farrell (Windgates) Independent	50	63
T Lacy (Naas) Independent	50	53

Kildare Observer, 12 June 1920

In one of the polling stations in a rural district in north Kildare, a lady entered to exercise the vote. She confessed to illiteracy. The presiding officer, as was his duty, asked her to whom she wished to give her first vote, and she answered without hesitation; [this continued] on until she had voted for five [candidates].

'And your sixth?' said the presiding officer.

'Now', said the harassed female, 'I know you are trying to make fun of me. I thought I had only one vote when I came in, and you've taken five from me already. I'm only an ignorant woman wid one vote, an' if yer not satisfied wid all I've given, then give them back to me and let me go about my business.'[4]

Another lady was the focus of a second vignette:

'Give me Mr M.'s paper', said a buxom lady walking into another polling station and addressing herself to the presiding officer.

'Surely you're not Mr M.' was the astonished official's reply.

'Of course, anyone but yerself can see I'm not Mr M. but he axed me to vote for him as I was coming in, and it's not in me or one belongin' to me to promise a thing I didn't mane to do. Out wid the paper now, and no more of yer nonsense.'

The laws of the franchise were explained to the lady, but she went away grumbling and thoroughly unconvinced.[5]

The journalist's view of the outcome would have mirrored those of the upper classes throughout the county:

This result cannot fail to produce its effect on the political situation in Ireland. It is evident that things cannot continue as they have been going, and we should think from the point of view of England that the only sane attitude would be to make an effort to ascertain how the national aspirations, as disclosed first by the Parliamentary struggle of a year and a half ago and now by the County Council and District Council elections, can be met. It is a fact that only about 50 per cent of the electors of Co. Kildare availed of the right to vote, but it is futile to conjecture what might have happened had there been a full exercise of the vote, and those who refrained from going to the polling booth have the least right to raise the question.[6]

With virtually the entire Council replaced, including the chairman and vice-chairman, the secretary sought a willing body to chair the first meeting. Mr Phelan proposed that Mr Buckley be appointed. When Mr Cusack seconded the proposition, it was carried unanimously. Ua Buachalla said 'he would prefer that some other member be appointed chairman, as he had no experience whatever in conducting business as a chairman'.[7] But after a response from Mr Mahon that 'they were all more or less in the same position',[8] ua Buachalla took the chair. And, perhaps not surprisingly, the first business he brought up for discussion was a request from the County Kildare Gaelic League that a deputation be met by the Council.

James Durney wrote that at this first meeting in Naas, it was decided to pledge allegiance to Dáil Éireann and to repudiate any claim by the British to legislate in Irish affairs. 'Every effort was made by the British to compel the council to recognise the British Local Government Board, including the issuing of writs. The new council deleted the resolutions condemning the Easter Rising, passed by the council in 1916 ... and the interest of the new members in the Irish language was demonstrated in the publication of the council's proceedings in both Irish and English in the *Leinster Leader*.'[9]

Delivery Duties for Michael Collins

While ua Buachalla continued to busy himself on many fronts, his eldest son, while in Dublin, was displaying the family trait of a zest for national independence. On the academic front, he was getting on with his engineering studies in Bolton Street. He continued to earn a living with John O'Neill, was an enthusiastic member of the Rathfarnham Company 4th Battalion and had moved into Cullenswood House (which was still owned by the Pearse family) with a few other former St Enda's pupils. He had distinguished company in Michael Collins, who had an office in the building, and Dick Mulcahy, who also resided there at the time. Mulcahy was appointed Chief of Staff of the IRA in 1919 and would succeed Collins after his death in 1922 as commander of the pro-Treaty forces during the Civil War. Both were well acquainted with Joe's father from their days in Frongoch.

Joe recalled being taken aside one night by Collins and told he had a job to do, which he was to undertake with Frank Burke:

> He gave us two revolvers each and said he wanted us to deliver them to an address on the other side of the city. He gave us detailed information on where to find it. We had to go in through an alleyway, into a little square in a poor part of Dublin. We knocked on the door and an old woman answered and she immediately told us to come in. She knew at once who we were, so we gave her the revolvers; somebody else was to pick them up. We walked across the city because it was easier to take to your heels if you were spotted. On a tram you were vulnerable.[10]

It was in the wide open spaces of the Dublin Mountains that his days of freedom came to an end – and with a little luck he might have avoided it. Heading for weekly manoeuvres, he called to Frank Burke's house and borrowed a bicycle which allowed him to save time on journeys, eventually joining up with the Rathfarnham Company and putting aside the bike for his return journey.

It was a Sunday morning and we had done some exercises, but were caught very badly coming down the mountain. The first thing we saw was a fusillade from a machine gun, which, fortunately, did not kill anyone. We did not have any guns with us. We never brought guns out on exercise because if you were caught you would lose them. And a gun was more important than a man at that time.

These fellows came up to us, about thirty in all. They were the very first of the specials, the auxiliaries, and a very peculiar bunch of men. They were well dressed, some had plus-fours. I'd say they were officers, soldiers of fortune. The second-in-charge wore a navy-blue suit, a pair of hob-nailed boots and a cap. He carried a rifle, a bandolier and a revolver. He was the nearest thing to a savage I ever saw.

They caught us up behind St Columba's College. We were walking down the mountain and some of the lads who should have been out with us were only coming up. One lad [Seán Doyle] whipped a hand grenade out of his pocket when he saw the position and took the pin out and went to throw it, but this fellow shot him between the two eyes. He might as well have been shooting a cat. I'd never seen a human being in a condition like this before, but I saw quite a few after.

We went into St Columba's College, where we were made to sit on the grass, covered by two machine guns, while they sent into Dublin for two lorries and then brought us to the Bridewell. We spent the night there and then were brought to Mountjoy where we spent four weeks. Our next move was to Collins' Barracks for the trial. As we travelled from Mountjoy, we got stuck in traffic and stopped at Cross Guns Bridge. There were six of us in the car and we thought we would make a dash for it when the guard opened the door because of the amount of smoke inside, but all we did was get jammed in our efforts, and [we] failed to get out.

Our time in court was short and sweet. The prosecuting counsel made his case and Jim Ryan, who was in charge of the group, told them to get on with it and do whatever they were going to do with us and not to waste our time because we did not recognise the court. We began to talk out loud among ourselves and this annoyed the officers very much and they said 'take them out' and we were returned to Mountjoy. We got two years each and were subsequently shipped to Wormwood Scrubbs, twenty of us in chains. We arrived in Holyhead to see Terence MacSwiney's body lying in the rain on a siding. Ryan called us to attention to salute the dead and say a Hail Mary. There must have been about fifty Black and Tans there as we were put on a train for London.

We arrived [at] about seven in the morning and they had police cars waiting, little open trucks. We decided we were not going to wear prison garb for anybody. We were brought down to the basement and told to peel off and have a bath. When we came out, our clothes were gone and prison clothes were there. We said we would not wear them, so they locked each of us in a cell, in December, without clothes. We were there for two weeks, freezing and without very much food, because the authorities said if we were not going to co-operate they were going to make things more difficult for us. Then a message came in saying that we were to wear them, that there was not much point going on like this. I'd admit that we were sorely tempted to give in at times, but for myself, I kept going by thinking what Pearse would have done in my position.[11]

His eldest sister, Síghle, received a pre-printed letter from Northampton, dated 8 November 1920, with only the italicised words written by Joe:

Dear *Sister*,

I am now in this prison and am in *good* health. If I behave well, I shall be allowed to write another letter about *a fortnight hence* and to receive a reply, but no reply is allowed to this.

Joseph Buckley.

At the foot of the page, however, he had added:

I am in very good health ever since I saw you last. I hope Father and all are well also. I will write a letter to you in about a fortnight. This is just to let you know I have changed my address. Remember me to Frank [Burke] etc.[12]

Little could Joe have realised that within two weeks of writing, Frank would be involved in one of the bloodiest massacres of the War of Independence, which was sparked by an early-morning series of killings the same day.

The shootings on 21 November 1920 first originated with the arrival in Dublin earlier in the year of a group of plain-clothes intelligence agents requested by the Dublin Castle administration to counteract the success that the IRA was enjoying. The unit, later to be called the Cairo Gang, suffered setbacks, but as the months passed their rate of detection worried Michael Collins to such a degree that he sought the names and addresses of all who were involved.

He then brought The Squad, a group of assassins working directly under his command, into play. In an interview with Tim Pat Coogan, their *modus operandi* was described by a member of The Squad, Vinnie Byrne: 'We were all young; 20, 21. We never thought we'd win or lose. We just wanted to have a go. We'd go out in pairs, walk up to the target and do it, then split ... nobody would get in our way. One of us would knock him over with the first shot, and the other would finish him off with a shot to the head.'[13]

At 9.00 a.m. on that fateful morning, they went into action. As front doorbells were rung and doors opened, the carnage began. An eyewitness described the bloody scene in one house as being 'like a badly conducted abbatoir'.[14]

The reaction of Michael Collins to the killings was succinct: 'My conscience is clear. There is no crime in detecting and destroying in wartime the spy and the informer. They have destroyed without trial. I have paid them back in their own coin.'

'Great God, I'm Shot'

The GAA had organised a challenge match between Dublin and Tipperary for Croke Park that afternoon, and although concerned after the morning's fourteen killings, the organisers decided to proceed with the game. At 1.30 p.m., before more than 10,000 spectators had gathered, orders were given to the Auxiliary Force to surround the grounds and warn by megaphone that every male attending the match would be searched. As the British neared the ground, they began to fire on what they reported were Volunteers near the turnstiles who had opened fire on them first. Following a number of interviews with Frank Burke, a series of articles appeared in *The Sunday Press* in 1968 by Pádraig Puirséal, in which he recalled the tragic afternoon:

> Frank, as usual on the left wing for Dublin, was delighted to find, as his immediate opponent on the Tipperary side, Mick Hogan from Grangemockler, with whom he had spent a couple of pleasant hours at a céilí in the Mansion House not too long before.

> Dublin were playing towards the Canal End, and into the teeth of a strong breeze, which was blowing towards what is now the Hogan Stand side. Indeed the ball never came near Hogan or Burke in the early stages, so they spent the time chatting, paying no great attention to a British army aeroplane that circled the field, seemed to depart, then came back again. At last, play arrived their way, but, even as they ran for the ball, shooting started from British troops or Black and Tans at the Canal End. At first Burke thought that they were firing blanks ... but the stampede of the crowd along the embankments quickly disillusioned him.

> With Stephen Sinnott, Mick Hogan and another player whom he could never quite identify, Burke ran from the left wing to mid-field. From there they could hear and see the bullets coming back off the Railway Wall. They threw themselves flat and began to crawl as best they could towards the exits, behind what is now Hill 16. Just as they neared the cycle-track that then ringed the playing-pitch, Hogan said, 'we may get shelter here'.

> Immediately afterwards he gasped, 'Great God, I'm shot'. Burke, seeing at a glance that his friendly opponent had been hit in the head, shouted for a priest, and a courageous clergyman promptly came dashing to the tragic scene from a group of spectators, who had been running across by the Railway Wall.

> Though Burke could still hear shots being fired, he now found himself being confronted by a Black and Tan, who poked a revolver against his stomach shouting, 'put your hands up! What team are you playing for?' When Burke answered, 'Dublin', the Tan, who had been joined by a comrade, made him run, hands aloft, round the field to the Dublin dressing-room, that revolver dug into his back.

They marched him into the dressing room, searched the clothes of three or four players, and then ordered them all to dress. Then, although random shots were still being fired, they were ordered to put their hands up again, and clear out.

So, on an evening of fog and gloom, Frank Burke finally worked his way across town to St. Enda's. There, his heart heavy as he thought of Mick Hogan, he faced another worry. As headmaster, he had given permission to a number of the St. Enda's boarders to attend the game ... mercifully, but for one minor injury, they had all gotten back safely.[15]

The London *Times* ridiculed Dublin Castle's version of events, as did a British Labour Party delegation visiting Ireland at the time. The British Brigadier, Frank Crozier, who was technically in command that day, later resigned over what he believed was the official condoning of the unjustified actions of the Auxiliaries. One of his officers told him that 'the Black and Tans fired into the crowd without any provocation'.[16]

Frank Burke was a Kildare man, born in Carbury, and a boarder at St Enda's. A bright student and outstanding sportsman, he continued to live in the college with many past pupils, while attending University College Dublin, departing in the morning by pony-and-trap and returning in the evening at whatever time suited them, and then dining with the Pearse family circle in the basement. Having completed his studies, he continued to live there when Pádraig Pearse offered him a job teaching Latin and Irish to the juniors. In 1920, Mrs Pearse appointed him headmaster, a post he held until the college closed in 1935.

When he finally retired from the sporting world, he had figured in five consecutive All-Ireland football finals for Dublin from 1920 to 1924, winning three in succession from 1921, and also collecting two junior medals. Between 1917 and 1921 he played in four All-Ireland hurling finals, winning two. He also won five Sigerson Cup titles and four of the Fitzgibbon Cup. One of the greatest exponents of hurling and football in the history of the game, Puirseal referred to him as the 'Quiet Man of Gaeldom'.

In later years, the relationship grew stronger between Frank and Joe and soon developed into a wonderful and long-lasting friendship that also incorporated their families, the cornerstone of which was the Friday night game of Spoil 15. Frank's son, Eanna, recalled that it was not just some Friday nights, it was every Friday night, and usually there were up to nine people around the table, generally not partaking of alcohol, but he confessed that the sessions were smokey. Besides ua Buachalla, two of his daughters, Máirín and Bríghid, were also occasional visitors.

After the 1916 Rising, which saw him fighting with Pearse, ua Buachalla and many St Enda's pupils in the GPO, he was shipped to Stafford Gaol where, ironically, he met his future wife. Born in Dungarvan, Angela Curran was one of a group of Irish girls in England who dared to visit the prisoners. Though the young teacher did not know him at that stage, one of the men to whom she was asked to visit was Frank Burke. And from that chance meeting blossomed a romance that was to last a lifetime.

It had a very welcome knock-on effect for Joe. A few years later Angela's mother arrived in St Enda's to see her daughter and Frank. With her was another daughter, Helen. It so happened that their visit coincided with Joe's. Obviously smitten when introduced to the young Waterford girl, another romance developed and they married in 1929.

Incarcerated in Northampton, Joe was allowed outdoors twice a day, an hour in the morning and again in the evening. He was also expected to work, which he and his fellow Irishmen refused to do initially.

After three or four months we changed our minds, because time was hanging heavily and the amount we would do would not make any difference. We got mail bags to make. We were supposed to make six in a day, but we only did one the first day, and never made more than three. In fact we could have made six in half a day. If a convict refused, though, he would not get either breakfast or dinner.

We each worked by ourselves in the cells and even though there was plenty of work outside, we were never let do it. We were permitted to get books, but the Protestant minister kept giving us tracts. I often gave them back to him and said I wouldn't let him proselytise me. Once, I asked to see the Governor and I told him we would not be bothered reading the books the minister was giving us. He wasn't a bad sort. He had been in Ireland and he appreciated our position. He did not look on us as criminals, though he didn't give us an inch at the same time. The books did improve; we got Dickens [...] but two a week was very little.

One day the Governor sent for me. I was brought to his office and there was only the two of us in his room. He said, 'I have a letter here for you from home. But I can't give it to you to read. I sent it up to the Home Office and they are not able to translate it'. So I said to the Governor 'give it to me and I'll translate it for you'. It was from my father and he simply refused to write in English. The Governor got to know his writing and whenever my father wrote, which was not very often, he would send for me and let me read it.

A postcard came one day, it was a picture postcard from Helen, and the chief warder who was steeped in jail routine said 'I thought there would be little pigs on this like you have in the kitchen'. I took a race at him but there was a warder on each side of the desk he was sitting at. They had me by the back of the neck in seconds. I got a dig at him alright, but it wasn't enough.

For weeks before we got out, I was planning how I could take my prison coat as a keep-sake. It was a short thing with arrows all over it. As I had no overcoat when arrested, and still had none, it was difficult to cover the prison coat and the warder spotted it. I asked him to close his eyes to it, but he wouldn't. Some of the others would have been game enough to let me take it.[17]

Joe returned to Maynooth shortly after the Treaty was ratified. A decision was taken that 400 political prisoners would be repatriated under an amnesty. He immediately became involved in the Treaty Debate, principally as a 'chauffeur'. His father, who never drove a car, was an ardent anti-Treaty advocate, and even after the decision had been taken, he travelled widely to speak to pro-Treaty people he knew and to many meetings, where he argued trenchantly that the Treaty was a flawed decision.

There might have been blue murder at the meetings, but he never fell out with anyone. One day when I was doing the books with him, two men arrived, one was called Smith and I forget the other fellow's name, two great Labour men. When the talk got round to politics, I remember my father striking the table with a bang and saying, 'if every man, woman and child in Ireland asked me to vote for the Treaty, I wouldn't do it because it's not for the good of the country'. At home he was the quietest man alive, but in politics he was adamant.[18]

For Joe, his weeks were occasionally spent in Maynooth, but gradually the Civil War drew him into the conflict in Dublin, and for much of the time he was on the run. The sight of men dying in pursuit of freedom for their country became part of his life.

CHAPTER 12

No Time for Trousers

Because of Domhnall ua Buachalla's Sinn Féin activities from 1914 onwards, his role in the 1916 Rising, his internment in Frongoch, an election to Dáil Éireann and involvement in the War of Independence, it was not surprising that the British forces took an interest in the wider ua Buachalla family.

Five years older than Domhnall, Cornelius was well known to the RIC and the Black and Tans in Kilcock, although he was never a member of the Volunteers or the IRA. Also a merchant and publican, he was similar in nature to his younger brother – quiet, principled, an enthusiastic supporter of Gaelic Games all his life and resolute in his refusal to do business with British companies. His great love of the Irish language, which manifested itself publicly with his name in Irish over the door despite being prohibited by law, prompted the Black and Tans to force him to take it down under threat of the gun. This was only a temporary gesture, however, as he soon had it replaced.

His son, Cathal, who was a few years older than his Maynooth cousin, Joe, had a dental practice located in his father's business establishment and was an active member of the IRA; in 1922 he would give sound advice to Domhnall after both escaped from jail. Patrick O'Keeffe, son of another publican whose premises continues to thrive in family ownership, recalled a raid in 1921, which drew Cornelius into the story:

> Our home was raided once or twice a week, so I had to sleep
> somewhere else [generally in one of a few houses his father owned in

the town]. The night Con Buckley was arrested, the Tans and [the] police raided the house where I was sleeping. It was a corner one on a terrace of houses. It had one door at the front and two on the side street; also a gate. I was awakened by heavy banging on the three doors and the gate. I jumped out bed, did not wait to put on my trousers, looked out the back, saw nobody, then ran for the back door of the next house, which I found open and went into the kitchen.

The tenant, Mrs Johnston, when she saw me, said 'Pat, you must have somebody's prayer, as I forgot to bolt the back door last night.' Looking through the widow, I could see [the] Tans and [the] police searching the yard I had just crossed. Then I heard them banging on the front door. I asked Mrs Johnston not to open the door for a few minutes. In the meantime, she gave me her husband's trousers to put on.

I saw the Tans going back into the house where I had slept. I was waiting for this and I left the house, crossed all the walls of the yards in the terrace and waited in hiding for a while. After some time I moved to a position where I could wait or escape to open country. I could hear the lorries pulling away. Presently, I went back to the house I had been sleeping in – and was informed [that] Con had been arrested.[1]

Whatever the reason for taking Cornelius, and it might well have been the frustration of not getting their hands on O'Keeffe, who was appointed a full-time adjutant at the Battalion Headquarters in Maynooth in 1922, he ended up in Rath Camp in the Curragh at the age of 60.

In Dublin on 29 January 1921, a military operation began at four a.m. in Glasnevin and Drumcondra, and concluded about mid-day with another brother of Domhnall's arrested. The *Irish Independent* recalled the morning's activities:

A cordon was drawn around Iona Road, Iona Drive, Iona Crescent, part of Lindsay Road, and part of St. Columba's Road. Lewis guns were mounted in the streets. Hundreds of troops were engaged, and every house, including the Presbytery, was searched. Milk was delivered by the military, but some milk and bread vans were [also] allowed through under escort. Business men and others in the occupied area were prevented from going to work until 12.30 p.m. The raid resulted in the arrest of Mr M. J. Buckley, City Engineer, 6 Iona Drive; Mr T. J. Morrissey, M. A., Four Courts official; and Mr Wilson, ex-Army officer. The latter was released on Saturday night. Mr Buckley is in Portobello Barracks.

There were instances where the same house was searched twice, the Crown forces returning some hours after the first visit. The operation, however, was conducted in a courteous manner. Young men who engaged in card-playing to while away the time during which they were detained at their homes were asked by an officer whether they belonged to the IRA. Householders were closely questioned as to recent visitors – relatives or otherwise – and their present whereabouts.

People going to Mass at St. Columba's, Iona Road, were turned back, but the Mass proceeded, though only the celebrant and clerk were there ... houses entered were completely surrounded as well as at the end of the streets. At Mr Buckley's residence, '*Garran an Cheoil*', the officer in charge asked to see Mr Buckley and when Mr Buckley answered, he was told, 'you have a uniform'. No uniform, it is stated, was found.[2]

A very thorough search was made at Mr Morrissey's house [the Four Courts official]. The study appeared to have been specially ransacked. Gaelic and Anglo-Irish publications, which Mr Morrissey as a pioneer student of Irish had stored – '*An Claidheamh Soluis*', '*The Gaelic Journal*', '*Banba*', etc. – were lying around in confusion. Amongst the seizures was a photograph of the late Kevin Barry.

The occupants of the house, 'Derevaragh', on Iona Drive, where Mr Wilson resided, were dumbfounded ... a lady in the house stated [that] Mr Wilson kept his revolver as it [had] saved his life more than once. 'As to our views', she said, looking at a large photograph of the late Queen Victoria, 'I don't wish to say much beyond the fact that a raid on a house like ours makes me indignant'.[3]

The fact that Michael was taken to Portobello Barracks suggests that he was a marked man, having been associated with his brother's election campaign and also the possibility that Maynooth connections might have been using his home as a 'safe house'.

That same weekend, Cullenswood House was ransacked after an initial search on the Saturday provided little joy for a strong military force. It was followed on Sunday morning by a systematic destruction of the walls and roof after the discovery of false walls which concealed corridors and a revolving wardrobe operated by hidden springs. Smoke was seen rising from the house in the early afternoon, but when the Tara Street and Rathmines brigades arrived they were turned back. St Enda's in Rathfarnham was also raided that day, the search lasting from 11.00 a.m. to 5.30 p.m.

As the War of Independence raged on, the British Government's solution to the 'Irish Problem' was to partition the country, with separate Home Rule parliaments in each jurisdiction. Sinn Féin nationalists participated but refused to recognise the new Home Rule parliaments. Instead, they treated the elections in both parts of Ireland as elections to the Second Dáil of one country. No polling took place in constituencies located in the south of Ireland as all 128 candidates, including ua Buachalla, were returned unopposed. In the Six Counties, violence preceded, accompanied and followed the election campaign. Catholics went to the polling stations in fear, yet they took twelve of the fifty-two seats, six going to moderate nationalists and six to republicans. The latter included Éamon de Valera, Michael Collins, Eoin MacNeill, Arthur Griffith, Seán Milroy and Seán O'Mahony.

While May had brought an electoral victory to the Republic, the same month had given the British Government a tactical advantage much greater than most of the ministers realised at the time, which Macardle referred to: 'The Partition Act, by establishing a separate government in the Six-County area, created a *fait accompli*, which elections and electorates were powerless to overthrow. Churchill realised it.'[4] From late spring until summer, the governments on both sides of the Irish Sea continued their diplomatic, albeit unproductive, dealings until a letter of rejection was sent by de Valera to Lloyd George on 24 August:

> On the basis of the broad guiding principle of government by the consent of the governed, peace can be secured – a peace that will be just and honourable to all, and fruitful of concord and enduring amity. To negotiate such a peace, Dáil Éireann is ready to appoint its representatives, and if your Government accepts the principle

proposed, to invest them with plenary powers to meet and arrange with you for its application in detail.[5]

A flow of correspondence continued until 30 September when de Valera concluded a letter with the words, 'we accept the invitation, and our delegates will meet you in London on the date mentioned "to explore every possibility of settlement by personal discussion".'[6] At a meeting of the Cabinet on 7 October, the delegates appointed as Envoys Plenipotentiary were Arthur Griffith, T.D., Minister for Foreign Affairs; Michael Collins T.D., Minister for Finance; Robert Barton, T.D., Minister for Economic Affairs; Edmund Duggan, T.D. And George Gavan Duffy, T.D. Their instructions were:

1. The plenipotentiaries have full powers as defined in their credentials.
2. It is understood before decisions are finally reached on a main question that a dispatch notifying the intention to make these decisions will be sent to members of the Cabinet in Dublin, and that a reply will be awaited by the plenipotentiaries before a final decision is made.
3. It is also understood that the complete text of the Draft Treaty about to be signed will be similarly submitted to Dublin, and reply awaited.
4. In case of a break, the text of the final proposals from our side will be similarly submitted.
5. It is understood [that] the Cabinet in Dublin will be kept regularly informed of the progress of the negotiations.[7]

A Heavy Responsibility

Talks commenced on 11 October at No. 10 Downing Street. Facing one another directly across the table were Lloyd George and Michael Collins. On 4 December came a defining moment, recalled by Robert Barton in Dáil Éireann on 19 December:

I broke my oath because I judged that violation to be the lesser of alternative outrages forced upon me, and between which I was compelled to choose. On Sunday 4 December the conference had precipitately and definitely broken down. An intermediary effected contact next day and on Monday at 3.00 p.m., Arthur Griffith, Michael Collins and myself met the English representatives.

In the struggle that ensued, Arthur Griffith sought repeatedly to have the decision between war and peace on the terms of the Treaty referred back to this assembly. This proposal Lloyd George directly negatived. He claimed that we were plenipotentiaries and that we must either accept or reject. Speaking for himself and his colleagues, the English Prime Minister with all the solemnity and the power of conviction that he alone, of all the men I met, can impart with word and gesture – the vehicles by which the mind of one man oppresses and impresses the mind of another – declared that the signature and recommendation of every member of our delegation was necessary or war would follow immediately.

He gave us until 10.00 p.m. to make up our minds, and it was then about 8.30 p.m. We returned to our house to decide upon our answer. The issue before us was whether we should stand behind our proposals for external association, face war and maintain the Republic, or whether we should accept inclusion in the British Empire and take peace. Arthur Griffith, Michael Collins, and Eamonn Duggan were for acceptance and peace; Gavan Duffy and myself were for refusal – war or no war. An answer that was not unanimous committed you to immediate war, and the responsibility for that was to rest directly upon those two delegates who refused to sign.

For myself, I preferred war. I told my colleagues so, but for the nation, without consultation, I dared not accept the responsibility. The alternative, which I sought to avoid, seemed to me a lesser outrage than the violation of what is my faith.[8]

He concluded with the words, 'I signed, and now I have fulfilled my undertaking, I recommend to you the Treaty I signed in London.'[9]

Although Gavan Duffy had not believed Lloyd George's threat of war, and stated that it was under duress, he subsequently agreed to sign. It was after midnight when Griffith, Collins and Barton returned to No. 10 Downing Street to sign the agreement, which, Churchill later wrote, surprised the British representatives. He recalled the moment:

As before, they were superficially calm and very quiet. There was a long pause, or there seemed to be, and then Mr Griffith said, 'Mr Prime Minister, the Delegation is willing to sign the agreements, but there are a few points of drafting, which perhaps would be convenient if I mentioned at once.' Thus, by the easiest of gestures, he carried the whole matter into the region of detail, and everyone concentrated upon these points with overstrained interest so as to drive the main issue into the background for ever ... we had become allies ... [10]

On 8 December 1921, the seven members of the inner Cabinet, together with Gavan Duffy and Erskine Childers, discussed the Agreement for five hours, after which the considerable efforts of Éamon de Valera, Austin Stack and Cathal Brugha failed to persuade them that the Peace Treaty be rejected. Within hours de Valera issued a Proclamation declaring that he could not recommend acceptance of the Agreement.[11]

The following day Arthur Griffith informed the country: 'I have signed the Treaty of Peace between Ireland and Great Britain. I believe that this treaty will lay the foundation of peace and friendship between the two nations. What I have signed I will stand by, in the belief that the end of the conflict of centuries is at hand.'[12] The Dáil was summoned to meet in the Council Chamber of University College Dublin on Wednesday 14 December to deal with the Treaty. Only those members who had duly taken the republican oath were called. The speaker, Eoin MacNeill, took the Chair and the roll call recorded the presence of 122 T. D.s, including ua Buachalla.

Something Less Than Freedom

Whereas talks on the Treaty at Westminster started the same day and were concluded with a vote two days later (House of Commons by a majority of 343; House of Lords by 119), the Irish Debate took twelve days of discussion and finished on 10 January 1922. It was Wednesday January 4, the seventh day in session, when ua Buachalla took the opportunity to pass judgement on the Treaty. His view differed radically from that of Lloyd George, who stated in the House of Commons a few weeks earlier, that in times of danger in the future 'I feel glad to know that Ireland will be here by our side and the old motto that "England's danger is Ireland's opportunity" will have a new meaning. As in the case of the Dominions in 1914, our peril will be her danger, our fears will be her anxieties, our victories will be her joy.'[13] Ua Buachalla's did not hold back:

I will begin by asking what was the mandate we, the members of the Dáil, got from our constituents in the last election? I know the mandate I got was to look for freedom, to strive for freedom for the country. When the plenipotentiaries left Ireland for the last time, I presume they had in their possession a document in which was stated the minimum demand Ireland was to make on England, and coming up to the last moment on the eve of the morning on which that document was signed, there was a threat held over the heads of these delegates ... therefore I conclude that the minimum demand which they had in their possession must have been minimised before these Articles of Agreement were signed. They must have been signed for something less than freedom for Ireland ...

How can it be said that we have freedom if we picture to ourselves John Bull standing four square in this country of ours, with a '*crúb*' of his firmly fastened in each of our principal ports? We are told that in each of these ports there will be what is called a 'care and maintenance party' – a very nice, mild term. What does it really mean, this care and maintenance party? It means a British Garrison in each of these ports with the Union Jack – the symbol of oppression and treachery and slavery in this country, and all over the world, but in Ireland especially – that this symbol of slavery will float over each of these strongholds, blockhouses of John Bull. Yet we are told we are getting freedom in these Articles of Agreement.

I recall one incident that happened during the last election while I was addressing a meeting in my constituency. A few of the khaki-clad warriors had fastened a Union Jack to the lamp-post beside the platform from which I was to address the meeting, and I remember stating distinctly to that assembly that I would not rest satisfied until every vestige of that rag was cleared out of the country. The assembly agreed with me, and before the words were scarcely out of my mouth, a rush was made by half-a-dozen boys from the crowd, and although the flag was defended by seven or eight of the warriors, the flag was torn down.

How can it be said that we are going to have freedom with this document when the flag which symbolises slavery continues to float over the country, here, there and everywhere, not alone in these four ports, but wherever there is a signal station or any other sort of station belonging to the British? The people of Ireland at this juncture have been stampeded by the rotten press of Ireland. Lloyd George is rubbing the palms of his hands and laughing, I doubt not, at the spectacle which is anything but creditable to [an] Ireland that has made such a fight up to this.

To my mind, the country wants a tonic of some sort to set it thinking. The country is not thinking. It has been stampeded and it now seeks to stampede its representatives. Well, there is one representative anyway that won't be stampeded. I stand today for the same object for which I stood on the platform throughout my constituency and for the same object for which my constituents elected me, and I mean to continue so. I shall vote against the Treaty.[14]

Arthur Griffith's motion to approve the Treaty was put to the Dáil on 7 January 1922, with the following words ringing in the deputies' ears:

I stand in this exactly where every leader of the Irish nation stood from the time of O'Neill to Patrick Sarsfield. Owen Roe O'Neill said: 'I do not care whether the King of England is King of Ireland so long as the people of Ireland are free. I do not care whether the King of England or the symbol of the Crown be in Ireland so long as the people of Ireland are free to shape their own destinies. We have the means to do that by this Treaty; we have not the means otherwise.'[15]

The result was sixty-four for approval, fifty-seven against. De Valera was first to speak after the result had been announced. 'It will, of course, be my duty to resign my office as Chief Executive. I do not know that I should do it just now.'[16] Michael Collins immediately said 'no' and added later, 'I do believe that some kind of an arrangement could be fixed between the two sides ... some kind of understanding ought to be reached to preserve the present order in the country, at any rate over the weekend.'[17]

As the House was about to be adjourned at 8.50 p.m., de Valera concluded, 'I would like my last word here to be this: we have had a glorious record for four years; it has been four years of magnificent discipline in our nation. The world is looking at us now ...' – at that moment he broke down.[18] Cathal Brugha took over with the statement:

'As far as I am concerned, I will see, at any rate, that discipline is kept in the army.'[19]

'Deserters all to the Irish Nation'

Two days later a vote was taken by Diarmuid O'Hegarty, Secretary of the Dáil, for the re-election of President de Valera. The resolution was lost by sixty votes to fifty-eight. Arthur Griffith reacted immediately with the words: 'I want the deputies to know, and all Ireland to know, that this vote is not to be taken as against de Valera (applause). It is a vote to help the Treaty, and I want to say now that there is scarcely a man I have ever met in my life that I have more love and respect for than President de Valera. I am thoroughly sorry to see him placed in such a position. We want him with us.'[20]

The following day, the twelfth day of the Treaty Debate and shortly before the luncheon break, Mr J. J. Walsh motioned that Griffith be appointed President of Ireland. After it had been seconded by Kevin O'Higgins, de Valera responded:

> 'As a protest against the election as President of the Irish Republic of the Chairman of the Delegation, who is bound by the Treaty conditions to set up a State which is to subvert the Republic, and who, in the interim period, instead of using the office as it should be used – to support the Republic – will, of necessity, have to be taking action which will tend to its destruction, I, while this vote is being taken, as one, am going to leave the House.'[21]

Mr de Valera then rose and left the House, followed by the entire body of his supporters. There was an immediate response to the departure:

> Mr Collins: Deserters all! We will now call on the Irish people to rally to us. Deserters all!

> Mr Ceannt: Up the Republic!

> Mr Collins: Deserters all to the Irish nation in her hour of trial. We will stand by her.

> Madame Markievicz: Oath breakers and cowards.

Mr Collins: Foreigners – Americans – English.

Madame Markievicz: Lloyd Georgeites.[22]

When the roll was called, sixty-one delegates responded. Griffith then spoke:

> As Premier I suppose I may say the Dáil and the Republic exist until such time as the Free State Government is set up. When that Free State Government is set up I intend that the Irish people shall have the fullest power of expression at that election. When the Dáil – the sovereign body of Ireland – passed the vote of approval of the Treaty, it was our business, and our duty to the Dáil, to see it carried through, and I regret, myself, that President de Valera resigned.[23]

After resuming at 4.20 p.m., and listening to a deputation from the Irish Labour Party and the Trade Union Congress, de Valera spoke again. 'I regret more than I can express the fact that I cannot consistently and sincerely congratulate the President on his election ... the difficulties which he has in his office are undoubtedly very, very great.' He continued:

> One who has had the burden of those duties on his shoulders understands what they are likely to be now, perhaps, better than anybody else; and I think I will be expressing the views of everyone here, not merely those on the majority side, but we here who stand definitely for the Republic, when I say that, appreciating to the full his difficulties in acting as President of the Republic of Ireland, as head of the established State, we shall not only not stand in his way in carrying out the duties of that office, but we shall do everything that is possible for us to secure to the full for the Irish people enjoyment of the liberty, which is their right as citizens of the Irish Republic.

> That must not, of course, be interpreted in any way as meaning that we are not to continue our own policy – that we are not to criticise and attack his policy in any respect in which it may appear to us to be contrary to the interests of the Irish people and the established government, which is the Republic ... [24]

The President responded: 'I desire to thank President de Valera for his words. I call him president still; because if he had not resigned yesterday,

I would never have asked him to resign.' And he concluded: 'Within the next three months we are going to have the heaviest task ever thrown on the shoulders of Irishmen. So at least give us a fair trial ...'[25]

While Dáil Eireann's Official Report on the Debate ran to 419 pages, the national and provincial papers were felling forests in their drive to keep readers fully informed of every detail that emanated from meetings in Westminster and Dublin. On 7 January 1922, the *Kildare Observer* carried an out-of-character banner headline declaring 'KILDARE FOR THE TREATY'. A sub-heading added, 'Meetings of Public Bodies, Sinn Féin Clubs and Farmers' Union in Support of Ratification'. The paper's first story was a resolution adopted at the Naas No. 1 District Council at the end of December declaring that 'we, in a special meeting, voicing the practically unanimous wishes of the people of the district, hereby call on the deputies of this area to vote for and use their influence to secure the ratification of the Treaty, which, although not satisfactory in every aspect, contains all the essentials of freedom.'[26] Four of the members, including Tom Harris, did not vote.

About 250 people filled the hall for the Naas Sinn Féin Club meeting and after the President, Rev. Fr Doyle C. C. called for a 'free and easy' discussion, he asked if there was anyone present who thinks the Treaty should not be ratified:

A voice: 'Yes, I am one'.

Chairman: 'Then it is as well that you state your case.'

The dissenter did not proceed to state his case and the Rev. Chairman said he would formally propose the following resolution: 'We, the members of the Naas Sinn Féin Club hereby express our conviction that the Treaty as signed by the Irish plenipotentiaries should be accorded approval by Dáil Éireann. Chaos appears to be the only alternative left ... when put to the meeting, only two hands were raised against it.'[27]

'Not What Men Offered Their Lives For'

The agricultural community gathered in Naas, where Joseph O'Connor proposed the resolution that 'we, the farmers of north Kildare in public meeting assembled, call upon the deputies representing this county in

Dáil Éireann to vote for the ratification of the Peace Treaty ... that copies of this resolution be sent to Messrs Donal Buckley, Art O'Connor, C. M. Byrne, Erskine Childers and R. C. Barton ... and also to Mr de Valera, Mr Arthur Griffith and the Minister for Propaganda.'[28]

At special meeting of Kildare County Council on 1 January, J. J. Fitzgerald told the meeting that he was speaking to Messrs. Buckley and O'Connor and 'Mr Buckley told me if he gets an expression of opinion from his constituents, it will cause him to think over the action he intended to take. Mr O'Connor told me if his constituents wanted him to vote a certain way he would reconsider his opinion.'[29]

Mr Fitzgerald's resolution 'that we, the Kildare County Council, are in favour of the ratification of the Treaty ... and call on the deputies for Kildare and Wicklow to support it', received enthusiastic backing, but Tom Harris had other ideas. 'I was out in 1916 and fought under Pearse and Connolly for the Republic. I worked hard to put in Mr Buckley as our representative in North Kildare, because he stood for the republican principles, and by de Valera. This Treaty is not what the men of Ireland offered their lives for.'[30] The chairman said that frankly, he was opposed to the resolution ... 'and as a republican he felt bound to oppose ratification'. The chairman dissented and Mr Harris did not vote, but the resolution was carried.

The strong ground-swell of support for acceptance of the Treaty in Kildare even stretched to the North Kildare Sinn Féin Executive, who unanimously passed the motion that

> we appeal to the leaders of all sections of opinion within Dáil Éireann to do all in their power to restore unity amongst the representatives of the nation. We pledge our unwavering support to the decisions of a unified Dáil, we express our conviction that the Treaty as signed by the Irish plenipotentiaries should be accorded approval by Dáil Éireann ... and if a deputy finds he cannot vote for the Treaty, let him at least not defiantly flout the will of his constituents; let him state his personal views, and abstain from voting.[31]

If the Executive had Domhnall ua Buachalla in mind when proposing the motion, and an expectation that he would follow their recommendation, they were mistaken. In fact, it would appear they did not really know the man they elected.

CHAPTER 13

An Insult to People's Intelligence

The *Times* reported that Dublin was agog with anticipation on 16 January 1922. 'From early morning a dense crowd collected outside the gloomy gates of Dublin Castle in Dame Street ... and only a few privileged persons were permitted to enter its grim gates.'[1] At 1.30 p.m., Michael Collins and other members of the Provisional Government were received by Lord-Lieutenant of Ireland, Lord Edmund FitzAlan-Howard, the first Catholic to hold the position since 1865, and 'were then formally and officially acknowledged'.[2] After centuries of British rule, it took just fifty-five minutes for the citadel to be returned to the Irish people.

In the same month, British troops began evacuating the country, as did the Auxiliaries and the Black and Tans. Civic Guards were sought to keep law and order and Eoin O'Duffy, Chief of Staff of the Republican Army, began a gradual reorganisation. In Kildare, a writer in the *Observer*, referred to Mr C. M. Byrne, T. D., as 'the only deputy representing the joint constituency of Kildare and Wicklow who wholeheartedly supported the ratification of the Treaty'. His speech the previous week at the Naas Sinn Féin Club was comprehensively covered in the paper, and readers were informed that Mr D. Buckley, T. D. was being given the same opportunity. But before doing so, the paper had a few judgements to hand down:

> We shall do Mr Buckley the credit of at once admitting our belief in his absolute honesty of purpose and of his patriotism. But we may

and do find fault with his reasoning in arrogating to himself, as did others, the right of deciding entirely on his own responsibility, and in conflict with the wishes and expressed desire of his constituents, what his attitude to the Treaty should be.

Mr Buckley said that when he was elected to represent the then constituency of North Kildare, the mandate as he understood it was 'to try and help to win freedom for Ireland as well as he could'. We believe that Mr Buckley quite accurately understood the mandate, but it will be noted there is a vast difference between winning freedom for Ireland and suggesting that the mandate was one for a Republic.

He voted against the Treaty because 'he knew that the people did not understand the Articles of Agreement' and he believed if the people went wrong that was no reason why he should go wrong. We acquit Mr Buckley of any intention to offer insult to the intelligence of the people, but we would point out that that is done by such statements as this. The fact, which appears to be completely lost sight of, is that the majority who voted for the Treaty were men just as patriotic, just as well versed in politics, just as intelligent and just as capable as knowing what was good and bad for the country as the men who voted against.[3]

Mr R. Dorrian, who introduced ua Buachalla on 25 January at the Naas Sinn Féin Club, said that he had been deputed to do so 'by the President, Father Doyle, who was absent through illness, and with whom Mr Buckley had arranged to come and address his constituents'. It was this speech which the *Observer* printed in full. Initially, ua Buachalla brought the gathering back to eve of the departure of the delegates for London after a Cabinet meeting:

That night they received instructions that on no account were they to sign any documents in London. Let those present bear that fact in mind. When they got the best terms they could, any documents for signature should first be brought back to the Cabinet in Dublin for approval. The threat of 'immediate and horrible war' by Lloyd George if the document was not signed was a bluff, but a bluff that succeeded. No country calling itself civilised could declare war on such a pretext, because a document was not signed by a certain hour, notwithstanding a refusal to allow the Irish delegates to carry out their instructions and bring it back for approval. The situation could have been saved if they admitted they had signed it under duress, submitted it to the Cabinet, and put it in the fire ...

The Articles of Agreement meant that for the first time in Irish history, the people of Ireland would, of their own free will, walk into the British Empire with their heads up and become British citizens. He ventured to say that their children, and their children's children, when they came to realise that fact, would come to say strong and galling things about them. Under the Free State Government they would have a governor-general living in Ireland, and he would have his following the same as the British lord lieutenant had in his time and that would be the British garrison in Ireland. Not alone would he have that – but some of their own people would go into that circle with their heads up because the Government gave them permission to do so.

The people of Ireland had been led astray by the Irish press, and particularly the *Freeman's Journal*. Seventy five per cent of the people were for the thing called the Treaty, not because they believed it to be a good thing, but because they dreaded the bogey that had been held up to them as the alternative – war.

It was very hard for them to realise what the power of England was in the press all over the world. She controlled half the press of America and a great deal of the Continent, and the cables through Reuter's were English, and every message that came through that agency was coloured to suit England's interests ...

What was the fight for? Was it to be made British citizens? Was it for this the men of 1916, Terence MacSwiney and Kevin Barry, went out to their death that Ireland might be free? Let them in God's name think for themselves ... let them think on straight lines, and not on lines of compromise and expediency. The country made a straight, stand-up fight for the last four or five years, and had taken a place in the world of which any country might be proud. We were the admiration of the world, especially countries trying to get out of the clutches of England – Egypt, India and South Africa.[4]

Turning to his decision to vote against the Treaty, he said:

> I consented to stand as representative for North Kildare after much persuasion. It was put to me that it was my duty to do so, and one of the reasons was, they thought, that I might get more votes than others and the object was to win the election. The mandate, as I understood it, was to try and help to win freedom for Ireland as well as I could.

> When I took my place in the Dáil along with the other members on a memorable occasion, we all stood up and held our hands above our heads and took a solemn oath, calling on God to witness that we would stand always for republican principles and the freedom of the country. When I took the oath I meant it, and I mean it still. I knew this Treaty would not give us freedom, and I voted against it. If the same thing were to happen again, I would do the same thing.

> I got several resolutions from different bodies in the country asking me to vote for the Treaty. I have never blamed anyone in the country for anything they did. We all act as we think best. But I knew the people did not understand these Articles of Agreement ... and I believed if the people went wrong there was no reason why I should go wrong.

> I am sure many of you, from the statements in the press during the debate, were under the impression that we in the Dáil were at one another's throats like cats. Such was not the case ... there was excitement at times, and men made the best case they could for their own side. In the heat of the excitement things may have been said that were better not said, but that was inevitable ... when the debate was over we all flocked out and mingled and chatted with one another. We haven't fallen out with one another.

> De Valera said he would not place any obstacles in the way of the majority unless they interfered with the Republican Government, which still exists, and shall exist until the Irish people throw it

overboard. Expediency or compromise never led a people to the goal of freedom. The straight path will lead us there. The fight will have to be continued ... the Treaty, if put into force, will give us some good things, control of education, finance, and a little army of our own, but our country will be dishonoured, and I put honour above anything else, and especially the honour of my country.

In 1914, a minority of the Volunteers stood by their country and refused to be stampeded by Mr John Redmond. Éamon de Valera was of that minority, and the minority was proved to be right. In 1916, a minority went out to fight for freedom. De Valera was of the minority, and that minority was proved to be right. In 1922, de Valera was still with the minority, and that minority that refused to accept the Articles of Agreement would yet be proved to be right.

Now, if all the people in this room disagree with me, I won't be any bit the worse friends with them, and I hope they won't be with me. If, in the Naas Sinn Féin Club, there is one solitary member of my way of thinking, I would like to have his name within the week.[5]

Ua Buachalla's speech, which started with the promise 'that he had only a few brief remarks to make', was lengthy by his normal standards. It mirrored the intentions of de Valera's new Republican Party, formed by those who had voted against the Treaty, 'to instruct the people in the implications of the Treaty and restore their courage, and to have the elections postponed until this could be accomplished, the Constitution published and the register revised; and they sought to devise some *modus vivendi*, some method by which the position of the Republic might be safeguarded and the country governed peacefully meanwhile'.[6]

'Straight as the Barrel of a Gun'

On 21 January the *Leinster Leader* reported the reaction of J. J. Fitzgerald to ua Buachalla's decision to vote against the Treaty. He said that in the lead-up to the 1918 election he had

> ... gone out working for Art O'Connor and Dan Buckley, and whilst they were out for a Republic, self-determination was mentioned far oftener than a Republic. He never worked that Dan Buckley should

express his own personal views, but the views of the people. He would be the last in the world to say a word against Dan Buckley, for the latter had no greater admirer and he knew Dan Buckley to be as straight as the barrel of a gun, but he could not see with him in his action regarding the Treaty.

The Treaty was not all that they wanted, but it was very near it. It was a great achievement because we could snap our fingers at England within five years ... and when the next scrap came they would not be meeting the enemy with out of date .45's but weapons of modern pattern.[7]

As *Cumann-na-mBan* re-affirmed its allegiance to the Republic, Michael Collins and Sir James Craig found no common ground in their Boundary discussions. The House of Commons got testy while debating the Irish Free State (Agreement) Bill and there was accord at the Sinn Féin *Ard-Fheis* on 21 and 22 February, which was attended by almost 3,000 delegates.

After a conference of some hours' duration between Arthur Griffith, Michael Collins, Éamon de Valera and Austin Stack, an agreement was reached by which the *Ard-Fheis* was to be adjourned for three months. In the meantime (a) the Officer board would act as a Standing Committee; (b) Dáil Éireann would continue to function in all its departments and no vote would be regarded as a Party vote requiring the resignation of the President and the Cabinet; (c) in the meantime no Parliamentary Election would he held, and that when held, the constitution of the *Saorstát* in its final form would be presented at the same time as the Articles of Agreement. There were no dissenting voices and the Agreement was ratified on 2 March. That same month, a letter was read at the Kildare County Council meeting from ua Buachalla, dated 14 March:

'*Do Liam E. Ó Cobaigh,*

A Chara,

I beg to acknowledge receipt of your letter of the 21st ult. conveying the unanimous decision of the Council that I be asked to reconsider my decision in the matter of the chairmanship. I delayed in replying in the hope that I might be able to see my way to accede to their wish.

I now find that it will be impossible for me to give the meeting anything like the regular attendance such meetings deserve – and must, therefore, hold myself excused for not continuing in the position as chairman. Need I say how I appreciate their and your desire that I should do so.[8]

If ua Buachalla's decision to vote against the Treaty had ruffled many feathers in Kildare, the reaction of the County Council to his letter was more positive:

Mr Colohan proposed that the Chairman be again asked to reconsider his resignation.

Mr Carroll: I second that. Tell him we won't accept it.

The motion was passed unanimously.[9]

Weeks passed as efforts were made to create a peaceful national compromise, with Griffith pushing for a June election although admitting that the outdated voting register would have to suffice, Collins calling for a plebiscite and, on 2 May, ten army officers, five from each side, exploring the possibility of a settlement. On 4 May, a truce was agreed as talks continued. Six days later the Dáil reported that it had failed to agree.

That Wednesday morning, ua Buachalla received a telegram which had been sent the previous night: 'Attend without fail party meeting tomorrow (Wednesday) morning, eleven o'clock.' It was signed 'Seant [Sean T. O'Kelly], Boland'. Despite the failure to reach an agreement, the desire to avoid a civil war predominated and de Valera's wish for the safety of the Republic received a boost when he put a question to Arthur Griffith in the Dáil on 17 May:

He enquired if Griffith did or did not want the co-operation of republicans on the understanding that they were not committed to the Treaty, and that the people should not be asked to commit themselves to the Treaty. Griffith replied that if de Valera meant to agree not to obstruct the people in expressing their views, his answer was 'yes'. To this Brugha retorted that it was the Treaty Party which wanted to prevent a million Irish adults from expressing their views by holding an election on the unrevised register.

Michael Collins made a long speech. He seemed sincerely anxious to arrange a coalition 'on the basis of goodwill and carrying out the advantages of the Treaty position … to consolidate their position, having in view the unity of Ireland'.

De Valera welcomed it: 'Being for the moment in a minority here, and realising that the interests of the country demand that there be stable government, if our assistance is required, so long as we are not committed further than I have stated, we are willing to give that assistance in any way in which we can benefit the country.'

The House received this offer with applause and with a feeling of hopefulness that an accommodation might yet be arranged. De Valera and Collins were requested to examine the possibility of finding a basis of agreement.[10]

Two days later the Dáil was informed that they had reached an agreement, and signed a pact. The June elections would not be seen as deciding the issue of the Treaty, but creating a government to create peace. The primary point of the Pact read: 'That a National Coalition panel for this Third Dáil, representing both parties in the Dáil and in the Sinn Féin organisation, be sent forward, on the ground that the national position requires the entrusting of the Government of the country into the joint hands of those who have been the strength of the national situation during the last few years, without prejudice to their present respective positions.'[11]

Unhappy with the settlement, Arthur Griffith amended his motion for an election in June, making it subject to the terms of the Pact. Seconded by de Valera, it was unanimously approved. This, constituting a decree of the Second Dáil for an election for a Third Dáil, made the Pact part of the law of the Republic and when it was ratified on 23 May, both Collins and de Valera expressed great enthusiasm for it, as did the members. The British Government and the Northern Unionists however, did not share in this enthusiasm.

The election campaign opened with a meeting at the Mansion House on 9 June, with both Collins and de Valera speaking from the same platform, but by the eve of polling day, no Constitution had been revealed and Collins had reneged on the Pact in a speech in Cork. On Polling Day, the *Irish Independent* carried a story under the heading 'Mr Collins' Plain

Talk', advising its readers to vote for candidates 'you think best of, whom you think will carry on best in future the work you want carried on'.[12]

The Constitution also appeared in the newspapers the same day as people went to cast their votes, which was far too late for a large proportion of them to read, let alone digest. The *Irish Independent* carried an article by Darrell Figgis, who returned as an Independent in the election. The article attempted to explain the Constitution for the paper's readers, and concluded with the line 'To be continued'.[13] On 24 June, the election returns showed the pro-Treaty side with fifty-eight seats, Republicans thirty-six, Labour Party seventeen, Farmers' Party seven, Unionists four (representing Trinity College) and Independents six.

If their belief in the Pact had been undermined, the Republicans were cast into limbo by the Constitution. Executive authority was vested in the King; the Oath was compulsory; the King had power of veto over all legislation and the representative of the Crown would be the Governor-General of the Irish Free State. All of which prompted Gavan Duffy to tender his resignation.

A Policy of Kick and Caress

If Domhnall ua Buachalla's election success in 1918 was marked by the greatest majority in the North Kildare constituency, the weight of being an anti-Treaty candidate in the Kildare-Wicklow campaign in 1922 decimated his support. In a 'Who's Who' of candidates in the *Kildare Observer* before the count, he was referred to as 'a well-known Irish-Irelander, a Gaelic speaker, Chairman of the Kildare County Council and a merchant in Maynooth. He voted against the Treaty in Dáil Éireann.'[14]

In his principal paper, he was proposed for election by Nicholas Travers, Portglorian, Kilcock, and seconded by Michael Stapleton, Main Street, Kilcock. The assentors were all Kilcock men – nephew Michael Buckley, Patrick Stapleton, Peter Flynn, Thomas Keely, Patrick Murray, John Gleeson and Patrick Johnson. In a second paper he was proposed by Diarmuid O'Neill, Weston Park, Celbridge and seconded by Elizabeth Wogan, Leixlip; in a third paper he was proposed by Rev. P. J. Kinane C. C., Maynooth and seconded by Henry Armstrong, Maynooth.

Of the other nine candidates, three were also Anti-Treaty – Robert Childers Barton, a farmer who lived in Glendalough House, Annamoe, Co. Wicklow, his cousin Erskine Childers, who lived in Bushy Park Road, Terenure, and Art O'Connor, Minister for Agriculture in Dáil Éireann prior to the split. Christopher Byrne, a farmer in Glenealy, Co. Wicklow, was the sole pro-Treaty candidate. Hugh Colohan, a brick and stonelayer and prominent Trade Unionist, and James Everett, Secretary of the Transport Workers' Union, represented Labour while the Farmers' and Ratepayers' Party ran three candidates – J. J. Bergin, a prolific writer on farming; Patrick Phelan, a member of the Kildare County Council, and Richard Wilson, a Rathdrum farmer. Michael Gallagher saw the 1922 election as

> A contest between two groups with different views on the place of politics. One saw Irish society in essentially monist terms, as innately conflict-free. It wanted any differences of opinion to be resolved within the framework of the all-encompassing 'national movement' and was suspicious of the very idea of political parties because the concept implied a fragmentation of the Irish people into different sections with different interests.
>
> The other took a more pluralist view, and saw the political process as existing in order to allow the peaceful resolution of conflicts that inevitably existed within Irish society. The fact that enough non-Sinn Féin candidates came forward to make the election a genuine test of the people's will ensured the second view prevailed, and established the new Irish state as a twentieth-century liberal democracy.[15]

From the early stage it was obvious that the four anti-Treaty candidates were in serious trouble. They mustered a meagre 6,568 votes between them compared to Christopher Byrne's 9,170 votes from supporters of the Treaty. Byrne, Colohan and Everett reached the quota and were elected on the first count, with Childers losing his deposit of £150. Ua Buachalla was eliminated on the sixth count; Wilson reached the quota on the eight count and Barton secured the final seat at 2.00 a.m. on Thursday of a count that commenced on Monday.

The electoral register was acknowledged to be seriously inaccurate and the franchise was extended to women if they were aged 30 or over. In the contested constituencies (eight of the twenty-eight were not contested) the pro-Treatyites won forty-one seats and the anti-Treatyites only nineteen. Not a single anti-Treaty candidate headed the poll in any constituency. Gallagher concluded that the election 'was significant in its own right from many perspectives. But perhaps its most important long-term consequence

THIRD DÁIL KILDARE-WICKLOW 1922		SEATS 5 QUOTA 5,753	
CANDIDATES	FIRST COUNT	FINAL FIGURES	
Christopher Byrne (Pro-Treaty)	9,170	
Hugh Colohan (Labour)	6,522	
James Everett (Labour)	5,993	
Richard Wilson (Farmers and Ratepayers)	3,035	6,700
Robert Barton (Anti-Treaty)	2,842	4,735
John Bergin (Farmers and Ratepayers)	2,013	3,723
Art O'Connor (Anti-Treaty)	1,776	4,360
Daniel Buckley (Anti-Treaty)	1,438	2,207
Patrick Phelan (Farmers and Ratepayers)	1,213	1,785
Erskine Childers (Anti-Treaty)	512	721

Irish Elections 1922–44: Results and analysis: Michael Gallagher

for Irish political history was that it asserted the primacy of the ballot box, at a time when this seemed very much in the balance'.[16]

Reaction to the outcome was positive in the media. The *Irish Independent* claimed that 'were the choice of the electors absolutely free and unfettered, the results would, we venture to claim, be an even more emphatic vindication of the sound sense of the people and a more irresistible demand for settled government'.[17] 'The success of the anti-Treaty Party's nominees has been the exception, not the rule. For the personality of many of the defeated anti-Treaty members, their former constituents have the highest regard; for their present policy they have little.'[18]

A statement from de Valera on 21 June contrasted sharply with the *Independent's* view and, ironically, was overshadowed by a four-column picture and report of Major-General Seán Mac Eoin's marriage in Longford to Mary Cooney.

> These results seem indeed a triumph for the imperial methods of pacification – outrage and murder and massacre, and then threat without concession – the policy of the kick and caress, with a kick in reserve. By the threat of immediate renewal and an infamous war, our people, harassed and weary, and fearful of chaos, have

in a majority voted as England wanted, but their hearts and their aspirations are unchanged, and Ireland unfree will never be at rest or genuinely reconciled with England.

England's gain is for the moment, and England's difficulty will still be prayed for as Ireland's opportunity. The men and women who have been rejected by the electorate have gone down with their flag flying, untouched by prospect of place or power, true to their principles, true to every pledge and promise they gave.[19]

On 21 June, Cathal Brugha, who was successful in the Waterford-Tipperary constituency, responded to a letter he had received from ua Buachalla:

Domhnall ua Buachalla: wishing you life and health!

A Chara,

That was received and I've sent a message to the people in the Four Courts today. It is said that that particular officer, P. Grogan, is one of the Free State people. Therefore it's the Beggar's Bush people who are responsible for this business. Notwithstanding that, our people will look after him if they can manage it. Perhaps you wouldn't mind writing to the Beggar's Bush people yourself?

Wasn't that a great election we had? The register was beautifully 'cooked'. Confirmation of that is ní Cheinnigh herself.

But it's the boys in the army who will settle the business in the end.

Mise,

Cathal B.[20]

While there was a hint of uncertainty in the letter concerning whether Grogan's needs would be rectified, and serious irony in his reference to the election, 'settling the business' certainly had a prophetic ring to it, but not with the desired outcome. Brugha was an advocate of the people of Ireland voting on whether to have a Free State or a Republic, and was also in favour of leaving the Four Courts before it was attacked and engaging in guerrilla warfare. However, within sixteen days of writing the letter, it was the 'boys' in the Free State army who would decide his future.

Repercussions for the Republicans

The following day, Sir Henry Wilson was shot dead on the footsteps of his home in London, a killing that was to have major repercussions for Republicans in the ensuing weeks. Oscar Traynor, O/C of the Dublin Brigade, tried to persuade the Executive to evacuate the Four Courts on June 27, without success. Pressure came on the Provisional Government from David Lloyd George to take action against the anti-Treatyites who had taken control of the Four Courts on April 14, and promised whatever military assistance was required.

On Tuesday 27 June, matters came to a head in Dublin as the day progressed. Eighteen-pounder guns, supplied to Michael Collins by the British, were put in place on the other side of the River Liffey and trained on the Four Courts. At 3.40 a.m. the following day the commandant of the garrison received a note demanding surrender; just after 4.00 a.m. the guns started firing. Although there had been skirmishes throughout the country before this, Dubliners awoke that morning to the start of Civil War. Military affairs in the city were under the control of Oscar Traynor. Brugha reported to Traynor and became a commandant in the Dublin Brigade.

Also back in Dublin at that time was ua Buachalla's son, Joe. Frustrated at not being allowed to take part in the 1916 Rising, he was now active again with the Rathfarnham Company and spent time in the Four Courts. The shelling of the building was constant right through Wednesday and Thursday, and on Friday morning the building caught fire. An attempt to move explosives within the building had only partly succeeded when the remainder came within the ambit of the fire. A terrifying explosion destroyed what remained of the building. The plight of those inside was now desperate and a despatch immediately went to Traynor. The response was predictable: surrender. 'To help me carry on the fight outside you must surrender forthwith. I would be unable to fight my way through to you even at terrific sacrifice . . . if the Republic is to be saved your surrender is a necessity.'[21] Shortly after noon on Friday 30 June, the flag of truce was raised and those inside the Four Courts marched out.

At this stage Joe had made his way to the city centre and while attempting to halt a movement of troops from Amiens Street towards

O'Connell Street, and fighting from inside Moran's Hotel in the company of two other young Volunteers, a grenade was thrown into the room beside them and the explosion killed both of his friends.[22] It was a stark reminder for the 23-year-old, if one was needed, of the proximity of death.

As the Four Courts smouldered, Government troops focused on a group of hotels close to the headquarters of the Dublin Brigade of the IRA as their forces fought for survival in the Hammam and Granville hotels. On the Sunday a group was ordered to depart with a white flag, while de Valera, Stack, Brugha and other leaders remained. The following day, de Valera, Stack and Traynor were among those who moved out and managed to make it to safe houses from where they communicated with Brugha. Their orders were to continue firing and to surrender when they could remain no longer. Despite an order on the Tuesday from Traynor to leave, Brugha ignored it, and it was not until the building was in flames the following day that he told his companions to leave. Liz Gillis described the final minutes:

> At around 7.00 p.m., and with the Granville completely consumed by fire, the roof collapsed. Soon afterwards, shouts of 'surrender' were heard. A white flag emerged in Thomas Lane at the rear of the Granville. Waving the flag, Art O'Connor led out his small party of Volunteers ... but Cathal Brugha was nowhere to be found ... he had chosen to remain in the building, and with him stayed Dr Brennan and Nurse Linda Kearns.
>
> The fire brigade quickly made their way to Thomas Lane and tried to gain entry into the Granville by the rear exit doors. As they broke down the doors there suddenly appeared a low-sized, smoke-stained man who rushed out with revolver drawn.
>
> In an effort to escape, Brugha made his way down Thomas Lane, running towards a party of troops. He was called on to halt but refused. A volley of shots rang out, but one bullet was all it took ... Nurse Linda Kearns and Dr Brennan ran to his assistance, but his femoral artery had been severed. Brugha was rushed by ambulance to the Mater Hospital and Linda Kearns stayed with him, holding the severed artery between her fingers. With that volley of shots in Thomas Lane, the battle for Dublin ended.[23]

Two days later, on the 7 July, Brugha, born in Dublin in 1874 of Catholic and Protestant parentage, and a pupil of Belvedere College, was dead.

With Joe 'on the run', his father had problems of his own in late June. The least of them was the election of a chairman for Kildare County Council, a matter that had not been resolved. Mr Phelan proposed that ua Buachalla, the outgoing chairman, be re-elected, and in doing so paid tribute to his fairness and impartiality. Mr Colohan seconded the proposition which was passed unanimously.[24] Ua Buachalla was late arriving and on being informed that he had been elected chairman, he asked that another person be appointed as he could not attend to the job as he would wish. The meeting declined to do so, insisting that he was the man for the job.

Before June was out, however, he was not in a position to attend any meetings as pressure came on the Republicans in Kildare. While travelling to a Board of Health meeting in Naas, Tom Harris was arrested along with J. P. Cusack. Both were brought to the military barracks where Harris was detained. Cusack was released and informed the meeting when he eventually arrived that 'it was scandalous that a man like Mr Harris, with eight years active service to his credit, should be thus insulted by men who were probably under the bed when he [Harris] was fighting and he thought it was the duty of the Board to protest'.[25] The meeting agreed and a letter was duly drafted.

The following day ua Buachalla was arrested. Much of his involvement in IRA activity was carried out with a group that included men from Leixlip, Kilcock and Celbridge – in particularly Mayo-born Commandant Patrick Mullaney, a school teacher from Leixlip, and Mick O'Neill.

Mullaney, O. C. of the north Kildare/Meath Brigade Column, and O'Neill, had been to Millmount in Co. Louth, and while returning by car they picked up ua Buachalla on their way into Kilcock. As they approached the village a roadblock brought them to a halt and all three were taken by Commandant Flynn to Kilcock jail, formerly the Ulster Bank, which was situated across the square from Domhnall's brother's premises. In an interview with Ernie O'Malley, O'Neill stated that they were then taken to the Curragh, but subsequently returned to Kilcock.

Two incidents in north Kildare a few days later brought the O'Keeffe brothers into the picture. After the Treaty vote, Patrick decided to return to help his father in the pub in Kilcock and Jim decided that he would take over his role as adjutant at the Battalion Headquarters in Maynooth. Patrick recalled the incidents:

Jim was standing on the footpath in Maynooth when two or three car-loads of Free Staters came along. Thinking that he would be an easy capture, they shouted 'hands up'. Instead, Jim, who had a grenade in his hand, let fly. It was on target, but did not explode. Jim immediately put his hand into his coat pocket, making out that he had a second grenade (which he did not). They jumped from their cars and looked for shelter in shops and houses near to them and [then] fled.

The next time I met Jim was at Trim Railway Station; he had been captured in Edenderry, and along with other prisoners, he was going to Dundalk Jail. When the Free Staters recovered from their fright in Maynooth they came to Kilcock, surrounded O'Keeffe's pub, charged in, and pushed their old friend, my father, up against the wall. I was behind the counter in my shirt sleeves, and asked them to let me into the kitchen to get my coat (I meant to escape) but they brought me out into the street and put me into an open lorry, and brought me over to the Ulster Bank ...

Thinking I was going to have a rough time, I said to Commandant Flynn, 'if you are going to shoot me, bring me out into the yard and do it now'. The challenge saved me punishment and I was put into a room with three other prisoners – Buckley, Mullaney and O'Neill. It was nice to be with true friends again. We were confined to this room for five weeks, having no exercise, except going to an outside dry toilet escorted by an armed guard. We were not allowed to close the door or be let out of sight.

We got a message that the bank was to be attacked. All the windows were sand-bagged with the exception of ours, leaving us no protection. My father's pub was fired into from the road on the south side of the canal, breaking the shop window [and] leaving a bullet hole in a drawer at the back wall. Parcels from my mother with bread or cake [for us] were cut up into pieces. No visitors allowed, no Sunday Mass. A professor from Maynooth College, after saying Sunday Mass in Kilcock, did call to see Dan Buckley.

Pat Mullaney and Mick O'Neill were transferred elsewhere, leaving Dan and myself. The windows in our cell were facing the street so we decided to try and get out. We got a hacksaw to cut the bars in one of the windows, but never got the opportunity to do so. We were now five weeks confined in this room and still getting no exercise. Dan sent an ultimatum to Commandant Flynn, saying that if we were not brought out for exercise by 6.00 p.m. that day, we would make an attempt to escape. Flynn must have thought it better to have two live prisoners on his hands than two dead ones, because at 5.55 p.m. we were allowed under armed guard to walk around the back garden. This was our first and last walk.

Next day, two or three cars were waiting outside to bring us to Dundalk. We were taken out into the street about 2.00 p.m. and Dan was put into one car and I into another, with our guards sitting [on] both sides of us. Commandant Flynn was sitting [beside] me with a grenade in his hand. We were brought via Maynooth and Lucan to Clonsilla Railway Station and put on a train.

The next stop was Trim, where my brother Jim, along with other prisoners, were put aboard. Our final stop was Dundalk, where all of us were put in jail. We were searched, our names taken, and the money we had was given to the Governor. I was put in a cell with Buckley. For our supper we got a mug of water and some dry bread. A mattress on the floor was our bed, and a bucket for our toilet. Next morning after breakfast we were told to clean up and empty all sops. After a short time all prisoners were brought out to the exercise yard, which was surrounded by a high wall. In the centre were four or five circles of stone flags for prisoners to walk on, a distance apart and in silence.

As time went on, our relations with the Governor and the prison staff were getting out of hand. We were some of the first IRA prisoners in a Free State jail not getting our demands, so we started a hunger strike. We strained the cell door by putting a Bible beside the hinge and pushing the door, and thereafter we were able to move it so that it could not be closed. Very quickly we were pulled out of our cells, some by the hair, and put down to the basement or punishment cells with six or more men in each cell. The first few days were very trying but our minds were made up not to surrender. After five days we got our demands.[26]

Oath of Allegiance

On 13 April 1922, the British Army had moved out of Dundalk Military Barracks and at mid-day, members of the Fourth Northern Division of the IRA, with their leader, Frank Aiken, moved in. He saw one insurmountable barrier to peace between the two Treaty parties – the Oath of Allegiance – but he was reluctant to take sides. He subsequently visited General Richard Mulcahy in Dublin and told him that if the Provisional Government did not give the anti-Treaty parties, both civil and military, a constitutional way of carrying on for the Republic, such as withdrawing the Oath for admission to Parliament, there would be no support, moral or material, for his Government. He was asked to return to Dundalk and write a full memorandum on the stance.

Early the following morning, a gun was put to Aiken's head after the gates of the barracks had been opened by some of his men who were under arrest for drunkenness. Aiken was now a prisoner; the pro-Treaty forces had taken over without any casualties and made all within prisoners. They were marched, heavily escorted, to the County Jail at the Crescent. The following day's papers reported a 'Great Coup' at Dundalk.

Having been paroled, Aiken received an offer from Mulcahy 'to have the prisoners in Dundalk released if they would sign an undertaking not to attack the Government'. General Aiken thought they would not wish to attack, but suspected that they would sign nothing until the Government withdrew from the Constitution the Oath of Allegiance. On return to Dundalk, he was informed by the Provisional Government's officers that he and his men were to be arrested. They were sent to the local jail.[27] On 28 July he was freed when a unit of men dynamited the prison wall and in a short space of time had released Aiken and approximately 100 fellow prisoners. He immediately appealed to former IRA members serving in the Provisional Government to 'down tools', maintaining that 'while you attack the men who can never accept the oath, you are in the wrong and must be met'.[28]

As his own division was under severe pressure from the Provisional Government's troops, Aiken was forced to take action. Just before dawn on the morning of 13 August four mines exploded simultaneously at the Dundalk barracks. Three soldiers were killed immediately and as the garrison came to life, they were confronted by anti-Treaty guerrillas. Patrick O'Keeffe recalled the moment when Aiken returned in force, and the aftermath of the explosion:

We were awakened by loud banging and shouting (coming from outside) and cries of 'get up boys, you are free'. Then the cell doors opened and we marched down to the barracks where we were supplied with guns to fight our way home. To me, this was a day in a lifetime, seeing over 200 IRA prisoners marching out, and about the same number of Free Staters marching in to take our place as prisoners. I can still see Aiken, dressed in a dark suit, watching us as we passed.[29]

Mick O'Neill recalled that they left the barracks early to get across the Boyne Bridge as soon as was possible. 'Aiken gave us arms and new boots, which nearly killed us. Michael Kennedy, now a T. D., was there and Jimmy Dunne of south Kildare, a new buck, a good man. At the bridge we met some lads loaded with stuff and they were dropping by degrees, they carried so much. At the pub on the Boyne we ate and drank minerals and I gave [the owner] a receipt.'[30]

About fifteen miles from Dundalk they heard a loud explosion, which they recognised as the destruction of the railway bridge. 'That night we slept in a hay field,'[31] O'Keeffe recalled. With this group was ua Buachalla, as enthusiastic and driven as his fellow escapees, but being about thirty years older than the majority, it was obviously taking a greater toll on his physical well-being. In addition, his busy lifestyle in local and national politics, in political meetings and elections, in IRA activities and in business – and having just come through a debilitating two months in jail – all these factors would have combined to throw doubts on his ability to elude the Free State forces. For that reason, he was offered sound advice by his nephew, Cathal, who was also in the escape group. Mick O'Neill recalled the young dentist suggesting to Domhnall that he should try to catch a train to Dublin rather than undertake a foot-slog over rough terrain. A practical man, ua Buachalla saw the merit in the idea, and when O'Keeffe turned down an invitation to go with him, he said his goodbyes and set out for a railway station south of Dundalk.

O'Neill had charge of a column of twenty men. He made it home to the family house at Weston Park with another escapee and, after a quick change of clothes, departed. He recalled that he was 'no sooner out of the place than it was surrounded'.[32] He went on to Elm Hall and moved further from home the following morning. Cathal Buckley was subsequently captured and imprisoned at Gormanstown until November of the following year.

Patrick O'Keeffe struck out with his brother and a group led by Jim Dunne. After two days without food or sleep, they were surrounded by 500

Free State troops in Meath. In the aftermath of a fight lasting almost five hours, they managed to break through the enemy ring, but a rearguard was put in place as a safeguard, which included the O'Keeffes.

> Each man had been provided with 250 rounds of ammunition and was armed with a rifle. When we surrendered, we had only seven rounds left and the rifles were jammed and red-hot. The Dublin Guards who had been attacking had lost three men, [who were] killed, and several wounded. The prisoners were lined up to be shot when the officer in charge of the Guards, Commandant Stapleton, arrived on the scene. He congratulated our men on the fight they had put up and accorded them good treatment.[33]

The O'Keeffes were brought to Drogheda and held in a school for a few weeks before being moved to the North Wall in Dublin and finally the prison ship, *Arvonia*, in Killiney Bay, which was crowded with prisoners from Cork, Kerry and Limerick.

> When we got on board there was hardly any room on top and bottom decks. It was like Hell on Earth ... we had to sleep where we were standing. Some got under the seats to sleep only to find that all the urine went down a channel underneath. We were like a lot of 'wicked dogs'. Bread was fired in, the best catcher getting the most. In a short time, most of the prisoners got the itch or scabies. A doctor came on board and ordered their transfer to the mainland. Jim scratched his arms, went to the doctor and was put on the transfer list.

> On the day the relief ship came, all the sick were put on board. I was very depressed over parting with Jim. Then the officer-in-charge said, 'there is room for two or three more, who will volunteer to come?' I accepted immediately along with Kitt Lynam. The ship sailed over to the North Wall where we disembarked and went by rail to the Newbridge Detention Camp.[34]

While the vast majority of the Dundalk escapees took a cross-country route to their native towns and villages, ua Buachalla headed for the coastline. Because he was a 56-year-old man with a grey beard, of slight build and no more than five foot eight inches in height, it would be reasonable to assume that he was a less than intimidating figure when passing the time of day with strangers; yet he remained aware of how vulnerable he was as the search for republican activists heightened.

Somewhere south of Dundalk he eventually managed to board a train which took him to Amiens Street and from there he disappeared through the Dublin streets, seeking the sanctuary of Castlewood Park in Rathmines where his sister Johanna and her husband, Conn McLoughlin, lived. No house could have been more welcoming; no bed would have provided greater comfort. Now, though, he was officially 'on the run', a prisoner at large, an absentee father, an unseated TD, a missing chairman, and a merchant divorced from his business.

CHAPTER 14

On The Run

Reassuring words eventually filtered back concerning Domhnall ua Buachalla's safety to Maynooth where his family were living with the fear that they might not see him alive again. Joe's involvement in the Civil War included action at the Four Courts and the Gresham Hotel, which ensured that he was subsequently a marked man. Consequently, much of the responsibility in managing household affairs would have fallen on the shoulders of the eldest daughters, 20-year-old Síghle and 16-year-old Bríghid, a student at the Presentation Convent, while Kevin, now 18, was in a position to assist in the business.

For their father, the fear of being discovered on the streets of Dublin forced him to spend considerable time indoors, but not idly. His passion for working with wood had its reward as he passed the days making finely crafted tables, one in particular – a chess table – which was inlaid and beautifully polished. The solitude, though, may have weighed heavily on him, and missing his children could have prompted a heartfelt inscription on a table he gave to Bríghid, one that is still in use today:

Dom inghean dhilis

Bríghid ní Buachalla

Beatha agus beannacht

Agus and bórd seo

Maille leis an nguidhe go raibh Grásta Dé

Agus A bheannacht aici I gcómhnaidhe

Gurab amhalig do'n t-é do rinne.

[To my faithful daughter

Bríghid ní Buachalla

Long life and blessing

And this table as well

Together with the prayer that the Grace of God

And His blessing be with her always.

May the same be with the one who made.]

His love and aptitude for woodwork was recognised in May of the following year at a Kildare Feis Committee Meeting, when a proposal by Senator Cummins that ua Buachalla be appointed one of the vice-presidents was passed. The following month they decided 'that a substantial prize – to be known as the Donal Ó Buachalla prize – would be awarded for the best exhibit of woodwork at the Feis.'[1]

After some weeks, with raids and arrests unrelenting and communication difficult, ua Buachalla did make the occasional visit to the Maynooth area. In a letter written many years later, Paddy Mullaney mentioned that they met after he escaped from the Curragh on 20 August and before being arrested again on 1 December, when his column had to surrender after a four-hour battle near Leixlip. These visits would have involved 'safe houses' which Domhnall could avail of. Willing facilitators would have been plentiful.

Bothered that the Free State authorities may have had an idea that he was living in Ranelagh, ua Buachalla eventually decided to leave Castlewood Park and move to another safe house. Military pension documentation of that period suggests that his benefactor was Frank Burke, headmaster at St Enda's, who was listed as a person willing to verify that at that time, Domhnall was '*a d'iarraidh a bheith saor ó charcair*' – 'avoiding capture'.

Those days of relative solitude would have given him time to reflect on the deprivation and destruction that had surrounded his life since the Easter Rising, particularly the periods he spent behind bars. Allied to that, as the months drifted by, he became a virtual spectator as comrades with whom he had fought for freedom, had been incarcerated with and had built a steadfast relationship with were now dead. Four in particular stand out, their ages ranging from 31 to 52, and only one of the four departed in peaceful circumstances.

On 5 June 1922, while Collins was repudiating the election Pact in Cork, ua Buachalla was one of six men who spoke from a platform in Naas, urging a huge crowd to support both the Pact and his fellow anti-Treaty candidates. Among the other speakers were Éamon de Valera, Austin Stack, Robert Barton and Harry Boland, who was elected to the First Dáil with ua Buachalla.

Less than two months later and only a few weeks after Cathal Brugha's funeral, Boland woke at 2.00 a.m. to the sound of a raid while staying at the Grand Hotel in Skerries. A large body of soldiers, backed up by an armoured car, surrounded the building and a party of six soldiers entered the room in which Boland slept. He made an unsuccessful attempt to seize a gun from one of the troops and then rushed out into the corridor. After firing two shots at random and calling on Boland to halt, the soldiers brought him down with a third shot. He died in St Vincent's Hospital on 2 August.

Ten days later, at the age of 50, Arthur Griffith passed away. Having orchestrated the rise of Sinn Féin and later led the delegation of Irish plenipotentiaries to negotiate the Treaty with the British Government in London, he subsequently drifted into poor health. A visit to a nursing home for tonsillitis followed, and while he seemed well as he set out to return to his office, this was not the case as the President of Dáil Éireann then fell forward, unconscious. Within hours, he was dead.

One of the pall-bearers who carried Griffith from the Pro-Cathedral in Dublin was Michael Collins, little knowing that within twenty days of the death of his erstwhile comrade, Harry Boland, and ten days after Griffith's demise, his own young life would be extinguished in the county that reared him. While Griffith's passing came as a major blow to a government striving to enforce the Treaty in the face of unprecedented hostility, the shooting of Collins at Béal na mBláth on 22 August 1922 rocked the nation. The Government's message on 24 August to its citizens read:

People of Ireland: The greatest and bravest of our countrymen has been snatched from us at the moment when victory smiled through [the] clouds upon the uprising of the Nation to which he had dedicated all the powers of his magnificent manhood.

The genius and courage of Michael Collins lent force and an inspiration to the Race, brought the long fight against the external enemy to a triumphant end, which had become almost a dream, and swept before it the domestic revolt, which tried to pluck from your hands the fruits of that triumph – your unchallenged authority in the land.

In every phase of the awakened activity of the Nation – constructive, administrative, executive, military – the personality of Michael Collins was vivid and impelling. He has been slain, to our unutterable grief and loss – but he cannot die. He will live in the rule of the people.[2]

These words contrasted with those of Liam Lynch, Chief of Staff of the IRA, who complimented his colleagues in the 1st Southern Division on the action at Béal na mBláth. However, he did add a rider that 'nothing could bring home more forcefully the awful, unfortunate national situation at present, than the fact that it has become necessary for Irishmen and former comrades to shoot such men as M. Collins'.[3] It is estimated that over half a million people either watched or were involved in the funeral, described by revolutionary, journalist and historian, Desmond Ryan:

Brains of lead and eyes of glass as the cortege, three miles long, moved swiftly with its army of wreath-laden, crepe-draped lorries, its seventeen bands moaning Handel's Funeral March, its archbishops and bishops in solemn canonical robes, its advance guard of cavalry, its generals, captains and grey-green firing party, fifty strong with rifles reversed, and buglers in the rear, its mourners afoot and in coaches, file after file of working men, clerks, students, clergymen, women, officials, all passing swiftly in the wake of the coffin on an eighteen-pounder gun-carriage … the sun pouring down on six miles of spectators as the procession flashed by with mournful pride to Glasnevin, where O'Connell's lime-white Round Tower soared sentinel to the newest corner and comrade in the Irish Pantheon.

Mourners afoot, mourners lining the streets, mourners on the roofs, with sun pouring down and the silence of doom over all as the funeral march stops and Dublin follows, looks on in wondering heartache and stupefied anger, sobs quietly and pays a last homage to Michael Collins in his coffin drawn by six stable horses to an eternal sleep in the heart of his nation, dark hair quiescent now, vibrating accent stilled, and determined jaw set forever.[4]

Whether ua Buachalla's association with Collins in Frongoch and the Dáil, and his son's collaboration with him while they were both resident in Cullenswood House overcame sufficiently any feelings of resentment the Civil War had generated to attend the funeral will never be known. The probability is that, had they been able, both would have made their way to the funeral that day.

A Friendly Welcome

The execution of Erskine Childers on 24 November had a deeper resonance for ua Buachalla. Two weeks previously, Childers was arrested by Free State forces in Glendalough House, Co. Wicklow, on the 10 November. He was tried by a military court on the charge of possessing a semi-automatic pistol on his person in violation of the Emergency Powers Resolution. Writing in *The Irish Press* in 1932, Sylvester Clarke, an associate of Childers in his final months, which were spent on the run in west Cork publishing a southern edition of *An Phoblacht*, recalled the gun: 'It was a little black automatic, effective only at very short range. It was a troublesome weapon. It fitted his waistcoat pocket so snugly that it could only be withdrawn with difficulty. One day it was so firmly wedged in that it took over ten minutes to remove it, and thenceforth he carried it pinned to his shirt-front beneath a lapel of his waistcoat. On no account would he part with it. "You see", he explained, "it is a souvenir which Michael Collins gave me during the trouble."[5]

Convicted by a military court and sentenced to death on 20 November, Childers was executed four days later at Beggar's Bush Barracks while his appeal against the sentence was still pending. In a spirit of reconciliation before his execution, he shook hands with the firing party. Dorothy Macardle wrote 'that even in England this execution was held by jurists to be a judicial murder'.[6]

Childers' demise, though, would not have greatly displeased Kevin O'Higgins, who stated on 27 September 1922 in Dáil Eireann that the able Englishman who is leading those who are opposed to this Government has his eye quite definitely on one objective … the complete breakdown of the economic and social fabric. So that this thing that is trying so hard to be an Irish nation will go down in chaos, anarchy and futility … he keeps steadily, callously and ghoulishly on his career of striking at the heart of this nation … and it is our duty to take what we consider are the most effective steps to check this headlong race to ruin.[7]

Childers was born in London to Robert Caesar Childers, a translator and oriental scholar, and Anna Mary Barton from Glendalough House in Wicklow. When Erskine was 6 his father died and his mother passed away six years later. The five children were sent to the Bartons at Glendalough where they enjoyed life, and Erskine Childers came to identify himself closely with his new country, despite being a product of the English upper classes. Initially a clerk at the House of Commons, he fought in the Boer War, joined the Royal Navy as a lieutenant in the Volunteer Reserve in 1914 and was awarded the D. S. C. (Distinguished Service Cross) in the Royal Naval Air Service.

In January 1923 ua Buachalla received a letter from Childers' wife Mary, who was living at their Dublin residence in Bushy Park Road:

A Chara,

Forgive my long silence. I have even now not been able more than to begin to answer all the wonderful letters that have come to us about my husband's death. I cared deeply for your message of sympathy, for your prayers and your close sharing with us in our grief and in the glory of his death; and I shall treasure your letter for our children to have.

Will you come to see me when this is possible? I think you know how friendly a welcome awaits you.

Is mise, le meas mór,

M. A. Childers.

PS: In a short time I will send you some things he wrote just before the end, which I know you would care to have.[8]

The papers Mary Childers intended to send never materialised, as a note on her letter written in 1940 by ua Buachalla indicated. The reason was revealed at the time of her death in 1964, when it became known that she desired any writings based upon the extensive and meticulous collection of papers and documents from her husband's involvement in Irish politics be locked away until fifty years after his death. In 1974 they were handed to Andrew Boyle, whose biography of Childers, *The Riddle of Erskine Childers,* was published in 1977.

Clarke's article in *The Irish Press* revealed that pressure from the Free State troops forced Childers to constantly change the location of his printing press in the south. From Ballymakeera he went to Renaniree, on to Coolmountain, then on to Dunmanway, to Kealkil and eventually Cork, a location which he felt was unsuitable as the probability of being caught was constant. Clarke went on to explain that for some time Childers had been planning to collect and collate information about the London negotiations that was known to few but himself. The essential documents were in Dublin and he decided to travel there, 'although everyone tells me in the most comforting way that if I am captured I will be shot'.[9]

On 25 October he set off with his old friend David Robinson, moving up-country on bikes, on foot, across a river in a flat-bottomed boat, in a hired car provided by republican well-wishers and, eventually reaching Glendalough House after dark on 3 November. His biographer, Andrew Boyle, recalled that 'Robinson insisted on prowling around the estate at all hours, "with Miss Barton's pistol in my hip pocket"', to enable his friend to rest and start his writing. There were Free State troops in the vicinity, and only when neighbours reported that the troops had marched off towards Dublin did Robinson decide to relax his vigilance.[10] Quoting Robinson, he continued:

> I had hardly closed my eyes when I heard Miss Barton rushing down the corridor. She said the Free State troops were in the house. I ran to the hall and saw them at the end of the stairs. I shouted to them 'Is Captain Byrne there?' as he had been a friend of Bob Barton's and was the only man who knew the layout ... he then came forward. I asked him what he wanted and he said 'we've come to raid the house'. Miss Barton joined me and asked him where was his warrant. 'This is no time to talk of warrants,' he said, and struck her with his rifle. At that moment, Erskine appeared from his bedroom nearby with the little souvenir revolver Michael Collins

had given him. They seized him. Then I was arrested. It was the early evening of November 10.[11]

Referring to Childers as a 'mischief-making murderous renegade', Winston Churchill believed that 'no man has done more harm or shown more genuine malice or endeavoured to bring a greater curse upon the common people of Ireland than this strange being, actuated by a deadly and malignant hatred for the land of his birth. Such as he is may all who hate us be'.[12] In Childers' farewell letter to his wife from prison, he stated:

> I have belief in the beneficent shaping of our destiny – yours and mine – and I believe God means this for the best: for us, Ireland and humanity. So in the midst of anguish at leaving you, and in mortal solicitude for you, beloved of my heart, I triumph and I know you triumph with me ... I hope one day my good name will be cleared. I felt what Churchill said about my 'hatred' and 'malice' against England. Don't we know it isn't true and what line I ever spoke or wrote justifies the charge? I die loving England and passionately praying that she may change completely and finally towards Ireland.[13]

De Valera had no doubts about a man whose son, Erskine Hamilton Childers, would become President of Ireland in 1973: 'He died the Prince he was. Of all the men I ever met, I would say he was the noblest'.[14]

As ua Buachalla mourned for the friends he had lost, all of them younger men, he would have been aware that the Constitution Bill introduced on 18 September by William Cosgrave was close to implementing the Treaty between Britain and Ireland. What he could not have perceived at that time was the significance it would have for him in later life. Included in Article 58 was the appointment of the Governor-General, his remuneration and where he would live. Thomas Johnson, on behalf of Cathal O'Shannon who was the Labour Party T. D. for Louth-Meath, moved that this clause should be deleted and was backed by Gavan Duffy who seconded the proposal – and objected strongly to the stipulation that the Governor-General was to be paid a salary of £10,000.

'In each of the three Dominion Constitutions,' he said, 'you will find an express provision for leaving it to the Parliament of the Dominions to decide how much this gentleman shall have. That is the express provision, and we must get into this Constitution an equally express provision for leaving it to the Dáil.'[15] The insertion of a provision concerning the Governor-General's establishment was also, he pointed out, a distinct departure from the practice in those Constitutions. The Government would not accept an amendment to the article. 'It is a vital clause on which we stand,'[16] Kevin O'Higgins stated. A decade later, the matter would again be a contentious topic for Dáil discussion – as would ua Buachalla's appointment to the position of Governor-General and, beyond that, his pension in 1937.

Cease Fire, Dump Arms

Éamon de Valera announced the re-organisation of Sinn Féin on New Year's Day 1923, stating that it was 'the only visible means by which the national forces can be again re-united, brothers reconciled, and the programme of national regeneration and social justice undertaken with enthusiasm and in earnest.'[17] No convention had been held since the *Árd-Fheis* of 22 May 1922, when the Collins–de Valera Pact was endorsed. The new offices were in Suffolk Street and the move was welcomed by republicans. But the ever-rising tide of bitterness that de Valera mentioned in an Irish-American paper, *The Irish World*, was clearly evident as the Republican Army increased activities, and executions by the National Army escalated.

A growing belief that the Civil War was becoming an exercise in futility in which brother was fighting brother took seed in Liam Deasy's mind. The Bandon-born Deputy Chief of Staff of the Irregulars was in the process of formulating his ideas for the Army Executive when he was arrested on 18 January 1923, tried a week later and sentenced to death. But the following day, as the Government became aware of his views, a stay was put on the execution, and Deasy was persuaded to sign the following document on 29 January 1923:

> I have undertaken for the future of Ireland to accept and aid in an immediate and unconditional surrender of all the arms and men and have signed the following statement: I accept and I will aid an immediate and unconditional surrender of all arms and men as required by General Mulcahy.
>
> In pursuance of this undertaking, I am asked to appeal for a similar undertaking and acceptance from the following: E. de Valera, P. Ruttledge, A. Stack, M. Colivet, Domhnall O'Callaghan, Liam Lynch,

Con Moloney, T. Derrig, F. Aiken, F. Barrett, T. Barry, S. MacSwiney, Seamus Robinson, Humphrey Murphy, Seamus O'Donovan, Frank Carty, and for immediate and unconditional surrender of themselves after the issue by them of an order on the part of all associated with them, together with their arms and equipment.

Liam Deasy.[18]

Rather than announce Deasy's change of direction immediately, the Government held it back until late on 8 February when 600 prisoners in Limerick Jail 'made an earnest appeal for peace in a communication sent to Major-Gen. Brennan'[19] and provided the press with both stories for the morning of 9 February. In conjunction with this news, the papers of that day also announced, through General Mulcahy, that 'the Government are prepared to offer amnesty to all persons now in arms against the Government'.[20] It was clever news manipulation, designed to enthuse the pro-Treaty population and entice those who were losing their appetite for defiance.

The papers also published a lengthy explanation from Deasy of his rationale for peace moves, which was introduced with a government warning that it 'contains statements and insinuations contrary to fact'.[21] In it he stated that the Free State Government had, 'by originating and pursuing a policy of murder, forced the hand of those whose outlook was national and not sectional' and that 'both sides had ample strength to carry on for an indefinite period'.[22]

The sole response to Deasy from his comrades was a letter signed by Liam Lynch on behalf of the Republican Government and Army Command, stating that his proposals could not be considered. Yet the wind of change continued to blow. Under the headings 'Proclamation' and 'Offer of Amnesty', the Government's enticement to the Republicans read:

(1) Bearing in mind the acceptance by Liam Deasy of an immediate and unconditional surrender of all arms and men, and knowing that the reasons dictating to him that the acceptance must weigh also with many leaders, and many of the rank and file who have found themselves led step by step into a destruction that they never intended, but which has been the sequel of the line of policy adopted by those to whom they looked for leadership.

(2) Notice is Hereby Given: That with a view to facilitating such a surrender, the Government are prepared to offer amnesty to all persons now in arms against the Government who, on or before Sunday18[th] February 1923, surrender with arms to any Officer of the National Forces or through any intermediary.[23]

The on-going horror of the war was epitomised by the Ballyseedy Cross Affair in Kerry shortly after midnight on 7 March 1923. Following the death of two Free State privates and three officers while searching for a republican arms dump at Knocknagoshal which was mined, nine prisoners were taken in a lorry from Ballymullen Prison in Tralee out to the Castleisland Road. The hands of the prisoners were tied behind their backs, and each man was tied by hand and leg to the person beside him. A rope was passed around the nine men holding them in a ring, their backs to a log which had a mine attached to it. The soldiers then retreated and exploded the mine.

Eight men were blown to pieces and the soldiers, thinking that all had been killed, filled nine coffins with the remains, unaware that Stephen Fuller had been blown clear by the force of the blast. Badly burnt, the native of Kilflynn dragged himself to safety in a nearby house and subsequently went on the run until the Civil War had ended. He lived to tell the horror story, which debunked the Free State Army's initial statement that the prisoners were clearing a mine which had been laid by their comrades in the IRA. Fuller was later a successful candidate for Fianna Fáil in the 1937 and 1938 elections.

The plight of the republicans countrywide prompted an executive meeting on 24 March in the Nyer Valley in County Waterford. Attendees included Liam Lynch, Austin Stack, Frank Aiken and Éamon de Valera, among a group of ten. A peace resolution was defeated but within three weeks the IRA's Chief-of-Staff, Liam Lynch, had been killed while fleeing from Free State troops in the Knockmealdown Mountains. The Republican Army Executive met again near Mullinahone on 20 April and after the election of General Frank Aiken to replace Lynch, it was agreed, with one exception, that the Army Council and the Republican Council should negotiate on two principles:

1. The sovereignty of the Irish nation and the integrity of its territory are inalienable.
2. Any instrument purporting to the contrary is, to the extent of its violation of the above principle, null and void.

On 26 April a unanimous decision was made in Dublin that de Valera should enter negotiations, with a temporary suspension of hostilities by the Republican Army to be put in place. He released a statement to that effect the following day, with Aiken adding an addendum for the Irish Republican Army:

> In order to give effect to the decision of the Government and Army Council embodied to attached Proclamation of this date, you will arrange the suspension of all offensive operations in your area as from noon, Monday April 30.

> You will ensure that – whilst remaining on the defensive – all units take adequate measures to protect themselves and their munitions.[24]

Proposals and rejections followed. *The Irish Times* suggested 'that the only real obstacle which remains is Mr de Valera's attitude to the Oath of Allegiance'.[25] Days later the Republican Cabinet and Army Council confirmed that peace would be maintained. An order was made on 24 May to 'cease fire' and 'dump arms'. In announcing it, de Valera told his army that 'the sufferings, which you must now face unarmed, you will bear in a manner worthy of men who were ready to give their lives for their cause. The thought that you have still to suffer for your devotion will lessen your present sorrow and what you endure will keep you in communion with your dead comrades who gave their lives, and all those lives promised, for Ireland.'[26]

Although the Civil War had officially concluded, the Free State Government had a 'mopping up' exercise in mind. Arrests continued; detention without trial also. And with no state of war in existence, they had a problem, which was quickly addressed. A Public Safety Act was passed through the Dáil on 2 July to legalise further detention.

Government strength was reflected at the Wolfe Tone Commemoration at Bodenstown Churchyard in late June. More than 1,000 troops were accompanied by bands from the Curragh, Athlone and Kerry, and special trains brought sizeable contingents of the public from Dublin and neighbouring districts to watch General Mulcahy, in the presence of President Cosgrave, place a wreath on the grave. The *Kildare Observer* reported that 'it was a magnificent display, carried out by troops whose training and service have made them second to none, and much enhanced the significance of this year's commemoration'.[27] This contrasted with the previous day, when the *Observer* reported 'a small gathering of mainly women', among them 'Mrs Pearse, Mrs James Connolly, Miss Mary MacSwiney, Miss K. Barry, Mrs McKee, Mrs Bryan, Mrs Cathal Brugha, Mrs Mellowes, Mrs Ginnell, Mrs Seumas O'Kelly, Mrs ffrench-Mullen, Miss Maloney and Mrs Stuart. A wreath from Mr de Valera was brought by Mrs Brugha.'[28] Talking to the press on 23 July, de Valera explained Sinn Féin's thinking:

> The war, so far as we are concerned, is finished ... If there were a free election, so that the republicans could adequately present their programme to the electorate, and if we were elected in a majority, our policy would be to govern the country on Sinn Féin lines as in 1919, refusing to co-operate with England in any way until England was ready to make with us such an arrangement as would make a stable peace possible; that is, an arrangement consistent with the independence and the unity of our country and people as a single State.
>
> If the present conditions of suppression continue, so that republicans are precluded from appearing before the electorate, and that we are elected in a minority, the elected republican members will all refuse to take any Oath of Allegiance to the King of England, will meet apart, and act together as a separate body, working along Sinn Féin lines for the honour and welfare of our country and for her advancement among the nations.[29]

By 15 August, de Valera had been jailed without trial and would not be released for almost a year. Nominated to stand in Clare on 27 August, and opposed by Eoin MacNeill, he drew unprecedented crowds to a rally in Ennis that day, before saying as he was taken away, 'I am glad it was in Clare that I was taken.'[30]

Ua Buachalla Back in Custody

Having eluded the Free State Army through the Civil War, Domhnall ua Buachalla would have had reason to believe that he might return to Maynooth and make up for lost time with his family, but if he did, the belief was, unfortunately, short-lived. In his interview with Ernie O'Malley, Mick O'Neill stated that ua Buachalla avoided arrest until after the Civil War, but with the announcement that a General Election would take place on 27 August, he was re-arrested and interned, although the official records in the Military Museum do not record the fact. It was Government policy at that time to seek out opposition candidates who had run in the previous elections, in particular those that had been elected, for internment.

By early August, Cumann na nGaedheal had selected three candidates to stand in Kildare – George Wolfe, Simon Malone and Thomas Lawler. Labour nominated Michael Smyth and Hugh Colohan while John Conlon was the choice of the Farmers' and Ratepayers. Contrary to expectations, and at a late juncture, the *Kildare Observer* reported that the Republicans were running three candidates. 'On Saturday last, Mr Charles Daly, Returning Officer, sat at the Courthouse, Naas, to receive nominations for the three seats to be filled … all the candidates, except Messrs. D. Buckley, Art. O'Connor and Thos. Harris (Republicans), who were interned, were present.'[31] Thomas Harris, of Caragh, they explained, 'had escaped some months ago from Newbridge Internment Camp' but was 'arrested on descending from the platform having presided at Miss MacSwiney's meeting in Naas a couple of weeks ago'.[32] The paper mentioned that, contrary to expectations, there were nine candidates nominated, Thomas Harris being added 'at the last moment'.

At one of the few anti-Treaty candidate meetings, Mrs Terence MacSwiney addressed a gathering in Athy, switching from an opening address in Irish to English, saying that some of those listening to her 'might not understand their language'.[33] She was forced, therefore, 'to speak to them in the language of the enemy', but she hoped 'it would not be necessary much longer to speak the language of the foreigner'.[34] She went on to emphasise that she was out for a Workers' Republic:

> For the present, they had to get the Government out and the way to do that was for them to vote Sinn Féin … She knew Arthur O'Connor very well; he was a great personal friend, he was a great supporter of the Irish language and he was in O'Connell Street during the fighting last year with Cathal Brugha. During that trying time, Arthur O'Connor fought bravely and worked very hard. Donal Buckley was also an old veteran in the movement and he was a fine type of Irishman. She did not know the other candidate, Thomas Harris, but from what she had heard of him, she was satisfied he was worthy of their support. Everything had been done to prevent them taking part in this election.[35]

Although the Civil War had ended, the Republicans were in no position to make a concerted or viable challenge to Cumann na nGaedheal, deprived as they were of so many experienced national leaders, and had to rely on the enthusiasm of youth and the drive of the women who had represented them at Bodenstown. While the Kildare papers filled many pages with reports on pre-election meetings in the county, the Republican candidates had been silenced.

An example of their loss of power was reflected at a meeting of the Naas Sinn Féin Club in June, when those present were asked to vote 'on the application of funds on hand in view of the winding up of the organisation and on the establishment of the new national organisation, Cumann na nGaedheal.'[36] When the Chairman, Rev. P. J. Doyle, C. C., asked an attendance of about seventy to vote on the passing on of the money to Cumann na nGaedheal, only eight – five men and three women – went to the side of the hall that was indicated for dissenters. The group was then asked to leave as the Sinn Féin Club meeting had concluded.

While the movement of funds from Sinn Féin to the Government Party was an indicator of how people in Kildare were likely to view the election, an eight-column advertisement in the *Irish Independent* on the morning of polling would have given ua Buachalla a lift – it was scripted by a staunch friend, Archbishop Mannix of Melbourne, a towering, and at times, controversial figure in the political and social life of Australia. It read:

ARCHBISHOP MANNIX says:

'Every Enemy of Ireland, without exception, is on the side of the

Free State. Don't be one of these enemies.'

VOTE FOR SINN FÉIN AND IRELAND A NATION.[37]

Another advertisement read:

LOADING THE DICE:

TERRORISM ALL OVER THE COUNTRY

The Sinn Féin seals for ballot boxes have been seized in Ballina.

No Sinn Féin literature has been allowed to be posted up all week in the great township of Rathmines, Co. Dublin.

Sinn Féin bill-posters in O'Connell Street, Dublin, Clonmel, Thurles and many parts of the city and country have been savagely beaten by men openly carrying revolvers.

Carlow Sinn Féin Election Rooms were practically gutted.

At Castlebar, all Sinn Féin literature and equipment was seized by armed bodies.

Reports of these widespread outrages on freedom of election cannot be published.

At the Central Headquarters of the whole Sinn Féin Party in Ireland, armed men ejected the staff and stopped all work for six hours at the most critical stage of election preparation.

Happily, YOU are safe.

Tyranny cows slaves; it only makes men more resolute to end it.

Shall England claim that the Irishmen of 1923 alone of all white races voted away their country's independence? Never!

Manhood of Ireland, assert what liberty is left you.

VOTE FOR SINN FÉIN

AND YOUR OWN UNPARTITIONED REPUBLIC[38]

Michael Gallagher wrote that the 1923 election was more significant than is often recognised:

It marked a vigorous effort by interest groups to win control of the Dáil, and to transform the whole basis of the Irish party system. Labour, which was still merely the political wing of the Trade Union

Movement, nominated over twice as many candidates as in 1922, and the Farmers' Party, representing the Farmers' Union, over four times as many as in 1922. Franchise rights were given to women between 21 and 30 for the first time. The number of Dáil seats soared from 128 to 153 and the constituency boundaries were re-drawn. Three were eight-seaters and Galway had a nine-seater.[39]

For ua Buachalla, the first count provided him with fifty-four votes more than he received in 1922 when the constituency was Kildare/Wicklow; elimination, which would not have come as a surprise, arrived after the fourth count. Art O'Connor dropped 740 from 1922 to 3,620, while the decision to bring in Tom Harris at the last moment rebounded, as he was eliminated on the first count with 206 votes and the loss of his deposit. The seat that Robert Barton won in 1922 was lost and Barton himself failed to get elected in Wicklow. Hugh Colohan (Labour), John Conlon (Farmers') and George Wolfe (Cumann na nGaedheal) had comfortable margins in taking the three seats.

A brick and stone-layer, Colohan had stepped into the political arena in 1922 when taking second place behind Christopher Byrne, the Pro-Treaty Sinn Féin candidate, on the first count. The foundation of his strength

FOURTH DÁIL KILDARE 1923		SEATS 3 QUOTA 4,674
CANDIDATES	FIRST COUNT	FINAL FIGURES
Hugh Colohan (Labour)	4,300	4,787
John Conlon (Farmers)	3,650	4,941
George Wolfe (Cumann na nGaedheal)	2,186	4,624
Arthur O'Connor (Republican)	2,276	3,620
Thomas Lawler (Cumann na nGaedheal)	1,920	2,643
Michael Smyth (Labour)	1,712	1,931
Daniel Buckley (Republican)	1,492	1,572
Simon Malone (Cumann na nGaedheal)	950	956
Thomas Harris (Republican)	206	206

Irish Elections 1922–44: Results and Analysis: Michael Gallagher

was the working-class vote – particularly in Newbridge and Athy – allied to the spin-off from the sizeable military presence on the Curragh, which provided employment on many fronts.

The *Leinster Leader* reported that 'there was the usual crop of amusing incidents. In Mayo, for instance, an old woman on entering the booth avowed her determination to vote only for Michael Collins and de Valera, while down in Kilkenny, an illiterate insisted on voting for Archbishop Mannix'.[40]

When the Fourth Dáil assembled on 19 September 1923, the William Cosgrave-led Cumann na nGaedheal had increased its representation by five to sixty-three; the Republican Party had moved up to forty-four, an increase of eight. De Valera received 45 per cent of the votes (17,762) in Clare; Professor Eoin MacNeill received 22 per cent (8,196). If these figures were slightly encouraging for the Republicans, they were mindful that the agreement to end the Civil War some months earlier had done little to free almost 15,000 men and women who remained in custody.

CHAPTER 15

Contrasting Views

International attention briefly settled on Ireland on 10 September 1923 when the Irish Free State was admitted to membership of the League of Nations, but the national emphasis had shifted from elections to the numbers still in confinement without trial. On 14 October, 462 men went on a hunger strike in Mountjoy and in quick succession other prisons and camps followed suit. Figures given at the time by Sinn Féin were: Cork 70; Kilkenny 350; Dundalk 200; Gormanston Camp 711; Newbridge 1,700; Tintown 1, 2, 3, Curragh Camp 3,390; Hare Park 100 and 50 women in the North Dublin Union.

The hunger strike did not receive unanimous support from the IRA, but the Chief of Staff, General Frank Aiken, maintained that the decision to go down the road of starvation was for each man and woman to make as an individual. He went so far as to tell the O/C of the Kilmainham prisoners that 'under no circumstances, even should a comrade die, are you to call off the hunger strike – of course you have no power to order any man off. I believe your fight will do more for the cause than a thousand years' war.'[1]

In Kildare, a County Council meeting report indicated that Tom Harris had been released in October and that the Government were trying to put the squeeze on Art O'Connor. The Council was debating what response they might make to a Sealed Order of the Local Government Department signed by Earnán de Blagd, removing O'Connor, Assistant County Surveyor, from office. Harris was quick to act, stating that the intent of the Ministry was in every way in keeping with the old Castle traditions:

I can see no other reason for Mr O'Connor's removal from office than that he is a political opponent. It is not through Mr O'Connor's own will that he was unable to carry out his duties. About sixteen months ago he was arrested in Dublin, fighting, as he believed was his duty, in support of the Government of the Irish Republic, which was attacked … once again might has overcome right.[2]

Support for Harris was vociferous, particular from the Labour members, Hugh Colohan and Michael Smyth, and a proposal from Joseph Cusack which read 'that we, the Kildare County Council, protest against the Sealed Order from the L. G. Department removing Art O'Connor from the office of Asst. County Surveyor, and that we demand his unconditional release in order that he can resume his duties, as, in our opinion, it is the wishes of the people of the county that he be retained in office.'[3]

Even though O'Connor had served the county exceedingly well for many years, the fact that it was passed unanimously by ten representatives from disparate parties testified that harmony was seeping back into daily life. A proposal from Grogan immediately afterwards was also passed: 'That this Council demands the immediate release of all political prisoners, including the 500 at present on hunger strike in Mountjoy and prevent further loss of life …'[4]

In the Dáil on 16 November, William Cosgrave insisted that there would be no respite for those who chose to go down the avenue of starvation. In response to Patrick Baxter, he promised brevity in his reply:

My statement will take only one minute … a hunger strike will not effect the release of any prisoner either now or in the future, and I would like to tell the Deputy who has just spoken that my view of his responsibility in this business is very great indeed. If a single prisoner on hunger strike dies, the attitude of the Deputy who has spoken, and of other people who, by their acts or resolutions or their talk about this gigantic failure, the most gigantic failure that these people who threatened the State ever entered into – this failure of the hunger strike – must not be overlooked.

About 300 out of 7,400 are on strike, and there are people in this country waiting to see who is going to die, some thinking it will mean the release of the remainder, and others thinking it will afford an opportunity to the face-savers to call off this hunger strike. They are held according to law, sir, every one of them. The law of this country, as passed in this Parliament, is not going to be repealed by speeches and appeals to sentiment. We are a free people now, entirely independent, and we are responsible for the conduct of this country. We are taking that responsibility and no appeal to sentiment is going to detract us from it.[5]

With winter conditions taking hold in jails and camps that ranged from basic to brutal, the Government were giving little succour to the interned, but on 18 November, following an appeal from Cardinal Logue that the Government should release before Christmas all those not guilty of crime, defiance weakened. When Commandant Denis Barry died on 20 November in Newbridge Camp after thirty-four days on hunger-strike, and Volunteer Andy Sullivan in Mountjoy after forty days, the prisoners' organisation in Kilmainham took a sensible course.

> On November 23 a number of men had been fasting for forty-one days and their recovery, even if they took food now, was in doubt: there were 167 men who had been fasting for over thirty-four days. Tom Derrig and D. L. Robinson, the leaders, asked permission to visit the prisoners for the purpose of calling off the strike. This was immediately arranged and they were escorted, still fasting, although they had been forty-one days without food, on a tour of the camps and jails. Only when they had made the round and called off the hunger strike everywhere did they take food.[6]

At a meeting of the Kildare County Council on 2 December, James Behan asked to have 'item fifteen on the agenda disposed of so that he would know whether he was entitled to be present at the meeting or not'.[7] The item was to consider the disqualification of Messrs. Buckley, Moran, Doran, McGrath and Behan, owing to non-attendance at meetings. The Chairman, Mr Phelan, said they were glad to have Mr Behan back. He thought Mr Behan, Mr Buckley and Mr Moran were absent through no fault of their own. No order was made.

The first public indication that ua Buachalla was a free man and had returned home was a letter written on 5 December 1923. It was read at a Kildare County Council meeting on 25 February 1924, in which he thanked the Council for inviting him back.[8] In March he again wrote to the Council, informing them that he would not be standing for re-election at the end of May; the Council minutes show that on the proposal of Patrick Whelan, seconded by Richard McCann, it was resolved that Michael Fitzsimons be appointed Chairman of the County Council in replacement of Domhnall ua Buachalla.

Before concluding, however, the Council agreed that a public meeting would be held in *Droichead Nua* on 4 May 1924, seeking the release of all political prisoners still incarcerated, and ua Buachalla was asked to be the principal speaker on the day. A numerically strong presence of political representatives heard him open the meeting by stating that 'he had come to let them know he was of one mind with those who wished to have the men in jails liberated. There was no longer any reason why there should be prisoners of war in Ireland. It was a shame for them to have to admit there were. It was a cause of shame to the whole country.'[9]

Later on, Michael Smyth proposed the following resolution: 'That we protest against the continued detention of political prisoners in Ireland and Great Britain; and we demand the immediate and unconditional release of all Irish political prisoners, whether sentenced or un-sentenced.'[10] Elaborating, he said:

> The resolution had been passed at several meetings of the County Council and by other public bodies during the last twelve months, but at their last meeting they did not believe it was any use in passing such resolutions and they decided to call the public meeting today, and he was sorry there was not a larger crowd present.
>
> It was a non-party meeting ... and there was no reason at all, now that the fighting had ceased over twelve months [ago], why these prisoners should be detained. They were told that they could not, with safety, be released, but in the face of that statement, during the past six months, thousands had been set at liberty. There were still seven or eight hundred men in jail. It was time the people took action – they were taking this matter lying down.[11]

James O'Connor, a brother of Art, said that 'the vast majority were men who stood between them and the Black and Tans, who fought the old fight and took different sides when things came to a crisis. Most of them had already spent terms in other jails and they had endured great hardships, as he knew well from listening to the stories of his brother.'[12] The resolution was passed by acclamation. Concluding, ua Buachalla said that he knew 'many young men were in jail because there was nobody to advocate their release' and appealed to those present 'to work and co-operate in demanding that the prisons be cleared'.[13]

Back home at this stage was his nephew, Cathal, who had been captured by Free State troops on his way back to Kilcock after escaping from Dundalk Jail. Interned in Gormanston Camp, he was released on 19 November 1923.

Ambitious Plans

More elusive during the Civil War was ua Buachalla's future son-in-law, Mick O'Neill, who was forced to go on the run. He continued to plot with Commandant Paddy Mullaney and the pair, in conjunction with two IRA officers who were formerly British Army airmen, were involved in an ambitious plan in November 1922, to capture Baldonnel Aerodrome (now Casement Aerodrome), a former British army Air Force Base, and bomb Beggar's Bush Barracks, the Curragh Military Camp and Leinster House. In his interview with Ernie O'Malley, O'Neill spoke of deserters from the Free State army coming to them at Hazelhatch by canal boat and how feasible he thought the operation was. James Durney recalled how Mullaney assembled his men in Celbridge:

> He was joined by Jim Dunne's column, Tom Harris with men from the 4th Battalion (Prosperous) and W. Byrne with the 6th Battalion column, bringing the number of republican troops to eighty. One hundred unarmed men were promised from the Dublin Brigade, but only twenty, under the command of IRA GHQ officer, Todd Andrews, turned up. The purpose of these men being unarmed was to enable them to carry off the stores and equipment they expected to capture.[14]

Andrews called off the operation as he felt they had insufficient numbers. The men returned to their areas, but were recalled on two occasions. 'The Kildare men were fiercely enthusiastic about the attack – the first large-scale action of its kind planned by the anti-Treatyites.'[15] Jim Dunne maintained that 'the bombing of Leinster House might have ended the war'.[16] He blamed Andrews for the failure.

The north Kildare/Meath Brigade men were a constant problem for the Free State Government, regularly damaging bridges and communications.

On 1 December 1922 they ambushed a ration lorry on its way to Maynooth, which became known as the Pike's Bridge Affair. The goods were taken, the lorry burned, and Vice-Commandant Lynam and his quartermaster were taken prisoners, the driver having escaped. Troops from Maynooth, Trim, Naas, Lucan and seven officers and forty men from Portobello Barracks, with a Whippet armoured car arrived. During a battle that raged for four hours, Private Joe Moran was shot in the head and killed, but the republicans – eventually realising their position was hopeless – surrendered. Durney wrote that

> twenty-two republicans, three of them badly wounded, were captured, complete with their arms: one Tommy gun, one Lewis machine gun, twenty-one rifles, one Mauser 'Peter the Painter' automatic pistol, five revolvers, five bombs and over 1,000 rounds of assorted ammunition. All were initially taken to Kilmainham Goal, where five were recognised and identified as deserters from the National Army ... they had deserted from their posts at Baldonnel Aerodrome several days earlier with their arms and joined Mullaney's column.[17]

They were convicted and executed by firing squad on 8 January 1923 in Portobello Barracks. Mick O'Neill, Paddy Mullaney and the rest of the column were taken to Mountjoy. Since they were captured under arms, they faced the death penalty, but after much agonising, debate and consultation, Commanding Officer Mullaney authorised his men to sign an undertaking, which read: 'I promise that I will not use arms again against the Parliament elected by the Irish people or the Government for the time being responsible to the Parliament, and that I will not support in any way such action. Nor will I interfere with the property of others ...'[18] Eight signed, but Mullaney and four others held out. In mid-March 1923, these five were informed that they were due for trial by military court at the end of the month. Trial would inevitably mean the death sentence. Finally, Mullaney authorised the remaining men to sign the undertaking, and did so himself.

Mullaney was sentenced to four years' imprisonment. Military records show that Mick O'Neill was sentenced to seven years penal servitude for 'armed attack on National Forces and possession of arms', as was Tim Tyrrell, who was one of the Maynooth men who walked to the GPO with ua Buachalla in 1916. O'Neill was eventually released on 7 June

1924, collecting £1.10 before departing, the residue in his prisoner cash account. There was a bonus a few weeks later when another £1 dropped through the letter box, with the authorities admitting there had been an error in calculating his account. Pressure from de Valera convinced the Government to allow the bodies of the five Volunteers executed after the Pike's Bridge Affair to be transported to their home towns. On 31 October 1924, the re-interment of 22-year-old Anthony O'Reilly took place in Donacomper graveyard, attracting a gathering that was estimated at 3,000. The *Leinster Leader* reported on the event:

> Business was completely suspended in Celbridge, shops were shuttered and windows were blinded during the period of the interment. Large contingents of IRA forces were present under Commandant P. Mullaney, Vice-Brigade Commandant, M. O'Neill ... members of Sinn Féin Clubs, *Cumann na mBan* and public bodies also marched in the funeral procession ... impressive scenes were witnessed at the graveyard as the remains was carried by members of the column through a double file of Volunteers to the graveside where Fr Furlong, C. C. recited the prayers. As the grave was filled in, Mr Donal O'Buachalla recited the Rosary in Gaelic ...

In the course of an oration in Irish and in English, Mr Buckley said that during the Anglo-Irish War, their feelings on an occasion such as this would have mainly been of pride for the man who had made the supreme sacrifice for the land he loved, but today their pride and sorrow were mingled with a greater grief that the deaths of Volunteer O'Reilly and his comrades should have been the work of Irishmen.

Their great pride, however, was that brave and gallant Irishmen like O'Reilly and his comrades were to be found who unflinchingly made the supreme sacrifice and faced death proudly for the cause of the Republic and the independence of the land they loved. The people should now, facing that grave, recognise the fact, if they had not already done so, that the name 'Free State' was a misnomer. So far from being free, it was the negation of freedom and represented tyranny and suppression in its worst form ... they would not be called upon to fight ... but peace would only come with the final triumph of the Republic ... there was now other work to be done, just as important as the work of the soldiers of the IRA, and in that work he asked them to join and give whole-hearted co-operation. They would thus bring the final day of triumph, which was steadily approaching them, nearer, and they would all witness the establishment of the Irish Republic.[19]

The Defiant Face of Maynooth

As the roads out of Celbridge disgorged the huge gathering that had attended O'Reilly's re-interment, ua Buachalla would have returned to Maynooth by car with the family's sole driver at the wheel. After studying engineering in Bolton Street, it was not surprising that Joe opened a garage beside the family business in Double Lane (now Buckley's Lane) and had just received permission from Kildare County Council to install petrol pumps outside the shop. Motor Traffic in *an Saorstát* doubled from 1923–24, and in terms of motor taxation, Kildare ranked eighth in the country, so with a prime site on the main Dublin–Galway road, diversification was a good business move.

Both Domhnall and Joe had been through a lot: they were both survivors of their country's most troubled years, both well acquainted with prison life and both were gunmen who had come face-to-face with death. Now, aged 58 and 26 respectively, both entered into a new phase of life. Awaiting their return was Domhnall Óg, 24, who was confined to living close to the house and shop; Síghle, at 22, a caring mother figure to her siblings and those employed in the business; Kevin, 20, the student; Bríghid, 18, just out of school and an ideal second-in-command to her elder sister; Máirín, 16, whose life would be dedicated to looking after '*Athair*', as he was addressed by his children throughout his life; and Séadna, 13, the most outgoing of all, who made life his playground, and everyone a friend.

When ua Buachalla told the mourners at the graveyard that 'they would not be called upon to fight', and that 'there is other work to be done', he would have been expressing thoughts that comforted him. By nature he was the quiet, cultural nationalist. Armed conflict would have been anathema to him. But fighting for the right to speak and write and identify with his native tongue was an imperative. To resist oppression and demand freedom, whatever the cost, warranted total commitment. It was these influences that transformed him into the rebellious nationalist. He might not have been at ease on the journey, but he was certainly willing to travel the hard road.

Having worked assiduously with like-minded men in preparing Maynooth for the Rising, he was happy to hand over to the battle-hardened Tom Byrne as they left the College, and subsequently was at the bidding of Connolly and Pearse in the GPO; through the War of Independence he was the defiant face of Maynooth in the centre of the town, the facilitator for those around him. And when the Treaty was welcomed by the majority, he stood with republican friends throughout the Civil War, the majority of whom were on the run or imprisoned.

There is a relevant line in ua Buachalla's sworn evidence, given before the Military Service Pensions interviewing officer on 22 December 1941, when he stated that he had no engagement with the Free State Forces. The report states that 'in fact, since Easter Week, Mr Buckley had no engagement with enemy forces of any description'.[20]

The term 'engagement' would imply facing the enemy with a gun, with the means to kill. So despite making munitions in his house, blowing up bridges and barracks, passing on guns from headquarters with instructions on who was to be 'taken out'; despite being prepared to defend his business with a gun, to shelter Dan Breen and to be involved in a number of ambushes, ua Buachalla's only known victims were shot at the corner of Parliament Street and McBirney's in Aston Quay in 1916. It is believed there were others during that week, which, by choice, he did not mention.

Killing British soldiers in a fight for national freedom was demanded of him in the line of duty. It would have been far more difficult for him to take the life of another Irishman in the Civil War. The fact that he was either imprisoned, or on the run, during that period took the gun out of his hands. His words in Celbridge certainly signified an acceptance that the day had arrived when there was no future in terminating life, that there had to be another way.

More than a decade had passed since he was imbued with the spirit of Pearse, when he was willing to walk with his neighbours and step in behind the leaders in the GPO. Now, although equally determined and knowing that more had to be achieved, he would also have realised that fortune had treated him kindly, that he was going home to embrace his seven children. He could have been Anthony O'Reilly at Pike's Bridge, or O'Reilly's friend, Leo Dowling from Carna, near the Curragh, who wrote to his parents on the eve of his execution from his cell in Kilmainham:

> I hope this letter won't make you unhappy. Well, we must always take things as they come as whatever is the will of God will be done.

Though 'tis a good thing to be happy in this world, 'tis better to be happy in the next. This world is really only a valley of tears, so you must not fret when you read this letter.

My dear mother, you know little about the charge against me. Well, after about one month my sentence has come and though 'tis the extreme penalty 'tis all for the best. Thank God I'll have the priest now in short[ly], and don't fret ...

Please God I'll be able to walk out tomorrow without flinching. I admit it appears a hard thing but it's the end and I like to die a soldier ... I will close now asking God to bless, protect and strengthen you, my own dear mother and father.

Your loving son,

Leo xxxx[21]

The decade would also have taken a physical and mental toll on ua Buachalla. Easter Week and Frongoch, Kilcock and Dundalk Jails, nine months evading national forces, internment and duties as a member of Dáil Éireann and Kildare County Council all intertwined with days and nights of subterranean activity.

More damaging than any physical hardship would naturally have been the loss of those closest to him. His father's and mother's deaths in 1915 and 1918 respectively might have been seen as nature's way of bringing ripe old age to a conclusion, but Sinead's passing in 1918, at the age of 48 must have been heart-rending, and it's possible that there was insufficient time for him to adequately grieve the loss in the turbulent years that followed. For a small and slight man, he had a big heart, and any thoughts of taking a back seat and slipping into early retirement would have been instantly dismissed. Nevertheless, in his wildest imaginations he could not have anticipated how life was going to treat him over the following twelve years.

A Confused Army of Officers

Of immediate – but more mundane – importance, was the sum of £26.4s., which had been taken from his room while he was away from home in

November 1922 a figure that would today convert to almost 1,700 euro. A headed business statement to Charles A. Brennan, Army Finance Officer, dated 5 May 1924, followed an earlier letter to the same address, requesting the army to reimburse him. It read:

Nov. 1, 1922 To amount of Cash taken from premises during raid by

Lieut. Patterson, Naas, £26.4s.

Copy of receipt for above

1 November 1922

Taken from the house of Mr D. Buckley

3 Flash Lamps

1 Pocket Book

1 Coil Wire

1 Bdle. Literature and the sums of

£22.9s. & £3.15s.

£26.4s.

Signed: James Pickering, Sergeant.

N.B. Above-mentioned James Pickering, Sergt. was on that day acting under command of Lieut. Patterson (of Naas).

D. ua B.

A subsequent internal memo read:

Case 19

Name: Donal Buckley, Main Street, Maynooth.

Amount: £24.9s.

Seized: 2 November, 1922.

This money was found in Mr Buckley's private room and was contained in two envelopes. In one there was £3.9s. and also a receipt for ammunition bought – the receipt had the initials T. H. (probably Thomas Harris, Caragh.) The other contained £21 and on the outside envelop was written '£2 paid to Mrs Sault whose husband was arrested by the Staters in July' ... Lt. Patterson made the seizure and he forwarded the money and all documents in connection therewith to Lt. Comdt. Dunne, Trim. Steps are being taken to get this money passed to the Army Finance Office.

A letter dated 29 February 1924 was sent to the Army Finance Officer from Collins' Barracks containing the following information:

Regarding the sum seized from Donal Buckley, Main Street, Maynooth – I beg to report that I have not yet succeeded in having it collected. Comdt. Dunne admits having seized the money, and states he forwarded it to the Command Intelligence Officer – Comdt. Shanahan.

Comdt. Shanahan denies having received the money. To fix responsibility, and to ascertain from whom the money should be recovered, I am convening a Court of Inquiry. I shall inform you of the result ...

For D. A. A. G., Dublin Command.

Comdt. Dunne's letter read:

To: Director of Intelligence, General Headquarters, Parkgate Street.

Loss of Irregular Monies

With regard to your query of 7th inst. concerning the loss of Irregular monies by ex-Comdt. Shanahan, Intelligence officer of the Easter Command, I beg to inform you that at the period stated, i.e.

November 1st 1922, I was acting as Divisional Intelligence officer of the last Eastern Divison.

On the 2nd November Comdt. Flynn who was I/O of the Maynooth area, reported to me that his I/O Lieut. Patterson had found in Mr D. Buckley's house at Maynooth a sum of £21, together with other documents relating to the purchase of arms, and there was no reason to doubt but that the cash was for illegal purposes. I instructed Comdt. Flynn to forward the cash to me, and I reported the matter to Comdt. Shanahan. A considerable time elapsed and not having got instructions from him as to its disposal, I enquired when at his office, and he instructed me to forward it to him, as there would probably be enquiries about it. On my return to Trim I sent my assistant, Lieut. Gibney, to Shanahan at Portobello Barracks with the cash and ordered him to obtain a receipt from Shanahan, which he did.

In January 1923 I was transferred to the Curragh and on my departure I handed over files etc. to Capt. Hughes, including a file relating to this cash, also receipt which was in the file. Ex-Lieut. Gibney and myself are available at any time to prove before any court that Shanahan received the £21 taken from Buckley's house.

B. Dunne. Comdt. Camp I.O.

Another letter on 6 May to the Director of Intelligence threw a damper on any hope of progress:

The preliminaries were being proceeded with when it was found that the two persons chiefly connected with the matter – Comdt. Shanahan and Lieut. Gibney – were demobilised on 7 March ... in the circumstances I am afraid I can do nothing further in the matter.

K. Gray, Captain.

On 15 May, Captain Gray sent another letter to the Army Finance Officer:

I regret I cannot comply with your request ... On receiving notice of his demobilisation, Comdt. Shanahan instructed the various District

I. O.s serving under him to destroy all files in their possession. His instructions were carried out by Capt. Hughes, who burned all Intelligence Files in Mullingar District, the file containing the receipt in question presumably being amongst the others.

The affair moved on when the Army Finance Officer received a letter on 21 June from the office of the Minister for Finance, signed by John Houlihan:

> I am directed to state that, in view of the correspondence which passed between you and the Command Adjutant of the Eastern Headquarters, and especially the fact that the two officers principally concerned have been demobilised, he does not see how anything can be gained by pursuing the matter further. Should the case be eventually decided in favour of Mr Buckley, the question will still remain to be considered whether the sum in question is to be charged against Army Funds.

The next missive to arrive on the desk of the Army Finance Officer was from Colonel F. MacEntee at the Office of the Adjutant General, dated 10 July, which stated that the matter was under investigation with the G. O. C. Eastern Command and he would issue a report shortly, which duly arrived:

> It seems highly probable that the money ultimately came into the hands of Commandant Shanahan, who is not now a member of the Army; we have not, however, any documentary evidence. Your suggestions, after perusal of file, are requested, please.

Letters continued to fly to and fro until one arrived at Griffith Barracks, dated 11 November 1925, from Joseph Shanahan:

> A Chara,

> Relative to the deduction of £21 from my Army Services Pension, I wish to state emphatically once more that no money captured outside the City of Dublin was ever handed over to me during my period of service in Portobello Barracks. During this period I only held the rank of Lieutenant and was only concerned with Dublin, as was my position when I was subsequently transferred to Keogh

Barracks. It was not until much later in 1923 that I was appointed Intelligence Officer of the Dublin Command.

On taking over in Collins' Barracks, I found one of the drawers of my desk locked. This desk, I might mention, was sent from Portobello Barracks some few days before. On bursting this locked drawer I discovered a sum of money amounting to £24 odd. This money was wrapped up in a sheet of blank paper, no indication being given as to its origin or the reason why it was left there. I immediately phoned the Director of Intelligence – Col. Neligan [a great ally of Michael Collins, who was known by the soubriquet, The Spy in the Castle] – informing him of my find. He instructed me to use it as I thought fit, in obtaining information which would be of use to our department. I can now state that I used it with a certain amount of success and also used some of my own money. The statement made by Col. Neligan, proving this latter statement, is already in your hands.

I do not in the least doubt that the money that was captured by Comdt. Dunne was sent to Portobello Barracks, but it was not handed to me and I did not know of its existence. The only way I can reconcile the money found in the drawer and the captured money, is that the amounts are somewhat similar and the desk was previously used in Portobello Barracks.

Trusting that this statement will finally dispose of a problem which has caused me a great deal of worry and pecuniary embarrassment.

Joseph Shanahan.[22]

So what started in 1922 in ua Buachalla's room had run until the end of 1925. Shanahan's letter was the final one in the file, and while John Houlihan's memo would suggest that ua Buachalla might have been refunded the money, it may have been too late, as the time for purchasing arms and ammunition had slipped by.

CHAPTER 16

Republicans Living in a Hostile Land

Not only had the election to the Fourth Dáil been a dispiriting one for Domhnall ua Buachalla, whose vote dropped to 8 per cent, it was also devastating for republicanism. Their flame had dimmed dramatically, not least because of the Oath and a Constitution that prevented them from taking their seats in the Dáil. As the Free State government enforced a suffocating regime, republicans were living in a hostile land and many went abroad to start a new life. The number of Irish emigrants to countries outside Europe had been under 20,000 in the year 1924, but had escalated to a figure in excess of 30,000 in 1925.[1]

As by-elections frequently cropped up from 25 October 1923, the status quo was maintained – until November 1924. When Hugh Kennedy, the sitting T.D. in Dublin South, was appointed Chief Justice, a youthful Seán Lemass topped the poll, an outcome characterised by his defeated Cumann na nGaedheal opponent, Séamus Hughes, as an endorsement of the policy of war.

In his first attempt to become elected, Lemass failed. The by-election in March of that year, saw James O'Mara win comfortably by a margin of 2,245 votes. This, however, was one of few setbacks in Lemass's political career, which culminated in him succeeding Eamon de Valera as Taoiseach in 1959. The loss of that by-election was not a huge blow; the great tragedy of his life was a domestic shooting accident when he was 16, which resulted in the death of his 22-month-old brother, Herbert. He also lost an older brother, Noel, a captain in the IRA, who was abducted in Dublin in June 1923 and summarily executed after the Civil War had ended. The mutilated remains were found on the Featherbed Mountain near Sally Gap in October of that year, and identified by his father from a garment he had been wearing. Three years later the family suffered the loss of another brother, Patrick, who died of natural causes at the age of 19.[2]

Further encouragement for the Republican Party on the same day originated when an army officer, Henry Coyle, was sentenced to three year's imprisonment for financial irregularities, which disqualified him from the Oireachtas. The people of the North Mayo constituency elected Dr John Madden by a margin of 870 votes. It was a reverse for Cumann na nGaedheal, who had a strong candidate in Professor Michael Tierney, a son-in-law of Eoin MacNeill and later President of University College Dublin.

These setbacks for the Government prompted a little unease, reflected in the words of a writer in the *Irish Independent* the following day: 'In every constituency, the anti-Treaty Party has shown more perfect organisation, more energy and more enthusiasm than their opponents ... is Cumann na nGaedheal going to profit by the lessons of those election results? No political party can ever afford to rest on its oars, least of all a party confronted with a powerful opposition ...'[3]

After a further nine by-elections, the opinion column was more upbeat. 'The voters have, by overwhelming majorities, reaffirmed their acceptance of the Treaty, their confidence in the Government's efforts for peace and prosperity, and their rejection of the futile policy of the Treaty's opponents.'[4] Nevertheless, the Republicans could point to Oscar Traynor's election in Dublin North and Samuel Holt's in Leitrim-Sligo. While they were coming from a low base, the party's vote had continued to escalate.

Any feeling of satisfaction from the elections that might have permeated Republican minds was fast disappearing as the year drew to a close. On 4 December, under a heading 'AGREEMENT SIGNED IN LONDON', the *Irish Independent* reported that the powers conferred on the Boundary Commission had been revoked, ensuring that the border was not going to be altered; that the Free State was released from the obligation to pay any share of the British War Debt, but that it would take over the British liability for compensation for malicious damage during the whole period of the Anglo-Irish war from 21 January 1919.[5] The Agreement was signed in the House of Commons by the *Saorstát*, and the six-county and British

Governments. It was hailed in Britain by all parties; President Cosgrave and Kevin O'Higgins saw it as a basis 'for a sure and lasting peace'; Sir James Craig spoke of it 'with feelings of rejoicing and relief'.[6]

Éamon de Valera responded to the Agreement by claiming at a meeting in O'Connell Street on 6 December: 'Let no Irishman think that we have gained anything further than avoiding the possibility of being cheated further',

> At the commercial rate of interest, say 7 per cent, such as capital employed in industry might be expected to yield, the accumulation would be over £3,000 million. That was the counter-claim put in by our delegation in 1921 and it was substantiated by colossal figures of Sir Robert Giffen showing the loss of industrial wealth ... but the worst of this bargain was that it would be said we had sold our countrymen for the meanest of all considerations – money.[7]

A group of Labour deputies, active in opposing the Pact, sought to enlist the assistance of the Republicans and summoned a meeting of all elected deputies to the Shelbourne Hotel on 10 December. More than fifty attended, about thirty-eight of whom were anti-Treaty, including de Valera. On the authority of a party deputy, the political correspondent of the *Independent* reported that a number of Republicans were willing to vote and that the subject had been on the minds of the party for some time. But while they talked, Dáil Éireann gave a Second Reading to the Bill, confirming the London Agreement. The number in favour of the Bill was seventy-one, with twenty against; so even with a full complement of forty-seven deputies present, the Republicans would have been outnumbered. The promise of a split in Sinn Féin soon became reality. Richard Dunphy recalled the lead-up to it:

> Revisionism had taken a firm hold in Dublin, where the Reorganization Committee, under Lemass, was engaged in a steady overhaul of the party, as can be seen from the 'Organisation Notes' published each week in *An Phoblacht*.

> The formal split came in March 1926, by which time Lemass was already heading his letters to the pro-de Valera faction with his preferred title for the new party – The Republican Party. A special conference was called to consider de Valera's motion that once

the Oath of Allegiance be removed, 'it becomes a question not of principle but of policy whether or not Republican representatives enter the Dáil'. The motion was narrowly rejected – 223 votes to 218. The next day de Valera resigned as Sinn Féin president. On 29 March, the leading revisionists, including Lemass, Gerry Boland, McEntee and P. J. Brennan, tendered their resignations from the Sinn Féin Standing Committee.

On 2 April a meeting was held to decide the name of the new republican organization: de Valera, sensitive to the mystic pull of the Gaelic and the political value of a certain ambiguity, insisted upon Fianna Fáil against Lemass's preferred title. Eventually a compromise was agreed – Fianna Fáil the Republican Party.[8]

The inaugural meeting was held on 16 May 1926 in the La Scala Theatre in Prince's Street, Dublin and from that day forward a powerful organisation took control, with the *cumann* or branch being the focal point. Fianna Fáil leader Micheál Martin recalled the words of Seán MacEntee during this period of intensive activity by the party's itinerant organisers: 'For more than five years hardly any of us were at home for a single night or any weekend. Lemass bought up four or five second-hand Ford cars, "old bangers"' and with them we toured every parish in the country, founding Fianna Fáil branches on the solid basis of old IRA and Sinn Féin members.'[9]

For ua Buachalla, a Ford car and driver was readily available at home. The fact that he was also totally committed to de Valera'a vision for the future made the decision easy for him when the Sinn Féin split occurred and signed the necessary pledge:

I, Domhnall ua Buachalla, hereby undertake that if elected I will support Fianna Fáil (Republican Party) in every action it takes to secure the independence of a United Ireland under a republican form of Government, and, in accordance with its constitution, I will not take any position involving an oath to a foreign power and I further undertake that if called upon by a two-thirds majority of the National Executive of Fianna Fáil to resign that office, I shall immediately do so.

He was immediately involved in putting the new organisation on a sound footing in Kildare. It grew in tandem with the rest of the country and by

May 1927, close to 800 *cumainn* were in operation following hundreds of public meetings used to spread the new gospel among the grass roots.

On 9 April 1927 the *Leinster Leader* told its readers that the General Election campaign for the Fifth Dáil had been set in motion the previous Sunday when 'an enthusiastic gathering crowded the Market Square in Kildare to its utmost capacity to hear the policy of Fianna Fáil propounded'.[10] The meeting was fixed for 6.00 p.m., 'but long before that hour motors and other vehicles were arriving in a steady stream by all roads ... the arrival of the Moone Fife and Drum Band further enlightened the animated scene, and the enthusiasm of the throng found vent in welcoming the standard-bearers – Donal Buckley, Maynooth, and James Cregan, an engine driver from Railway Cottages, Kildare and a member of Kildare County Council'.[11] They had been selected at a convention in March, with Seán T. O'Kelly presiding on behalf of the National Executive.

> As the candidates mounted the stand, they were followed by Seán Lemass, Tom Harris and many other prominent politicians. James Behan, a member of Kildare County Council from Monasterevan, who opened proceedings, immediately informed the meeting that 'the principles guiding Fianna Fáil were the same today as they were in the past, when standing united they almost achieved the goal they had set out to reach ... he could not help feeling that they were rapidly getting back to the position they occupied in 1918, when imperialism under the guise of false nationalism was swept aside and the way cleared for a general advance to full nationhood.'[12]

Last to address the meeting, ua Buachalla brought his audience back to 1918 and the first day he entered the Dáil. He informed the gathering that

> when he took his seat he had raised his hand and solemnly taken an oath, and when he took that oath he meant to keep it. When the Treaty debates were in progress, following December 1921, he was approached by people who brought all the pressure they could to bear on him, to prevail on him to break his oath, but he refused to do so. If he was returned again by the people of Kildare, he would renew his oath against all foreign dominations and the defence of the Republic ... he was not seeking re-election now to represent any class or section of the people. All were alike to him, and he

would devote himself to the interests of the farmers, labourers, shopkeepers, tradesmen, all creeds and classes …[13]

Turning to 'the purest people of their race', the inhabitants of the Gaeltacht, he spoke of how the Free State administration had failed them:

> The land they tilled was barren for the most part, their holdings were small and uneconomic, and existence was hard and difficult. Those people were the descendants of the old Irish families who had been driven by Cromwell to 'Hell or Connacht'. When their claims to better treatment had been proved by a commission set up to investigate their conditions, the recommendations were turned down, and the Minister of Agriculture declared there was not sufficient land to go around in order to improve the people's lot. The people may die of starvation, while the rich lands were given over to the bullock.[14]

Before concluding, he said that the meeting was a surprise to him in its dimensions and gave him more hope than he felt for a long time, and that 'the forces of nationalism were again resurgent, and that these would give the final blow to imperialism in this election'.[15]

The following Sunday in Athy it was the Churchtown Pipers' Band that warmed up another sizeable audience, and just as ua Buachalla started to speak there was, as the local reporter put it, 'some diversion caused by blows being struck, but quietness was quickly restored'.[16] He spoke about a nation struggling to feed itself and focused on the O'Sullivan family in Berehaven, Co. Cork, three of whom had died of starvation. 'It was known six months before that these people were in poor circumstances, but because they had some land, they could not get relief. Could such a thing happen in any civilised country – that a man and his family should be let die from starvation?'[17] He continued:

> In Germany, where there are seventy million people, the administration work is done by General Hindenburg at a salary of £7,000, and here in this little nation of twenty six counties, we have a Governor-General, a man whom the nation could easily do without, drawing £37,000 a year for ruling three and a half million. It was a monstrous thing that the country should be ruled in such an extravagant fashion.[18]

He then turned his attention to the Ministry of Fisheries:

> The total expenditure of this Department was £102,971, salaries and allowances amounted to £21,826, travelling, £3,000, incidental expenses, £200, telegrams and telephones, £250, fishing development, £34,025, rural industries, £31,120, sea fishing protection service, £9,500, contribution to the International Council, £550, the study of Sea Mirror Marine Works, £2,500; total, £102,971.

> The Department consisted of a minister, a private secretary, secretary, staff officer, two higher executive officers, six junior executive officers, nineteen clerical officers, writing assistant, shorthand typists, typists in addition to the outdoor staff … the money expended on this particular branch had not been to help the fishermen of Ireland, but give good fishing to the 'plus fours' and 'Oxford bags'.[19]

The split in Sinn Féin saw the party enter the election with only fifteen candidates, its aim to retain seats held at the dissolution. In no area did it make more than one nomination. In contrast, Fianna Fáil ran eighty-seven candidates, nine less than Cumann na nGaedheal. In summarising matters that affected the election, Michael Gallagher wrote:

> Cumann na nGaedheal's style of government managed to antagonise an ever-increasing number of interests, and some of these rallied behind the National League. The League had been formed in September 1926 under the leadership of William Redmond, and appeared to mark an attempt to revive the old Irish Parliamentary Party. However, it also developed policies in favour of the rights of tenants and publicans, winning the endorsement of groups representing both interests. Another small party to contest the election was Clann Éireann, which favoured much the same policies as Fianna Fáil.[20]

An immediate priority for Fianna Fáil was to find the necessary finance to fund a campaign. To that end an appeal appeared in the local paper on 30 April 1927, offering the people of Ireland 'an opportunity of arresting the downward process of the nation into national bankruptcy, which has resulted from the Free State administration, and of turning it along a path of prosperity and independence'. Subscriptions could be sent to Donal Buckley in Maynooth and Professor R. P. Farnan at Bolton Castle, Moone.[21]

On the first day of May, the bandwagon moved from Prosperous to Allen and Allenwood. The *Kildare Observer* suggested that 'if public manifestation of support counts for anything, the Fianna Fáil organisation and its candidates have every reason to be satisfied with the reception accorded to them and their policy'. Ua Buachalla turned his attention to the Minister for Foreign Affairs:

> He told us a few weeks ago that he did not know of any country in the world that had progressed so much as Ireland in the past four years. What brazen effrontery a man must have to stand on a public platform in Ireland today and make such a statement, in face of the widespread economic distress that prevails. In the past four years of foreign misrule, the population of the country has declined by 210,000 ... the best bone and sinew of the land, the young and healthy and most energetic are gone ... in the past four years the number of acres under tillage has declined by 170,000, and the number of farm animals by 557,000 ... the burden of taxation tends to crush all industrial initiative ... and worst of all, some people in some parts of the west and south are actually starving.[22]

Two weeks later in Poplar Square, Naas, he had the Freemasons in his sights:

> The Senate, as at present constituted, was dominated by the Freemason element, and since the Free State was established, Freemasonry has grown in strength and today they had far more lodges in the country than ever before. So, Fianna Fáil, if given the proper support, would defeat these sinister influences in their national life, and break down the main barrier that stood between them and those imperial and alien powers that were the implacable barriers to everything Irish.[23]

At Rathangan the following week, two parties arrived simultaneously in search of votes. Philip Ryan was present to speak on behalf of Art O'Connor, who had remained in the Sinn Féin camp, and was now running against ua Buachalla; two friends who believed passionately in a self-governed thirty-two-county Ireland, but with contrasting views on how it should be achieved. One holding fast to set principles; the other believing that a new path could lead to the same objective. A compromise was immediately reached. Tom Harris, a guiding force behind the Fianna Fáil campaign, offered Ryan the opportunity to speak first. When he finished, Harris showed that the bond between the parties remained strong by agreeing with everything that had been said by Ryan regarding Art O'Connor's work and ability 'in the cause they all had at heart – the freedom and independence of the country'.[24] Nevertheless, while there was harmony on the day, O'Connor was a serious obstacle for ua Buachalla as he had headed the Sinn Féin candidates in the 1923 election, amassing 2,276 votes, 784 more than his erstwhile colleague.

Very noticeable in the final days of the campaign was a surge in Fianna Fáil advertising in the *Irish Independent*, where they had been taking serious criticism in leader articles and general reportage. On 3 June, in a departure from the paper's tradition, they permitted Fianna Fáil to place an advertisement, which covered two-thirds of page one of the paper with a banner headline, 'FIANNA FÁIL IS GOING IN', and a sub-heading 'FIANNA FÁIL IS WINNING EVERYWHERE'.[25] Beneath it was another advertisement, possibly prompted by the newspaper's proprietor, with the message 'Mr de Valera, who burned your house yesterday, complains today of the smell of petrol'.[26]

On 6 June, Fianna Fáil topped a half-page advertisement with a quote from Kevin O'Higgins made on 29 May 1927:

> 'We fought the Civil War, interned 12,000 men, executed seventy seven, and spent £25,000,000 of your money – for what? To put the plain people of Ireland in the saddle.'

Beneath it were the words:

> 'The tremendous price in blood and money taken from the Irish people by the Free State Government has accomplished nothing because the Oath of Allegiance to a foreign king keeps the Irish people out of the saddle.'

On voting day, Fianna Fáil made their final play for the nation's support by taking another full-page advertisement in the *Independent*. The election campaign had drawn to a conclusion in a blaze of propaganda, with William Martin Murphy pocketing a sizeable sum in advertising revenue, much of it from Fianna Fáil, who had been fundraising abroad. The voices of 376 candidates fell silent: in thirty constituencies, 152 would get the approval of the electorate.

In the hours after polling stations closed in Kildare, the Naas Courthouse became the focal point for gardaí, election officials and the agents of the candidates as the boxes arrived, and at 10.00 a.m. the following morning, the Returning Officer, Charles Daly, supervised the checking of ballot boxes. To the surprise and annoyance of many, the counting of votes did not commence until Saturday morning, but within a few hours ua Buachalla would have been relieved. The votes were stacking up well for him: he would be elected. Sinn Féin's nationwide collapse had seriously affected the highly respected Art O'Connor, who was struggling, as were Cumann na nGaedheal, but it was almost impossible to predict who would top the poll.

By early afternoon, ua Buachalla was running neck-and-neck with Hugh Colohan, and as the count finished he had a margin of just fifteen votes over his closest rival. He totalled 4,127 (18.62 per cent) to the Labour candidate's 4,112 (18.55 per cent), but both were well short of the quota, 5,542. The fact that James Cregan was the second candidate to be eliminated provided ua Buachalla with 810 second preference votes; from Art O'Connor he benefited to the tune of 760. Combined, these figures brought him to 5,732 – 190 over the quota. Sinn Féin had gone under, Labour held firm, Cumann na nGaedheal received a wake-up call – and Fianna Fáil had arrived.

As it was almost 7.00 p.m., the count was adjourned until Monday. While George Wolfe (Cumann na nGaedheal), Hugh Colohan (Labour) and John Conlon (Farmers') had the Sabbath to pray and ponder how the numbers would fall the following day, ua Buachalla was in a position to gather the Party team for a celebration – and reflect on an outstanding campaign that suggested they would be around for some time to come.

On the Monday morning, Hugh Colohan was powered over the line when he collected 1,697 votes after the elimination of Michael Smyth. That paved the way for George Wolfe to take the third seat without reaching the quota: the sitting T. D., John Conlon, was stranded. The fact that Art O'Connor did not resign from Sinn Féin when the option arose cost him many votes and eased the way for ua Buachalla.

Having headed the poll, ua Buachalla opened the ritual of thanking the returning officer, stating that 'Charles Daly had shown tact, courtesy and a business-like manner' in fulfilling his duties. He went on 'to express earnestly the hope that Fianna Fáil in its advent to a share of

FIFTH DÁIL KILDARE 1927 (JUNE)	SEATS 3	QUOTA 5,542
CANDIDATES	FIRST COUNT	FINAL FIGURES
Daniel Buckley (Fianna Fáil)	4,127	5,732
Hugh Colohan (Labour)	4,112	7,226
George Wolfe (Cumann na nGaedheal)	2,438	4,496
John Conlon (Farmers)	2,310	3,956
Michael Smyth (Labour)	1,865	2,342
James Bergin (Cumann na nGaedheal)	1,559	1,726
Rupert Trench (National League)	1,415	1,854
Art O'Connor (Sinn Féin)	1,133	1,287
John Bergin (Protectionist)	1,129	1,409
James Cregan (Fianna Fáil)	1,098	1,109
George Henderson (Independent Farmer)	979	979

Irish Elections 1922–44: Results and Analysis: Michael Gallagher

the government of the nation would succeed in lifting the country out of the gloom of the past few years, and also that the other parties in the Government would co-operate with them, and that the combined efforts would succeed in putting Ireland once again on the path to real freedom, progress and prosperity'.[27]

Outside of local politics, other factors influenced the outcome of the election, which the *Irish Independent* was quick to expound on:

> It is the lot of every Government that has been in office for some years, and that has carried through a heavy programme of legislation, to incur some disfavour. The most salutary reform is unpalatable to some section[s]. One cannot tamper with the rent laws without treading upon the feet of either landlord or tenant. One cannot alter the liquor laws without offending either traders or temperance advocates; and one may easily displease both.

> But the reverses that the Ministry has suffered are not altogether explained by the normal consequences of legislative activity ... we are forced to conclude that the overbearing attitude of certain

ministers weighed heavily against Cumann na nGeadheal. There were times when this aggressive truculence amounted almost to insolence, unbecoming [of] the dignity of the office that they held. Some members of the Ministry have on occasion displayed the petulance of schoolboys when subjected to reasoned criticism ... and even their leader has not always been above reproach.[28]

Summing up the results, Michael Gallager said they were notable in three respects: 'Volatility was exceptionally high, reflecting the still somewhat inchoate nature of the battle lines of the party system ... Fianna Fáil practically retained the 1923 republican vote and completely eclipsed Sinn Féin, which won only five seats ... Cumann na nGaedheal slumped to a little more than a quarter of the votes, with especially heavy losses in Dublin.'[29]

The final figures were: Cumann na nGaedheal forty-six, Fianna Fáil forty-four, Labour twenty-two, Independents sixteen, Farmers' eleven, National League eight, Sinn Féin five and Ceann Cómhairle one.

On 23 June 1927, ua Buachalla and the forty-three other successful Fianna Fáil candidates entered Leinster House, where they were met by Col. Brennan, Captain of the Guard, and escorted to a committee room where they spoke with the clerk and assistant clerk. The latter officials emerged in a few minutes and ordered the doors leading to the Chamber to be locked. Other doors in other passages were also locked, and strong guards were placed on them.[30] What were termed 'warm arguments' by the paper developed between officials and the Fianna Fáil deputies, all of whom refused to subscribe to the Oath. Several, including de Valera and Seán T. O'Kelly, attempted to proceed in the direction of the Chamber, but were prevented from doing so.

Backed by qualified support from the Farmers' Party, the National League and some Independents, and with Labour opposed, Cosgrave was re-elected by sixty-eight votes to twenty-two, his offer to stand aside and allow the opposition to form a Ministry not being availed of. And having again appointed Kevin O'Higgins as his Vice-President, as well as managing the workload in Justice and External Affairs, the President would have felt comfortable leading Cumann na nGaedheal into another term of office.

Assassination on a Leafy Road

The external affairs portfolio demanded an early visit to the League of Nations in Geneva for O'Higgins. Naval disarmament was up for discussion in late June, an engagement he felt he could not ignore, but one he did not relish because of the time it would take, especially when there was so much still to be done at home. Early the following month he was again fully engaged in national duties and on Sunday 10 July 1927, he left his home, Dunamase, on Cross Avenue, Blackrock and headed down the leafy road for his usual five-minute walk to the parish church. Alone with his thoughts, little did he know that he had the undivided attention of five republicans.

Turning into Booterstown Avenue, he was confronted by three armed men. What ensued, according to a police statement the following day, shocked the nation:

> A motor car belonging to a Captain McDonnell was stolen in the city on Saturday night ... and shortly before midday yesterday morning this car was driven from Blackrock Road to Booterstown Avenue. It was occupied by three men. The car was parked in Booterstown Avenue, above the junction with Cross Avenue.
>
> Five men were engaged in the occurrence. Two of these men acted as scouts. One of them signalled to the three men when he saw Mr O'Higgins coming down Cross Avenue on his way to Mass at Booterstown Church at about 11.55 a.m. The three men fired on Mr O'Higgins as he turned the corner into Booterstown Avenue. Mr O'Higgins ran across the road and fell on the footway beside the lamp-post outside the gates of Sans Souci, a large residence which was later demolished and is now Sans Souci Park, a small housing development.
>
> The three men then left him, assuming he was dead, and made for their car. Mr O'Higgins raised one of his hands slightly as he lay on the ground. Seeing the movement, the three men immediately ran back to him and each fired one shot at Mr O'Higgins. One bullet penetrated his head through the ear, another bullet entered the body above the heart, and the third pierced the abdomen.[31]

Historian John P. McCarthy recalled the immediate aftermath:

> Eoin MacNeill, whom the gunmen passed [while] running towards their car, was one of the first to arrive on the scene. O'Higgins

remained conscious, although wounded seven times, including a wound in front of the right ear, and suffering a great loss of blood. His first remark to MacNeill was 'I forgive my murderers'. He also told MacNeill to tell his wife Brigid that he loved her eternally. He also gave instructions regarding certain papers on his person.

Several others then came on the scene, including a doctor who had been at Mass and Canon Breen, the pastor of the church, who gave the last rites and who also heard him assert 'I forgive them all'. An ambulance came, which took him to his nearby home where he survived, under the attention of two Dublin surgeons, for nearly five hours.[32]

What the jury at the coroner's court in the Town Hall in Blackrock the following day referred to as a 'cruel outrage' was immediately condemned by Éamon de Valera. 'The assassination of Mr O'Higgins is murder, and is inexcusable from any standpoint.'[33] McCarthy wrote that a less generous but not unique attitude was reflected in the retrospective commentary by C. S. ('Todd') Andrews, an adjutant to republican leader Liam Lynch during the Civil War and later the director of Bord na Mona and executive chairman of CIE: 'It would be hypocritical to pretend that the death of O'Higgins caused a tear to be shed by any republicans; nor were many shed by the general public or his colleagues. He was not a well-liked man. The assassination was worse than the crime, it was a mistake.'[34]

Suspects were hauled in for the murder of the 35-year-old O'Higgins, but none were arrested. The perpetrators – Bill Gannon, Timothy Coughlan and Archie Doyle – were revealed more than fifty years later when a biography of Harry White, a Belfast republican, was published. It was subsequently stated that the killing was contrary to IRA Army Council policy.

Profound Effects

While the days following the assassination were filled with outpourings of anger, grief and tributes as O'Higgins was laid to rest in Glasnevin, the decision of the Government to propose a constitutional amendment on 20 July requiring Dáil candidates to declare before nomination their intention, if elected, to take the prescribed oath, had a profound effect on national politics. In moving the second reading of the Public Safety Bill on 26 July, President Cosgrave said:

The assassination of the Vice-President of the Executive Council is still fresh enough in the public mind to make it a comparatively easy task to establish that the State and the public safety are endangered to such an extent as to throw the duty upon the Government of bringing forward special legislative measures designed to deal with the danger, and to throw upon the Oireachtas the duty of protecting the representatives of the State by granting the powers sought.[35]

The move forced Fianna Fáil's hand. Impotent if they stayed outside, yet held there by principle, it was time to reconsider. Ua Buachalla was one of forty-two T. D.s summoned by de Valera to a meeting in Dublin on 10 August. Shortly after midnight, with the media waiting eagerly for headline news, the momentous decision was issued:

The Fianna Fáil deputies have met and given careful consideration to the position of national emergency, which has been created by the legislation now being pressed through the Free State Parliament. They recognise that this legislation may imperil the general peace and cause widespread suffering; that it disfranchises, and precludes from engaging in any effective peaceful political movement towards independence, all Irish republicans who will not acknowledge that any allegiance is due to the English Crown. Nevertheless, they have come unanimously to the conclusion that even under these circumstances, it is not competent for them, as pledged Republicans and as elected representatives of the republican section of the community, to transfer their allegiance.

It has, however, been repeatedly stated, and it is not uncommonly believed, that the required declaration is not an oath; that the signing of it implies no contractual obligation, and that it has no binding significance in conscience or in law, that in short, it is merely an empty political formula, which deputies could conscientiously sign without becoming involved, or without involving their nation, in obligations of loyalty to the English Crown.

The Fianna Fáil deputies would certainly not wish to have the feeling that they are allowing themselves to be debarred by nothing more than an empty formula for exercising their functions as public representatives, particularly at a moment like this. They intend, therefore, to present themselves at the clerk's office of the Free State Dáil 'for the purpose of complying with the provisions of Article 17 of the Constitution,' by inscribing their names in the book kept for the purpose, among other signatures appended to the required formula. But, so that there may be no doubt as to their attitude, and no misunderstanding of their action, the Fianna Fáil deputies hereby give public notice in advance to the Irish people, and to all whom it may concern, that they propose to regard the declaration as an empty formality, and repeat that their only allegiance is to the Irish nation, and that it will be given to no other power or authority.[36]

Speaking at the celebration of the INF Benefit Society's jubilee in Melbourne a few weeks later, Most Rev. Dr Mannix got to the core of the republicans' decision with greater brevity. Change came, he said:

Because entry to the Dáil had become an absolute necessity. The republicans detested the British Dáil and its oath so much and so justly that they would not touch either until the hateful contact had become an absolute necessity. They entered the Dáil mainly to prevent legislation, which would for all time disfranchise Irish republicans. In that aim they had, he thought, succeeded. It was of course a bitter experience for the republicans: but if a man really needed an operation, it was no use for him to say that he could not submit to the humiliation of the operation table. The operation was necessary for Ireland, and now that it was over, it seemed to him that the patient, though not yet out of danger, was doing as well as expected.[37]

An overnight stay in Dublin on 10 August 1927 gave ua Buachalla time to reflect on the dramatic events of the day and how the fall-out from the murder of O'Higgins had forced his party into a *volte-face,* something that would have troubled him. But pragmatism took him down the road that de Valera had chosen. He was not as upbeat about the decision as President Cosgrave, who remarked the following day: 'I am pleased to see them coming into the Dáil, and I think it is the best thing that has happened during the last five years.'[38] Labour's Thomas Johnson mirrored the view of many citizens:

The entry of Fianna Fáil deputies into Dáil Éireann is a political event of the first importance, opening up an entirely new and more helpful prospect. The situation calls for calm and serious consideration. In my view, it is now possible to do what has not been possible hitherto – to break away from the tragic past and to prepare for a happier future.[39]

Shortly before 11.00 a.m. the next day, ua Buachalla arrived at Leinster House where the party whips – Frank Aiken, Gerald Boland and Seán Lemass – were in conversation with Thomas Johnson and Captain W. A. Redmond, leader of the National League. Colm O Murchadha, Clerk of the Dáil, then took control and administered the Oath of Allegiance, to which the Fianna Fáil deputies subscribed their signatures. This continued until 1.35 p.m. when de Valera arrived and by 2.00 p.m. they had all left the building. *The Irish Times* reported that 'their coming and going had passed almost unnoticed. There were no crowds in the adjoining streets to witness the entry of Fianna Fáil into the Parliament of the Free State.'[40] Later, the party held a lengthy meeting but no statement was made, which prompted the paper's political reporter to write that 'Mr de Valera and his friends are past masters in the art of keeping secrets.'[41]

Ua Buachalla was back the following morning, but not before his leader who arrived at 10.00 a.m. and immediately went to the Committee Room of the Labour Party, where he was joined at 10.30 a.m. by Thomas Johnson; minutes later the coalitionist family was complete when Captain Redmond arrived. They talked until noon.[42] Conferences continued at a hectic rate before lunch was taken at 1.30 p.m. and as the parties entered the chamber just before 2.30 p.m., the House was accommodating more people than ever before; among those who could not obtain seats were the foreign consular representatives in Dublin. One journalist wrote about an 'atmosphere of tense excitement' as the Fianna Fáil representatives 'took possession of the former leading opposition party seats with the Farmers' Party, the National League and the Independent Deputies all mingled together on the centre blocks of seats'.[43]

The battle for power, however, was deferred. The Government did not move the vote for the Creameries Scheme, involving more effective regulation of the dairy industry and persons and co-operative societies within it. The question of the confidence of the House in the Ministry was avoided. Mr Johnson then gave notice to bring the matter to issue on Tuesday when he would move a vote of no confidence in Mr Cosgrave's administration – 'that this House is of the opinion that the Executive Council has not retained the support of a majority of Dáil Eireann'.[44]

Tuesday provided the fireworks. When the motion of no confidence in the Executive Council ended in stalemate, seventy-one votes to seventy-one, the Ceann Cómhairle's vote was registered against the resolution. All parties voted in full strength except the National League, one member of which, John Jinks, in spite of his leader's announcement, abstained; and Labour, who were without Thomas O'Connell, who was in Canada. James Fitzgerald, Minister for Defence, although recovering from an illness, walked into the Chamber with the aid of a stick.

The political Correspondent of the *Independent* described it as 'a great occasion in the life of our elected Assembly ... it will add volumes to its prestige, already high, for the debate on the whole was on a lofty plane, and was conducted with dignity ... Fianna Fáil gave a most striking example of self-restraint and discipline.'[45] The House adjourned until 11 October, with the President intimating that if Cumann na nGaedheal did not win the two by-elections, a general election was in the offing.[46]

If some of the wind was taken out of Fianna Fáil's sails at the failure to bring down the Government, they were becalmed on 25 August when the results from Dublin County and Dublin City South came in. They gave emphatic backing to Cumann na nGaedheal in the by-elections, increasing the party's vote as Dr Thomas Hennessy and Gearóid O'Sullivan were returned. Encouraged by the outcome, the Government immediately dissolved the Fifth Dáil after a life of just two months, well aware that it was still on rocky ground, and set a polling date of 15 September 1927. Explaining his decision, President Cosgrave said:

> The entry into the Dáil of the members of the Fianna Fáil party and the alliance between that party, the Labour party and the National League group has created an entirely different situation to that which was envisaged by the electorate at the General Election.
>
> On the one hand it is quite clear that the present Government could not hope to carry out their programme in the new circumstances. There is no margin of safety ... the alliance which was disclosed at the last sitting of the Dáil can muster seventy-two votes out of a house of 146. Any three members, ill or absent, any two Farmers or Independents voting against the Government, means its defeat.

On the other hand, there does not appear to be any basis for stable government in the alliance. The three parties which have combined to form it have nothing in common but a desire to defeat the present Government. The National League group were returned on the basis of a complete acceptance of and loyalty to the Treaty, and on a programme of reduction of expenditure. The Fianna Fáil deputies were returned following the most definite public statements that they would refuse to take the Oath. The programme of the Labour party differed from both.

I undertook to the Dáil that if the Government were defeated at either of the by-elections, the Dáil would be specially summoned. Instead, the Government won both seats by very large majorities. The people in two very large and important constituencies have pronounced against the proposal to replace the present Government.[47]

As Cosgrave rolled the dice and gave all political opponents just three weeks to persuade the nation that he was not the man to govern for another term, he hit a brick wall. A telegram from the Minister for Posts and Telegraphs, J. J. Walsh, who was in Lucerne, stated that he was resigning from the Government Party, making it patently clear that he was unhappy with the Government's opposition to protectionist policies. It forced Cosgrave to stand for election in Cork Borough as well as Carlow-Kilkenny, his own stronghold.

Political Abstractions and Old Shibboleths

For ua Buachalla, it was probably an election he could have done without. The Government's decision to make it a short and sharp campaign would have put serious pressure on the 61-year-old to get his election team into the field and resist the surge in popularity that the Dublin by-election successes created. He would also have to defend the Fianna Fáil decision to take the Oath, a move that would have been anathema to many of his supporters. Gone, though, was any challenge from Sinn Féin, who decided that they did not have the financial resources to undertake another campaign.

Fianna Fáil records show that ua Buachalla was their only official representative in Maynooth at that time, but the Naas *Comhairle Ceanntair* was a strong driving force behind his campaign. Its committee consisted of Chairman, Rev. T. Burbage, Broadford, Moyvalley; Vice-Chairmen, Tom

Harris and ua Buachalla; Treasurer, J. Connell, Robertstown; Secretary, M. J. O'Donoghue, Naas.

Thomas Murphy replaced James Cregan as ua Buachalla's running partner; Cumann na nGaedheal decided that George Wolfe would be their sole candidate; Independents Rupert Trench, John Bergin and George Henderson opted out; and Art O'Connor no longer had a party to represent. Within the space of a few months, voters were faced with a reduction of five candidates on the ballot paper – and the *Kildare Observer* pushed the Government line as powerfully as ever.

> It is inconceivable that our people should be again deceived by political abstractions or cajoled by old shibboleths into withholding support from the Cumann na nGaedheal Party, which is at present the only safe party with which to entrust the destinies of the nation. In time, no doubt, Fianna Fáil will have learned wisdom and gained experience as active members of the Dáil, but until that time comes, and until they realise that we are a Free State in fact as well as name, it would be most dangerous to hand over to them the control of our affairs, of our property, even of our very lives.[48]

In the same week that the article appeared, ua Buachalla, sharing a platform in Naas with de Valera, warned President Cosgrave that the republicans were wide awake to the snap election, and that the action of Minister Walsh showed how the wind was blowing.

> The Minister for Posts and Telegraphs had cleared out – he had deserted the sinking ship – and left his comrades to go down in it. Writing from Lucerne as to the reasons which prompted his action, Mr Walsh states, 'whatever doubts I have had hitherto on the economic policy of the Government, I have none today, seeing that the Party itself has gone bodily over to the most reactionary elements in the State, who will henceforth control its policy. A government cannot depend on the votes of ranchers and importers.' This election, continued ua Buachalla, was going to be a fight between Irish nationalists and British imperialists.[49]

Having mentioned the great work accomplished by Most Rev. Dr Mannix in contributing £1,000 'as a first instalment' towards the election fund and the fact that Dr Mannix would 'do what he could to release Ireland from the stranglehold of the Masons', ua Buachalla said that 'he hoped the people would show that the Public Safety Act, or the spearhead of Mr Cosgrave's campaign, did not represent the feeling of the country'.[50] He suggested that if they voted Fianna Fáil, 'the sky would not fall'.[51] Stepping up to address the constituents after ua Buachalla, de Valera said that the Act

> tore up twenty-two out of the thirty-two Articles of the Constitution. Those people talked about law and order, but they had no regard for it, as, obeying orders from England, they attacked the Four Courts on the 28 of June 1922, two days before the re-assembling of the Dáil, without consulting the assembly. They had proved insincere in their desires for peace, because on every occasion, instead of responding to an effort to restore peace, they had used the military forces at their command, and they apparently intended to do the same in the future.[52]

Days later in Athy, President Cosgrave was, in contrast, maintaining that Cumann na nGaedheal stood for honesty and 'for putting down the gunman no matter what the cost, and no matter who he was, and who was standing behind him ...'[53]

The decision of Cumann na nGaedheal to run just one candidate in Kildare was a success when it came to polling day. Having finished third in the June election with 2,438 first preference votes (11 per cent), George Wolfe topped the poll this time with 6,497 (29.6 per cent). The fact that there were five less candidates also contributed greatly to the figures. Ua Buachalla finished second with 6,250 first preference votes (up from 18.6 per cent to 28.5 per cent). Both got in on the first count. Thomas Murphy managed a 2.8 per cent increase as second candidate and the party had the highest aggregate vote.

The *Leinster Leader* noted that Cumann na nGaedheal had far more cars to assist voters to get to the stations, that their organisation had improved greatly since June and suggested that the county was 'generally surprised' at Wolfe heading the poll. The paper also noted the extent to which women exercised the franchise, stating that 'they may be said to have voted to a man'.[54]

Speaking at the conclusion of the count, ua Buachalla said that 'Kildare, again, he was proud to say, had shown up well for the republican

SIXTH DÁIL KILDARE 1927 (SEPTEMBER)	SEATS 3	QUOTA 5,493
CANDIDATES	FIRST COUNT	FINAL FIGURES
George Wolfe (Cumann na nGaedheal)	6,494	
Daniel Buckley (Fianna Fáil)	6,261	
John Conlon (Farmers)	3,284	4,555
Hugh Colohan (Labour)	3,251	5,667
Thomas Murphy (Fianna Fáil)	1,694	2,397
Michael Smyth (Labour)	985	1,058

Irish Elections 1922–44: Results and Analysis: Michael Gallagher

movement ... a sign that the people were swinging back to their old allegiance. He was glad also that Labour had succeeded in getting direct representation in the Dáil, particularly since Fianna Fáil had helped them to that position'.[55]

When the Sixth Dáil met on 11 October 1927, the division provided Cumann na nGaedheal with a majority of six, having the support of the Farmers' Party and most of the Independent deputies. Watching affairs in the visitors' area was the Labour leader, Thomas Johnson, who had failed to get re-elected, and was replaced by Thomas O'Connell, who went through many uneasy hours before winning the fifth seat at the South Mayo count. The election, Michael Gallagher wrote,

> ensured that future lines of the party system became much more rigidly defined, 'as the political picture, hitherto highly fluid, settled down into a pattern whose outlines were very clear'. Both major parties made large advances – in contrast to the June election, they won more than 60 per cent of the votes in twenty-two of the twenty-eight territorial constituencies – while all other groups fell back. Cumann na nGaedheal gained votes in every constituency [its advances being greatest in Dublin] and Fianna Fáil in every constituency except Dublin County; neither party lost a seat in any constituency.[56]

The final figures were: Cumann na nGaedheal sixty-one; Fianna Fáil fifty-seven; Labour thirteen; Independents thirteen; Farmers' Party six; National League two.

To mark their performance in the Kildare election, Fianna Fáil held a celebratory demonstration in Naas on 2 October 1927, led by the Kildare Pipers' Band, who paraded through the streets beforehand playing popular airs. Tom Harris presided, and in the course of an animated speech, he was critical of a very hostile press, but pleased that voters were gradually opening their eyes to what has happening to the country.

> Who supported the Cumann na nGaedheal Party? They had the old ascendancy class, the ex-landlords and remnants of the old Southern Unionist Alliance, the party who at every turn in Irish history had strangled, or attempted to strangle, the national aspirations of the country. They came out of their big demesnes and brought their motor cars; they even came from the Continent.

> At the last election, all the imperial elements were in motion – the Tories, West Britons and recreant nationalists united against them [Fianna Fáil] – but they had failed. He knew there were some good nationalists who voted against them at the last election, but their eyes were being opened, and in a short time they would all be together as in 1921 – all united under one banner, the sovereign independence of this country.[57]

Within a few years, the energetic and talented Caragh man would play a major role in Kildare and national politics – and his presence would have a profound effect on ua Buachalla's future.

CHAPTER 17

A Country to Know, to Love and to Serve

Despite the hasty nature of the September election, Fianna Fáil would have seen the outcome as satisfactory, yet they went into the Dáil on 11 October 1927 in the knowledge that they were likely to be in the opposition benches for the best part of five years. Their Executive Council met on 6 October to prepare for the long haul and the following day Éamon de Valera addressed a full meeting of the successful candidates at No. 34 Lower Abbey Street.

One of de Valera's first duties was to name the committees and as an ardent advocate of the Irish language, Domhnall ua Buachalla would have had a preference for Education. He was not disappointed. Under the chairmanship of Proinnsias Ó Fathaigh, he was in a panel that included Seán Brady, Thomas Powell, Patrick Boland and Mícheál Clery. A week later, it was decided that Education would be amalgamated with the Gaeltacht and Fisheries, which gave him a voice in a wider range of affairs. De Valera also appointed him to Defence with Frank Aiken (chairman), Frank Kerlin, Seán Hayes, Dr Patrick O'Dowd, Seumas Colbert, Frank Carney and Tom McEllistrim.[1]

The meeting was also informed that the Executive Council had unanimously decided 'that a minimum of £2 per month be contributed by each *Teachta* to the party funds'.[2] Little did they realise how difficult it would be to enforce this decision, and for the duration of the Sixth Dáil, the minutes constantly recorded shortfalls and various suggestions on how the situation could be remedied. More welcome was the decision taken a few days later, after a lengthy discussion, 'that it would be our policy, when we would be in a position to put it into effect, to pay a maximum of £1,000 a year to the Ceann Cómhairle, ministers, or any other officials of the Oireachtas.'[3] An amendment, proposed by Sean T. O'Kelly and seconded by Frank Carney, to have a maximum of £1,500 a year in the case of the President, was defeated 'by roughly forty-nine votes to eight'.[4]

In a break from Dáil work, ua Buachalla formally opened the Naas Fianna Fáil Club on 7 November. During a lively speech, he took the opportunity to have a sideswipe at the morals and social mores that were acceptable in England and now threatened the fabric of society in Ireland.

> Too long have we been without the (social) *Cumann*, not alone in *Nás na Ríog*, but throughout the whole country. In my opinion, the people of Ireland, especially in the country-parts as distinct from the cities, the middle and humbler classes, have not sufficient legitimate recreation, either indoor or outdoor: recreation that is untainted by foreignism – and when I say 'foreignism' I refer to vulgarity, the putrid mental and moral form that comes through the medium of her press, her filth that comes to us from magazines and novels, her smutty cinema pictures and questionable mode of dress. A *Cumann* such as this can do much to counter those degrading influences.

> But it is only after you have been some time working will you realise its possibilities for good to the community. You must concentrate on restoring to the Irish people the old, Irish civilisation, which was clean and Christian and mind-elevating. Let your debates and lectures deal with subjects of Irish interest: of Irish trade and commerce, nationality as applied to the creation of patriotic spirit and national outlook, and Irish history to teach us that we have a country to know, to love and to serve.

> If Ireland is to survive as a distinct nation, we must restore the language to its rightful place ... we must foster our own native games ... we must give Irish music, song and dancing pride of place in our homes and in our halls.[5]

Back in Lower Abbey Street, money was a constant topic at meetings, and as 1928 progressed, the need for funds for a national paper was seen as paramount. On 19 July, de Valera informed a Fianna Fáil meeting that £70,000 had been collected – although twelve counties had only collected more than half their quota. Despite the financial problems, *The Irish Press* was officially registered as a company on 4 September 1928.[6] Later in the year, frustration prompted a motion from Thomas O'Reilly, seconded by ua Buachalla, that:

> The Fianna Fáil Party is of the opinion that as the carrying on of conversations with Free State ministers in the halls of Leinster House is unbecoming and demoralising, deputies should not carry on conversations nor arrange for interviews with Free State ministers in any place whatever, except in so far as members of the Party may be obliged to act with such minister at committee meetings or at public functions.[7]

After some discussion, Seán Lemass proposed an amendment: 'That it be the rule of the Party that members should not conduct any business with Cumann na nGaedheal's ministers or deputies in bar or restaurant and that fraternisation under any circumstances be not permitted.'[8] On a show of hands, it was carried.

When the Fianna Fáil T. D. for Leitrim-Sligo, Samuel Holt, died on 18 April 1929, the party's representation in the Dail was reduced, with Seán Mac Eoin taking the seat for Cumann na nGaedheal. This followed earlier by-election successes for them – in April 1928 and March 1929 – in Dublin North. Vincent Rice won the seat vacated by James Larkin (Independent) and Thomas O'Higgins replaced Alfred Byrne (Independent). As was the custom when a fellow-member died, a decade of the Rosary was said for Holt, and it was agreed that a collection should be made for the family. The sum gathered was £204, a substantial figure at that time.

Much of ua Buachalla's Dáil work dealt with the needs of his constituents, from pension claims to drainage schemes, land improvement loans to road grants, but from time to time he made his views known concerning matters that were dear to his heart. In June 1929 a vote was about to be taken on funding for afforestation when Dr Jim Ryan moved that the estimate be referred back for reconsideration. He felt that sufficient work was not being done for afforestation.

17. Gortleitreach, Monkstown, Co. Dublin, Domhnall ua Buachalla's residence during his term as Governor–General. *(Family photo)*

18. The *Evening Standard* delved into 'paddywhackery' when Domhnall ua Buachalla was appointed Governor–General, with a cartoon and caption which read: 'Arrah! It was an iligant cirimony, the swearing-in of the Governor–General. His Excellency took the oat' in his own private language (which no one but himself could understand at all at all) whoile the mimbers of the Government sang an Oirish version of the National Anthem – God Save the King from matters which don't consarm him. Despite the vigilance of the troops the proceedings were interrupted by a child coming to buy a penn'orth of acid drops for Mr. Twomey.'

19. The youngest of the ua Buachalla family, Séadna, c. 1935. *(Family photo)*

20. A historic moment for Domhnall ua Buachalla as he signs the Constitution (Amendment No. 27) Bill, 1936, abolishing the post of Governor–General. *(Family photo)*

21. With tongue in cheek, *Dublin Opinion* suggested that Domhnall ua Buachalla might have considered asking the Government for a 'farewell broadcast' before leaving office in 1936.

22. Domhnall ua Buachalla's son, Joe, receiving the Liffey District, L.D.F. flag at Maynooth College in March 1943 after it had been blessed by the Very Rev. Edward Kissane, President of the College, following a march of 600 members from the Presentation Convent. *(Photo: The Irish Press)*

23. Domhnall ua Buachalla chatting with the Very Rev. Edward Kissane and Major–General Hugo MacNeill after his son, Joe, Leader of the Liffey District, L.D.F. received the unit colour in Maynooth College in 1943. *(Family photo)*

24. Domhnall ua Buachalla with his sons, Joe and Kevin, his daughter Máirín and Kevin's wife, Peggy, in Rome for an audience with Pope Pius X11 in 1950. *(Family photo)*

25. Twelve of the fifteen Maynooth Volunteers who walked to the GPO in 1916 photographed many years later in Croke Park. Back row: Pat Weafer, Tom Byrne, Joe Ledwidge, Tom Mangan, Mathew Maguire. Front row: Pat Kirwan, Tom Harris, Jack Maguire, Patrick Colgan, Domhnall ua Buachalla, Tim Tyrrell, Liam O'Regan. *(Photo: The Sunday Press)*

26. Domhnall ua Buachalla's son, Joe, with his wife, Helen in 1960. *(Photo: Fintan Buckley)*

27. Cardinal Agaginian, Éamon de Valera, Domhnall ua Buachalla and his daughter, Máirín, at a Patrician Year garden party in 1961. *(Photo: The Irish Press)*

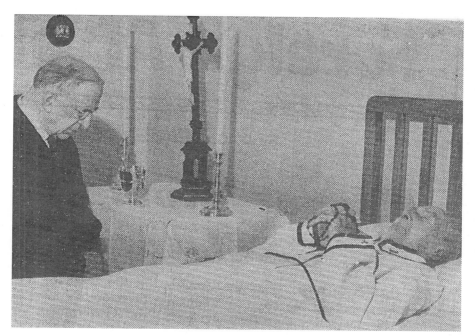

28. Éamon de Valera kneels in prayer at the bedside of Domhnall ua Buachalla in the Pembroke Nursing Home, Dublin on 30 October 1963. *(Photo: The Advocate, Australia)*

29. Éamon de Valera and Seán Lemass at Laraghbryan Cemetery, Maynooth where Domhnall ua Buachalla was laid to rest with full military honours. *(Photo: The Sunday Press)*

30. The monument in the Town Square which honours Maynooth's fifteen Volunteers who walked to the GPO for the Easter Rising in 1916. From top: Domhnall ua Buachalla, Tom Byrne, Patrick Colgan, Jack Graves, Tom Harris, Patrick Kirwan, Joe Ledwidge, Jack Maguire, Mathew Maguire, Tom Mangan, Ted O'Kelly, Liam O'Regan, Oliver Ryan, Tim Tyrrell and Pat Weafer. *(Photo: Author's Collection)*

He immediately had an ally in ua Buachalla who spoke at length about the excellent work being done in Czechoslovakia. 'In recent years, the Government, I understand, have taken over upwards of 5,000,000 acres of privately owned forests ... the country is between one and half to two times the size of Ireland and has an annual cut of 200,000,000 cubic feet.' He called for 'a faculty of forestry to train young Irish men to think in terms of trees in Ireland ... we require a Forestry Department and then a commission to glean information from whatever sources possible ... if we take up forestry earnestly and as it ought to be taken up, we will stop a great proportion of emigration'.[9] Despite the pleas for greater investment, the Government won the vote, as was the norm, with seventy votes to fifty eight.

Although ua Buachalla spent considerable time in Dublin attending Fianna Fáil meetings and Dáil sittings, as well as dealing with constituents in Maynooth and keeping an eye on his business, he had more pressing demands in 1929: two of the family, Joe first, and then Síghle, were preparing for married life.

After Frank Burke returned to Dublin from Frongoch, he struck up a warm relationship with Angela Curran, a Waterford-born teacher who had been living in Birmingham and who regularly brought food parcels to the prisoners while they were in Stafford Jail. They married in 1923. Naturally enough, Joe also got to know Angela but, more importantly, he became acquainted with her sister, Helen, occasionally meeting her in St Enda's where Frank was now headmaster and living with Angela in a bungalow on the grounds. Time passed, another relationship developed and in 1929 they married.

It was no surprise that their first boy was called Domhnall. He had three brothers – Colm, Fintan and Joe – and a sister Ann, who sadly died at 27. Domhnall went on to play senior championship football with Offaly while he was working for D. E. Williams, a grocery business that was owned by the Williams distillery family of Tullamore Dew fame.

However, mindful that he was a Kildare man first, he had the nerve to sew the Kildare crest to his Offaly jersey on the eve of his debut for his adopted county – and survived to tell the tale. Some years later he returned to play for Kildare and later emigrated to America, where he was invited to join the Kerry team. On the day he first turned out for Offaly, younger brother Fintan played minor championship football with Kildare.

Fintan and Colm attended Newbridge College where they became accomplished rugby players with two other Maynooth boys, Tony and Tim Twomey. The quartet also played for the local GAA team, *Crom Abú*. Now enjoying two sports, the four joined North Kildare Rugby Club and were members of a side that won the Provincial Towns Cup. Their celebrations were short-lived, however, as they were suspended by the GAA – together with their club – for breaking Rule 27 (a ban on playing or attending rugby, soccer, hockey and cricket games). As Tony Twomey was at that time a talented member of Lansdowne Rugby Club, both Colm and Fintan decided that they would also move to rugby headquarters.

While the family would have been disappointed at the suspension of Colm and Fintan, it would not have unduly bothered their grandfather. In the weeks and months after the boys started playing rugby at Newbridge, a certain coolness developed over the fact that the boys had been allowed to take up a 'foreign game' in the first place. Grandfather was not best pleased with his grandsons, but with time came acceptance; in fact, ua Buachalla had to take care of many grandchildren – and their friends – in his Eglinton Road home later in life before they were picked up by parents after Leinster Schools' Cup matches in Donnybrook.

The second member of the family to leave home was Síghle, who had taken care of her siblings during the latter stages of Sinéad's illness and after her death, through the months of her father's enforced absences, and the years following 1924 when life settled into more peaceful patterns. It was in St Kevin's Church in Harrington Street, Dublin, on 31 October 1929, that her father gave her hand to Mick O'Neill.

While ua Buachalla was very much involved with Mick, and his brother Diarmuid, both members of the Volunteers from 1914 on, the friendship probably originated some years earlier. The 1911 Census indicates that Diarmuid was the owner of a spacious residence with out-offices and farm-buildings in Maynooth, having arrived from Russacussane, near Kenmare in Co. Kerry, with his wife, formerly Emily Murrogh-Bernard, a relation of Mary Robinson, President of Ireland from 1990 to 1997. The O'Neills were first cousins of the O'Connor Scarteen brothers, Tom and John, who lived in Main Street, Kenmare. Having fought in the War of Independence, the O'Connors joined the Irish Free State forces and were unarmed when shot dead in their home during the Civil War, ironically, it was said, by a man who had previously been a close friend. The killings epitomised how the Treaty had sundered so many relationships.

After a few years in Maynooth, Diarmuid decided that he needed a larger holding so he sold out and bought a 100-acre farm, Weston Park, between Celbridge and Lucan, which is now an airport. Mick gave a hand on the land but his priority at that stage was to qualify as a veterinary surgeon. It was not surprising, therefore, that a strong bond developed between ua Buachalla and the brothers as their political persuasions were similar, and this empathy manifested itself as the country moved closer to the Rising, in particular on the weekend of Pentecost Sunday, 1915.

A decision had been taken by Pádraig Pearse, in conjunction with Éamon de Valera and Tom McDonagh, that they would travel from Dublin to Limerick by train as a morale-boosting show of strength for the Volunteer movement. With return tickets priced at five shillings, over 300 members made the trip and as they were welcomed by the local Volunteers, numbers had increased to over 500.

When Mick heard about the excursion, he suggested to ua Buachalla that they should also travel and agreement was reached. Unlike the Dublin contingent, however, their choice of transport was the bicycle. So 49-year-old Domhnall and the 23-year-old Kerryman headed south from Maynooth, giving themselves ample time to eat, rest and swap life stories. Unfortunately, the reception by the banks of the Shannon was not what Pearse had anticipated and 'as the Volunteers marched through the city, missiles of various kinds were thrown at them and they were made the objects of many insulting remarks. In the evening, as they drew close to the railway station, hostile crowds gathered and endeavoured to prevent them from entering the gate of the station.'[10]

The following day provided the cyclists with much to discuss on their return journey and recalling the events many years later for Ernie O'Malley, Mick mentioned that Pearse had said to them as the stones were flying, 'What can you expect? Don't blame the people, for they haven't seen the light yet. You'll have to endure a lot more before the country is free.'[11]

These words might well have echoed through the ensuing nine years for the two intrepid travellers whose lives ran the full gamut of war before resuming normality in 1924 when both had total freedom again. Having abandoned his veterinary plans for a few years working on the land, and later a life in business, Mick, it seems, was continually drawn back to Maynooth, and eventually to marriage.

Síghle was a gentle, caring person; he, an extrovert with a great sense of humour and an infectious laugh. His daughter Nóirín spoke of him as 'a man who played hard and worked hard' and was grateful that he was present when her mother went into labour with her. Before the home-confinement nurse arrived, her father had done an excellent job assisting his wife through child-birth and was able to hand over a healthy young girl when the nurse eventually came through the door. The couple initially settled in Cooldrinagh, Lucan, before Mick built a bungalow in Páirc na gCrann, Celbridge. From there, the family, which was blessed with five children – Maedbh, Nóirín, Brídín, Eoghan and Niall – finally moved to Clondalkin.

A pleasant footnote to the relationship with Mary Robinson came during her term as President of Ireland when she invited Domhnall ua Buachalla's grandchildren for afternoon tea to honour the only Governor-General or President of the country not to have lived in Árus an Uachtaráin.

Assassination in a London Hotel

A little over sixty years later, tragedy struck the extended O'Neill family when Mick's 27-year-old grandson, Diarmuid, was shot dead in London. A volunteer in the Irish Republican Army, he was a son of Eoghan who had moved to England early in life, married Theresa (Terry) Mulhere, and raised three children, Diarmuid, Siobhán and Shane. On a Panorama television programme in the wake of the killing, Shane spoke of a close family and wonderful holidays in a 200-year old cottage they had close to the sea in Donegal; of a brother, four years older, who was 'great to me', who 'looked after me'. Neighbours in the Irish community knew a family 'that was not over-emphatic' about its Irish roots, and were 'greatly surprised' when the events unfolded.

Educated at the London Oratory School, where he was remembered as cheerful and outgoing, Diarmuid developed a keen interest in politics from the age of about 13. His father remembers him 'constantly airing his views at mealtime, which were very much pro-Labour and, in particular, pro-Tony Benn, whom he greatly admired'.[12] Aware of his grandfather and great-grandfather's roles in Irish history, he spoke passionately about the IRA hunger strikers and had a strong aversion to the use of plastic bullets in the north. As his teenage years slipped by, his interest in Irish culture and nationalism increased, and led to fundraising for the families of prisoners and selling republican papers in London. Basque nationalism also engaged him and he visited Spain on occasions with his Basque-born girlfriend, Karmele Ereno. She spoke about being 'shocked to find that he was in the IRA' after his death.

After school he took up employment in the Bank of Ireland branch in Shepherd's Bush, where he was involved in a £75,000 cash fraud, with a sizeable sum going to Northern Ireland. This led to nine months in a young offenders' institution.

He was unarmed when shot and killed by the London Metropolitan Police specialist firearms unit, SO19, in a hotel in Hammersmith on 23 September 1996 during an operation code-named 'Tinnitus'. It followed six weeks of twenty-four hour surveillance – with some rare exceptions – that began on 11 August when Brian McHugh and Patrick Kelly arrived in London to take charge of explosives and munitions. The IRA wanted them in safe-keeping as efforts for a renewed ceasefire continued, although the police saw them as potential bombers. A fourth member of the group was James Murphy.

Knowing that they had a lorry with explosives in a lock-up garage and that O'Neill, who normally lived at his home in Fulham, was going to stay that night in a hotel with McHugh and Kelly, a decision was taken by the police to arrest all three in the hotel. A plan for an armed entry had been organised for several weeks, but the first briefing on 22 September for S. O. officers was held at 9.00 p.m. and it was only then that Officer 'Hotel', the leader of the team designated to enter the room, became aware that a specific C. S. irritant had been authorised by D. C. S. Bunn, who was in overall charge of the operation. An extensive report by Amnesty International in 2000, which called for a review of the police investigation into the killing, was revealing:

> At 4.30 a.m. SO19 arrived at the hotel. Two teams were formed, one of which was responsible for gaining access to the room and arresting the suspects. It consisted of Officers 'Alpha', 'Delta' 'Gulf', 'Hotel', 'Kilo', 'Lima', 'Mike', 'November' and 'Oscar', most of whom did not bring their respirators and none of whom was wearing one when the raid started. The other team was positioned outside the premises. When the replica key failed to unlock the door [to the bedroom] ... a decision was taken to make use of the enforcer and the R. I. P. [gas]rounds.

> [During cross-examination, D. C. I. Mark Williams stated that at 8.00 p.m. officers at Old Street were told that C. S. gas was not an option 'as permission for its use had been refused'. Officer 'Delta' confirmed this by saying that he was told at the 9.00 p.m.

briefing that a request for C. S. gas had been refused. D. C. S. Bunn acknowledged that he had not been trained in its use and was unaware of the different types of gas.]

An order was given to fire five rounds through a side window as a distraction whilst Officer 'Alpha' attempted to smash down the door with the enforcer. Officer 'Delta' – a member of the entry team – also discharged five rounds into the room. The enforcer had only punched holes into the door ...

The spreading C. S. gas not only affected the suspects inside the room but also had a devastating effect on the police officers in front of the door as it had seeped out through the holes caused by the enforcer. The contamination of the lobby outside the room was such as to force most of the officers to leave the scene to be sick outside. Officer 'Kilo' stated he had difficulties breathing, was choking and his eyes were streaming. Only officers 'Oscar', 'Lima' and 'Kilo' withdrew to an adjacent corridor to get some air before returning. 'Hotel', the officer in charge of the operation, remained outside until he heard shots being fired in the building.

Although it is evident from the recording of the incident [through bugs placed in the hotel room by MI5 some weeks earlier] that the suspects inside indicated their surrender immediately after the discharge of the R. I. P. rounds, the officers remaining in the proximity of the room stated that they increasingly feared being fired at. The officers perceived their commands – which were contradictory in themselves as the recording shows – as not being responded to by the suspects ...

As two of the suspects lay face-down on the floor and the third, Diarmuid O'Neill, responded to the officers' request to open the door, the accounts of different officers of what happened next diverged. Officer 'Mike' claims to have seen Diarmuid O'Neill display one of his hands through the hole in the door, whilst others did not recollect this ... it can be taken as an established fact that for some reason – reportedly because it had been battered and broken by the enforcer – Diarmuid O'Neill was not able to open the door fully.

Officer 'Mike' stated that he saw Officer 'Kilo' kicking the door open before the shooting, whereas 'Kilo' himself did not recollect having done so. Conversely, he stated that he remained across the lobby, several feet from the door, during the time he was discharging his weapon. According to him, the door was open as he fired.

Officer 'Kilo' stated that immediately before he fired at Diarmuid O'Neill, he saw him displaying 'aggressive body language', standing in a 'classic boxer's stance with his arms down', which suggested to Officer 'Kilo' that 'he was holding a weapon'. On the other hand, he and other officers stated that it was very hard to see, because their visual perception was impaired by the cloud of C. S. gas. Officer 'Kilo' also claimed that Diarmuid O'Neill was not complying with his orders and stayed stationary throughout the rounds of fire.[13]

Diarmuid O'Neill was dragged down the stairs and outside the building. The result of the post-mortem showed a 'patterened' bruise to his scalp which, in the opinion of the pathologist for the British Home Office, may have resulted from 'an individual treading on his head'.[14] He died later in hospital. McHugh, Kelly and Murphy received a combined sentence of sixty-two years.

In 1997, an investigation into the circumstances surrounding the killing was supervised by the Police Complaints Authority and conducted by the Criminal Investigation Bureau of the Metropolitan Police. After almost two years, it concluded with a report which led to the Crown Prosecution Service deciding that there was not enough evidence to prosecute the police officers involved in the killing.[15]

In October 1999, Hammersmith Coroner Dr John Burton asked the Home Office to set up a public inquiry into the death. When his request was rejected, he proceeded to hold a Coroner's Inquest into the death. It commenced on 31 January 2000 and resulted in a verdict, which in effect amounted to a 'lawful killing' verdict by the Coroner's jury on 18 February 2000.[16]

Amnesty International believes the inquest 'failed to allay its concerns, as serious issues surrounding the circumstances of O'Neill's death remain unresolved. Amnesty International is thus concerned that the full facts of the killing remain unknown, given the inconsistencies between officers' accounts and forensic evidence.'[17] This would be very much at odds with a senior police officer involved who said, 'I don't admit that anything went wrong – somebody has died, yes, but nothing went wrong.'[18]

Early on the morning of the raid, Diarmuid's bother Shane was awakened in his apartment in London by a noise that sounded like a firecracker. Little did he realise that the house was surrounded by police who had broken in through the front door. Held for six days in Paddington Police Station and initially denied legal representation, he was not told of his brother's killing for over forty-eight hours. After a protracted battle to be allowed outdoors, he overheard one officer say to another, 'that's the brother of the guy we killed'.[19]

In west Cork, where they moved after a lifetime's work in London, Eoghan and Terry awoke very early on 23 September and sat down to a cup of tea in the kitchen as they listened to the morning news. They heard the newsreader mention a shooting in London but paid little attention and retired again. Later in the morning, Eoghan saw two gardaí and a detective walking up the driveway of the house and realised that something was amiss; his immediate fear was that one of the children had been in an accident.

After a short delay as the garda spokesman composed himself, Eoghan and Terry were told that 'Diarmuid was dead and Shane had been arrested after a shoot-out with the police in London.' Aside from the inaccuracy of the information that was fed from London, the news left them devastated. It was a moment in life they would take to the grave, a father and mother who had 'no, no, no idea whatsoever' that their son was so actively involved in IRA affairs. Within days, their house in London had been seized by the police and boarded up. When they were informed six weeks later that they could return to it, the building and gardens had been 'thrashed' to the extent that the estimate to repair the damage was £34,000. They didn't receive compensation.

Diarmuid O'Neill is buried in St Mologas' Cemetary, Timoleague, County Cork: the memorial card for his funeral opened with the words:

> We did not see you close our eyes
>
> We did not see you die,
>
> All we know was you were gone
>
> Without a last goodbye …

And concludes ...

Your life was full of kindly deeds

A helping hand for others' needs,

Sincere and true in heart and mind

Beautiful memories left behind.

Out of Bounds

For the Irish Government, finance became a time bomb on 28 March 1930 when President Cosgrave announced to the Dáil the resignation of his Cabinet in order to give the House an opportunity to elect a new executive. He pointed out that the Government could not accept the responsibility of financing the Old Age Pensions Bill, passed the previous night against the Government's wishes, as it 'would impose a burden of £300,000 on the taxpayer'.[20] The Cabinet, he said, was not prepared to impose fresh burdens on agriculture and industry by a measure which would not even have the merit of benefiting the more necessitous and deserving old-age pensioners.

Although the Executive Council appreciated that the vote was due to the fact that a number of the Government members were unavoidably absent, it felt the House, in view of the decision, should be given the opportunity of electing another executive. The acting Fianna Fáil leader, Seán T. O'Kelly, agreed that the President had taken the proper course in some ways, but not with delaying it until the following Wednesday. Within minutes, Domhnall ua Buachalla and his fellow deputies were in conclave in another room. The Party agreed unanimously that de Valera, who was in America, would be proposed, and the minutes also recorded that they would back Labour if de Valera was defeated. However, that decision was reversed on 2 April at another meeting when it was decided that the Party should abstain from voting on a motion that Mr O'Connell be elected.[21]

The outcome in the Dáil was a decisive vote of confidence for maintaining the status quo, although the debate 'was of a lively and occasionally bitter nature'.[22] First to be nominated, de Valera got the backing of fifty-three of his followers. With the exception of two who abstained, the other ninety-three deputies voted against him. Three hours later O'Connell's bid for the presidency attracted thirteen votes, with seventy-eight against. It was almost midnight when Cosgrave had the backing of eighty deputies, sixty-five voting against his re-election.[23]

With the summer months approaching, ua Buachalla was asked at a Fianna Fáil meeting to do an audit of accounts for the six months ending 30 April, with the assistance of Matt O'Reilly and Daniel Bourke. The report showed that there was an effective shortfall of £280, mainly due to the wages bill having increased and a figure of £126 owed by four members. £700 of the £1,000 promised had been paid to the Fianna Fáil Organisation. Obviously impressed with the audit, the Maynooth T. D. was asked to look after financial arrears. By February of 1931 the scale of payments had increased, with T. D.s living in Dublin having to pay £3 and Senators £5, effectively to meet the annual payment of £1,000.[24]

One of the more lively debates in 1931 concerned the Intoxicating Liquor Bill, which prompted a variety of views. Drinking habits, in fact, were not unknown on Fianna Fáil agendas during the Sixth Dáil. Early on, de Valera appealed to members not to take any drink whatsoever in the bar at Leinster House, yet there was the occasional reprimand at meetings for members who were 'under the influence'. That is, until 16 May 1929, when it was decided 'that the bar at Leinster House be definitely out of bounds for members of the Party'.[25]

The Liquor Bill debate in 1931, and whether the country should be permitted to raise a glass to St Patrick on his Feast Day, left *Teachtaí Dála* in no doubt about ua Buachalla's stance on the subject. He was not a teetotaller, at least not in his latter days, but his consumption was modest in the extreme.

> I had not intended to say a word on this Bill, because I had not thought that any Irishman with respect for his country or himself, or even for the poor working man for whom this opening of the public-houses is supposed to be a concession, would advocate their opening on St. Patrick's Day. We have all been concerned for the interests of the working man. Now we seem to be interested in putting great temptation in his way.
>
> We all know that when England was in control in this country and when there was any sign of the country prospering, England deliberately increased the number of public-houses here, or, at least,

advocated their increase and condoned the increased consumption of drink. With what object? With the object of degrading the country and its people and making it easier to keep us in subjection. When the public-houses were closed on St. Patrick's Day, the self-respect of the public increased very much. The civic spirit and the public life of the country improved immensely ...

Deputy Redmond said that the people of Scotland celebrated St. Andrew's Day, and in order to do that, allowed the public-houses to open. Does Deputy Redmond not know how the people of Scotland – I was going to say celebrate – degrade St. Andrew's Day because public-houses are open and the people can get as much drink as they want? If we want to earn respect from other countries we must respect ourselves first, and we cannot do that if we encourage the people to drink on St. Patrick's Day. I hope that this bill will be defeated by a large majority.[26]

The Breakthrough

The death of Hugh Colohan on the 15 April 1931, Labour's first successful candidate in Kildare in 1922 brought two very able politicians face-to-face for the first time at the hustings – William Norton of Labour and Fianna Fáil's Tom Harris. The third candidate was Cumann na nGaedheal's experienced campaigner, John Conlon.

Self-educated, Norton was born in Dublin in 1900, left school at 13 and served as secretary of the Post Office Workers' Union from 1924–48. He was elected for Dublin County at a by-election in 1926, but lost his seat at the June General Election the following year. He would go on to lead the Labour Party, was twice Tánaiste in Inter-Party Governments and was recognised as one of the country's great parliamentarians.

Tom Harris was 21 when he marched with ua Buachalla to the GPO in 1916. In the intervening years he worked tirelessly in election campaigns for the Maynooth man. A talented orator, he spoke powerfully throughout the county on behalf of the Republican candidates and also served the people of Kildare at County Council level. His decision to run for election after the setback of 1923 would have been a measured one, primarily based on the fact that the time was right and that he had a seriously good prospect of success. He was also aware of the strong support behind him at

Fianna Fáil headquarters in Dublin. While the cornerstone of his support was the Fianna Fáil vote, his daughter – and historical author – Annie Ryan suggested that much of the army vote in the Curragh would have gone his way. In addition, he was a farmer, or as Annie put it, 'not so much [a] conventional farmer as an experimental one',[27] yet still a Fianna Fáil candidate who had land. The enthusiasm among his supporters to win the seat was vividly reflected at a meeting in Athy on 21 June 1931:

> Shortly before Éamon de Valera's arrival, a body of men, well over a thousand walking four-deep and headed by three bands, marched out to meet him, and as the cars containing the party drove up, the cheers were deafening. Mr de Valera smilingly raised his hat and bowed his acknowledgement of their greetings and then, accompanied by the members of his party and the members of the local committee, he walked through the town – the band playing national airs – marching at the head. The procession drew up at the platform under the shadow of the Town Hall and as the music ceased, the cheering of almost five thousand people rose in the air, hats and caps were waved aloft and cries of 'Up Dev' and 'Good Old Dev' and 'de Valera Aboo' were heard. For five minutes after the party had ascended the platform the cheering continued and only ceased by the band striking the National Anthem.[28]

Also on the crowded platform was Frank Aiken, but it was Dr Jim Ryan who first addressed the gathering, pointing out 'that they were getting the chance of showing whether or not they were satisfied with the Government of the country for the past nine years'. He recalled the Rising:

> I remember in 1916, Tom Harris came up with Donal Buckley, they came to fight for the independence of our country, and I remember also when leaving the post office after we had surrendered, he got wounded and was put beside James Connolly who had been wounded the previous day. I remember leaving him behind for the British military to take away to hospital – they took them to the Castle hospital. There are people going round today who tell you they are the disciples of the late James Connolly and spokesmen of Irish labour, and tell you that you must not vote for Harris. I ask you, is there one who went as far with James Connolly in Easter Week?[29]

Five nights later in Leixlip, it was de Valera, ua Buachalla and many other prominent figures who were extolling the virtues of Harris and Fianna Fáil. And while the party would have had reason to be confident of having a second T. D. elected in the county, the opposition was formidable.

It was an hour into the morning of 1 July 1931 – and after a recount – that Harris, proposing a vote of thanks to the returning officer and staff, said that his success 'was a protest against the extravagant administration of the present Government ... they [Fianna Fáil] had to fight the alliance between Cumann na nGaedheal and the party which he called the Labour-Imperial Party ... and that what Kildare had done that day, the rest of the twenty-six counties would do tomorrow if they had the chance.'[30] The 'Special Representative' wrote in *The Irish Times* that

> there was a distinctly Kildare atmosphere in the Dáil the following day. Even the approach to Leinster House held motor cars which bore the slogan – SPEED THE PLOUGH, VOTE FOR HARRIS – and the dust of many miles of summer travel in the short grass county [...] At the end of the thirteenth question (which was the last on the list) Mr Gerald Boland, the Chief Whip of Fianna Fáil, took the blushing stranger by the hand (so to speak) and led him down the centre gangway to the Speaker's Chair, where he duly presented Mr Harris. There were loud cheers from the Opposition benches ... a clamour of 'Resign! Resign!' ... but Mr de Valera retained his usual attitude of aloof dignity during this outburst, [and] he was seen to smile.[31]

Of possibly greater interest was a paragraph which read, 'Behind the scenes, however, I understand that there were moments of strong emotion when the bets which had been made on the Kildare election were being

KILDARE BY-ELECTION 1931 (JULY)	SEATS 1	QUOTA 12,543
CANDIDATES	FIRST COUNT	FINAL FIGURES
Tom Harris (Fianna Fáil)	10,041	11,612
John Conlon (Cumann na nGaedheal)	8,374	11,103
William Norton (Labour)	6,669	

Kildare Observer

loyally settled. In one case a deputy had laid sixty pounds against forty – and lost. Little wonder that there were libations to the gods.'[32]

Before Harris had an opportunity to become accustomed to the routine of a Dáil deputy, the summer break had arrived, which would run until early October. This provided him with the opportunity to thank the 'marching army' that had elected him, and also prepare for a general election the following year in which he would now be collaborating with ua Buachalla. It was certainly a formidable partnership with the wind in their sails, yet both would have had nagging doubts about the feasibility of getting two safely over the line in a three-seat constituency.

Although it was later than de Valera might have anticipated, *The Irish Press* hit the streets for the first time on 5 September 1931. The launch date was well chosen, the eve of an All-Ireland hurling final between Kilkenny and Cork, an event that sat comfortably with the readers sought by the paper. The *Irish Independent* was engaging with the sport more and more; *The Irish Times* happy enough to pay little heed. Of greater relevance to the majority of citizens was the fact that the *Independent* was anti-republican and strident in its criticism of the 1913 Lock Out; *The Irish Times* pro-unionist and Protestant. A sizeable gap in the market existed.

Margaret Pearse pushed the button to start the presses rolling, watched by the editor, Frank Gallagher. Cork-born, a close friend of de Valera and a member of Sinn Féin, he frequently wrote under the pseudonyms David Hogan and Henry O'Neill. He was interned in Mountjoy during the War of Independence and took part in a mass hunger strike of republican prisoners who wanted political status. At a Fianna Fáil meeting in December, Gallagher was introduced to the deputies by de Valera, who urged them to think how best they could help to improve circulation and advertising. Whatever their input was, those running the paper were instantly successful, despite exclusion from using a special train which delivered newspapers from Dublin to provincial Ireland.[33]

O'Rahilly takes Republican Line

Perhaps the greatest boost that *The Irish Press* got was the announcement that a general election would be held on 16 February 1932, which was earlier than expected. This would not only provide an on-going source of lively copy, but also act as an agent to push the republican line for the first time. An example of this was an article carried on the eve of the election, written by Professor Alfred O'Rahilly, an advocate of the

Anglo-Irish Treaty who was elected to the Fourth Dáil in 1923 as a Cumann na nGaedheal candidate, but resigned the following year.

> Whether you agree or disagree with me, I claim to be a model voter. I admit I have not risked getting influenza by listening to speeches; but I have carefully read the newspapers and I have studied the election literature ... and finally I have made up my mind.

> I believe I am speaking for a great number of decent-minded people when I say the vast bulk of the Cumann na nGaedheal propaganda has consisted of vile caricatures, unjustified abuse and hysterical misrepresentation. I have sought mostly in vain for rational arguments amid this reeking mass of unchristian vilification. Of course there are arguments for Cumann na nGaedheal; but those that I have tabulated have largely been cogitated by myself.

> There is one argument that appeals to many; I am told that tomorrow aeroplanes will drop leaflets telling us that 'the gunmen are voting for Fianna Fáil'. I confess it leaves me stone-cold. It is as if the British Government of the eighties were to say 'the Fenians are voting for Parnell' ... I propose in the interests of peace to vote for Fianna Fáil.[34]

The article carried the heading 'The End of a Neutral' and would not have seen the light of day if *The Irish Press* had not arrived on the streets of Ireland. It was a reward for de Valera's persistence in his pursuit of the mighty dollar, which financed the company.

Ten days earlier, Barry Brown, the Returning Officer in Kildare, had received nominations for the three seats. As anticipated, ua Buachalla and Harris were the Fianna Fáil candidates. Unlike September 1927 when Cumann na nGaedheal put up one candidate, George Wolfe, they changed tack and selected Michael Fitzsimons and Sydney Minch. Labour took a contrary view, going from two – Hugh Colohan and Michael Smyth – to one – William Norton. The Farmers' Party was not represented. The tactical changes made Fianna Fáil's second seat look tenuous. Although a first-time pairing, the Harris–ua Buachalla ticket was powerful. Their campaign was well orchestrated, with a constant flow of the Fianna Fáil hierarchy joining them at meetings throughout the county. Writing about matters that influenced the election, Michael Gallagher pointed to rising paramilitary activity:

In late 1931 the Government introduced draconian security legislation involving military tribunals that could impose the death penalty. Shortly before the election, with rather characteristic heavy-handedness, it prosecuted *The Irish Press* before a tribunal on a charge of seditious libel. It also introduced a budget that raised taxes and adumbrated cuts in public service pay.

Fianna Fáil entered the election in a confident mood, having won two of the three most recent by-elections. It had added policies on social and economic issues to its long-standing commitment to amend the constitution, and expected to capitalise on the unpopularity of the Government. Labour's fortunes were at a low ebb and ran only thirty-three candidates, while the Farmers' Party was on the verge of extinction, several of its T. D.s having defected to Cumann na nGaedheal.[35]

Although it was February, the correspondent for the *Kildare Observer* reported that polling day was a day when 'to be let out of doors was a treat not to be missed'. He also pointed out that in the South Kildare constituency, 80 per cent of the votes were cast, the overall figure being 72 per cent, an increase of 7 per cent on 1927.

For ua Buachalla, however, the sunshine of Tuesday turned to hovering dark clouds on Wednesday as the count got under way. From an early stage he would have been aware that Harris was maintaining the impetus of his by-election success, that Norton's star was rising, that Cumann na nGaedheal had polled well. The prospect of a second seat for Fianna Fáil evaporated.

SEVENTH DÁIL KILDARE 1932	SEATS 3	QUOTA 6,050
CANDIDATES	FIRST COUNT	FINAL FIGURES
Tom Harris (Fianna Fáil)	6,510	
William Norton (Labour)	5,496	5,875
Sydney Minch (Cumann na n Gaedheal)	4,653	7,777
Daniel Buckley (Fianna Fáil)	3,802	4,313
Michael Fitzsimons (Cumann na nGaedheal)	3,735	3,743

Irish Elections 1922–44: Results and Analysis: Michael Gallagher

Tom Harris topped the poll with 6,510 votes, 2,708 ahead of his running partner and 1,014 in front of Norton. Although ua Buachalla got 409 of Harris's surplus of 460, the subsequent elimination of Fitzsimons elevated Minch to 7,777 – substantially over the quota of 6,050 – for the second seat. Ua Buachalla was then eliminated and Norton knew he was returning to the Dáil, for what would be a distinguished innings.

One of the Fianna Fáil posters used during the campaign had a picture of both candidates at the top, and a 400-word exhortation to dump the present Government. It also asked people to vote No. 1 and 2 'in order of your choice'. When it came to decision-making, Kildare went for a dynamic candidate who not only impressed them in the 1931 by-election, but also in the years preceding when he was pivotal as an election strategist and voice of persuasion on the election platforms from 1918 on. In a sense, Harris was the natural successor to ua Buachalla, an ambitious and energetic 35-year-old, aware that his time had come, knowing that his 66-year-old mentor who had been at his side since the early months of 1916 was close to the point when retirement was an option. The only interruption to their association arrived during the Civil War, a conflict Harris disapproved of. His popularity saw him returned at every election until 1957, when he failed to get sufficient support and decided to retire.

While ua Buachalla would have been aware that his seat was in jeopardy, elimination cannot have been easy to accept. Within weeks Fianna Fáil would be in power. What was once a vision had now become reality. But it had come too late for him. The comforts of home, the proximity of family and grandchildren, more time to relax, to re-focus – all would have had an appeal to a man of his age. But he was different. There was more to be done. Now he was on the outside and time was marching resolutely on. Within a week, he had a letter published in the *Leinster Leader:*

The Editor,

A Chara,

With your kind permission I should like to return my sincere thanks to the host of workers in Kildare who spared no effort in the recent election to secure the return of the two Fianna Fáil candidates – Mr Tom Harris and myself.

That their efforts were not crowned with complete success was no fault of theirs. The result, however, proves the necessity for continuous work in the future, particularly in the matter of attention to the new register, from which not a single name qualified for entry should be omitted. I desire also to convey my gratitude to the many sincere friends, not only in the constituency but throughout the country, who so kindly conveyed in writing their expression of regret at my non-return.

We must all rejoice, however, in the fact that a really National Government will in a few days take over control of Ireland's destiny; that with a National Government there will be joy in the hearts of our people in America and throughout the world who had to flee their country during the past ten years, and who yearn to return to the land of their birth; that the people of Ireland have once again set their feet on the road to freedom; and that, with God's help, and a proper sense of national duty, that goal will soon be attained.

On my own behalf I only have to say that in the future, as in the past, every effort of mine shall be only too willingly directed towards that goal.

Domhnall ua Buachalla.[36]

Reunion of the National Forces

The election figures in Kildare were mirrored throughout the country. Front-page headlines progressed from 'Fianna Fáil Outdistances All The Other Parties' on 19 February to 'People Rejoice in Victory of Fianna Fáil' on 22 February. For the Cosgrave Government, it was a major setback, one which suggested they could be in opposition for some time. For the first time, Fianna Fáil took more than 40 per cent of the vote in a general election. Michael Gallagher pointed out that they gained votes in every constituency, 'and whereas it had headed Cumann na nGaedheal in only eleven of the twenty-eight territorial constituencies in September 1927, it was now ahead in twenty-one. Moreover, its considered policies had evoked a response from National University graduates, who had hitherto given fairly solid backing to Cumann na nGaedheal'.[37]

On 4 March 1932, de Valera addressed the people of America and Canada on radio, thanking those 'whose loyalty and generous support throughout the years have brought the cause of Irish independence so far on the road to victory'.[38] He continued:

> Every friend of Ireland is, I am sure, overjoyed, as I am, at the thought of the reunion of the national forces here – particularly in this year of St. Patrick's centenary and of the Eucharistic Congress – the reunion of those forces so disastrously divided by the Treaty of 1921. For ten years our nation has been struggling in agony in an attempt to free itself from the dilemma in which it was then placed – with an Oath of Allegiance hateful to all who prized independence standing in the way of acceptance of the one rule of government by which discipline and ordered progress could be secured.
>
> This oath will now be removed and every section of our people will at last, without coercion of conscience or sacrifice of principle, be able to send their representatives to the People's Assembly, where national policy and the direction of the national advance can then be re-authoritatively determined by majority vote.[39]

Seven days later, de Valera was back in Dublin and back in the Dáil amid scenes of celebration and satisfaction that were reminiscent of the past. After Frank Fahy had been elected Speaker, the proposition was made that de Valera be elected President of the Executive Council. Before the vote, 'short addresses by Mr Cosgrave and others, and an eloquent speech by Mr Norton' were delivered and then the motion, supported by some Independents, was carried by eighty-one votes to sixty-eight. A 'Special Correspondent' provided a colourful introduction to the afternoon's proceedings.

> The House is empty except for the Press Gallery. Outside, one can hear the deep voices of the crowd cheering its favourites, shouting angrily at some who it dislikes. The quiet in the House is accentuated by those noises from the gates. It is 2.55 p.m.
>
> The public galleries are crowded and silent. One feels the strangeness of this empty chamber ... Many who helped to write the play now to be staged are there – Liam Pedlar, Donal Ó Buachalla, Eamonn

Donnelly, many others, but above all Mrs Pearse and Miss Pearse, looking down – with what thoughts?

The shadows of the lobbies disappear softly; the lights have come suddenly on. The deputies are moving. Dr Myles Keogh is first. Mr Osmond Esmonde strolls in … Dan Breen, Seán Moylan and Oscar Traynor together. Seán Lemass hurries down the steps, Mr Ruttledge greets him, smiling. Seán T. Ó Ceallaigh comes with Dr Ryan. Quickly down the gangway, in neat black, Éamon de Valera, his face young, serious, peaceful. Frank Aiken follows in saffron tweed, towering, dark … The House is full. No doubt where the mastery lies, and it is the mastery of youth over middle age. A curious thing is the youth of the outgoing Ministry, with behind them a middle-aged, even elderly Cumann na nGaedheal Party, while opposite is a party with hardly a white head, leaders and led are all of one era, one time, one thought. The whole political situation is summarised in that – a Ministry which once belonged to a young, idealistic movement and breaking away, tried to lead old age.[40]

Within hours of the new Ministry being named, the Minister for Defence, Frank Aiken, and the Minister for Justice, James Geoghegan, K.C. appeared in Arbour Hill Prison. By 4.00 p.m. the following day all twenty political prisoners in the Free State were released, seventeen from Arbour Hill, two from Portlaoise and one from Mountjoy.[41] Sidelined for so many years, no time was being lost.

Ua Buachalla was also quickly back at grassroots politics. He attended a meeting of the Kildare Branch of Fianna Fáil in *Droichead Nua* on 28 February, where it was decided to appoint collectors in each polling district to work on the outstanding election debts and to have the collection closed by 13 March. To deal with the workload, 'two Honorary treasurers were appointed – Domhnall ua Buachalla of Maynooth and Miss Darby of Athy'.[42] He had not gone away – and no job was beneath him. The following month, the accounts for the three parties appeared in the *Kildare Observer*, and it was made clear that they could be inspected at the Court House in Naas, if desired: Buckley and Harris £164.18s.; Fitzsimons £22.18s.10p.; Minch £318.8s.4p.; Norton £441.17s.8p.[43]

The final figures; the book closed. From the euphoria of Sinn Féin's triumph in 1918 to the breakthrough by Fianna Fáil, ua Buachalla had been the constant in Kildare. With his party now dictating policy in

Dublin and de Valera orchestrating it – and despite the election setback – Maynooth would, finally, have a more settled, more tranquil atmosphere since the evening, sixteen years previously, when he marched defiantly with like-minded men to the GPO.

Yet, within weeks he was appointed one of two commissioners to report on industries and other matters concerning the Gaeltacht, an undertaking that appealed greatly to him, and one he attacked with energy. The title of the job was 'Temporary Inspector for the Survey of Industrial Activities in the Gaeltacht', but the appointment did not please everyone. A letter to the *Irish Independent* on 12 July 1932 read:

> Sir,
>
> 'Commissioners' have been appointed for the Gaeltacht. It is strange that the selection was not made from men from the Gaeltacht who have a practical knowledge of the kelp and the Carrageen industry – men such as Martin McDonogh, Dr Tubridy, Mr J. W. Mongan and others. I am not aware that seaweed or Carrageen moss grows in Maynooth.[44]

Little did ua Buachalla know then that this was not the only curveball life was going to throw at him that year.

CHAPTER 18

Life in the Park Ends

With power came change. One of Fianna Fáil's primary concerns after the election was the Oath of Allegiance and the presence in the Viceregal Lodge of a Governor-General, a symbol of loyalty to the Crown. Éamon de Valera saw the position as 'an altogether useless one. I shall endeavour to have it abolished.'[1]

The incumbent in 1932 was James McNeill, who had been a student at Belvedere College and Emmanuel College, Cambridge, before entering the Indian Civil Service, and then returning to Ireland in 1915. The majority of his work was done in the Bombay Presidency where he was involved in fighting the plague by inoculation, rural and urban communities and local land systems. He was also assigned to special duties in the West Indies and Fiji.

A brother of Eoin MacNeill, he spent a short time in jail after the Dublin Castle administration became suspicious of his activities, but any role he had was of minor consequence. After holding a diverse array of positions in Dublin, the Executive Council asked him to take up the post of representative of the *Saorstát* in London on 20 December 1922, where he performed admirably, most notably with 'the establishment of a bureau which was helping to extend trade with Great Britain and the overseas Dominions'.[2] On 16 December 1927, his appointment to succeed Tim Healy as Governor-General was announced.

As soon as Their Excellencies had settled down in the Viceregal Lodge, the customary deputations began to present themselves.

Among those who stayed with the McNeills were Lady Gregory, Lord and Lady Buxton, Lady Lavery, Countess Annesley, Lord Passfield, the Marquis and Marchioness of Aberdeen and Temair, Count and Countess McCormack and Mr and Mrs G. K. Chesterton.

The McNeills invited people to lunch and gave receptions, dinners and garden parties ... McNeill spoke at meetings and dinners, attended exhibitions, garden parties, receptions, dances and sporting events ... his wife [Josephine] normally accompanied him and also maintained her own round of social engagements.[3]

It is not surprising, therefore, that the household staff was sizeable: those who were paid monthly included the butler, valet, cook, assistant cook, vegetable maid, kitchen maid, plate maid, staff maid, stillroom maid, assistant stillroom maid, head housemaid, first housemaid, two housemaids, lady's maid, laundry maid and assistant laundry maid. Those who were paid weekly included the under butler, first footman, second footman, three odd men, charwoman, first chauffeur, second chauffeur and the farm man.

For a position de Valera saw as 'useless', the cost was substantial, and there were increases in some of the above figures during McNeill's time in office, as well as the replacement of cars by the State, with the purchase of one large limousine and two saloons (Armstrong-Siddeleys) in 1928 and a Ford van in 1930. By October 1932, de Valera had abolished the positions of comptroller, assistant private secretary, medical attendant and clerk, and reduced the chaplain's salary to £150 per annum.[4]

Although he had 'no personal grudge against James McNeill',[5] differences of opinion and contrasting views persisted. Ironically, what brought matters to a head was the incident at the French Legation on 23 April, when Seán T. O'Kelly and Frank Aiken walked out upon the arrival of the McNeills, and the ensuing correspondence between McNeill and de Valera. When this correspondence, which the President declared were confidential state documents and which could not be published, were made available to the press – with the exception of one marked 'personal' – a watershed had been reached.

Despite efforts by the Government to stop publication, word soon spread and the following day the Executive Council authorised publication of the entire correspondence. The Governor-General spoke of 'calculated discourtesy'; de Valera must have reasoned 'an appointed and unwanted

ANNUAL COST TO THE STATE OF THE GOVERNOR-GENERAL'S OFFICE, NOVEMBER 1932

(a) Salary	£10,000
Estimated value of exemption from income tax of £6,000	1,500
(b) Salaries, wages and allowances of official staff	1,395
(c) Allowance for maintenance of domestic establishment	3,000
(d) Travelling expenses	175
(e) Telegrams and telephones	190
(f) Motor car replacement fund: Grant-in-aid	240
(g) Stationary Office Vote	65
(h) Rates	775
(i) Posts and Telegraphs Votes	65
(j) Army Vote	840
(k) Cost of upkeep and maintenance of the Viceregal Lodge (including Garden produce to estimated market value of £1,000 supplied free to The Governor-General) - £9,867 – less letting of land - £160	9,707
TOTAL	£27,952

Government Memorandum, Dept. of the President, 26 November 1932

official ... had deliberately acted contrary to the formal advice and direction of a government elected by the people'.[6] He decided that McNeill must go.

On 3 October 1932, McNeill was received by the King in London and subsequently invited to lunch with Their Majesties. Some hours later it was announced in London and Dublin that 'in accordance with the advice tendered to His Majesty by the President of the Executive Council of the Irish Free State, the King has approved of Mr James McNeill relinquishing the Office of Governor-General of the Irish Free State'.[7]

Seán T. O'Kelly, who would reside in the Viceregal Lodge from 1945 to 1959 as President of Ireland, suggested to McNeill that 1 November might be a suitable date to leave the Phoenix Park, which McNeill agreed with.

As the McNeills prepared to depart, and speculation about the possible successor heightened, de Valera sought an avenue whereby he might use a brief window of opportunity to dilute or abolish the position of Governor-General. He did this by drawing in particular on the expertise and offices of Hugh Kennedy, the Chief Justice, John Dulanty, the Irish High Commissioner in London, Joseph Walshe, Secretary at the Department of External Affairs and Michael McDunphy, Assistant Secretary to the Executive Council.

Suspecting that de Valera might ask him to take on the powers of Governor-General, Kennedy made a suggestion which involved an 'Attorney of the King', a person who would hold an office not unlike that proposed in Article 75 of the draft Constitution brought to London in May 1922. If the British could be persuaded to adopt this solution, the title of 'Governor-General' would be abolished and the principle of the strict separation of the executive and judicial powers upheld.[8]

The solution was not acceptable. Nor was another, suggested by de Valera:

> The President of the Executive Council should be the person in whom the powers and authorities should vest and that he would exercise them until such time as, after further consultation, such more permanent arrangements can be made as will be more in harmony – than those hitherto existing – with the establishment of permanent friendly relations between the Irish Free State and Great Britain. It is further proposed to advise His Majesty that the Oath of Allegiance should be eliminated from the procedure of investment.[9]

That, too, was unacceptable to the King, as was 'a Commission, which consisted of the President of the Executive Council, the Speaker of the Dáil and the Chairman of the Seanad'[10] as it would not be in accordance with the Treaty and the Constitution. In all cases, the taking of the Oath of Allegiance became an insurmountable obstacle. With de Valera in Geneva from 16 November until 1 December, a meeting of the Executive Council held on 24 November approved an order advising the King to appoint Donal Buckley to be the Governor-General of the Irish Free State as from 25 November 1932.[11]

On the same day, a submission by Vice-President O'Kelly was laid before his Majesty. It opened as follows:

Certain parliamentary measures will have to be signed before the end of the current month. The appointment of a person who will succeed to the powers and authorities of the Governor-General has therefore become an urgent necessity. The Executive Council of the Irish Free State accordingly intend forthwith to advise His Majesty either to amend the Letters Patent in such manner as to allow the Chief Justice to exercise the powers and authorities and to leave no doubt outstanding about the automatic vesting in him of such powers and authorities, or to appoint Donal Buckley, Esquire, of Maynooth in the County of Kildare, as Governor-General as on and from the 25th November.

The Commission appointing the said Donal Buckley, Esquire, is attached hereto for His Majesty's signature. The Signet Seal to be used will be that approved by His Majesty for use in the Irish Free State.[12]

Choosing ua Buachalla was not a last-minute decision by de Valera. Despite the hectic diplomatic activity in October and November between Dublin and London in search of a solution that would satisfy him, Brendan Sexton believes that it was after returning from London on 17 October that de Valera was in a position to give the matter his full attention.

The name that came first to his mind, he was later to recall, was that of Domhnall ua Buachalla. He sent for ua Buachalla [apparently around the 24 October] and – in the words of the Earl of Longford and Thomas P. O'Neill – 'asked him to act if the necessity arose'.[13]

Years later de Valera spoke of the moment: 'It was a request completely unexpected by him and at first he could not answer. I asked him to think about it and I did not use any persuasion. He thought it over and later he said: "I am willing to do anything that you think ought to be done for Ireland".'[14]

Sexton went on to write that 'the important word here is "later" ... as he [ua Buachalla] hated the idea of assuming the Governor-Generalship':

... it may indeed have taken him some weeks to come to a decision. And de Valera may have been waiting for that decision when his proposals of 25 October, 5 November and 14 November were presented to the British. Ua Buachalla did not inform his family until the last moment of 'the very hard thing' that he was about to do.[15]

A letter received by ua Buachalla, written on 22 December 1932 from Joe Connolly, who was working with de Valera in Geneva, also indicates that the decision to take the job was probably made in November.

A Dhomhnall Dhíl,

I have been planning to write to you since I got back from Geneva and I was sorry I did not get mine in before yours of the 21ˢᵗ arrived … I was with the Chief in Geneva when your appointment was going thro' and we talked much and often about you. I need not assure you how much he appreciated what you did but I might add that he feels as I do that we have one right man in the job, and one that can be trusted as perhaps no other in the country can be trusted. God spare you to us and to the country and my blessing on you for undertaking an awkward task in difficult circumstances. I had an interesting and exacting time in Geneva and am now trying to pull up arrears.

I hope to see you soon and meantime my sincere good wishes for every happiness at Christmas and always.

Joe Connolly.[16]

Many years later, in October 1968, a series of articles appeared in *The Irish Times* – 'The Gerry Boland Story' as told to Michael McInerney – which carried a suggestion that raised the hackles of the ua Buachalla family, and in particular Joe:

It was shortly after that incident [the row between James McNeill and Government Ministers, Aiken and O'Kelly] when it was clear that the Governor-General was going, that Mr Boland received a friend of Mr Domhnall Ó Buachalla, a vigorous IRA veteran who had led a Kildare contingent to the GPO in 1916. [The person referred to by Boland would appear to be Tom Byrne.] The friend said that Mr O Buachalla had retired from business, but would be glad to take on some job in the national interest which would give him some small income. Mr Boland told the friend that he thought he might indeed 'have something suitable for him in the near future'. Shortly afterwards, Mr O Buachalla was invited to become Governor-General, instead of Mr MacNeill.[17]

The letter immediately prompted the following response on 15 October which was sent to No. 102, Howth Road, Dublin 5, by Joe.

A Chara,

I have just read the 'Gerry Boland Story, No.4' as told to Mr McInerney in *The Irish Times* of October 11th. In the paragraph headed 'New Crises' you have mentioned my father's name and given an account of the series of events which led to his appointment as Governor-General.

The facts as stated in the article are completely untrue and I can definitely state that neither you, nor any member of the Government, knew the President's mind in the matter until after he had spoken to my father. I would have thought that you, who knew him so well, would have been the last man to belittle his character as to accept the statement from anyone 'that he would be glad to take on some job in the national interest that would give him some small income'.

I feel that my father's public life does not need any defence and I have no wish to discuss the matter. I have full knowledge of the events which led to him agree to fill the position and they are completely at variance with the story as told in Mr McInerney's article.

I now ask you to issue a statement in the Daily Press, making good the damage your article has done to my father's character. I have no other reason for writing this letter.

Mise le meas,

Seosamh ua Buachalla.[18]

No statement was issued in the *Daily Press* in subsequent days, nor was there a personal letter to Joe from Mr Boland on the matter.

It was to No. 108 Rock Road, Booterstown, Co. Dublin, the residence of ua Buachalla's brother, Michael, that the Commission arrived on the morning of 26 November. The swearing in was observed by J. P. Walshe and Seán Moynihan, Secretary to the Executive Council. Ua Buachalla handed the Commission to Chief Justice Kennedy – who read it and found it to be in order – and thereupon took the Oath of Allegiance and the Oath of Office, which Kennedy tendered and administered to him as required in the prescribed forms, but in the Irish language. Ua Buachalla signed it thus:

> *Bheirim-se, Domhnall ua Buachalla, mo mhóid go ngéillfead go fírinneach agus go mbéad, dílis de Shoillse, Rí Seoirse V, dáoighri agus da chómharbaí do réir dlighe.*
>
> *Go gcabhruighidh Dia liom dá réir.*[19]
>
> [I, Domhnall ua Buachalla, do solemnly swear that I will comply honestly and truthfully, that I will be true to His Highness, King George V, to his offspring and successors.
>
> May God help me in this regard.]

On Monday 28 November, *The Irish Press* reported that 'the name of the new Governor-General came as a complete surprise on Saturday when two days' exciting speculation was ended by the official announcement'.[20] The *Times* looked more haughtily on the appointment:

> The circumstances attending the appointment ... make it clear that the King has pursued to the end the only dignified and constitutional course which was left open to him by the quarrel between Mr McNeill and Mr de Valera. It would have been intolerable that His Majesty should have allowed himself to become embroiled in that quarrel.
>
> It is perhaps hardly less intolerable that he should be troubled at all with a situation which has long since become *opéra bouffe*. But the time that has elapsed since Mr McNeill's departure suggests that a

good deal of trouble has, in fact, been taken to maintain the façade of a Dominion Constitution in the face of a strong effort to break it down ...

Mr Buckley's career is described in Mr Dulanty's *communique* with so discreet a selection of emphasis and omission that it becomes difficult to understand why no reference is permitted to the fact that the new Governor-General has already taken the Oath of Allegiance. That, for what it is worth, and the fact that Mr Buckley is a separate entity from Mr de Valera, are the two constitutional points involved as far as the Sovereign is concerned.[21]

Much more indignant was the editorial writer in *The Irish Times*, who questioned ua Buachalla's ability to reconcile ardent republicanism with the Oath of Allegiance and suggested 'that it be left to Mr Buckley's conscience'.[22] He was also disappointed at the new Governor-General's 'lack of any of the traditional qualifications for this great office'. Warming to the subject, he continued:

We may infer, therefore, that, with Mr Buckley's appointment, the social importance of the Viceregal office – maintained with high dignity, and with much national profit through some centuries – will be extinguished ... The Governor-General no longer will be a living bond between the King and the Irish Dominion.

Until he [de Valera] gets his full mandate, the Governor-Generalship cannot be abolished. It can be assailed, however, by such a progress of neglect and diminution as will make its death – when Mr de Valera obtains his free hand – a natural and even desirable thing ... the gradual approach of theoretical independence, in the supreme degree, seems to be bringing small wealth or happiness to the Free State; but 'the mind is its own place', and, perhaps, her bankrupt citizens will draw spiritual comfort from the shuttered windows of the Vice-Regal Lodge.[23]

Both de Valera and ua Buachalla could positively identify with much of what had antagonised the writer.

On 28 November at 4.00 p.m. in the Conference Chamber of the Supreme Court, at the request of ua Buachalla, Hugh Kennedy 'did with all solemnity read and publish the Commission under the sign manual and signet of the King, appointing Your Excellency to be the Governor-General of the Irish Free State in the presence of all such judges of the Supreme Court of Justice, of the High Court of Justice, of the Circuit Court of Justice and of the District Courts of Judges, the Master of the High Court and Registrars and other officials of the Courts of Justice, as attended there in response to an invitation issued by me.'[24]

Ua Buachalla did not inform the King's private secretary of his installation. When he received what was in effect an invitation to an audience with His Majesty, he replied in polite and non-commital terms.

On his appointment it was decided that he would not live in the Viceregal Lodge, but would select a suitable residence as soon as possible, and he would also use the term *Seanascal* rather than Governor-General. This name prompted the Hon. Edward Cadogan (Conservative, Finchley) to ask the Secretary of the Dominions in the House of Commons 'whether his attention had been drawn to the announcement'.[25] A few days later it was briefly referred to:

> Mr J. H. Thomas: I understand that the term *Seneschal*, in the Irish spelling, has been used since the establishment of the Irish Free State as the Irish translation of Governor-General, and, so far as I am aware, no alteration has been made in this position.
>
> Mr Cadogan: Will the right hon. Member give us a translation in his own language?
>
> Mr Thomas: I would hate to shock the House.
>
> Lieutenant-Commander Bower [Conservative, Cleveland]: Is he aware that one of the definitions is a military commander, invested with judicial powers; and does he not think the gentleman referred to rather over-states the importance of his office?
>
> Mr Thomas: I have ceased to think on this.[26]

No doubt, it would have pleased ua Buachalla that the honourable gentlemen had taken time out from ruling the Empire to discuss the Irish language. *Time* Magazine gave America a view on the appointment.

King George appoints as Governor-General of the Irish Free State, or any other dominion, any man whom its premier may choose. Last week, scrawny President Éamon de Valera, whose office is equivalent to premier, chose his old friend Daniel Buckley. The move was a surprise to Dublin, a tactical victory for the de Valera Republicans. One of their objects is to abolish the post of Governor-General entirely. By supporting a man that all Ireland knows took the Oath and will fill the office with his tongue in his Gaelic cheek, they are very near to success.[27]

Within days, Messrs. Battersby and Co. had completed arrangements for ua Buachalla to live at Gortleitreach, Monkstown, Co. Dublin. Initially, the Bord of Works architect and Chief Valuer, Mr Robinson, inspected a number of houses in Dublin before the list was whittled down to a choice between Gortleitreach [ua Buachalla's spelling] and Victoria House in Dalkey. Robinson accompanied ua Buachalla and de Valera to view both residences before they made a decision – and it's possible the name of the Dalkey property might not have sat comfortably with either man.

Describing Gortleitreach in an article for the Dun Laoghaire Borough Historical Society in 2011, Mary Grogan wrote that 'from the front it looked like a miniature of the White House in Washington'. Built for the Stewart family, who were the hereditary agents for Lords Longford and De Vesci, it was

a handsome house of Georgian character, two stories over basement, and looked out over Dublin Bay past De Vesci Terrace. The main house was built by 1846; a wing and a large conservatory were added later. A surviving account book for the year 1856 shows that £102.14 was spent on the garden, £100.15 on the stable, £23.13 on coal and £14.15 on gas. Nearby Willow Bank was a small development of four semi-detached houses, which were built in 1865 and let by J. R. Stewart of Gortleitragh to a 'very high-class' tenantry.[28]

After the house went back on the market in 1937 it became the home of Dr Eduard Hempel, Adolf Hitler's diplomatic representative in Ireland. He became an acquaintance of ua Buachalla, inviting him to have lunch on 19 August 1941 and later exchanging Christmas greetings. It was in Gortleitreach that de Valera paid his condolence on the death of Hitler, though pointing out later that it was 'important that it should never be inferred that these formal acts imply the passing of judgements, good or bad'.[29]

John P. Duggan wrote that Hempel 'served Ireland well. Ireland was lucky to have had him. He was lucky to have been in Ireland.'[30] Hempel's final letter to ua Buachalla arrived from Germany in 1950. 'To kind remembrance, our very best greetings for Christmas and wishes for the coming year to you, dear Mr Buachalla, and to your family, together with a hearty farewell'.[31]

If ua Buachalla's appointment did not meet with unanimous approval, there was a warm and enthusiastic response from around the country, particularly in Dublin and on the western seaboard, the latter no doubt influenced by his recent work as commissioner. The telegrams came first, letters followed, and then the overseas post from many countries, particularly America. The source of one of the initial telegrams was no surprise:

Melbourne, Australia

An old friend of yours congratulates you and the de Valera Government. The old order changeth, thank God – Archbishop Mannix.

New York, USA

A thousand congratulations. Memories of Broadstone, our march to Richmond and later Frongoch came crowding back. Wish you every success in the task you have undertaken for Dark Rosaleen – Tommy O'Connor.

Grattan House, St Stephen's Green, Dublin

Dear Mr Buckley, Lady Esmonde joins in congratulating you on your appointment as Governor-General. May you enjoy good health and happiness in your new office – Thomas Grattan Esmonde.

Doon Cottage, Cashel, Connemara, Co. Galway

I tender my sincere congratulations ... hope we will have another drive along the hillsides by next summer – Mark E. Keely.

Boulea, The Commons, Thurles, Co. Tipperary

Your services to the nation are esteemed by me and by all true republicans who believe in ultimate freedom. May you be as leading a light and as gallant a soldier as in the past, when Ireland triumphs over her enemies and is a free nation – Seán F. T. Bulman.

Newtown House, Blackrock, Co. Dublin

A Chara, The King doesn't know you as well as I do! – Con Ó Laoghaire.

Ballybrack, Co. Dublin

The news today is what I expected, you were always a Governor-General ... have had the honour of being your friend and have seen you day by day in the little church in Maynooth – and serving my Mass too – I shall say Mass for you tomorrow, that God in His grace may strengthen you. I'm damn sorry now I sent back my horse ... we may ride again ... the 3rd Southerns are still living – *An tAth.* Tomas Ó Grúagain.

Mainistir N. Proinsias, Cloch na Rón, Cuan na Mara

Congratulations and felicitations *adfinitum* to you as a recognition of brave deeds and to our little nation to have such a sincere and genuine *Gaedheal* at the helm ... in you we have achieved the glorious dreams of the past – the resurrection of the hopes and wishes of long lost friends. Snobbery is dead, eat and make merry over its tomb – Br. Laoiscach.

Pluckerstown House, Naas, Co. Kildare

I, Mrs and family were delighted to see that President de Valera and his Government conferred on you the highest honour. Little we thought last summer when you asked us to pray for the success of your mission to the west that it would turn out so successful ... we can say we had the pleasure of you once cutting turf with us – Bob Ivers.

Drumsna, Co. Leitrim

An old friend takes the liberty of congratulating you as *Seanascal* ... you may remember my late husband, T. Garland, who was station master at Leixlip up to two years ago. How very glad he would be now to know of your having such an exalted position. Through you good kindness we got back the subscription we gave to Dáil Éireann – Kate Garland.

No. 5 Lower Merchants Road, Co. Galway

Having known you personally since June 1910, when I first tested your weighbridge at Maynooth and annually calling at your place in the capacity of Inspector of wts. and ms., [weights and measures] from Naas, until I was compelled to resign in 1920 for my national sympathies, I had to vent my happy feelings at seeing an honourable, sincere, Irish patriot getting the honour you richly deserve – Martin Faherty.

No's. 5, 6 & 7, Upper O'Connell Street, Dublin

I hasten to congratulate you because it shows the great confidence shown in you by Dev. It is a position requiring great moral courage to accept in the circumstances, but you may rest assured [that] there will be understanding on the part of those who know you, and you need not bother about the others. My aunt has grown about ten years younger since she heard the news because she thinks you will have about £40,000 per annum and says you deserve it – Michael Fay.

Dunfierth, Enfield, Co. Meath

Heartiest congratulations. When T.D. for Kildare, Your Excellency interested yourself for me and other local people, as to obtain for us farms of land on the Cloncurry Estate. Congratulations is only poor recompense for doing such as Your Excellency did ... but they are genuine feelings – John McNally.

Askeaton, Co. Limerick

May it please Your Excellency I to write the following as I am troubled with a very hard beard. I would be very thankful if you would send me a razor as I cannot afford to get a suitable one – Michael Quinn.

Castlewarden Estate, Newcastle, Co Dublin

On behalf of myself and the other tenants of the above estate, I offer you our hearty congratulations ... we have not forgotten that it was only through your intervention and that of our worthy President that we were saved from eviction by the previous government. Although the matter has not yet been settled, we are hopeful of being treated in a Christian manner by the present Executive – J. Dowdall.

No. 18 Mountjoy Place, Newport, South Wales

I hope you will forgive the liberty I am taking in addressing you. I served with you, and under your dear father, as shop assistant in 1892–93. (You may remember me). May God bless you and give you health, strength and wisdom to keep our dear flag flying, and also to sever the few remaining links that bind our beloved country. One line of acknowledgment would be cherished by me, and my children, as long as life lasts – John Cleary.

Suite 1500, Cadillac Square Building, Detroit, USA

I sincerely congratulate you ... it was particularly appealing to see [that] your appointment received the endorsement of President de Valera. On his visit here three years ago, it was my son Gerald Emmet who introduced him to the public over the radio station NMBC. Since that time the boy – at 39 – was slain by gangsters. Gerald was a crusader and was engaged, successfully, in cleansing this city of underworld politicians – J. C. Buckley.

Blackwood, Robertstown, Naas, Co. Kildare

It may interest you to know that your old constituents around here are simply delighted at the news; personally, although a lot has happened during the past six months to give me pleasure, nothing so far has happened to come near my delight when your appointment came on the wireless from London on Saturday night. I laughed myself sick at the thought of the rebel representing his Satanic – excuse me – His Britannic Majesty. You are the third

Governor-General – and I feel sure you will be the last. The Final Step is not far away.

Your appointment will hasten that day; you have done many brave acts in your life, but this last is, in my opinion, the bravest of all – for no doubt there will be attempts to misrepresent your motives. You no more represent the English King than you do the man in the moon. I believe the heart of every decent man in our country goes out to you – R. P. Cusack.

This selection of telegrams and letters reflects the pleasure ua Buachalla's appointment gave to the heartlands of nationalism. They could relate to him on many levels – as a shop-keeper, a friendly neighbour, a family man, devoted to the Irish language, religious, proud of his country and willing to put his life on the line for it. He was a man who cared, and they knew it. They respected him. And that recognition would certainly have helped him deal with the slings and arrows of those who would declaim him, who would miss the pomp and pageantry of royalist days.

An example of this was a cartoon published in the *Evening Standard* on 29 November 1932, which had ua Buachalla standing behind the counter in his shop in shirt sleeves and top hat, with one hand in the air and the other on a telephone directory, as the Chief Justice reads the 'Oat of Allegience'. Standing behind the Chief Justice as witnesses are a number of politicians, among them Éamon de Valera, Seán T. O'Kelly and Seán Lemass. With a heading 'HISTORICAL OCCASION IN IRELAND', the caption read:

Arrah! It was an iligant cirimony, the swearing-in av the new Governor-Giniral. His Ixcillincy took the oat' in his own private language (which no one but himself could undershtand at all at all) whoile the mimbers of the Government sang the Oirish version av the National Anthem – *God save the King from interfering in matters that don't consarrn him.* Despite the vigilance av the troops, the proceedings were interrupted by a choild coming to buy a penn'orth av acid drops for Mr Twomey.

Written beneath the cartoon by ua Buachalla is '*Sampla de cultúir Shasana*'. [Example of British culture.]

Agreement on a Salary

Having decided that the position of Governor-General would be abolished, de Valera set about dismantling it with clinical precision. He spoke to ua Buachalla about what lay ahead when first asking him to take on the assignment, and in early December at a lengthy meeting, he elaborated on his vision for the future, and how a succession of decisions would continue to undermine and eventually destroy what had been a highly visible and glamorous institution of the Crown. On 13 December 1932, Michael McDunphy, Assistant Secretary to the Executive Council, wrote the following letter to de Valera:

President:

1. Some time ago I provided the Governor-General with a formula which has proved very successful to himself and his household in fending off importunate visitors, namely that: the Governor-General will under no circumstances receive anybody accept [sic] by appointment.

He asked me today whether similar assistance could be given him in the matter of social functions. I mentioned that I was contemplating a formula which, subject to your approval, would run somewhat as follows:

'It is the desire of the Governor-General to reduce to the minimum, compatible with the requirements of his office, his attendance in an official capacity at receptions and other functions of an official or social character. In pursuance of this intention he proposes to limit his commitments of this nature to such as he is advised by the Executive Council are necessary or desirable in the State interest.'

He expressed himself as very pleased with this, and stated that if put into operation, would save him an immense amount of trouble and transfer from him to the Executive Council the onus of deciding troublesome matters of this nature.

2. The formula could be suitably embodied in letters from the Governor-General's Private Secretary in reply to invitations, whether

in respect of purely social or official or quasi-official functions, as in the case of those given by foreign representatives. Each such invitation could then be transmitted by the Private Secretary to this Department for the Executive Council's decision.

3. As a matter of courtesy, the Department of External Affairs could explain the position in advance to foreign representatives accredited here, so that in the event of such a representative wishing to invite the Governor-General to a function, the views of the Government could be obtained formally beforehand.

4. On the general question of control, I think that it is in accordance with your view that all official communications to the Governor-General should emanate from this Department as the mouthpiece of the Executive Council, and that other Departments who wish to have communications transmitted to him should operate through this department. Any other procedure would militate against unity of control and lead to needless confusion. M. McD.[32]

A hand-written reply to the original letter arrived the following day from the President's secretary:

M. McDunphy,

The President has considered the formula suggested in paragraph 1 of your minute. He feels that it will be sufficient that the Governor-General, when declining invitations, shall state that he is unable to accept, without giving reasons. It is, of course, understood that the Governor-General, in dealing with invitations sent to him in his official capacity, shall act only after ascertaining informally the views of the Executive Council. The President will discuss the suggestion in paragraph 3 with Mr Walshe or Mr Murphy.

He agrees with the view expressed in paragraph 4.[33]

The Governor-General's Private Secretary, Mr P. Moriarty, took up his duties on 20 December, a more highly-paid official than his predecessor. The reason for the increased salary was 'in order to secure more effective control by the Government over the Governor-General'.[34] An example of how invitations were dealt with is provided in the correspondence between Moriarty and McDunphy in July 1933:

> Mr McDunphy,
>
> I enclose herewith two cards of invitation received by *An Seanascal* from the Most Rev. Dr Byrne, Archbishop of Dublin, for the favour of your early attention.
>
> P. Ó Muircheartaigh.
>
> *Rúnaí Príobháideach,*
>
> With reference to your note of the 15 instant regarding the enclosed invitations from His Grace the Archbishop to the *Seanascal* to a garden party in honour of the President and members of the British Medical Association to be held at Blackrock College on Friday July 28th , I have to inform you that the question has been submitted and a decision given that His Grace should be informed that the *Seanascal* will not be able to attend.
>
> M. McD.[35]

When it came to deciding on a salary, the Governor-General was asked by de Valera 'to state what he considered to be an appropriate recompense for his services'. His answer – which he was to confirm in writing on 26 June 1933 – was that he would take only £2,000 net per annum of the salary to which he was entitled ... As the total net amount actually paid to the Governor-General by 30 June was £5,299.6s.2p. and as the amount payable on the basis of £2,000 per annum would have been £1,201.19s., the sum to be refunded was therefore £4,098.4s.5d. On 28 July 1933 a cheque for that sum was sent to Government Buildings by His Excellency's private secretary. By then, de Valera had explained in Dáil Eireann that they were bound to offer £10,000 per annum but that 'he was not bound to receive it'.[36]

He would also receive £1,200 per annum for the maintenance of his official residence and establishment. This was intended to cover the 'renting and upkeep of his residence, the payment and boarding of his domestic staff and the employment of a chauffeur at £200 per annum'.

He also purchased the 'dearer of the Armstrong-Siddeleys and the Ford van, which had been part of his predecessor's fleet'.[37] The idea of a chauffeur was later dispensed with and a member of Special Unit, No. 53672, Private J. Cassells, was appointed as military chauffeur/bodyguard on 4 February 1933.[38] He resided in Gortleitreach, and was required to hand over his revolver to the Private Secretary when leaving the establishment in off-duty hours. His official staff consisted of a private secretary, a chaplain, two gardaí, a military chauffeur-bodyguard, a typist, cook, maid and gardener.

Sexton wrote that the statement that his 'sole function' was 'to sign acts of the Oireachtas' was not correct. 'Ua Buachalla dissolved and summoned the Oireachtas, sent money messages, signified the King's Assent to Bills, appointed the President and appointed ministers, judges and members of the Constitution (Special Powers) Tribunal. He also made orders and miscellaneous appointments, issued Letters Patent and accepted both a Letter of Recall and a Letter of Credence.'[39]

'No Pastry for the King'

As the year came to a close, two of ua Buachalla's daughters – Bríghid and Máirín – who lived with him in Monkstown until the position of Governor-General was abolished, prepared their new residence for occupation and selected house staff. And while he would not be receiving any guests on behalf of the Irish Free State, he had younger and more important people to become acquainted with – his grandchildren.

James Durney recalled that 'he endeared himself to the Dublin masses by refusing to send King George the traditional Christmas pastry of "four and twenty woodcocks, baked in a pie"' for generations the annual gift of Irish viceroys. Dublin instantly rang with a new version of the rhyme:

> When the pie was opened
>
> The birds began to sing:
>
> Three cheers for Donal Buckley
>
> No pastry for the King! [40]

Word of ua Buachalla's break with tradition eventually reached Australia, where an exile wrote a seven-verse poem, which appeared in *The Advocate* in Melbourne, beginning:

> The Queen was in the parlour,
>
> The King was at the door,
>
> Excitement filled the palace
>
> From roof to basement floor,
>
> The Queen continued rocking,
>
> But the King looked down the street,
>
> He might have asked the butler,
>
> Yet he was too discreet.

The poem went on to record the reaction of the King . . .

> The butler brought the message,
>
> There would not be a pie,
>
> 'E says 'E's unacquainted
>
> With Your Majesty.'
>
> The King near burst out laughing
>
> But he was too discreet,
>
> As he wrote in his notebook
>
> 'That's a lad I want to meet'.[41]

A few weeks before leaving his temporary accommodation in Booterstown for good, a decision about where the brothers, Domhnall and Michael, would attend Christmas Mass arose. Michael said he had a preference for Midnight Mass in a chapel in Drumcondra, which had been customary for him for many years. On reaching an agreement, the pair walked to the car on a bitterly cold Christmas Eve, and drove past the guard on duty who was shivering as snowflakes drifted onto his exposed hut. About two hours elapsed before they returned, and as they headed for the door, Domhnall turned to Michael and suggested that they bring in their 'minder' and give him a drink to ease the pain of the sub-zero temperatures.

Michael duly returned with a hot toddy, which was gratefully received, and quickly dispatched. Within minutes, however, their guest had dropped to the floor, comatose. Two worried hosts were later relieved to see him come around and eventually saw him safely home, yet were still anxious about his state of health, and their role in his collapse. The problem was solved on Christmas Day when they discovered that he had moved almost as quickly as the car when it headed for Drumcondra the previous night, but branched off about 100 yards down the road, and nipped in through the front door of The Punch Bowl. Apparently, he knew he'd have time for one or two . . .[42]

As ua Buachalla settled into his new surroundings in January, de Valera was busy asking the country to give Fianna Fáil an overall majority in the Eighth Dáil on 24 January 1933. As well as the Oath abolition, retention of Annuities, full protection of the home market for agriculture and industry, the saving of the language, the setting up of industries in the Gaeltacht and a reduction in the number of T. D.s, he also promised the abolition of the Senate. Despite the attractive package, the party fell one short of the required seventy-seven seats, and again had to rely on Labour's support. Subsequent by-election successes would give them independent power.[43]

A 'Special Description by J. A. P.' in the *Independent* as business resumed on 8 February recorded that there was 'a crowded House [only five members absent], a crowded Public Gallery, and a division lobby thronged with Senators (who, I think, adjourned early in the hope of better sport in the Dáil)'.[44] He continued: 'We settled down to business. The Clerk went through the usual formulae – reading the Governor-General's (or should one say, the *Seanascal's*) Proclamation convening the Dáil, in Irish and English, and then the names of all the deputies returned [less than half-a-dozen of which were in the Gaelic].'[45]

After Seán Moylan proposed de Valera for President, and Michael O'Clery seconded the motion in Irish, 'the leader of the opposition rose. Mr Cosgrave's indictment of the de Valera Government, delivered with an utter lack of emotion, as if he fully realised the futility of tilting at windmills, occupied barely two minutes, but was distinctly incisive.'[46]

Aware that his duties should be low-key, 'Domhnall Ó Buachalla drove up alone to Government Buildings, and on alighting from his car, hurried up the steps to avoid photographers. [This he failed to do as a picture of him appeared in *The Irish Press* the following day.] He went to Mr de Valera's room. When de Valera returned to the Dáil, Mr Ó Buachalla slipped away from Government Buildings. A crowd of sightseers loudly applauded when he appeared, but police shepherded the throng back to make way for him.'[47]

In Kildare, Tom Harris increased his vote by 1,289 in heading the poll, and was followed – as in 1932 – by Sydney Minch and William Norton. In the absence of ua Buachalla for the first time since 1918, Fianna Fáil broke with tradition in nominating Brigid Darby, but the electorate could not be persuaded to empower a woman.

Although virtually consigned to anonymity, ua Buachalla had a role to play on 13 May 1933 when the State welcomed M. Pierre Guerlet, the new French Minister Plenipotentiary and Envoy Extraordinary, to the Irish Free State. 'The booming of fifteen cannons, fired in slow succession at Island Bridge, signalled the arrival' while 'there was a brilliant scene as the Minister was escorted by cavalry through streets lined by cheering people'. M. Guerlet 'was dressed in diplomatic costume of gold-braided blue, arrived in his car escorted by a troop of Free State cavalry – a picturesque sight in their striking uniforms and trappings'.[48]

Although he had come to present his credentials to *an Seanascal*, he was greeted by Michael McDunphy on alighting from the car and led inside, where he was received by de Valera and Seán T. O'Kelly. In the Council Chamber, M. Guerlet delivered the letters of recall of his predecessor, M. Charles Alphand, and then his own letters of credence. He expressed the regret of M. Alphand that, owing to ill-health, he had not been able to take leave of *an Seanascal* in person.

'Having already been able to appreciate the value of Irish hospitality, I am as happy as I am proud to see this mission confided to me', said M. Guerlet, addressing ua Buachalla in person. He concluded a brief speech with the words, 'permit me to express to Your Excellency the sincere good wishes that I feel for you personally and for the prosperity of the Irish Free State'.[49]

Having responded first in Irish, ua Buachalla continued in English, saying he was glad to know that His Excellency the President had chosen M. Alphand for a very important mission in the diplomatic service for his country. 'I regret that M. Alphand's state of health has not permitted him to take leave in person and I would be grateful if you would convey to him my own good wishes and those of the Government of the Irish Free State for his complete restoration to health.'[50] Speaking about the traditional friendship of the two countries he said:

> The fulfilment of your mission will be made easier still by those friendships and associations which you have already formed during the time in which you have been with us in another capacity ... your efforts, Mr Minister, to advance as far as possible the economic, intellectual and cultural relations between our two countries, will receive from the Government here the fullest support and co-operation.

> I thank you for your good wishes for myself and the prosperity of Ireland, and I shall be glad if you will convey to His Excellency the President of the French Republic the good wishes of the Government and the people of this country, both for His Excellency personally and for the welfare and prosperity of the French Republic. I bid you welcome.[51]

The conciliatory tone of the Governor-General's speech, wrote Brendan Sexton 'and the fact that this was the only occasion on which ua Buachalla was involved in such proceedings, gives the impression that de Valera was trying to make amends for the unseemly incident at the French Legation'.[52] The controversial spat centred on O'Kelly and Aiken walking out of the legation when James McNeill and his wife arrived during a dance given by M. Charles Alphand. 'In this crude and insulting fashion did the two ministers let it be known that they did not wish to publicly associate with the Governor-General.'[53]

The degree to which ua Buachalla adhered to de Valera's instructions is reflected in the fact that he arrived at Government Buildings a few minutes after the President, stayed in the background until it was time to address M. Guerlet, and did not appear in any picture with him. The desire to implement a common objective was unrelenting.

Dissipating Misconceptions

The next occasion for pageantry involved Mr W. W. McDowell, the United States Minister to the Free State, who arrived at Government Buildings on

28 March 1934. On this occasion, ua Buachalla was kept out of sight, but newspaper reports the following day forced the Government to comment:

> To clear up a misunderstanding arising from press reports of the presentation of credentials by Mr McDowell, United States Minister, to Mr de Valera instead of to the Governor-General, the Department of External Affairs, Dublin, issued the following statement:

> Until the autumn of last year it was the Governor-General who received foreign ministers. It was then decided that ministers should, in future, present their Letters of Credence to the President of the Executive Council instead of to the Governor-General. In November, arrangements to bring about this change were made in the customary constitutional manner. The British Government has nothing whatsoever to do with such matters.[54]

Simultaneously, the following statement was issued:

> The American Legation wishes to dissipate any misconceptions which may have arisen in connection with the presentation by the Minister of his Letter of Credence. The Legation was fully aware of the change in procedure and desires to state that there was not the slightest want of consideration or courtesy towards the Minister on the part of the Irish Free State Government.[55]

McDowell and de Valera were no strangers. They met twice in Butte in 1919 when de Valera was raising money and McDowell was Governor of Montana. On 25 July, the American met the train and the pair drove through the streets, where de Valera addressed a crowd of 10,000 people. The following day he addressed a joint session of the Montana State Legislature. Between his July visit and a return in November, Butte had raised for the Irish Freedom Fund $12,061.75, and by May 1920 the Butte Irish Bond Drive had, between cash raised and pledged, a figure of $108,700.[56]

A Negative Response

In ua Buachalla's private papers, there is an *Irish Press* cutting which was devoted to the premiere screening in the Savoy Cinema in Dublin of *Grand Hotel*, the film version of Vicki Baum's novel, which recorded the 'fact' that he attended in the company of 'his son Joe and party'. Written in the margin beside the story is a refutation of the story, and an explanation, starting with the words '*Ní raibh an Seanascal ag an bpeictúir seo*'. It would be reasonable to assume that these facts were pointed out in a letter to the Government the following day.

Refusing invitations, no matter how politely done, drew opprobrium. It started when the rugby fraternity read that he would not be attending Lansdowne Road for the Home Nations Championship match in 1933 against Scotland. James Meehan from Belfast, in a letter to the *Irish Independent*, aired his feelings:

> It speaks very badly after President de Valera's broadcast stating that equal justice is being meted out to all citizens. Rugby players and supporters are of every race and religion in the Free State. It is a game played in Catholic and Protestant colleges, and I believe President de Valera was once a rugby player.
>
> The Governor-General represents all citizens of the Free State, whether they play rugby or Gaelic football, and they are all equal taxpayers and citizens before the Law. No act could do greater harm to that ideal preached by President de Valera for the joining up of the Six Counties with the rest of Ireland if bigotry and intolerance is shown by the powers that be in such a trivial matter as welcoming sportsmen coming to play a game of football from Gaelic Scotia.[57]

In March, *The Irish Press* reported that 'he cannot see his way to accept the address of loyalty', which Trinity College had proposed to present to him, his reason being that 'he has decided to carry out the duties of his office in a quiet manner, and not to receive addresses or become patron of any body'.[58]

In April he had to reject a request to attend Kildare's racing festival at Punchestown. In May it was the turn of the Royal Dublin Society, but de Valera and a number of ministers were enthusiastic attendees at the Spring Show; the Irish Lawn Tennis Association was also informed that he was unable to attend upcoming international matches.

Another Kildare racing venue, the Curragh, was in the picture in October when Seán MacEntee, Minister for Finance, introduced a supplementary estimate in the Dáil for £105, which was required for a Plate to be run at the course, and which would be called the 'Saorstát Plate'.

Readers of the *Irish Independent* were informed 'that an added interest is lent to the estimate by the fact that this Plate is in part a substitution, at public expense, for the Plate formerly known as the Governor-General's Plate, which the former Governor-General used to provide out of his own pocket. The present Governor-General, Mr Buckley, although he is a Kildare man, is apparently not inclined to keep up the custom'.[59]

Not all of his decisions, however, had a negative tone. In a case which attracted nationwide attention, John O'Connor of Tralee was arrested in January on a charge of larceny and possession of arms. He subsequently went on hunger strike while on remand in Cork Jail. When the case came before Mr Justice McElligott in Tralee on 29 April 1933, he told the court that while he regarded a hunger strike as being destructive of the very foundations of democratic government, 'O'Connor is a young man of character, of ideals, and I believe that in pursuit of these ideals he would persist in the course he has adopted to the last extreme.' He went on to say:

> I would regard it as a criminal folly if any government elected by popular franchise should yield to the weapon of hunger strike, as it would render the employment of the law impossible; yet on this occasion in view of the fact that O'Connor has been in custody on remand for three months – I would not have imposed on him a greater sentence if he had been convicted – I propose to ask the Governor-General to remit the unexpired portion of the sentence I have passed on him and release him pending his trial.[60]

By 10.00 a.m. on Monday morning, having spoken to the Government, ua Buachalla signed the documents and O'Connor was released.

Two days later he put his name to a much more contentious piece of legislation. The Bill for the removal of the Oath of Allegiance taken by members of the Oireachtas was finally passed by seventy-six votes to fifty-six on the 3 May 1933. De Valera moved the necessary resolution (which recalled how the Bill had been held up by the Seanad), stating that the Government was elected at the last two elections to get rid of the Oath, and this Bill was the last step in doing so. He said that the Government was interested in getting rid of the Oath because they knew 'that the majority of the people did not want any confession of allegiance to a foreign king on the part of their representatives'.[61]

In a declaration regarding arms, he said there was no excuse for anybody to prepare in any way for the use of force. No government could permit to go unchecked such a movement for the use of force. Before the debate concluded, however, the Civil War made its way into the dialogue:

Mr Cosgrave: You began it, and we ended it.

President: No; we are ending it here today, thank God.[62]

On 31 October 1933, with one dissenting voice – that of Sir John Keane – three bills amending the Free State Constitution were passed by the Senate, which continued the process of diminishing the role of the Governor-General. The first removed the right given to the Representative of the British Crown to authorise all appropriations of public moneys. It was a right not in fact exercised by the British Crown but by the Free State Executive Council. Yet the continuance of the clause in the Constitution was an acceptance of British supervision over expenditure here. The elected representatives of the people, in law as well as in fact, had now alone the disposal of the State appropriations.

The second Bill concerned political structure. Under Article 41, the British Crown, through its representative, had the express right to withhold the Crown's assent to any measure which the people's elected deputies had passed, thereby preventing it becoming law. The amendment removed from the representative of the Crown any authority, except to sign every bill presented to him, its nature notwithstanding, thus making the people's representatives the final architects of the people's laws. The third amending Bill abolished the Free State citizen's legal right under the Constitution to appeal to His Britannic Majesty in Council against the decisions of the Free State Courts.[63]

Although the *Daily Express* ran a story that 'Mr Donal Buckley, the Governor-General of the Irish Free State had declined an invitation from the King to attend the forthcoming wedding in London of the Duke of Kent and Princess Marina', and that the reply 'was addressed to his Majesty in Gaelic, with an English translation',[64] it was denied in a statement from the Government Information Bureau.

Nevertheless, the following day the *Irish Independent* maintained that 'it was in a position to state that an invitation was received by the Governor-General'. However, one day later they revealed that they 'received a communication from the Department of the President, signed by Seán Ó Muimhneachain, stating that there is no truth in the statement that "an invitation to attend the Royal wedding was received by the Governor-

General", and admitted that we accept the statement'.[65] Their final word, though, was a finger-wagging exercise: 'It would appear that the Irish Free State alone of the Dominions has not been invited to be represented at the ceremony. This is a slight upon the nearest Dominion, which other members of the Commonwealth will undoubtedly resent.'[66]

In March 1934, the *Evening Herald* carried a story that *an Seanascal* had taken to the skies, literally. '*D'eitell Domhnall ua Buachalla, Seanascal, I gceann des na heiteal-lánaibh* "Everson Services" ... *agus rinne sé scrúdughadh ar an eiteallán nua,* "*Spiorad Éireann*", *a rinneadh Mac ui Fhoghludha*'.[67]

[Domhnall ua Buachalla flew in one of 'Everson Services' aeroplanes ... and examined the new aeroplane 'Spiorad Éireann', which was made by Mr Foley.]

It was followed up in *Dublin Opinion* under the heading, 'A Flight of Fancy':

> 'Step in, your Excellency', said the pilot. 'I hope the noise of the engine won't worry you. I regret that I cannot carry out my duties in a quiet manner. We are now passing over the Phoenix Park. Look down carefully, and you'll see the house where you don't live ... Sit tight now; we're going up and up ... and up! You're sure the altitude isn't affecting you?'
>
> 'Not at all', said the Governor-General; 'a big rise is nothing to me!'[68]

Under Section VI of the 'Instructions passed under the Royal Sign Manual and Signet to the Governor-General of the Irish Free State, December, 1922', Ua Buachalla was obliged to get permission if he ever wished to leave the country during his period in office. In March 1934 he did intend to take the boat from Dun Laoghaire to Holyhead, but as it was his intention to return within twenty-four hours the President's view was that there was no need for a formal application. It is possible he was going to meet his son, Séadna, who was working in Britain, for a few hours, but he never did travel as his daughter Máirín revealed to Brendan Sexton. In fact, he never left the country during his term of office.[69]

CHAPTER 19

Séadna Emigrates

During a debate on the estimates for the President's Department on 29 May 1935, Éamon de Valera informed the Dáil that before his term of office expired, a new Constitution would be introduced, which 'so far as internal affairs are concerned, will be absolutely ours'.[1] He continued: 'No one deplores the fact that extraordinary measures have to be used today more than I do, and no one in the country would be happier if it were possible to get on without these extraordinary measures, but there must be order. We undertook duties as a Government and there is no way out for us. We have got to fulfil these duties or get out.'[2]

Before going on to talk about major aspects of Government policy, he said he wished to refer to quite a negative reference made by Roscommon Independent Deputy, Frank MacDermot, during the debate:

> I think it is my duty to say that Domhnall Ó Buachalla is one of the finest types of Irishmen in the country. When men were required he was there and there is no one from overseas or anywhere else whom we would choose before him for any position.

> Domhnall Ó Buachalla, at his [de Valera's] urgent request, and much against his own will, accepted the position. He hoped at the appropriate time to ask the Irish people to show to Ó Buachalla the appreciation he deserved. It was particularly mean to refer to the salary he was receiving in the way Deputy MacDermot had done.[3]

Immediately, MacDermot was on his feet.

> Before the President continues, perhaps you will let me say what I
> said yesterday, that my remarks were not intended as any kind of
> reflection on Mr Buckley. I spoke of the preferability in my view of
> getting an Irishman from overseas to fill the post. I had no desire
> to pass any reflection whatever on the present occupant of the post.
>
> As regards the financial matter, I was casting no sort of aspersion
> upon him personally. My point was that it seemed to me that it was
> impossible for Mr Buckley in present circumstances to spend the
> salary, which with allowances was in the region of £4,000 a year. If
> he spent it on entertainment, the Government would throw him out
> of office. My remarks about salary were in the nature of an attack on
> the Government and not on the man.[4]

De Valera said he was glad that the Deputy had tried to make that clear
once more.

> There had been until recently a certain courtesy shown towards the
> person who held the position of Governor-General. There was not
> a position in the country that Domhnall Ó Buachalla could not fill
> with dignity and honour to the nation and no one from overseas
> or elsewhere could fill it better than he could. If he did not come
> out and do things in public, it was because it was the policy of the
> Government that he should not do it.[5]

McDermot was born in Dublin in 1886 and educated at Downside School
and Oxford University before qualifying as a barrister. He moved on to
banking in New York from 1919 to 1927, returned to Ireland where he
failed to get elected for Belfast West in 1929, but was successful in 1932
as an Independent in Roscommon. The following year he was back in
the Dáil as a member of Fine Gael, and subsequently a persistent critic
of Fianna Fáil, de Valera, and both the abolition of the Oath and the
position of Governor-General. Life in the bosom of Fine Gael eventually
turned sour, and his differences led to him joining Fianna Fáil, with de
Valera appointing him to the re-established Seanad in 1938.

If the *Seanascal* was an easy target for criticism in the Dáil, at home it
would have been unthinkable. But it did happen, and it came from his

youngest son, Séadna. He recalled that his father was disappointed with the result of the exams he sat with a view to getting a job in banking – and it upset him to the point that it was written into his notebook. The reality is that Séadna was probably not cut out for life behind a desk or one spent dealing in finance. He was a man of action with a great sense of humour, one who interacted very well with people, had a great interest in nature and loved the outdoor life. As a young boy he recalled entering the store in Maynooth from the main yard one day:

> I heard a noise and while searching about, I guessed it was a female mouse going to build a nest. I was correct. I got a wooden box and divided it into three compartments, i.e. a playroom, a kitchen and a bedroom. I built the playroom in such a way that she could not get out. In the other section of the box I had the two rooms with glass giving me a view of what was going on. I made a small ladder for the mouse to get into the bedroom.

> I put her into the playroom with a ball of newspaper. During the night she had chewed the paper to pulp. Later in the day I looked in again and the mouse had six young ones. I fed the mouse on milk and bread. The following day my father told me that I would be going to Ring to school, so I decided to release the mice. I opened the door of the house and out ran mama followed by the six. In half an hour all six had returned.[6]

His stories mirrored the passing years and included a hurling match he played for Kildare against Offaly in which 'my front teeth were smashed and while the rest of the team were eating in Naas I had to suffer in silence, watching them. I went to Kilcock where my cousin Cathal was a dentist and he helped out. He removed the stumps and made a temporary plate – and the pain of that operation is something I will never forget.'[7]

Later he recalled a Sunday morning in winter spent shooting with Joe's rifle. He had dismantled the gun and secreted it in his coat, pumped a soft tyre on the bike, put a cock pheasant into a deep pocket and was about to return home after an enjoyable morning's sport when a car, driven by the local sergeant, pulled up behind him. Asked if he had been out shooting, Séadna looked down at the tail of the pheasant sticking out of the coat and reluctantly nodded his head.

Ordered to leave his bicycle at the local farm, he 'was driven in state' to the barracks in Maynooth, where the details of his arrest went into the daybook, with the sergeant telling him that 'he had been trying to catch him for three years' and he could now expect 'six months in prison and a £200 fine'. The charges were: 1. Having a gun without a licence. 2. Ammunition without a certificate. 3. Shooting in the close season. 4. Shooting on land without permission. The case was heard in a busy Kilcock court where the sergeant accused Joe of being 'up every morning on other people's land while they were at Mass'.[8] What the sergeant might not have been aware of was that the judge, Kenneth Reddin, was a past-pupil at St Enda's, had fought in the Easter Rising and been jailed in Stafford; and that a friend of Séadna, Con O'Leary, had made the judge aware of the accused's background. The fine, at £3, was probably appropriate, but may not have satisfied a resolute sergeant.

With the bank no longer an option, Séadna decided to go to Bennett College and here he received a diploma in the theory of welding and later attended Bolton Street School of Technology. Much to the surprise – and probable dismay – of his father, he took the boat to Britain and got employment with Metropolitan Vickers at Trafford Park in Manchester before moving on to Cammell Laird at Birkenhead, where he worked on the aircraft-carrier, *HMS Ark Royal,* which was completed in 1938 and torpedoed in 1941 off the coast of Gibraltar by German submarine *U-81.*

From there he travelled north to Renfrew in Scotland and was taken on at Babcock and Wilcox. Asked to go on night work as a supervisor, he managed to get transferred to the Fusion Service. He later arrived back in Dublin to work on installing four boilers for a cracking plant which refined oil, a job that had gone to his company through the good offices of Seán Lemass. His wanderlust complete, he married Kathleen McNamara, settled down in a house overlooking the grounds of Monkstown Rugby Club/Pembroke Cricket Club in Wilfield Road, Ballsbridge and spent the rest of his life working nearby for the ESB at the Ringsend Power Station. Ua Buachalla did get over his son's period in exile, and probably never bothered to resurrect the benefits of a job in banking.

On 25 June 1935, the fourth eldest of the ua Buachalla children married, which would have been a pleasant social distraction for ua Buachalla himself at that time. Kevin was educated by the Christian Brothers in O'Connell School, which at one time was referred to as 'the working man's Belvedere College', due to its outstanding reputation and the fact that it was non fee-paying. Both schools could boast the fact that

James Joyce was a past-pupil. Quieter by nature than Joe and Séadna, Kevin married Peggy Clarke from Ballybunion. The couple lived in Ranelagh, where Kevin was a member of the local Fianna Fáil Cumann. Ironically, his studies also led him into the ESB – working for a time with Séadna at the Ringsend Station.

While Dáil deputies spoke of the elusive Governor-General, his presence was recorded on a number of occasions in the provincial press. In 1934 he visited many parts of Kerry, including Ballybunion, while staying in Glenbeigh. He also visited Cork and Cavan. In 1935, during his holiday tour in the south, a local paper reported that he had stayed in the house of his cousin, Mr R. Buckley, Powerstown House, Drumcradh. Accompanied by other members of the extended family – Mr J. Buckley, M. R. I. A., London and Miss B. Buckley, Powerstown House – he motored to Kildorrery where he was joined by another cousin, Mr D. J. Buckley.

Close to Skennakilla, in Ballydaheen, he was attracted to 'a rare type of dwelling house, occupied by Mrs Noonan. It is two-storied, well thatched, and possesses an air of unmistakable comfort. The original building has undergone some facial alterations, but enough remains to show that it was erected more than two hundred and fifty years ago, and was once a residence of considerable importance.'[9] Although hospitably entertained by its owner, the reporter told readers that ua Buachalla was not disposed to accept the meaning of the place name, 'Ballydaheen', as the 'homestead of little David'.

Their next stop was Labbamolagga, where the well-preserved remains of one of the most ancient and interesting oratories in Ireland, as well as ruins of early Christian and Pagan times were viewed. On they went to Darragh Churchyard, to Ardpatrick, where he was recognised by many people, and then to Fantstown Castle. His final destination was Kilmallock, 'the picturesque town gate that spans the main street, King John's Castle, where the sound of the anvil is daily heard, the famous ruined Dominican Priory, the ancient Catholic church with its incorporated round tower, Sarsfield House and other interesting buildings ...'[10]

He took time another day to visit the Christian Brothers' Schools in Doneraile, where he was received by Rev. Br. Nolan, Superior, and in each class he was given 'a rousing reception by the pupils'.[11] Among them were five relations – Robert, James and Donal Buckley of Annakisha, Patrick Buckley of Powerstown and Conor Quirke of Castletownroche. Before departing, 'His Excellency, addressing the senior pupils in Irish, expressed his pleasure at the enthusiasm with which Irish was being studied in the school, and earnestly exhorted the pupils to avail to the full the opportunity within their grasp to making Irish their every-day language . . . and in appreciation of his visit, the pupils were given a free day.'[12]

On the same holiday, he visited Mallow to see Mr William J. Griffin, M. C. C., a life-long friend of the family, and went on to the sugar factory at Newberry. When he learned that the coal for the factory was obtained from Wales, he asked if Irish coal could be used. The factory manager explained that Castlecomer could not supply sufficient coal. The boilers had been built so that they could use Irish anthracite when the supply was available, which would happen in time. He had previously been through the Carlow factory, where Irish coal was being used.

Later, 'he conversed in Irish with the press representatives. "He was", he said, "pleased with the tour of the factory and he took a keen interest in all branches of Irish industry and had found it delightful and enlightening to see the factory".'[13]

Although generally out of sight – if not out of mind – in Ireland, ua Buachalla was remembered in London. Charles James O'Donnell, formerly of the Indian Civil Service and Liberal M.P. for Walworth 1906, and a son of Captain Bernard O'Donnell, Northumberland Fusiliers, of Carndonagh, Co. Donegal, left estate in Great Britain of the gross value of £23,334. The recipients of this vast amount included the National University of Ireland for genealogical research into his ancestors, ten Catholic Churches and an annuity of £500 in rotation to some of Ireland's and Britain's main universities to establish O'Donnell lectures in Celtic history and literature.

His final bequest of £1,000 went to the Governor-General of the Irish Free State, but not for his own use. He requested ua Buachalla to spend £500 repairing the tombs of the Princes O'Neill and O'Donnell in the church of San Pietro in Rome, and to place a marble tablet, to the value of £100, in the Votive chapel in Vienna in memory of Count Maximilian O'Donnell, who saved the life of the Emperor Francis Joseph in 1852. The remaining money was to be used for the maintenance of tombs of other great Irishmen. Whether they were to be selected by ua Buachalla was not stated, but the will ensured that the *Seanascal* would be busy for some time carrying out the wishes of the Donegal benefactor, even if the work was not directly related to his official paymaster.[14]

London was again the focus on 20 January 1936 when a bulletin was issued from Sandringham House at 9.25 p.m., stating that 'the King's life is moving peacefully towards its close'.[15] The Prince of Wales sat talking to his mother, Queen Mary, as they waited for those fateful words that would make him King Edward VIII of England. They arrived shortly before midnight. George was 70 and had reigned for twenty-six years. The following morning a telegram was delivered to ua Buachalla:

> London C T O, Absolute Priority, OHMS
>
> Most immediate.
>
> *Seanascal*, Dublin.
>
> Profoundly regret to state that his Majesty King George the Fifth passed away just before midnight. Please inform President, Executive Council.
>
> Wigram.

The President of the United States also wired a message:

> On the occasion of the death of his Majesty King George, I wish to extend to Your Excellency and to the people of the Irish Free State on behalf of the people of the United States and in my own name an expression of sincere sympathy in your great loss.
>
> Franklin D. Roosevelt.[16]

On 6 February in the Dáil, Frank MacDermot was anxious to find out about messages of sympathy for the King. He asked the President 'whether he received any message or messages from the head of any foreign State or Government in connection with the death of the late King; and, if so, what was the text of such message or messages and of the reply thereto.'[17]

Having quoted the telegram from Roosevelt to the *Seanascal*, he said the response was: 'I am very grateful for your Excellency's kind message of sympathy on the death of his Majesty King George V.' He also pointed out that he had received a similar telegram from America, and given the same response.[18] De Valera had also sent a message of sympathy to Queen Mary. 'On behalf of the Government of *Saorstát Éireann*, I desire to express to your Majesty our sincere sympathy with you and the Royal Family in your great sorrow.'[19] The following reply was received:

'I am deeply touched by the kind message you have sent me on behalf of the Government of *Saorstát Éireann*. I greatly appreciate your sympathy with me and my family in our irreparable loss.

[Sgd.] Mary.'[20]

King George paid a brief visit to Ireland shortly after his coronation in 1911. In 1921 he travelled to Belfast to open the Six-County Parliament. Regarding the events leading up to the Truce, he was kept informed through his personal friendship with the Viceroy, Lord FitzAlan. In his speech, believed to have been framed with the express intention of creating an atmosphere suitable for negotiations, King George said: 'This is a great occasion for the Six Counties, but not for the Six Counties alone, for everything which interests them touches Ireland ... I appeal to all Irishmen to pause, to stretch out the hand of forbearance and conciliation, and to join in making for the land they love a new era of peace, contentment and goodwill.'[21]

Michael Comyn, K. C., Vice Chairman of the Seanad, also spoke about the King's contribution to affairs in Ireland:

> In the summer of 1921, a number of IRA prisoners were under sentence of death in Ireland. When the number had mounted to forty-two, a writ of prohibition in the case of Clifford and Sullivan was moved by me in the Irish Courts and carried to the House of Lords. During the long hearing, the King personally intervened and secured an assurance from the Prime Minister that no execution should take place and that peace would be made.[22]

The Free State was represented at the funeral by the High Commissioner in London, John Dulanty, and a tribute was sent to Windsor in the form of a shamrock of yellow narcissi, daffodils and tulips tied with green and yellow ribbon and inscribed 'From the Government of *Saorstát Éireann*'.

King Edward Desires Friendly Relations

Four months later, a meeting took place in Dublin between Joseph P. Walshe and Sir Harry Batterbee, who was Assistant Permanent Undersecretary of State for Dominion Affairs to his brother-in-law Sir Edward Harding, which resulted in a confidential letter – with the title 'Our Political Relations with the British' – being sent to de Valera. Walshe wrote:

Sir Harry Batterbee phoned me on Tuesday afternoon from the Adare Hotel and asked me to dine with him in the Shelbourne on Wednesday night so that we might have an opportunity of talking over things in general. I asked him to come and have a meal in my house instead, where we should be much more to ourselves and would be free from disturbances ... I picked him up at the train at 7.30 p.m. and we talked until about midnight. He said that he was hoping very much that it would be possible to come to some sort of political agreement before long.

King Edward, immediately after his accession, had expressed a very strong desire to establish friendly relations with *Saorstát Éireann* ... Batterbee himself had been asked to dine with the King for the purpose of giving him all the information he could about the existing situation.

Recently, Batterbee had a chat with Mr Baldwin. There were, I gathered, other officials present ... Batterbee suggested to Mr Baldwin that he should make a statement setting out that Great Britain would place no obstacle in the way of the establishment of a united Ireland ... I urged Batterbee that the idea of coercing Ulster did not exist except in the imagination of some Tory propagandists ... that there was no intention in *Saorstát Éireann* of attempting any coercion of the Six Counties.[23]

Later in the letter he wrote:

On the Governor-General question I had said to him that it was our view, and must be the view of all liberal-minded people, that Great Britain had no right whatever to interfere or to dictate what form our system of government should take. On this he said: 'But isn't that a very strong reason for our having an impartial representative in Dublin who will convince our Cabinet that such is your attitude, and no doubt, it is a justifiable attitude?'

As you will remember, we have discussed this matter of a British High Commissioner in Dublin, and there did not seem to be much reason for encouraging the project, but I am beginning to think that it would be better for us that the British should hear from a properly accredited representative what is happening in this country than from the mischievous interferers who now seem to be their chief sources of information.[24]

At a Cabinet meeting a month later, on 5 June 1936, de Valera mentioned (and the Cabinet agreed accordingly) that he proposed to address a communication to King Edward VIII in regard to the intention of the Government to introduce a Bill in the Dáil, at the beginning of the autumn session, for the purpose of setting up a new constitution. The King would be informed:

(a) That this Constitution would deal with the internal affairs of *Saorstát Éireann*;

(b) That amongst the provisions of the new Constitution would be the creation of the office of President elected by the people and the abolition of the office of Governor-General.

Dulanty delivered this communication on 8 June and two days later, 'as a matter of courtesy', gave an outline of the constitutional proposals to Malcom MacDonald, the Secretary of State for Dominion Affairs.[25]

On 24 June 1936, while moving an estimate of £1,327 for the office of Governor-General, de Valera told the Dáil that 'the Governor-General will be replaced by an elected representative of the people who will act as the ceremonial head of the state'. The President said 'that there should be someone outside and above political parties to act on public occasions as a ceremonial head of the State. The kind of person holding such an office should have a more important function than that of appending his signature to Bills or officiating at a garden party.'[26] He then went on to say:

> I think that the person to act as the head of the State here should be directly elected by the people and be responsible to them as a supreme guardian of their constitutional rights. I had the creation of such an office in mind in 1921, and I have often felt since that if such an office had then existed, our people might have been spared the misery that followed later ... The full proposals will be submitted to the Dáil in a few months and ample time will then be afforded for their discussion ... I hope the members of the Opposition will

consider them on their merits and with a single-minded regard to the permanent interests of the country.[27]

Not surprisingly, Frank MacDermot was first to respond, moving an amendment that the estimate be referred back, but admitting he was pleased that the President had committed himself to the view that there should be a person who could be described as the head of the State, a person outside party politics.

> The total cost to the State under all headings for the Governor-General's office was approximately £4,000. It might seem a little ungracious to question this expenditure, especially on this occasion ... but the most outstanding, sensational and perhaps the only activity that had been connected with his tenure of office is the exchange of cablegrams between him and President Roosevelt ... which the Government so sedulously concealed from public notice until he [Mr MacDermot] elicited the information by parliamentary question.[28]

The words 'secrecy' and 'misrepresentation' continued to dominate proceedings:

> Mr de Valera: What did the Deputy mean by 'hiding away'? Is not our whole policy known to the people of the country? It was quite consistent with that policy. A telegram was received for a head of a State and a courteous reply was needed and was sent in response. I also got a similar telegram as President of the Executive Council and replied to the Secretary of State ...

> Mr MacDermot: When I said the telegram was concealed what I meant was that it would not have been published, but for the questions I asked about it and I think that the President implied that that is so.

> Mr de Valera: The Deputy is very clever in using his words. What is the meaning of the word 'concealed'? I take it 'conceal' means a deliberate attempt to hide away from the people.

> Mr MacDermot: Yes.

Mr de Valera: I say that is untrue.

Mr MacDermot: Would they have been published if I hadn't asked the question?

Mr de Valera: I say that it is untrue to say that these telegrams were deliberately withheld from the people. They were not published. None of them was published because non-publication of them was directly in line with our whole attitude on the question, and when I was asked for them, I gave them without apology in the same terms as I have given them now.[29]

The vote on a payment of £1,327 for the office of Governor-General was agreed, Mr MacDermot asking to be recorded as dissenting.

Passing through London the following month, de Valera took the opportunity to tell MacDonald that in his new Constitution, the Crown would cease to perform any function, or to have any functions performed on its behalf, in the internal affairs of the Free State. But in matters of common concern between the nations of the Commonwealth, the Free State would co-operate fully and for these purposes the King would be recognised as the head of the Commonwealth.[30]

On 17 November, MacDonald told the Irish Situation Committee that de Valera would soon introduce new Constitutional Legislation, with the Second Reading before Christmas, but the abdication crisis upset the timetable. Within months of ascending to the throne, King Edward VIII was proposing marriage. Unfortunately, the lady in his life, Wallis Simpson, had two divorced and living ex-husbands. It did not help his cause either that she was an American socialite.

Further conflict faced Edward as titular head of the Church of England, which at that time opposed the remarriage of divorced people if their spouses were still living. On the political front, he was aware that if the marriage went ahead, Prime Minister Stanley Baldwin would resign. Such an outcome would force a general election and further damage his standing as a politically neutral constitutional monarch.

On 29 November Sir Harry Batterbee saw de Valera in Dublin. The message from Prime Minister Stanley Baldwin, had three alternatives: 'That Mrs Simpson would become Queen; that there should be a morganatic marriage; that the King should abdicate.'[31] The Irish attitude was one of detachment. MacDonald informed de Valera on 4 December that abdication would occur in a matter of days. De Valera sent a message which stated that

> he could not at any time or in any circumstances be responsible for legislation recognising a King in Ireland. Batterbee was despatched to Dublin and made clear that, if the Free State Parliament passed no legislation, Edward VIII would remain King of the Free State and that Mrs Simpson, if the King married her, would become Queen. Confronted with this intolerable prospect, de Valera decided to speed up the introduction of his constitutional legislation.[32]

Windsor and the Pangs of Parting

The realisation that his days as Governor-General were numbered would have pleased ua Buachalla. A position he never sought, but felt duty-bound to accept, was about to be abolished. The abuse that followed the appointment – and ensuring that the position became less visible as the years passed – would have been an irritant, but no more. Satisfaction lay in successfully implementing de Valera's strategy. As he prepared to leave, so too did King Edward VIII. On 11 December 1936,

> an atmosphere pregnant with the pangs of parting surrounded Fort Belvedere, where the standard of the Duchy hung listlessly ... final arrangements were made for his departure after his farewell message to the Peoples of the Empire over which he had reigned ... shortly after midnight he sailed from Portsmouth Harbour in the Admiralty yacht *Enchantress*, escorted by the destroyer Wolfhound ... Mr Edward Windsor had gone to his destiny ...'[33]

That same day the *Seanascal* was driven from Monkstown to the Dáil, which assembled at 3.00 p.m. The Public and Strangers' Galleries were packed and the Press Gallery was fuller than on any occasion since the removal of the Oath Bill debate. Members of the House had been summoned by telegram and, in addition, a message was broadcast to deputies to hold themselves in readiness. The attendance in the Distinguished Strangers' Gallery included the American Minister, Mr A. Mansfield Owsley; the French Minister, M. Pierre Guerlet; the Consul General for Italy, Signor Lodi Fe; the Consul General for Poland, Count Dobarynski and the German Charge d'Affaires, Herr Schroetter.

By 10.30 p.m. the Constitution Amendment (No. 27) Act had passed all stages. Shortly after the Dáil rose, the Bill was signed by ua Buachalla as his last act as the official representative of Edward VIII, whose abdication would be accepted by an Act to be passed through the Dáil the following day.[34] In signing the Bill, ua Buachalla deprived himself of all his major powers under the Free State Constitution. From that point on, the King of England would only represent the Free State in external affairs as the link symbolising the Association of the Commonwealth of Nations. 'The Executive Authority (External Relations) Bill, 1936 was passed the following day by Dáil Éireann and signed by the Ceann Cómhairle. De Valera emphasised that the Bill's main purpose was to make clear, beyond all shadow of doubt, that the executive authority resided in the Executive Council, the body elected by the representatives of the people.'[35] And yet, doubt still existed.

> During the second stage of the Constitution (Amendment No. 27) Bill 1936, de Valera said that in the case of the Governor-General 'the appointment and executive power's provisions' were being deleted. Whether 'the Governor-General' was 'immediately ended by that' was 'another question'. The amendment did not expressly state what functions in connection with legislation disappeared. There were certain statutory functions 'which would require a consequential Act to clear up'. If it should be necessary to bring in a consequential Act to deal with the situation, they were prepared to do so.

> De Valera and his advisers, in other words, do not appear to have been at all sure as to whether the office of Governor-General would still be in existence after the Bill had received the King's assent. The British, on the other hand, were in no doubt once they had become acquainted with the text of the legislation. A memorandum prepared on 14 December by the Attorney-General, Sir Donald Somervell, declared categorically the Governor-General as Representative of the Crown, having been deprived of his functions in the Constitution, was abolished by the deletion of Article 60.[36] By 21 December, the matter had been resolved.

> On that day, de Valera saw ua Buachalla in Government Buildings and informed him that he had been advised that the office of Governor-

General had been abolished as and from 11 December by the Constitution (Amendment No. 27) Act 1936, and that ua Buachalla's occupancy of the post had terminated as from the same date. He further stated that it was his wish that ua Buachalla should terminate his occupancy of Gortleitreach and retire into private life as soon as could be conveniently arranged so that anything that might be construed as a continuation of official existence might quickly disappear. Ua Buachalla undertook to comply with de Valera's wishes.[37]

In doing so, though, he had a problem. No longer employed by the Government, his income had ceased, yet he was tied to a five-year lease on the house in Monkstown, having been advised by de Valera when taking up the post of the probable time-frame required before his work would conclude. The final year's rent would have to come out of ua Buachalla's pocket – for a residence that was far too big for his needs and much too costly to maintain, particularly as it would be necessary to retain at least a maid and the gardener. He made some progress on that front in late December when Messrs Battersby & Co. Ltd, acting for the owners, agreed to conclude the agreement in mid-June.[38]

Nevertheless, the former *Seanascal* was being set adrift by the State at 71 with an outstanding financial burden, which was not of his making. Allied to that, it had been necessary to hand over his business to his eldest son after accepting the position of Governor-General in 1932. Although not apparently sympathetic when ua Buachalla first explained his predicament in relation to the house in Monkstown and also the need for a small pension, de Valera was unlikely to overlook the sacrifice that the *Seanascal* made when agreeing to be the country's third Governor-General. Subsequent suggestions that he was pursuing High Court litigation on the matter have never been validated and there is nothing in his papers to suggest that he did; nor was there much delay in de Valera assenting to his request.

At a Cabinet meeting on 15 January 1937, authority was given for the preparation of a Bill to vest in the Executive Council, with effect as and from the date of the enactment of the Constitution (Amendment No. 27) Act 1936, all powers duties and functions, with certain specified exceptions, which immediately prior to the passage of that Act were vested in or were exercised or capable of being exercised by the King or by 'the King's Representative' in relation to internal *Saorstát* matters, under whatever title or titles, and whether pursuant to statute, charter, prerogative, custom or other authority.[39]

On 2 March 1937, at a Cabinet meeting in the Council Chamber, the final item to be discussed was 'Governor-General: Financial Provision'. Now fully aware of ua Buachalla's outstanding debt on Gortleitreach, the fact that he no longer was a Maynooth merchant, and that he had not been provided with a pension, de Valera put forward a proposal for consideration to his colleagues – Seán T. O'Kelly, Patrick Ruttledge, Seán Lemass, Seán MacEntee, Dr Jim Ryan, Frank Aiken, Thomas Derrig, Gerald Boland and Oscar Traynor – which met with approval:

> Arising out of the abolition of the post of Governor-General and the termination of office of the holder thereof, Domhnall ua Buachalla, in consequence of the enactment of 11 December 1936 of Constitution (Amendment No. 27) Act, 1936 (No. 27 of 1936), it was decided that financial provision should be made for Mr ua Buachalla as follows: a lump sum of £2,000 and a pension of £500 per annum.[40]

The Executive Powers (Consequential Provisions) Bill, 1937, was introduced on 11 May and became law on 8 June. On introducing the second reading on 18 May 1937, the Minister for Justice, Patrick Ruttledge, mentioned that 'it also makes provision with reference to the late Governor-General, which I do not want to deal with now. I can deal with that when replying.'[41] If he thought that the discussion was going to slip quietly by, he was mistaken.

'Unsavoury Piece of Jobbery'

The official Debate Report contains almost 30,000 words, which were delivered over a period of almost three hours. Vitriol poured from many tongues, directed generally at de Valera and his Government, but also at ua Buachalla, despite the occasional qualification of him being a 'gentleman'. The following are selected extracts:

> Mr Frank McDermot: At the time the Governor-General was appointed, did he make a condition that if he accepted that office, he should be provided for life?
>
> Mr Patrick Ruttledge: I do not think there was an understanding like that.

Professor John O'Sullivan: It is surely rather peculiar that a man who has got for four years a salary of £2,000 a year for doing nothing, an allowance of £2,000 a year to live in a house so as to help him to do nothing, should now get a gratuity of £2,000 for doing nothing and £500 a year to enable him to do nothing for the rest of his life ... and mind you, this Bill comes before the House with the unanimous blessing of the Fianna Fáil Party.

Mr McDermot: I feel obliged to say frankly that it has the appearance of an unsavoury piece of jobbery. I hope it is not that. I am not stating it is that, I am only stating that, in default of explanations ... that is what it looks like.

Dr Thomas O'Higgins: Donal Buckley appears to me to be a business man. It is a pity that he was subsidised in idleness ... he appears to be the man we have missed for the last five years, because, on its face, this document has all the evidence of having been dictated by a shrewd and hard businessman.

The President: I cannot put it any more generally than [£2,000 was used] for the purpose of his establishment. It is interesting to take some figures which I asked to be prepared for me. Taking it in comparison with the sums that were paid in the past –

Mr James McGuire: You cannot compare them.

The President: Why not?

Mr McGuire: Because he was doing nothing.

The President: What was he not doing – going to Punchestown?

Mr George Bennett: Perhaps I should preface my remarks by indicating that anything I will say will have no personal reference to Mr Donal Buckley, although I might be tempted to say very strong things. I can only describe this as the most scandalous proposition that has ever been brought before this House. The President has made no proper effort to justify it ... As far as Mr Donal Buckley is concerned, my recollection of him when last I saw him in this

SALARY AND EXPENSES FOR GOVERNORS-GENERAL 1923–1936

1923–1924	£24,309-18-9
1924–1925	£34,447-16-6
1925–1926	£27,626-5-8
1926–1927	£26,650-14-5
1927–1928	£26,639-5-4
1928–1929	£28,098-9-2
1929–1930	£26,122-14-9
1930–1931	£25,743-18-4
1931–1932	£25,665-4-5
1932–1933	£21,522-19-7
TOTAL	£266,827-6-11
1933–1934	£4,674-7-0
1934–1935	£4,160-19-2
1935–1936	£4,166-9-10
1936–1937	£3,225-4-4
TOTAL	£16,227-0-4

The Irish Press, 19 May 1937

House was an affable, genial Irish gentleman against whom I could not say a word. He was at that time a member of this Dáil, enjoying no salary but an allowance of £360 a year to meet his expenses as a deputy.

Mr Daniel O'Leary: I am not going to have a silent vote on this Bill. I look upon this Bill as being the result of the greatest piece of corruption that has ever happened in this country ... we see here that the Governor-General is to get a pension of £500. I should like to know from the President what that would amount to at the present rate of interest, if it were capitalised?

Mr McDermot: The Deputy must remember that it is only an annuity.

Mr O'Leary: Well, would it not work out the same way?

Mr McDermot: It must be remembered that, to buy an annuity of that or a like amount, for a man of 70 years of age, would cost less.

Mr O'Leary: Yes, but then, in this case, there is the question of a lump sum, and that, at 10 per cent, would be about £8,000, before you were finished with it. However, what I was going to say is that, at this rate, there will be no end to the corruption that is going to prevail in this country.

Mr William Norton: I am not going to be tempted, no matter what my indignation may be in regard to this Bill, into making any derogatory references to Mr Donal Buckley. I believe him to be an eminently respectable gentleman, held in high esteem by a very large section of the community, of which I am glad to say I am one, but one must consider this Bill apart altogether from one's admirations or feelings towards the recipient of these sums. One must look at this as a matter of principle, and, looking at it as a matter of principle, I cannot for the life of me understand what justified the Executive Council in formulating such outrageous proposals as are contained in the Bill . . .

I understand that the ex-Governor-General is a native of Maynooth. In Maynooth, a man with a wife and five children will only get 12s 6p a week unemployment assistance. A sum of 12s 6p a week in Maynooth, to which the Governor-General will probably go back to reside, is expected to keep a man with a wife and five children. But when it comes to an ex-Governor-General, he cannot exist on less than £500 a year . . . I challenge the Government to take off the Whips and try to get this Bill passed on a free vote.

General Seán MacEoin: I think that the proper justification for this compensation and this pension would be as compensation for imprisoning Dan Buckley for four years in Monkstown.

Mr O'Leary: Without any cause.

General MacEoin: Illegally. If the Government can put forward that as a reason, I certainly will vote for this, because I think it was an outrageous hardship on the poor old man to bring him to Monkstown and keep him a prisoner ... except you let him out for a trip down to Lahinch or some place like that – but even then his escort was with him: he was not let free even for that time.

Mr James Dillon: So far as Mr Buckley is concerned, I wish him a long life to enjoy it. I hope he will beggar the Treasury before he lies down to die ... It is nothing short of grotesque when one throws one's mind back to the song and dance that was made about the disinterested rejection by this noble-hearted patriot of the remuneration granted to other Governors-General. Now a Bill is being brought in to pay his debts, to give him a lump sum, and to furnish him with a life pension ...

This Bill will leave a nasty taste in everybody's mouth, and to tell the truth, the most regrettable part of it is that this decent man should be the subject of as much ridicule and jest as he must be throughout the country when the people come to read this.

Mr Ruttledge: [summing up]: I do not think much of the hypocritical statements to which we have listened in this House today. As a matter of fact, I think that, in putting forward these hypocritical statements, the people who have put them forward will not find the favourable reaction they hope to get from the people of the country.[42]

When the question was put, the Dáil divided: *Tá* fifty-six; *Níl* twenty-seven.

The following day, the *Evening Mail's* leader article was run under the heading 'The Martyr's Crown' and enjoyed the opportunity to take a sideswipe:

... the Governor-General was as much to be pitied as any bag-snatcher or cycle thief in Mountjoy. His staffed commune, with their fellows, freely play lawn tennis and enjoy the fresh air and pleasant scenes at the seaside and in the country, but Domhnall ua Buachalla could only sit in his lonely retreat ... the hermit of South County Dublin ... he has suffered for four years in the cause of making the

King's representative the object of ridicule … now that he is free once more to gaze upon the world with all its mothly rout, let us not deny him his reward.[43]

Dublin Opinion bade farewell with its cover cartoon, which depicted him leaving Gortleitreach with hat, coat, umbrella, a chessboard under his arm, a weeping cat by his side, and a caption: 'Maybe I ought to have asked them for a farewell broadcast.'[44]

Mean Tongues and Mean Minds

On 14 June 1937, de Valera dissolved the Dáil and went to the country on 1 July, seeking a return to power for the Fianna Fáil Party and the ratification of the Constitution of Ireland. What *The Irish Times* described as 'one of the swiftest and most strenuous election tours ever conducted in the Free State'[45] was concluded on the eve of polling in College Green where he addressed 'a meeting that is said to have been the largest election gathering held in this country within memory'.[46]

The paper reported that 'College Green was densely packed from Trinity College to Anglesea Street, and the crowd also extended into College Street, Grafton Street and all the smaller streets in the neighbourhood of College Green. Several speakers had addressed the meeting before Mr de Valera arrived, but when he came in sight the crowd seethed towards him, and it was only with great difficulty that the large force of Civic Guards preserved an avenue to the platform.'[47] Having asked for support for his Party and the new Constitution at length, he took three questions before departing, the second of which was: 'What consideration was shown to the ratepayers in connection with granting a pension of £10 per week and a sum of £2,000 to Donald [sic] Buckley?'

> Without the work Donald Buckley did, you would not be asked tomorrow to enact a free Constitution. If he had been a gentleman who would have garden parties and all the rest of it, then we would have heard nothing of the £10,000 a year to which he was legally entitled. Buckley was entitled legally to it, and could not be deprived of it, and whoever took his place would be entitled to it – to a yearly salary of £10,000 over and above whatever might be spent on his establishment.

He did not take that money; he took only the money which was necessary for the Government's point of view, to see that the position he was occupying was going to be occupied in the best interests of our people, so as to rid us forever from a Governor-General. One single year's payment would, at Buckley's age, purchase for him not merely £2,000, which we say we should give him, but in addition to that, would more than purchase an annuity which would give him the £10 per week ...

I asked that man, in the national interest, if for no other cause, because he was a man who had shown himself in his conduct in Easter Week, to be a man who loved his country; and when we wanted a man who could be trusted not to succumb to the allurements which would be put before him once he got into that office, I turned to him.

From the moment he got into it he was being taunted with the fact that he was a nonentity and was not appearing in public, and every effort was made to seduce him from the position, from acting as we wanted him to act, so as to end that office altogether. We knew that would be done, and we wanted a man who was certain not to yield to any of these things, and naturally, when I wanted a man, I looked for a 1916 man. I asked him to do that work, pointing out its importance nationally, and I asked him to do it as I would have asked a volunteer to go out and take a position of danger. I said: 'You are a 1916 man, I am going to ask you to do a much harder thing for Ireland than you did voluntarily in 1916. If anything should make it necessary, will you do it?' He said: 'Anything you think is necessary for me to do for Ireland, I am prepared to do it'.

We took this man, at his age, away from his business and his home, and put him into this position. Are we going to be so ungrateful now as to turn him out and not make any provision at all for the years that remain? I say we would be acting disgracefully as a nation if we did. We knew when we were bringing in that Bill that mean tongues and mean minds would be trying to make the most of it in the election.

But we would be meaner than they are, meaner than the meanest of them, if we let a man who rendered that service go without provision for him. I would not regard as lavish the giving of that sum to enable him to be saved for the future from some of the humiliation which he had suffered whilst he had remained in that office. He did his duty so well that there will never again be a Governor-General.

If the old Constitution remains, these people will want to give another £10,000 a year to a Governor-General that they would select, and you may be perfectly certain the money they would grudge for the upkeep of a man selected by the people, they would not grudge to somebody who would be a centre for shoneenism.[48]

The question on ua Buachalla's pension may well have come at random from the crowd, but it was one that de Valera would have welcomed, as it provided an opportunity to react to the abuse inside – and outside – the Dáil. And what better stage than a pre-election rally before an audience of thousands.

The text of the draft constitution, with minor amendments, was approved on 14 June by Dáil Eireann (then the sole House of Parliament, the Senate having been abolished the previous year). Put to a plebiscite on 1 July 1937, the day of the General Election, it was approved by a majority of 158,160 votes (685,105 to 526,945), failing to get a majority in five of the thirty-four constituencies – Dublin Townships, Dublin County, Cork West, Sligo and Wicklow. De Valera described the outcome as 'a source of joy to everyone who has been working in the cause of Irish independence'.[49]

He would have been less satisfied with the result of the General Election, failing to get the majority that was generally anticipated. Fianna Fáil's sixty-nine seats were matched by the other parties, and when Frank Fahy was re-elected Ceann Cómhairle, they were in a minority. In opposing de Valera for the position of President, William Cosgrave spoke of 'the ultimate destruction of parliamentary institutions'[50] by Fianna Fáil, but once again William Norton avowed 'that the party's position was the same now in 1937 as it had been in 1932'.[51] He would lend his assistance to any proposal which would lead to a 'fair and honourable solution of the economic war', and would fight with equal determination any move which would prejudice the freedom, prosperity and happiness of the Irish people. Before the Dáil dispersed, de Valera was re-elected President by eighty-two votes to fifty-two, promising that there would be no change in the personnel of the Government.

Although ua Buachalla had managed to bring forward his departure date from Monkstown to June, he continued to press Messrs. Battersby & Co. Ltd for an earlier release, and received the welcome news that they would be happy to see him depart on 4 March 1937. But there was a rider, which came in the form of a demand for £139.17s.3p for 'delapidations' since 1932, which included some damage to furniture, glass, garden equipment etc. His immediate reaction was that £10 should cover the cost. The Taoiseach advised him 'to arrange through his solicitors the most favourable settlement that might be found practicable'[52] and settle the bill. The final figure, which took many months to agree, was less than originally demanded.

The quality of the antique furniture and fittings was exceptional and when Battersby's auctioned the contents over two days later on in the year, it drew a large attendance 'with several well-known cross-Channel and Continental buyers present, as well as connoisseurs and dealers from Dublin, Cork and Belfast'.[53]

Having handed over the business in Maynooth to Joe, and also the family residence beside the College, he was now a homeless ex-*Seanascal*, and needed time to decide where he wished to spend the remaining years of his life. Aware that Bríghid was soon to be married, he knew that the foreseeable future involved himself and his youngest daughter, Máirín. Although his first preference might well have been to head back to the plains of Kildare, he realised that Máirín wished to continue working in Dublin – initially she was involved in the launch of *The Irish Press* and later worked for the Irish Sugar Company – and so he returned to his brother's house in Booterstown as an interim abode.

Within a matter of weeks a detached residence – *Lios na Craoibhe*, Stillorgan Park, Blackrock – was purchased, and it was there that the wedding breakfast for Bríghid was held on 28 November 1938 when she married Séamus O'Sullivan from Killorglin, the third Kerry native to be welcomed into the ua Buachalla family.

CHAPTER 20

Dublin Castle Falls to the Gael

At 72, Domhnall ua Buachalla deserved a little down time. Although his latter days in Monkstown were far from demanding, and he found occasional respite from metropolitan censure in the company of friends and relations in rural settings, his life from the start of the twentieth century made no provision for leisure time. Now, in the knowledge that little more could be demanded of him, he was in a position to enjoy whatever simple pleasures lay ahead.

The most significant of these pleasures arrived on 25 June 1938 in Dublin Castle, where he was one of about 200 guests. Standing on a dais, a quiet-voiced man spoke briefly in Irish:

> *I láthair Dia na nUilechumhacht, táimse á ghealladh agus á dhearbhú go sollúnta is go fírinneach bheith I mo thaca agus I mo dhidín do Bhunreacht Éireann, agus dlíthe a chaomhnú, mo dhualgais a chomhlíonadh go dilís coinsiasach de réir an Bhunreacht is an dlí, agus mo lándícheall a dhéanamh ar son leasa is fónaimh mhuintir na hÉireann. Dia do mo stiúradh agus do mo chumhdach.*[1]

[In the presence of Almighty God I do solemnly and sincerely promise and declare that I will maintain the Constitution of Ireland and uphold its laws, that I will fulfil my duties faithfully and conscientiously in accordance with the Constitution and the law, and that I will dedicate my abilities to the service and the welfare of the people of Ireland. May God direct and sustain me.]

He then stretched out his hands, and into them the Chief Justice placed the Great Seal of his office. With this simple ceremony, the new Irish State and the new Constitution came fully into being, with Douglas Hyde, the unanimous choice as first President. *The Irish Press* caught the mood of the day:

> Six silver trumpets flashed in the lights, and as their peals rang out, stirring the old banners on the walls, Dublin Castle fell to the Gael. And so the wheel of history has come full circle. Dublin Castle, founded in stormy tumult, for centuries a defiant fort on a hill, has seen the fruit and vindication of that long struggle.
>
> Hurdled fort of the Danes, moated stronghold of the Normans, but always [an] unchanging symbol of the oppression of the Gael. Kernel of Ireland's political history, it has seen the whole bloody pageant of warring policies. Rebellion and Confiscation, Plot and Conspiracy. Its dungeons crammed with noble Irish hostages and luckless Armada refugees. Its battlement walls spiked with their tarred heads.
>
> It has seen Lord Deputies sailing up the Liffey, hot with the latest edict; Geraldines passing to their doom. York and Lancaster, Cromwellian and royalist, Dutch King and Scottish King. Viceroys of later years. All now have passed, and the storms that they raised in their time have settled down to a murmur in the dust.
>
> The thread of freedom was picked up where it was shattered at Kinsale when An Taoiseach hailed the President of the resurgent nation as 'the successor of our rightful princes'. The breach is closed at last.[2]

What was remarkable about the choice of *An Craobhín Aoibhinn* to fill the role was the alacrity with which Cosgrave and de Valera agreed that he was the right man, with the principal doubter being Hyde himself, who told reporters that 'if my acceptance will be of any use to the country, I will gladly accept. My one objection is the fact that I am so old.'[3] He was 78 at the time. *Dublin Opinion* satire suggested that Hyde is 'such a quiet old gentleman, we may soon be wishing for the brave old days when we had Domhnall ua Buachalla dashing around all over the place'.

That night, in excess of 1,500 guests gathered in Dublin Castle to celebrate the occasion, one that 'some newspapers and gossip mongers had talked of as de Valera's "sop" to the Protestant Ascendancy, to the Gaelic revivalists, to Trinity intellectuals, and to the Church of Ireland . . .'[4] But the authors disagreed:

> No, de Valera had chosen Hyde for himself – for his experience, his judgement, and his political skills, honed over a period of nearly half a century; for his ability to move easily and smoothly in circles which de Valera had never been part; for his shrewd understanding of Americans, Canadians, the British, the French, and the Germans at a crucial time in modern history when an independent Ireland was about to take stage.[5]

If that day and night had enthused ua Buachalla, he probably derived equal satisfaction on 26 September when he was one of 400 guests at Áras an Uachtaráin. Having shunned the Viceregal Lodge when appointed Governor-General, he was 'one of the first to arrive'[6], no doubt keen to see the luxury enjoyed by Tim Healy and James McNeill at a gathering for old friends and co-workers of Hyde in the Irish Revival Movement. 'Georges and Williams, a Charlotte, an Albert, and the one and only Victoria, gazed superciliously from the walls on the thronging, victorious Gael; and the old tongue echoed, floating on a wave of Irish music, where once had walked the representatives of monarchs who had used more than influence to extinguish both forever.'[7] There was no formality about this occasion.

> Men from Connemara, Kerry and Donegal, and all the Gaeltacht, and, indeed, from all the provinces, mingled in tweeds and serges with the Gaels of Dublin, Government officials, Gaelic League leaders, civil servants, teachers and workers. The vast ballroom of the Viceroys was used as a refreshment room, and, as if to emphasise the change-over, even the labels on the sandwich plates were written in Gaelic. On the spacious lawns there were more meetings, where tragic and glorious history was re-enacted and old acquaintanceships renewed.[8]

Ua Buachalla's friendship with Hyde developed with letters passing between them, and in January 1941, the President responded to a birthday greeting with an invitation to visit him at the Áras. A note written later on the invitation refers to '*cúpla uair aoibhinn agam – agus cupán tae*' [a few delightful hours for me – and a cup of tea], which is not surprising considering it was a meeting of the last Governor-General who had orders to remain out of sight, and the first President who wondered if he was too old for the job.

A Return to Front-Line Activity

Although time was marching on for ua Buachalla, the physical demands of life were apparently not taking too great a toll, so much so that he joined the Local Security Force in 1940. It was created in May of that year as an auxiliary police service in response to security threats posed during what was termed 'The Emergency' in Ireland, or the Second World War to the wider world. Recruiting forms were dispatched to Garda stations on 31 May, and by 16 June, more than 46,000 had enrolled nationwide.

His primary instructions were 'to observe everything on sea, on land, and in the air, to pay particular attention to coastal shipping, motor vehicles, cyclists, pedestrians, especially to strangers'. The equipment would be group property – torches, patrol records, binoculars, etc. – which would be handed over from patrol to patrol. With the instructions came 'an earnest request to attend in Blackrock College at 8.00 p.m. on 11th inst. when an important lecture would be given by a senior official of the Garda. Afterwards, members who had not yet made the Declaration would be attested.'[9]

Another letter on 25 June informed him that he would be required for duty from 7.00 p.m. to 11.00 p.m. each Tuesday, and on presenting himself at the Blackrock Station, he would receive instructions as to the nature and extent of his patrol. In conjunction with this work, he subsequently joined the Order of Malta. By July 1941 he received a certificate for passing the prescribed examination to the satisfaction of the Chief Medical Officer, Conor O'Malley.

Although in good health and enjoying life in his new surroundings, the same could not be said of his son, Domhnall. He had required care from his early days and in later years his condition deteriorated to the extent that he needed full-time attention. On 12 March 1942 Domhnall passed away, a grievous loss to all the family who had for so long eased his path through life.

On the 29 March 1942, ua Buachalla had reason to celebrate a milestone in his eldest son's life. About 600 members of the Local Defence Force paraded from the Presentation Convent grounds at one end of the town to Maynooth College where Joe, Leader of the Liffey District, received a Unit Colour, presented by Very Rev. Edward Kissane, D. D. L. S. S., President of the College, who blessed it in front of the professional staff as well as 600 students and visitors.

The Local Defence Force was the 'A' Group of the Local Security Force that had been transferred to the Army in January 1941 as the Second World War developed. With its military status and responsibility, it was integrated into the combat organisations under full military discipline. The main L. D. F. weapons were the rifle, bayonet and grenade. In 1943 its strength rose to 103,530 but then declined as the European battle front receded from Irish shores. It was the first time a military parade took place in the College and the 'townspeople watched the units enter to the background of the towering ivy-covered ruins of the ancient castle of the Geraldines'.[10]

In his address, Dr Kissane said the L. D. F. had been called into existence by 'The Emergency' that threatened the state. They had made sacrifices during the last few years and had hardships; but they had endured them willingly, and buoyed by the ideals which they had chosen, they had gained self-discipline and the companionship of comrades inspired with the same ideals. One of the section leaders was Patrick Weafer who had marched to the GPO in 1916 with ua Buachalla and his comrades, many of whom were also present at the address.

At that time, the men who were involved in 1916, the War of Independence and the Civil War were in the process of making their applications for a Military Pension, ua Buachalla included, and in September 1942 he was given credit 'for all his services up to the period ended 31st March, 1923'[11] with an annual payment of £29.5.11, but this 'was abated' as the Governor-General pension had come into operation in 1937. There was a sequel to the first pension in April 1963, of which ua Buachalla was probably unaware. A letter arrived on the desk of the Secretary of the Military Pensions Board from Balla in Co. Mayo, signed by Paddy Mullaney, his Meath Brigade Officer.

A Chara,

It recently came to my notice that the Military Service Award to Domhnall Ó Buachalla of Maynooth was for only his 1916 service. As

O/C and Verification Officer for the Maynooth Company as well as for others in the 1st Meath Brigade, I was never questioned about his service pre-Truce and Civil War period. Considering I was arrested with him on the 1st day of the Civil War and that he escaped from Dundalk and joined me after I escaped from the Curragh, why was I not asked to verify and why was he not given credit for these periods?

Unfair and wrong and unjust.

P. E. Mullaney.[12]

In fact, ua Buachalla had been credited for this period, but he would certainly have been pleased to know that his commanding officer was thinking of him in his 97th year.

Fifteen years after receiving his £500 pension, ua Buachalla officially spoke to de Valera about its devaluation and suggested to him that it might be increased. Although mentioned at a Government meeting, nothing happened for a few years, but by 1960 it had been increased by £121; without any Dáil discussion.[13]

Notwithstanding the peace and tranquillity of *Lios na Craoibhe* in Stillorgan Park, there was sufficient upkeep and maintenance to prompt ua Buachalla and Máirín into searching for a more compact home which would better suit Máirín's job in the city. In January 1947 they became aware that two sites were available at the Donnybrook end of Eglinton Road, backing on to the Dodder River, and after negotiations with the owner, who was also a building contractor, they purchased No. 4 in 1949. Their only regret came some years later when permission was granted for a sizeable office block at the end of the site, which totally disfigured a leafy, suburban road. One of the reasons for the choice of Eglinton Road was its proximity to the parish church, but ua Buachalla had also received permission to have an oratory in the house. In times of poor health he would get a local priest, or one of his two Jesuit friends – Fr Peter Jacob and Fr Jack Kelly – to say Mass.

The location was an inspired choice. It was a warm, welcoming home in which both were extremely happy. Máirín had the choice of driving, taking the bus or walking to work. Meanwhile, her father had his workshop, which was equipped with just about every tool required for crafting wood, (all arranged meticulously) and it was there that he spent endless hours, along with time devoted to a garden which swept down to the river.

In Touching Distance of the Grim Reaper

For a man who came safely through the Easter Rising, the War of Independence and the Civil War, it was in his Donnybrook home that he came within touching distance of the Grim Reaper. He had access to what was a building site beside him before the blot on the landscape mushroomed, and from time to time he would wander in. One day, spotting a stump of lead piping sticking out of the ground, he decided that he might have some use for it in the future. So with hacksaw in hand, he set about cutting it, unaware that it was live and available for the builders whenever they recommenced work. Minutes later he struggled to his feet in shock and made his way into the house to Máirín with his hair and beard badly singed, visibly weakened and unsure of what had happened. But for his rubber-soled boots, he would probably have met his Maker that day. The hacksaw was a write off.

Indoors, in a study where a fire burned for much of the year, he read and wrote at an elegant desk he had crafted. And it was from here that a stream of letters was directed to *The Sunday Press* from the mid-fifties, almost weekly, for many years. The vast majority of them dealt with the Irish language; others with the need for greater patriotism, place names in Irish, education and emigration, for which he was the recipient of criticism from some readers. And then there was the 'h' letter. This referred to the introduction of the h-spelling to the Irish language, which many thought impractical. The 'h' was introduced to replace the *séimhiú*, or dot, as part of developments in the fifties and sixties to make the language more accessible to people and simplify spelling; also because the cost of publishing in the Gaelic script had become excessive. In January 1961 he wrote:

> Having just finished reading a recently published and interesting Irish book printed in the 'h' language, it struck me to count the number of h's in the last page; the number was 145. I then opened the book at random three times, counting the number of h's on one page each time; the numbers were 131, 146, 125, the average for the four pages being 136.

> There are 163 pages in the book, not including twelve picture pages. Multiply 163 by 136 and we get approximately the total number of h's in the book. It is 22,168 (twenty-two thousand one hundred and sixty eight!!!!).[14]

As he laboured away through the letters-page preaching sound cultural and religious standards, he received a particularly important one from de Valera, inviting him to attend his inauguration as President of Ireland on 25 June 1959 and later to have lunch at Áras an Uachtaráin with other guests who included Senator Margaret Pearse, Senator Nora Connolly-O'Brien, daughter of James Connolly, and Kathleen Clarke, widow of Tom, who was a close friend of ua Buachalla leading up to the Rising.

More surprising was another letter received shortly afterwards from de Valera, asking him to be a member of the Council of State, a body established to advise the President in the exercise of his or her discretionary powers. The Council usually consists of a number of government officials, who sit *ex-officio*, as well as certain former office holders and up to seven individuals of the president's own choosing. Every member must subscribe to a stipulated declaration of office before participating.

On 13 September of that year he was back in the Áras attending a lunch given in his honour by the President, where his lifetime contribution to Ireland – and indirectly his loyalty to de Valera – was recognised. It was a final gesture by the Chief for his 95-year-old friend whose night prayers always concluded with a request that Dev be kept safe for the good of the country.

In 1963, ua Buachalla made his last visit to the Áras for a reception in honour of John F. Kennedy during the historic state visit, and was in Dublin Castle the following day when the United States President received the degree of Doctor of Laws (LLD) from both the National University of Ireland and the University of Dublin, as well as the Freedom of Dublin. It was Kennedy's speech in the Dáil that made the greatest impression on ua Buachalla, so much so that he got a friend in Dáil Éireann, Donnchadh Ó Bríain, to send him a copy of the official address. He would certainly have appreciated the sentiment expressed in the words: 'There are those who regard this history of past strife and exile as better forgotten, but to use the phrase of Yeats, "let us not casually reduce the great past to a trouble of fools, for we need not feel the bitterness of the past to discover its meaning for the present and the future".'[15]

As the days shortened in 1963 and the autumn closed in, ua Buachalla's health declined. Mass in the oratory became the norm, members of his family visited more regularly and his health was discussed in hushed tones. He was moved to the Pembroke Nursing Home on 30 October and died peacefully in the care of Rev. Mother Mary Paula and her staff.

The following day, the Department of the Taoiseach announced that he would be accorded a State Funeral and de Valera visited the nursing home to pay his respects. A poignant photograph of his visit shows ua Buachalla laid out in a white vestment with rosary beads in hand, a crucifix and candle on a table beside him, and the President on his knees in prayer, head bowed. From there the President went to Eglinton Road and spent some time with the ua Buachalla family: sons Joe, Kevin and Séadna; daughters, Sheila, Bríghid and Máirín.

Full military honours were accorded at the removal of the remains on Friday 31 October. Six military policemen carried the coffin draped in the Tricolour, which they placed on a gun carriage. A firing party rendered honours and the cortège moved off through Fitzwilliam Square South, Leeson Street, Morehampton Road and finally to Donnybrook Church, where it was received by Very Rev. C. P. Crean, P. P. Here, an escort of troops from the Eastern Command and Air Corps again rendered honours and the No. 1 Army Band struck up the Dead March.

After Requiem Mass the following morning in a packed church the remains were brought back through the Phoenix Park – where a twenty-one-gun salute rang out in tribute. The coffin was met by an Army escort and band from the Curragh, who preceded the gun-carriage to the cemetery about a mile outside the town. IRA veterans from north Kildare and Meath formed a guard of honour as the remains was carried into the cemetery. Among them were surviving members of the small group that had marched to the GPO in 1916: Tom Harris, Tom Mangan, Tim Tyrrell, John Maguire and Pat Weafer.

The attendance included de Valera and his wife, Sinéad, An Taoiseach Seán Lemass, former President Seán T. O'Kelly and his wife, members of the Cabinet, the Judiciary and both Houses of the Oireachtas. At the graveside, a volley was fired by the troops from the Curragh, prayers were recited by the Very Rev. W. O'Riordan, P. P., and, before his remains was laid to rest beside his wife, Sinéad, who had died forty-five years previously, the President spoke briefly about his friend:

> Even though he was a man of few words, he was a man that got things done, and it would not be right to leave here without a word or two to say goodbye to this hero lying here today. Domhnall ua Buachalla was a gentleman, also a man who steadfastly stood for justice, a man that was very dependable, a man of his word.

> One of the most loyal people of that great generation that founded *Conradh na Gaeilge* to save the language, founded *Óglaigh na*

hÉireann, took part in the Easter Rising and continued with the fight for freedom until freedom was obtained for us in this part of the country. It is Domhnall ua Buachalla's name that is on *Acht na Dála* to end control of a foreign authority in this country.

He loved his native country. He had a long life and he spent his time working for the good of his fellow countrymen. We are all under a great compliment to him and we thank God for such a great man. That his soul will be among all the heroes gone before him who gave their souls for the freedom of our nation.[16]

It was the great Dromore-born writer from County Tyrone, Benedict Kiely, who touched on the essence of the man:

Domhnall ua Buachalla left his home in Maynooth on a spring night in 1916 and crossed the quiet fields to the city that was about to explode in fire and fighting. He came home again for the last time on a morning of autumn rain with the last leaves colouring the trees along the village street, and out by the college and along the western road, where in the shadow of old, ivied walls, which must have inspired his younger days with a sense of his country's past, he was laid to rest.

Soldiers of the Irish Army that in his time, and thanks to the courage and sacrifice of he and his comrades, had taken their rightful place in the country's life, marched before him to the grave. The three ritual volleys were fired and the bugles spoke farewell over the flat Kildare fields; a fitting farewell to a man whose memory went back so far, who was born indeed, just before the Fenian year when Irish soldiers, as outlaws, were abroad on the winter hills.

Their memory, the stories of the Fenians told afterwards in quiet midland places, moulded and tempered his spirit, and gave him the resolution that Pearse noticed when he spoke of him as 'the most determined man'.

As the echoes of the bugles died away, a man who had been his friend for many years spoke to me at the graveside. He talked of the spring night of decision when Domhnall crossed the fields to

Dublin. He was no young, reckless fellow. He was a man settled in life, past middle-age, married, the owner of a prosperous business. He had every human reason for leaving the fighting and the risks to younger men.

He had made, and one might have thought, almost lived, his life in that ordered village where the college bells divide the day and on the main road to Dublin and in the heart of a fat and prosperous land. That was his reality.

Across the fields in the warm spring night, gathering ominously around Dublin, there were only orators' words, and danger and the memory of brave, defeated men. His friend told me how Domhnall had spoken to him of the agony of that moment of decision. Then he said goodbye to his wife, looked not back again in case his resolution would weaken, turned his back on all the known things he had made, and faced towards the city and doubt and, for all he knew, disgrace and death. It was not to be that way.

He was to live to an honoured age, to charm younger men (among whom I am proud to include myself) with his courtesy, wit and hospitality, to instruct them with talk of his own long memories, and of earlier years, of which he in his youth had absorbed the memories, again from older men.

He lived in Dublin city by a small river, and with his passion for greenery and growing things, he had built his own garden to be along that river, as if garden and river had been there together since the beginning of time. For he had always the sense of order of a man from spacious, well-planned fields; and as the funeral passed through the village and along the college wall and was met by the soldiers, it seemed that this moment was carefully preordained in the long story of this man's years, and of many of the most vital years in his country's history.[17]

ENDNOTES

Chapter 1

1. Author's Collection.
2. *Ibid.*
3. The ua Buachalla Collection, Kilmainham Goal Museum 2011, 0803.
4. O'Buachalla Collection 2011, 0804.
5. *Collected Works of P. H. Pearse, Political Writings and Speeches* (Dublin: Phoenix Publishing Company, 1924), pp. 106–7.

Chapter 2

1. Author Interview with Bobby Buckley (2013).
2. Killavullen and Annakissa Community Council History, accessed 2013.
3. Cork newspaper cutting, unidentified, n.d.
4. *Ibid.*
5. *Ibid.*
6. John Mitchel, *Last Conquest of Ireland (Perhaps)* (Dublin: Dublin University College Press, 2005), p. 219.
7. William Edmundson, *A Journal of the Life* (London, Hinde, 1774), p. 4
8. *Ibid.*
9. Lena Boylan, 'Joshua Jacob, 1801–77' *Journal of the Co Kildare Archaeological Society* (1983–84), p. 350.
10. *Ibid.*
11. *Ibid.*
12. *Ibid.*
13. *Ibid.*
14. *Ibid.*, p. 351.
15. *Ibid.*
16. *Ibid.*

17. *Ibid.*
18. *Ibid.*, p. 353.

Chapter 3

1. Author's collection. (Notes written by Domhnall ua Buachalla's son, Joe; circa 1940).
2. Bureau of Military History, WS, 850 (Patrick Colgan), p.1.
3. Pat Bell, *Long Shies and Slow Twisters – 150 Years in Co. Kildare* (Kildare; Templemills Press, 1993), p. 14.
4. O'Buachalla Collection, 2011, 1030.
5. Author's Collection (Notes written by ua Buachalla's son, Joe).
6. BMH, WS, 194 Domhnall O'Buachalla, p. 1.
7. Author's Collection.
8. O'Buachalla Collection, 2011, 0557 a/b.
9. *Westmeath Examiner*, 14 June 1930.
10. O'Buachalla Collection, 2011, 0556 a/b/c.
11. Author's Collection.
12. Seamus Cullen, *Kildare Nationalist*, 'Kildare – Always Popular with Visiting Royals', 17 May 2011.
13. BMH, WS, 850, Patrick Colgan, p. 4.

Chapter 4

1. Author's Collection.
2. Ibid.
3. Ibid.
4. Dorothy Macardle, *The Irish Republic* (London: Victor Gollancz, 1937), p.61.
5. Ibid., p.61.
6. O'Buachalla Collection, 2011.0805.
7. Author's Collection.
8. O'Buachalla Collection, 2011.0808.
9. Ibid., 2011.0809.
10. Ibid.
11. Ibid., 2011.0810.
12. Ibid., 2011.0812.
13. Ibid., 2011.0813.
14. Ibid.
15. Ibid.
16. Ibid., 2011, 0820.
17. *The Irish Times*, 17 March 1906.
18. *Leinster Leader*, 2 December 1905.
19. *Freeman's Journal*, 9 January 1906.

20. Ibid., 14 February 1906.
21. Ibid.
22. *Cork Constitution,* 15 February 1906.
23. *Irish Law Times and Solicitors' Journal,* 24 February 1906.
24. *An Claidheamh Soluis,* 17 February 1906.

Chapter 5

1. O'Buachalla Collection, Kilmainham Gaol Museum, 2011; document 0855.
2. *Ibid.,* 2011 0848.
3. *Ibid.,* 2011 0550. (Original in Irish).
4. *Ibid.,* 2011 0548. (Original in Irish).
5. *Ibid.,* 0553. (Original in Irish).
6. Author's Collection (Notes written by Domhnall ua Buachalla's son, Joe, circa 1940).
7. *Ibid.*
8. *Ibid.*
9. *Ibid.*
10. *Ibid.*
11. *Ibid.*
12. Elaine Sisson, *St. Enda's and the Cult of Boyhood* (Cork: Cork University Press, 2004), p. 4.
13. *Ibid.*
14. Emmet Larkin, *In The Footsteps of Big Jim: A Family Biography* (Dublin: Blackwater Press, 1966), p. 122.
15. E. MacNeill, 'The North Began', *An Claidheamh Soluis,* 1 November 1913, p.6.
16. Dorothy Macardle, *The Irish Republic* (London: Gollancz, 1937), Statements and Documents, p. 946.
17. *Ibid.,* p. 947.
18. *Ibid.,* p.104.
19. Bureau of Military History, WS, 850, Patrick Colgan, p.5.
20. Tom Garvin, *The Evolution of Irish Nationalist Politics,* (Dublin: Gill & Macmillan, 2005), pp. 105–10.
21. *Ibid.*
22. *Leinster Leader,* 20 September 1913.
23. BMH, WS, 194, Domhnall ua Buachalla, p. 1.
24. BMH, WS 850, Patrick Colgan, p. 6.
25. *Ibid.,* p.6.
26. P. S. O'Hegarty, *A History of Ireland under the Union* (London: Methuen, 1952), p. 946.
27. *Irish Independent,* 21 September 1914.
28. BMH, WS, 194 (Domhnall ua Buachalla), p.1.
29. BMH, WS, 158 (Séamus Kenny), p. 2.

30. Author's Collection.
31. BMH, WS 850 (Patrick Colgan), p.6.
32. *Ibid.*
33. Macardle, *The Irish Republic,* p. 141.
34. BMH, WS 194 (Domhnall ua Buachalla), p. 1.
35. Author's Collection (Notes written by ua Buachalla's son, Séadna; circa 1975).
36. Ibid.

Chapter 6

1. Bureau of Military History, WS 320 (Tom Harris), p. 1–3.
2. BMH, WS 416 (Mrs James Ryan, nee Máirín Cregan), p. 2.
3. *Ibid.,* p. 3.
4. *Ibid.,* p.7.
5. O'Buachalla Collection, 2011.1009, 01–2.
6. BMH, WS 564 (Tom Byrne), p. 16.
7. *Ibid.,* p. 17.
8. BMH, WS 850 (Patrick Colgan), pp. 7–8.
9. BMH, WS 564 (Tom Byrne), pp. 8–9.
10. 320 (Tom Harris), pp. 5–7.
11. BMH, WS 564 (Patrick Colgan), p. 10.
12. *Ibid.,* p. 12
13. BMH, WS (Domhnall ua Buachalla) p.2.
14. BMH, WS (Patrick Colgan), pp. 8–9.
15. *Ibid.*
16. *Ibid.*
17. *Ibid.*
18. *The Irish Press,* 26 May 1933
19. BMH, WS 850 (Patrick Colgan), p. 14.
20. BMH, WS 564 (Tom Byrne), p. 20.
21. BMH, WS 850 (Patrick Colgan), p. 15.
22. *Ibid.,* pp. 15–16.
23. BMH, WS 320 (Tom Harris), p. 7.
24. BMH, WS 850 (Patrick Colgan), p. 16.
25. *Ibid.*
26. Imperial War Museum, Art IWM PST 13595
27. BMH, WS 850 (Patrick Colgan), p. 17.

Chapter 7

1. Bureau of Military History, WS 850(Patrick Colgan) p. 17.
2. BMH, WS 96 (John Hanratty) p. 8.
3. BMH, WS 850 (Patrick Colgan), p. 18.

4. Author's Collection (Notes taken by Matt Feehan, circa 1958).
5. BMH, WS 194 (Domhnall ua Buachalla) p. 4.
6. BMH, WS 850 (Patrick Colgan) pp. 21–2.
7. *The Sunday Press*, Michael O'Halloran series on Domhnall ua Buachalla, April/ May 1960.
8. *Ibid.*
9. BMH, WS 194 (Domhnall ua Buachalla), p. 5.
10. Author's Collection (Notes taken by Matt Feehan, circa 1958).
11. BMH, WS 194 (Domhnall ua Buachalla) p. 5.
12. *Ibid.*, p. 6.
13. *The Sunday Press*, April/May 1960.
14. *Ibid.*
15. Macardle, *The Irish Republic*, p. 182.
16. *Ibid.*, p. 184.
17. BMH, WS 194 (Domhnall ua Buachalla) p. 6.
18. *The Sunday Press*, April/May 1960.
19. BMH, WS 194 (Domhnall ua Buachalla) p. 6.
20. *Ibid.*, p. 7.
21. BMH, WS 320 (Tom Harris) p. 9.
22. BMH, WS 850 (Patrick Colgan) p. 28.
23. *Ibid.*, p. 29.
24. *Ibid.*, p. 30.
25. *Ibid.*, p. 55.

Chapter 8

1. W. J. Brennan-Whitmore, *With the Irish in Frongoch* (Dublin: Talbot Press, 1917), p. 30.
2. *Ibid.*, p. 31.
3. Bureau of Military History, WS 850 (Patrick Colgan) p.55.
4. *Ibid.*
5. Tim Pat Coogan, *Michael Collins: A Biography* (London, Hutchinson, 1990), p. 49.
6. *The Sunday Press*, 22 May 1960.
7. James Durney, *On The One Road* (Kildare: Leinster Leader, 2001), p. 39.
8. *Ibid.*, p. 33.
9. Macardle, *The Irish Republic* (London: Victor Gollancz, 1937), p. 212.
10. Brennan-Whitmore, *With the Irish in Frongoch,* pp. 204–5.
11. *Ibid.*, p. 206.
12. BMH, WS 194 (Domhnall ua Buachalla) pp.7,8.
13. Author's Collection (Notes written by Domhnall ua Buachalla's son, Joe, circa 1940).
14. *Ibid.*

15. *Ibid.*
16. *Ibid.*
17. *Ibid.*
18. *Ibid.*
19. *Ibid.*
20. *Ibid.*
21. Macardle, *The Irish Republic,* p. 243.

Chapter 9

1. Author's Collection (Notes written by Patrick O'Keeffe).
2. Dorothy Macardle, *The Irish Republic* (London: Victor Gollancz, 1937) p. 250–1.
3. Denis Gwynn, *The Life of John Redmond* (London,: G.G. Harrap, 1932), p. 17.
4. *The Irish Times,* 16 August 2014.
5. *Ibid.*
6. Macardle, *The Irish Republic,* p. 262.
7. *Ibid.*
8. O'Buachalla Collection, 2011 0565a/b.
9. Author's Collection (Notes written by Séadna, ua Buachalla's son, circa 1975).
10. *Ibid.*
11. Ida Milne,'A Glimpse of Hell', *Irish Daily Mail,* 4 May 2009.
12. BMH, WS 850 (Patrick Colgan) pp. 61–2.
13. *Ibid.,* p. 62.
14. *Leinster Leader,* 23 November 1918.
15. *Ibid.*
16. *Ibid.,* 30 November 1918.
17. *Ibid.*
18. *Ibid.,* 7 December 1918.
19. *Ibid.*
20. *Ibid.,* 30 November 1918.
21. *Ibid.,* 7 December, 1918.
22. *Ibid.*
23. *Ibid.,* 14 December 1918
24. Thomas P. Nelson, Kildare County Council, 1899-1926, (PhD Thesis, National University of Ireland, Maynooth, 2007), pp. 103, 104.
25. *Ibid.*
26. *Kildare Observer,* 21 December 1918.
27. *Ibid.*
28. *Kildare Observer,* 4 January 1919.
29. *Ibid.*
30. Macardle, *The Irish Republic,* p. 279.
31. *Leinster Leader,* 4 January 1919.

32. *Kildare Observer,* 4 January 1919.
33. *Leinster Leader,* 4 January, 1919.
34. *Kildare Observer,* 4 January 1919.
35. *Leinster Leader,* 4 January, 1919.
36. *Ibid.*
37. *Kildare Observer,* 11 January 1919.
38. *Ibid.*
39. Maire Comerford, *The First Dáil* (Dublin, Joe Clarke Publications, 1969), pp.52–3.
40. Macardle, *The Irish Republic,* pp. 285–6.
41. Comerford, *The First Dáil,* p.53.
42. *Ibid.*
43. Macardle, *The Irish Republic,* p.299.
44. *Ibid.* 304.

Chapter 10

1. Dan Breen, *My Fight For Irish Freedom* (Dublin: Anvil Books, 1981), p. 46.
2. Bureau of Military History, WS 850 (Patrick Colgan) pp. 63, 64.
3. Breen, *My Fight For Irish Freedom,* p. 86.
4. BMH, WS 194(Domhnall ua Buachalla) p.7.
5. BMH, WS 850 (Patrick Colgan) p.64,65.
6. Author's Collection. (Notes written by Séadna, ua Buachalla's son, circa 1975).
7. Breen, *My Fight For Irish Freedom,* p. 88.
8. *Ibid.,* pp. 88–9.
9. BMH, WS 850 (Patrick Colgan) p.65,66.
10. Henry Hanna K. C., Denis Pringle, *The Statute Law of the Irish Free State, 1922–1928,* (Dublin: Alex Thom & Co., 1929).
11. Macardle, *The Irish Republic,* p. 317.
12. *Ibid.,* p. 318.
13. *Ibid.*
14. Author's Collection.
15. *Daily Mail,* 15 December 1919.
16. *Leinster Leader,* 14 February 1920.
17. Author's Collection.
18. *Ibid.*
19. MSPC, Domhnall ua Buachalla, 34 REF8261.
20. *Leinster Leader,* 13 March 1920.
21. *Kildare Observer,* 27 March 1920.
22. *Ibid.,* 10 April 1920.
23. *Ibid.*
24. *Leinster Leader,* 22 May 1920.
25. BMH, WS , 769 (Stephen O'Reilly) p. 1.
26. *Ibid.,* pp. 1,2.

27. *Ibid.*, pp. 3,4.
28. Author's Collection.
29. *Ibid.*
30. *Evening Times,* 27 January 1921.
31. John Drennan, *Cannonballs and Croziers – A History of Maynooth* (Community Council, ISBN 0 9524953 0 9) p. 130.
32. *Ibid.*

Chapter 11

1. *Kildare Observer,* 29 May 1920.
2. *Ibid.*
3. *Kildare Observer,* 5 June 1920.
4. *Kildare Observer,* 12 June 1920.
5. *Ibid.*
6. *Ibid.*
7. *Leinster Leader,* 26 June 1920.
8. *Ibid.*
9. James Durney, *On The One Road* (Kildare: Gaul House, 2001), p. 64.
10. Author's Collection. (Notes written by ua Buachalla's son Joe, circa 1940).
11. *Ibid.*
12. *Ibid.*
13. *The Sunday Press,* 18 February 1968.
14. T.P. Coogan, *Michael Collins; A Biography* (London: Hutchinson, 1990), p.116.
15. C. Connolly, *Michael Collins* (London: Weidenfeld & Nicolson, 1996), p.65.
16. T. Ryle Dwyer, *The Squad and the Intelligence Operations of Michael Collins* (Cork: Mercier Press, 2005), p. 140.
17. Author's Collection.
18. *Ibid.*

Chapter 12

1. Author's Collection (Notes written by Patrick O'Keeffe).
2. *Irish Independent,* 31 January 1921.
3. *Ibid.*
4. Macardle, *The Irish Republic* (London: Victor Gollancz, 1937), p. 473.
5. *The Irish Times,* 27 August 1921.
6. *Ibid.*, p. 543.
7. *Ibid.*, p. 549.
8. Dáil Éireann Official Report: Debate on the Treaty, Dec. 1921–Jan.22, (Dublin: Talbot Press, 1922), p. 49.
9. *Ibid.*
10. Macardle, *The Irish Republic,* p. 611.

11. *Ibid.,* p. 618.
12. *Ibid.,* p. 619.
13. *Ibid.,* p. 626.
14. Dáil Éireann Official Report: Debate on the Treaty, p. 213.
15. *Ibid.,* p. 344
16. *Ibid.,* p. 346
17. *Ibid.,* p. 347.
18. *Ibid.*
19. *Ibid.*
20. *Ibid.,* p. 379.
21. *Ibid.,* p. 410.
22. *Ibid.,* p. 410.
23. *Ibid.,* p. 411.
24. *Ibid.,* p. 414.
25. *Ibid.,* p. 415.
26. *Kildare Observer,* 7 January 1922.
27. *Ibid.*
28. *Ibid.*
29. *Ibid.*
30. *Ibid.*
31. *Ibid.*

Chapter 13

1. *The Times,* 16 January 1922.
2. *Ibid.*
3. *Kildare Observer,* 28 January 1922.
4. *Ibid.*
5. *Ibid.*
6. Dorothy Macardle, *The Irish Republic* (London, Victor Gollancz,1937) p. 683.
7. *Leinster Leader,* 21 January 1922.
8. *Kildare Observer,* 18 March 1922.
9. *Ibid.*
10. Macardle, *The Irish Republic,* p. 739.
11. *Ibid.,* p. 741.
12. *Irish Independent,* 16 June 1922.
13. *Ibid.*
14. *Kildare Observer,* 10 June 1922.
15. Michael Gallagher, *Irish Elections, 1922–44: Results and Analysis* (Limerick: PSAI, 1993), pp. 1–2.
16. *Ibid.,* p. 2.
17. *Irish Independent,* 21 June 1922.
18. *Ibid.*

19. *Irish Independent*, 22 June 1922.
20. O'Buachalla Collection, Kilmainham Gaol Museum, 2011. 0587.
21. Liz Gillis, *The Fall of Dublin* (Cork: Mercier Press, 2011), p. 81.
22. Interview with Fintan Buckley, Joe's son, by Adhamhnán Ó Súilleabháin, June 2013; re father's involvement in Civil War.
23. Gillis, *The Fall of Dublin*, p. 116.
24. *Kildare Observer*, 24 June 1922.
25. *Leinster Leader*, 1 July 1922.
26. Author's Collection (Notes written by Patrick O'Keeffe).
27. *Macardle, The Irish Republic,* p. 793.
28. *Ibid.*, p. 794.
29. Author's Collection.
30. University College Dublin Archives, O'Malley Papers (Mick O'Neill), P17 b/107, pp. 48.
31. Author's Collection (Notes written by Patrick O'Keeffe).
32. University College Dublin Archives, O'Malley Papers (Mick O'Neill), p17 b/107, pp. 48.
33. Bureau of Military History, Witness Statement 1571 (Jim Dunne).
34. Author's Collection (Notes written by Patrick O'Keeffe).

Chapter 14

1. *Leinster Leader*, 2 June 1923.
2. *Irish Independent*, 24 August 1922.
3. Colm Connolly, *Michael Collins* (London, Weidenfeld & Nicolson, 1996), p. 94.
4. Desmond Ryan, *Michael Collins* (Dublin, Anvil Books, 1994), p. 149.
5. *The Irish Press*, Christmas Number, 1932, p. 44.
6. Dorothy Macardle, *The Irish Republic* (London: Victor Gollancz, 1937), p. 846.
7. Dáil Éireann, Parliamentary Debates, Vol.1, No. 13, 27 September 1922.
8. O'Buachalla Collection, Kilmainham Gaol Museum, 2011. Document 0590.
9. *The Irish Press,* Christmas Number, 1932, p.44.
10. Andrew Boyle, *The Riddle of Erskine Childers* (London: Hutchinson, 1977), p. 319.
11. *Ibid.*
12. *The Times*, 13 November 1922.
13. Andrew Boyle, *The Riddle of Erskine Childers*, pp. 16–17.
14. Anthony Jordan, *Eamon de Valera, 1882–1975: Irish Catholic Visionary* (Mayo, Westport Books), p. 127.
15. Macardle, *The Irish Republic*, p. 828.
16. *Ibid.*
17. Macardle, *The Irish Republic*, p. 861.
18. *Irish Independent*, 9 February 1923.
19. *Ibid.*
20. *Ibid.*

21. *Ibid.*
22. *Ibid.*
23. *Ibid.*
24. *Irish Independent,* 28 April 1923.
25. *The Irish Times,* 10 May 1923.
26. *The Irish Times,* 25 May 1923.
27. *Kildare Observer,* 30 June 1923.
28. *Ibid.*
29. *Irish Independent,* 23 July 1923.
30. *Clare Champion,* 18 August 1923.
31. *Kildare Observer,* 25 August 1923.
32. *Ibid.*
33. *Leinster Leader,* 25 August, 1923.
34. *Ibid.*
35. *Ibid.*
36. *Kildare Observer,* 23 June 1923.
37. *Irish Independent,* 27 August 1923.
38. *Ibid.*
39. Michael Gallagher, *Irish Elections 1922–44: Results and Analysis* (Limerick; PSAI, 1993). pp. 23–4.
40. *Leinster Leader,* 1 September 1923.

Chapter 15

1. Bryce Evans, Stephen Kelly (eds), *Frank Aiken, Nationalist and Internationalist* (Kildare, Irish Academic Press, 2014), p.105.
2. *Kildare Observer,* 20 October 1923.
3. Ibid.
4. Ibid.
5. Dáil Éireann Debates, Vol.5, No.13, 16 November 1923.
6. Dorothy Macardle, *The Irish Republic* (London: Victor Gollancz, 1937), pp. 901–2.
7. *Leinster Leader,* 1 December 1923.
8. *Kildare Observer,* 1 March 1924.
9. *Leinster Leader,* 10 May 1924.
10. *Ibid.*
11. *Ibid.*
12. *Ibid.*
13. *Ibid.*
14. James Durney, *The Civil War in Kildare* (Cork: Mercier Press, 2011), p. 102.
15. *Ibid.*
16. *Ibid.*
17. *Ibid.,* p. 105.
18. *Ibid.,* p. 106.
19. *Leinster Leader,* 8 November 1924.

20. Military Service Pensions, File Ref MSP34, REF8261, Ass. Files 34E7032
21. Durney, *The Civil War in Kildare*, p. 106.
22. Military Archives, Cathal Brugha Barracks, file 'Seizure of Money Public Safety (Emergency Powers) Act, AFO 269, File a/652, Donal Buckley, Maynooth'. 22 November 1922.

Chapter 16

1. Dorothy Macardle, *The Irish Republic* (London, Victor Gollancz, 1937) p. 918.
2. Eunan O'Halpin, 'Seán Lemass's Silent Anguish', *The Irish Times*, 21 July 2013.
3. *Irish Independent*, 21 November 1924.
4. *Irish Independent*, 14 March 1925.
5. *Irish Independent*, 4 December, 1925.
6. *Ibid.*
7. *Irish Independent*, 7 December 1925.
8. Richard Dunphy, *The Making of Fianna Fáil: Power in Ireland, 1923–1948* (Oxford: Clarendon Press, 1995), pp. 70–1.
9. Mícheál Martin, *Freedom to Choose, Cork and Party Politics in Ireland, 1918–1932* (Cork, The Collins Press, 2009), p. 137.
10. *Leinster Leader*, 9 April 1927.
11. *Ibid.*
12. *Ibid.*
13. *Ibid.*
14. *Ibid.*
15. *Ibid.*
16. *Leinster Leader*, 23 April 1927.
17. *Ibid.*
18. *Ibid.*
19. *Ibid.*
20. Michael Gallagher, *Irish Elections 1922–44; Results and Analysis* (Limerick: PSAI Press, 1993), p. 55.
21. *Kildare Observer*, 30 April 1927.
22. *Kildare Observer*, 7 May 1927.
23. *Kildare Observer*, 21 May 1927.
24. *Kildare Observer*, 28 May 1927.
25. *Irish Independent*, 3 June 1927.
26. *Ibid.*
27. *Leinster Leader*, 16 June 1927.
28. *Irish Independent*, 16 June 1927.
29. Gallagher, *Irish Elections 1922–44*, p. 55.
30. *Kildare Observer*, 25 June 1927.
31. *The Irish Times*, 11 July 1927.
32. John P McCarthy, *Kevin O'Higgins: Builder of the Irish State*, (Kildare: Irish Academic Press, 2006), p. 287

33. *The Irish Times,* 12 July 1927.
34. McCarthy, *Kevin O'Higgins: Builder of the Irish State*, p. 288.
35. *The Irish Times,* 27 July 1927.
36. *The Irish Times,* 11 August 1927.
37. *Kildare Observer,* 8 October 1927.
38. *The Irish Times,* 12 August 1927.
39. *Ibid.*
40. *Ibid.*
41. *Ibid.*
42. *Irish Independent,* 12 August 1927.
43. *Ibid.*
44. *Ibid.*
45. *Ibid.*
46. *Ibid.*
47. *Irish Independent,* 26 August 1927.
48. *Kildare Observer,* 10 September 1927.
49. *Ibid.*
50. *Ibid.*
51. *Ibid.*
52. *Ibid.*
53. *Ibid.*
54. *Leinster Leader,* 24 September 1927.
55. Ibid.
56. Gallagher, *Irish Elections 1922–44*, p. 95.
57. *Kildare Observer,* 8 October 1927.

Chapter 17

1. University College Dublin Archives, P176/443, 7 October 1927.
2. *Ibid.*
3. University College Dublin Archives, P176/443, 1 October 1927.
4. *Ibid.*
5. *Kildare Observer,* 12 November 1927.
6. University College Dublin Archives , P176/443, 7 October 1928.
7. *Ibid.,* 29 November 1928.
8. *Ibid.*
9. Dáil Éireann, Parliamentary Debates, Book 30, 26 June 1929, pp. 1765–6.
10. P.J. Ryan,The Old Limerick Journal, Winter Edition, 2003, p.3.
11. University College Dublin Archives O'Malley Papers (Mick O'Neill), p17b/107, p.41.
12. Interview with the author, 14 July 2013.
13. Amnesty International April 2000 AlIndex: Euro 45/41/00, pp. 4-7.
14. *Ibid.*

15. *Ibid.*, p. 1.
16. *Ibid.*, p. 2.
17. *Ibid.*, p. 11.
18. *Ibid.*
19. Interview with the author.
20. Dáil Éireann Parliamentary Debates, 28 March 1930, Vol. 34, p. 276.
21. University College Dublin Archives, P176/443, 28 March 1930.
22. *Irish Independent*, 3 April 1930.
23. *Ibid.*
24. University College Dublin Archives, P176/443, 15 May 1930.
25. University College Dublin Archives, P176/443, 16 May 1930.
26. Dáil Éireann, Parliamentary Debates, Book 37, 26 February 1931, p. 791–2.
27. Interview with the author.
28. *Leinster Leader*, 27 June 1931.
29. *Ibid.*
30. *The Irish Times*, 1 July 1931.
31. *Ibid.*, 2 July 1931.
32. *Ibid.*
33. University College Dublin Archives, PI76/44317 December 1931.
34. *The Irish Press*, 15 February 1932.
35. Michael Gallagher, *Irish Elections 1922–1944, Results and Analysis* (Limerick: PSAI Press, 1993), p. 125.
36. *Leinster Leader*, 5 March 1932.
37. Gallagher, *Irish Elections 1922–1944*, p. 125.
38. *The Irish Press*, 4 March 1932.
39. *Ibid.*
40. *Ibid.*
41. *The Irish Press*, 11 March, 1932.
42. *Kildare Observer*, 5 March 1932.
43. *Ibid.*, 9 April 1932.
44. *Irish Independent*, 12 July 1932.

Chapter 18

1. *The Irish Press*, 30 January 1933.
2. Brendan Sexton, *Ireland and the Crown 1922–1936* (Dublin: Irish Academic Press, 1989), p. 113.
3. *Ibid.*, pp.116–17.
4. *Ibid.*, pp. 117–18.
5. *Ibid.*, p. 124.
6. *Ibid.*, p. 129.
7. *The Irish Press*, 4 October 1932.
8. Sexton, *Ireland and the Crown 1922–1936*, p. 138.

9.   *Ibid.*, p. 139.
10. *Ibid.*, p. 149.
11. National Archives of Ireland: Executive Council Minutes, C.6/68, item, 'Appointment of Donal Buckley.'
12. Sexton, *Ireland and the Crown 1922– 36*, p. 151.
13. *Ibid.*, p. 153.
14. *The Irish Press*, 21 April 1949.
15. Sexton, *Ireland and the Crown 1922–1936*, p. 153.
16. Author's Collection (Letter from Civil Servant, Joe Connolly, to Domhnall ua Buachalla, 22 December 1922).
17. *The Irish Times*, 11 October 1968.
18. Letter belonging to Fintan Buckley, Joe's son. 15 October 1968.
19. University College Dublin Archives, Kennedy Papers, 1261, p. 4.
20. *The Irish Press*, 28 November 1932.
21. *The Times*, 28 November 1932.
22. *The Irish Times*, 28 November 1932.
23. *Ibid.*
24. University College Dublin Archives, Kennedy Papers, 1261, p. 4.
25. *The Irish Times*, 2 December 1932.
26. *Ibid.*, 7 December 1932.
27. *Time*, 5 December 1932
28. Mary Grogan, 'Gortleitragh House' Dun Laoghaire Journal No. 20, (2011), p. 59.
29. *Ibid.*, p. 63.
30. John P. Duggan, *Herr Hempel at the German Legation in Dublin, 1937–45.* (Dublin: Irish Academic Press, 2003).
31. O'Buachalla Collection, Kilmainham Gaol Museum, 2011. 0723.
32. Author's Collection.
33. *Ibid.*
34. Sexton, *Ireland and the Crown 1922–1936*, p. 156.
35. National Archives of Ireland, TSCH/3/S8574, Governor-General, Instructions to Private Secretary.
36. Sexton, *Ireland and the Crown 1922–1936*, p. 156.
37. *Ibid.*, p. 157.
38. National Archives of Ireland, TSCH/3/S8549, Governor-General.
39. *Ibid.*, p. 157.
40. James Durney, *On The One Road*, pp. 146–7.
41. *The Advocate*, Melbourne, date unknown.
42. Related by John Buckley, nephew of Domhnall ua Buachalla, Radio Éireann interview, 21 May 1985.
43. *The Irish Press*, 21 January 1933.
44. *Irish Independent*, 9 February, 1933.
45. *Ibid.*
46. *Ibid.*

47.   *The Irish Press,* 9 February, 1933.
48.   *Ibid.,* 15 May 1933.
49.   *Ibid.*
50.   *Ibid.*
51.   *Ibid.*
52.   Sexton, *Ireland and the Crown 1922–1936,* p. 124
53.   *Ibid.*
54.   *The Irish Press,* 30-31 March 1934.
55.   *Ibid.*
56.   Irish Heritage Club, Seattle, Washington.
57.   *Irish Independent,* 27 March 1933.
58.   *The Irish Press,* 3 March 1933.
59.   *Irish Independent,* 12 October 1933.
60.   *The Irish Press,* 1 May 1933.
61.   *Irish Independent,* 4 May 1933.
62.   *Ibid.*
63.   *The Irish Press,* 1 November, 1933.
64.   *Daily Express,* 19 November 1933.
65.   *Irish Independent,* 20 November 1933.
66.   *Ibid.*
67.   *Evening Herald,* 17 March 1934.
68.   *Dublin Opinion,* April 1934.
69.   Sexton, *Ireland and the Crown 1922–1936,* p.154.

Chapter 19

1.   *The Irish Press,* 29 May 1935.
2.   *Ibid.*
3.   *Ibid.*
4.   *Ibid.*
5.   *Ibid.*
6.   Author's Collection (Notes written by ua Buachalla's son, Séadna, circa 1975).
7.   *Ibid.*
8.   *Ibid.*
9.   *Cork County Chronicle,* 28 September 1935.
10.   *Ibid.*
11.   *Ibid.*
12.   *Ibid.*
13.   *Ibid.*
14.   *Daily Express,* 5 March 1935.
15.   *The Irish Press,* 21 January, 1936.
16.   O'Buachalla Collection, Kilmainham Gaol Museum, 2011 1018.
17.   Dáil Éireann, Parliamentary Debates, Vol. LX, 187.
18.   *Ibid.*

19. *The Irish Press,* 22 January, 1936.
20. *Ibid.*
21. *The Irish Press,* 21 January 1936.
22. *Ibid.*
23. University College Dublin Archives P150/2183 No. 333
24. *Ibid.*
25. Brendan Sexton, *Ireland and the Crown 1922–1936* (Dublin: Irish Academic Press, 1989), p. 161.
26. *The Irish Press,* 25 June 1936.
27. *Ibid.*
28. *Ibid.*
29. *The Irish Press,* 25 June 1936.
30. Sexton, *Ireland and the Crown 1922–1936,* p. 162.
31. *Ibid.,* p. 163.
32. *Ibid.*
33. *The Irish Press,* 12 December 1936.
34. *Ibid.*
35. Sexton, *Ireland and the Crown 1922–1936,* p. 165.
36. *Ibid.,* pp. 165–6.
37. *Ibid.,* p. 166.
38. NAI TSCH/3/S8576, Internal Memo, 8 March 1937.
39. Sexton, *Ireland and the Crown 1922–1936,* p. 166.
40. National Archives of Ireland (CAB 7/396) S.9677/4.
41. Dáil Éireann Parliamentary Debates, LXVII, 591–663, 18 May 1937.
42. *Ibid.*
43. *Evening Mail,* 19 May 1937.
44. *Dublin Opinion,* January 1937.
45. *The Irish Times,* 1 July 1937.
46. *Ibid.*
47. *Ibid.*
48. *The Irish Times,* 1 July 1937
49. *Ibid.*
50. *The Irish Times,* 8 July 1937.
51. *Ibid.,* 22 July 1937.
52. *Ibid.*
53. National Archives of Ireland, TSCH/3/S8547, 7 July 1938.
54. *The Irish Press,* 6 October 1937.

Chapter 20

1. *The Irish Press,* 27 June 1938.
2. *Ibid.*
3. *Ibid.*

4. Janet and Gareth Dunleavy, *Douglas Hyde – A Maker of Modern Ireland* (Berkeley: University of California Press, 1993), p. 3.
5. *Ibid.*
6. *The Irish Press,* 26 September 1938.
7. *Ibid.*
8. *Ibid.*
9. O'Buachalla Collection, Kilmainham Gaol Museum, 2011 1074.01.
10. *The Irish Press,* 29 March 1943.
11. Military Service Pensions, 34/S.P./91 41.
12. Military Service Pensions, 34/S.P./91 41, E7032.
13. NAI, TSCH/3/S8536A.
14. *The Sunday Press,* 22 January 1961.
15. Dail Éireann, Official Report, Address by the President of the United States – 1915. Vol. 302 No. 14.
16. *The Irish Press,* 3 November 1963.
17. *The Sunday Press,* 2 November 1963.

BIBLIOGRAPHY

1. Primary Sources and Archival Institutions

Kilmainham Gaol Museum, Dublin
O'Buachalla Collection

Military Archives, Cathal Brugha Barracks, Dublin
Seizure of Money – Donal Buckley, Maynooth (AFO46/Public Safety/48)

Military Service Pensions Collection (MSPC)
Domhnall ua Buachalla (34REF8261)

Bureau of Military History (BMH), Witness Statements (WS)
Tom Byrne (WS 654)
Pat Colgan (WS 850)
Jim Dunne (WS 1571)
John Hanratty (WS 96)
Tom Harris (WS 320)
Seamus Kenny (WS 158)
Domhnall O'Buachalla (194)
Stephen O'Reilly (1,761)
Mrs James Ryan (Máirín Cregan) (WS 416)

University College Dublin Archives (UCDA)
Kennedy Papers (P4)
O'Malley Papers (P17)
Fianna Fáil Party Papers (P176)

National Archives of Ireland (NAI)
Department of the Taoiseach (DT)
Cabinet Minutes (CAB)

Parliamentary Sources
Dáil Éireann (DE)

Private Papers
Joe Buckley (copy in possession of author)
Séadna Buckley (copy in possession of author)

Interviews
Bobby Buckley (2013)
Fintan Buckley (2013, 2014)
Helen Buckley (2014)
Eoghan O'Neill (2013, 2014)
Shane O'Neill (2013)
Seamus Cullen (2013, 2014)
Brendan Sexton (2014)

Great Britain
Amnesty International (AI Index: EUR 45/41/00, April 2000)

Newspapers, periodicals, magazines
Advocate, Melbourne
An Claidheamh Soluis
An Phoblacht
Clare Champion
Cork Constitution
Daily Express
Daily Mail
Dublin Opinion
Dun Laoghaire Journal, No. 20
Evening Herald
Irish Press
Irish Independent
Irish Times
Kildare Observer
Leinster Leader
Old Limerick Journal, Winter Edition, 2003
Sunday Press
Times (London)
Westmeath Examiner

2. Secondary Sources

Bell, Pat, *Long Shies and Slow Twisters* (Celbridge: Templemills Press, 1993).

Boylan, Lena, *Journal of the Co. Kildare Archaelogical Society, Joshua Jacob, 1801-1877.*

Boyle, Andrew, *The Riddle of Erskine Childers* (London: Hutchinson, 1977).

Breen, Dan, *My Fight for Irish Freedom* (Dublin: Anvil Books, 1981).

Brennan Whitmore, W. J., *With the Irish in Frongoch* (Cork: Mercier Press, 2013).

Coogan, Tim Pat, *Michael Collins: A Biography* (London, Hutchinson, 1990).

Corry, Eoghan, *Kildare GAA: A Centenary History* (Kildare: CLG Chill Dara, 1984).

Duggan, John P., *Herr Hempel at the German Legation in Dublin, 1937-1945* (Dublin: Irish Academic Press, 2003).

Dunleavy, Janet Egleson and Gareth W., *Douglas Hyde: A Maker of Modern Ireland* (University of California Press, 1991).

Dunphy, Richard, *The Making of Fianna Fáil Power in Ireland 1923–48* (Oxford: Clarendon Press, 1995)

Durney, James, On The One Road, Political Unrest in Kildare 1913–1994 (Kildare: Gaul House, 2001).

___*The Civil War in Kildare* (Cork, Mercier Press).

___*The War of Independence in Kildare* (Cork, Mercier Press, 2013).

Evans, Bryce and Kelly, Stephen (eds), *Frank Aiken: Nationalist and Internationalist* (Dublin: Irish Academic Press, 2014).

Gallagher, Michael, *Irish Elections 1922-1944: Results and Analysis* (Limerick: PSAI Press, 1995).

Garvin, Tom, *The Evolution of Irish Nationalist Politics* (Dublin: Gill & Macmillan, 2005).

Gillis, Liz, *The Fall of Dublin* (Cork: Mercier Press, 2011).

Henry Hanna, KC and Denis A. Pringle, *The Statute Law of the Irish Free State, 1922–1928* (Dublin: Alex Thom & Co., 1929).

Larkin, Emmet, *In The Footsteps of Jim Larkin: A Family Biography* (Dublin: Blackwater Press, 1966).

Macardle, Dorothy, *The Irish Republic* (London: Victor Gollancz Ltd., 1937).

Martin, F. X., *The Irish Volunteers 1913–1915: Recollections and Documents,* (Dublin: Irish Academic Press, 2013).

Martin, Micheál, *Freedom To Choose, Cork and Party Politics in Ireland, 1918–1932* (Cork: Collins Press, 2009).

McCarthy, John P., *Kevin O'Higgins: Builder of the Irish State* (Dublin: Irish Academic Press, 2006).

Ó Beacháin, Donnacha, *Destiny of the Soldiers* (Dublin: Gill & Macmillan, 2010).

Pearse, Pádraig, *Collected Works of P.H. Pearse, Political Writings and Speeches* (Dublin, Cork, Belfast: Phoenix Publishing Co., 1924).

Ryan, Desmond, *Michael Collins* (Dublin, Anvil Books, 1994).

Sexton, Brendan, *Ireland and the Crown 1922-1936* (Dublin: Irish Academic Press, 1989).

INDEX

Note: Tables and plate entries appear in bold, i.e. the ninth plate is indicated thus: **P9.**